Further praise for *Risky Business*

'Alvarez's own voice is quiet, wise and utterly authoritative. He has that supreme essayist's skill of making the reader feel in direct conversation with the writer. And he has a marvellous range of sympathy . . . you gain a powerful insight into their different skills and different worlds . . . It is superbly tuned' David Flusfeder, *Daily Telegraph*

'Never before has art seemed to involve so much *muscle* . . . Forget the mystery of creation. This is a writer who knows about graft and understands that without it, nothing much will happen, even for a genius . . . These essays, so quietly revealing, deserve to lie between soft covers. And if lots of copies also happen to get shifted, so much the better. It would be nice to prove to their author that someone, somewhere, does notice the trouble he takes' Rachel Cooke, *Observer*

'Marvellous . . . compelling . . . he is thrilled by the "perfect balance of precision and pleasure" which informs the writing in *The Worst Journey in the World*. Much the same could be said about his own prose in this compelling and wide-ranging book' Matthew J. Reisz, *Independent on Sunday*

'Unostentatiously brilliant, cosmopolitan reviews . . . What's best in these essays isn't the tough talk but the hard-won intellectual and moral balance: in a word, taste. Alvarez writes wonderfully' Jeremy Treglown, *Spectator*

'Alvarez's fresh and confident literary judgements are the book's real selling-point' Robert Hanks, *Independent*

'Climbing, playing cards, flying about in decrepit aircraft, reading too much poetry – Al Alvarez has done all these risky things and more, so that we don't have to, but can listen instead to the wonderful tales he spins from them . . . surprisingly moving' Steven Poole, *Guardian*

'Alvarez always has something to say in pin-sharp prose that goes beneath the surface. It's true that essays seem out of fashion. But they shouldn't be, given the ease of digestion of these short bites, and the pleasure of time spent in lucid and intelligent company that comes with reading them' Victoria Moore, *Daily Mail*

'Here is Alvarez – still writing, playing poker, and full of liveliness and charm' Charlie Campbell, *Literary Review*

BY THE SAME AUTHOR

GENERAL

Under Pressure: The Writer in Society: Eastern Europe and the USA
The Savage God: A Study of Suicide
Life After Marriage: Scenes from Divorce
The Biggest Game in Town
Offshore: A North Sea Journey
Feeding the Rat: Profile of a Climber
Rain Forest (with paintings by Charles Blackman)
Night: An Exploration of Night Life, Night Language, Sleep and Dreams
Where Did It All Go Right?
Poker: Bets, Bluffs and Bad Beats

CRITICISM

The Shaping Spirit
The School of Donne
Beyond All This Fiddle: Essays 1955–1967
Samuel Beckett
The Writer's Voice

NOVELS

Hers
Hunt
Day of Atonement

POETRY

Lost
Penguin Modern Poets, No. 18
Apparition (with paintings by Charles Blackman)
Autumn to Autumn and Selected Poems 1953–76
New and Selected Poems

ANTHOLOGIES (editor)

The New Poetry
The Faber Book of Modern European Party

RISKY BUSINESS

People, Pastimes, Poker and Books

Al Alvarez

BLOOMSBURY

To Frank Kermode

First published 2007
This paperback edition published 2008

Bloomsbury Publishing Plc,
36 Soho Square,
London WID 3QY

A CIP catalogue record for this book
is available from the British Library

ISBN 978 0 7475 9311 9

10 9 8 7 6 5 4 3 2 1

Typeset by Hewer Text UK Ltd, Edinburgh
Printed by Clays Ltd, St Ives plc

The paper this book is printed on is 100% post-consumer waste recycled

www.bloomsbury/alvarez.com

CONTENTS

Preface

IT IS NEARLY FORTY years since I last put together a collection of essays, not because I stopped writing them but because the audience for essays seemed to have withered away. Back in the late sixties, when university English departments were small and the study of literature had not yet become just another academic discipline with a specialised language of its own, literary criticism was still a subject that people who read books took seriously. It was thought of as an interesting minor art-form in its own right, writers writing about other writers, an honourable profession.

Honourable or not, by the time the essays were published, in 1968, Ecclesiastes 12, always my favourite chapter of the Bible, was increasingly on my mind, especially its writerly conclusion: 'Of making many books there is no end; and much study is a weariness of the flesh.' By then I had been studying books, writing about them and also writing books of my own about other people's books for twenty-odd years – as a student, as a university teacher, as a literary journalist and poetry editor and critic for the *Observer* during the golden period when the paper regularly published a great deal of verse, much of it by poets not much known in Britain at that time – Robert Lowell, John Berryman, Sylvia Plath, Zbigniew Herbert, Miroslav Holub. But two decades is a long time in poetry criticism and by 1968 I was truly weary of it; I wanted to move on and write about other subjects that interested me. So I called the collection *Beyond All This Fiddle* in homage to Marianne Moore's famous poem on 'Poetry', which begins: 'I too dislike it: there are things that are important beyond all this fiddle.'

I didn't dislike poetry, of course, but I had trouble with the fiddle, which seemed, in the context, to have two very different meanings. The poet's fiddly pursuit of perfection – every word in its inevitable, right place – was, as they say, something I could relate to. My problem was with the other kind of fiddle – the politics and jostling for position peculiar to small closed worlds. Having left the closed world of academia to become a freelance writer, I had no intention of being swallowed up in the closed world of poets and bookmen. Freelance, as I understood the word, meant being independent, living a life on my own terms, without bosses or colleagues or anyone's timetable but my own. And because I had spent my teens shut up in wartime England and hadn't even crossed the Channel until I was eighteen, independence also meant getting out to see what there was to see and trying my hand at whatever was on offer. Literature was a fine and private place, but there were other worlds out there full of talented people who had nothing to do with the arts and I wanted to write about them, too.

It turned out not to be as easy as it sounds, especially with a family to take care of. So I have called this collection *Risky Business* because, among other reasons, that's what the freelance life is without the safety net of a regular pay cheque. That I have managed to get by is largely thanks to Robert Silvers, the magnanimous and open-minded editor of the *New York Review of Books*, who for more than forty years has let me write at length not only about literature, which he probably reckoned I knew something about, but also about what, for him, were the indecently eccentric subjects that also interested me – mountaineering, polar exploration, flying, poker. For ten pleasurable years, I did something similar at *The New Yorker*, initially encouraged by another great editor, the late William Shawn, a chronically shy and nervous man, for whom my choice of topics was not so much eccentric as downright unhinged. He himself would never have dreamed, say, of hanging out with mountain climbers, or professional poker players in Las Vegas, or with engineers and roughnecks on oil installations in the North Sea, but he liked the idea of my going places for him and reporting back. Not many of the pieces I wrote for *The New Yorker* were about books; most of them were about people and places, and the three longest ended up as books – *The Biggest Game in Town, Offshore, Feeding the Rat*. All of them, unusually for me, were a pleasure to write.

As I get older and less mobile, going places is no longer an option but people fascinate me more and more. Reading over the essays I've written, I see that that has also been my constant preoccupation as a literary critic – not biography but the way character expresses itself in language. Character, of course, is not the same as personality – the cartoon idiosyncrasies that make good copy and help sell books. It is an inward quality, an indication of how you behave both in the world and in how you write, and it expresses itself in your tone of voice – in modesty or the lack of it, in awareness of how words interact on the page and in the disinterested need to make each work as perfect as you can in its own terms.

With this in mind, I have selected pieces for this collection from literally hundreds of essays I've written over the years. Only one of them appeared in my earlier collection: 'Beyond the Gentility Principle', the introduction to my Penguin anthology *The New Poetry*. I wrote it in 1961, a particularly dreary moment in British poetry, in the hope of stirring things up; and because the anthology was widely used in schools, it seemed to have succeeded – at least for a time. I reprint it now because it lays out the principles – or prejudices – I started with, and provides a context for some of the pieces that follow. The essay on 'Risk', which first appeared in *GQ*, also provides a context, though of a different kind, and I used some material from it in my autobiography, *Where Did It All Go Right?* I also incorporated material from 'No Limit' and from my introduction to Herbert O. Yardley's *The Education of a Poker Player* in another book, *Poker: Bets, Bluffs, and Bad Beats*. The other articles appeared, often in slightly altered or abbreviated form in the *New York Review of Books*, *The New Yorker*, the *New York Times*, the *Observer* and the *Guardian*. My thanks to all the editors concerned for their permission to reprint them here.

I am immensely grateful to Chiki Sarkar and Mary Morris, my editors at Bloomsbury, who waded through the untidy mess of typescripts and clippings I dumped on them and tactfully helped me weed out the ones that worked from the ones that didn't.

2006

Risk

IN MY EARLY THIRTIES, after my first marriage broke up, I acquired a brief reputation as a wild man: I drove fast cars, played high stakes poker, and spent more time than I could decently afford off in the hills, climbing rocks with the boys. Admittedly, this reputation only applied in the London literary world, where the standards, by any stretch of the imagination, were not high. As far as the hard men on the climbing scene in the 1960s were concerned, I was a minor player. They accepted me because I was a good man to have second on the rope – strong and not prone to nervousness – and also perhaps because most of them were fugitives from the straight world of business, engineering, plumbing, medicine or teaching, and I worked in what they considered an odd, faintly exotic trade. When it came to piss-ups and really hard routes, I wasn't in their league. Even so, the Welsh hills and the Cornish sea-cliffs were the places I was happiest, and where, I felt, my real life was led. Writing was just a way of filling in time between weekends.

A happy second marriage changed all that. Yet even thirty years later, in my sixties, I still tried to get to the rocks any Sunday when the weather was halfway decent, although my stamina and flexibility were sharply diminished, and the cliffs I went to – a little sandstone outcrop called Harrison's Rocks, near Tunbridge Wells – would fit comfortably into the foyer of a modern skyscraper. And whenever I was deprived of my weekly fix by work or rain or my increasingly decrepit body, I suffered withdrawal symptoms: restlessness, irritability, a glum conviction that my week had been spoiled.

Climbing, I mean, is an addictive sport, although what it is that gets you hooked is by no means clear. Some people climb to get away – not 'Because it's there', but 'Because I'm here'. Others climb because they are turned on by the degree of physical and mental self-control needed to get up a difficult piece of rock in good style, with minimum effort and minimum fuss. The worst climb to prove something, to show they are tougher and stronger and more skilful than they might otherwise appear. The best climb simply for the fun of it, because they like the company, the hills, the curious on-off physical rhythm – blinding effort on the pitches, long periods of goofing-off on the belays – and the general anarchy of the climbing world. Most of us probably climb for a mixture of all those reasons. But there is one thing we have in common – the thing, I suspect, that initially turned us on to the game and then kept us coming back to it – the adrenalin rush. Climbing is a risky pastime – if something goes wrong, you may get hurt – and risk produces adrenalin, and the adrenalin high is addictive.

I was sixteen when I first went to the mountains in North Wales. The trip was organised by my school, and the master in charge was a gung-ho, old-style, spirit-of-the-hills freak – he had been a reserve on a pre-war Everest expedition – whose idea of fun in the hills was to see how fast we could slog up to the summit of Tryfan and back down to the Ogwen Valley. I loathed the boring, remorseless grind as much as I loathed him.

But one day he took us up a rock route on the Idwal Slabs. The hard bit – the crux – was a steep little wall, with what seemed like a good deal of empty air below it, and widely spaced holds that looked far too small for my clumsy nailed boots. I studied it a long time, convinced that I was going to fall off. Then I strolled up it without any effort at all, as easily as if it had been flat. What I felt, as I pulled onto the ledge at the top, was a surge of pure elation and well-being, the kind of glow and happiness I suppose a drug-addict must get from a fix. I was hooked and all I wanted to do was repeat the experience. But the weather closed in, we went back to the mountain-bashing, and it was not until the end of my first year at Oxford, four years later, that I climbed again. After that, however, I didn't stop, although, as I gained experience, the situations that produced that lovely surge of elation became steadily more improbable.

The elation is heightened by the fact that climbing is a peculiarly uncluttered sport; it depends on the climber, not the equipment. When I began, all that was needed was a rope, boots, carabiners and a few nylon slings to hook around flakes of rock to protect you against a fall. Since then, the safety gear has improved enormously, and the modern hard men are festooned with gear when they hit the rocks:

artificial chockstones – called 'nuts' and 'friends' – bags of chalk to improve their grip, and other arcane goodies – sticht plates, nut-keys, descendeurs. Some of them also dress up in glaring Lycra tights and snappy singlets that show off their muscles, although the prevailing style – in Britain, at least – is still government-surplus shabby. Yet no amount of flashy gear will get you up a climb, and the well-being you feel is intensely private and physical. No doubt, every athlete feels the same on his best days, but in climbing that style of contentment is attainable long after you pass your physical prime.

There is also the pleasure of the company you keep in the hills. Climbing, after all, is a maverick sport, and the people who do it consistently are interesting and rather private. Some lead very successful lives, because the kind of drive that will get you up a mountain will also stand you in good stead in a career. But there are many natural anarchists in the climbing world, who have chosen to grub along outside the system in order to be able to make their own timetables and not to answer to any boss. What all of them have in common – the employed and the unemployable – is a taste for black humour and a wicked eye for pretension. Climbing has its phoneys, but they don't have an easy time. It is also a curiously classless activity. What you do away from the rocks simply doesn't count. The group I climbed with regularly at Harrison's Rocks included a freelance computer programmer, a security guard, a municipal gardener, an odd-job man, a business tycoon and a schoolboy. The tycoon and I, being older and less competent than the others, were benignly tolerated.

In recent years, there has been a great leap forward in climbing standards. Routes that were once climbed by artificial means – by hammering pitons into cracks, and hanging *étriers*, miniature nylon ladders, from them – are now climbed free, by simple muscle-power. This is the result of the introduction of indoor climbing walls on which the young tigers train every day of the week, whatever the weather. These artificial walls have had much the same effect on climbing as the birth control pill had on sex-life in the '60s: they have made it possible to do what you like, when you like, without fear of the consequences. People who train regularly on climbing walls perform at such a high standard that there are now, in effect, two quite separate types of climbing – with training and without – and a whole category of very hard climbs – Extreme – with more subdivisions than all the old-style grades put together.

Yet the rewards are much the same, whatever standard you climb at. You get to wild, beautiful, lonely places, and the people you go with are mostly funny and irreverent and impervious to pretension. Climbing is also a physical activity of a special, rather intellectual kind. Each pitch is a series of specific local problems: which holds to use, and in which combinations, in order to climb it safely, and with the least expenditure of energy. Every move has to be worked out by a kind of physical strategy in terms of effort, balance and consequences. You have to think with your body, and think clearly, because if you get it wrong there is sometimes a risk of being hurt.

It was that aspect of climbing that I always found peculiarly satisfying – perhaps because I am a professional writer, and writing is a solitary, joyless occupation. For five or six days each week, I sit at my desk and try to get the sentences right. If I make a mistake, I can rewrite it the following day or the next, or catch it in proof. And if I fail to do so, who cares? Who even notices?

On a climb, my concentration is no less, but I am thinking with my body instead of with my addled head; and if I make a mistake, the consequences are immediate, obvious, embarrassing, and possibly painful. For a brief period and on a small scale, I have to be directly responsible for my actions, without evasions, without excuses. In the beautiful, silent, useless world of the mountains, you can achieve a certain clarity, even seriousness of a wayward kind. It seems to me worth a little risk.

That, at least, is how I used to justify my addiction to the sport. But maybe I was kidding myself. I realise that the elation I first experienced as a schoolboy on the Idwal Slabs was an adrenalin rush, the great surge of hormone that increases heart activity and muscular action, and generally prepares the body for 'fright, flight or fight'. What had produced it, I think, was not so much the physical effort as the exposure – the sensation of all that free air and empty space below the little wall. Instead of frightening me, the exposure turned me on. (If it doesn't turn you on you will never be a climber, no matter how physically adept you may be, because you will always secretly be scared.) But the real point was, when the elation came I recognised it; I had been there before.

Since then, I have thought a lot about that adrenalin high – I have also spent a good deal of effort recreating it, by one means or another – and I think I now know why it felt familiar. It brought back the first and more or less only memory I have of my early childhood. When I was about twelve months old, I had a major operation to remove a lymphatic growth from my left ankle. I remember nothing about the surgery, of course, but what I do remember, *vividly*, is re-learning to walk. *Re*-learning, because my first steps were presumably taken indoors and very young, whereas the scene I remember takes place at the King Henry's Road entrance to Primrose Hill. I assume I must be two or three years old. My nanny is kneeling a few yards away, beckoning. There is a dangerous stretch of gravel between her and me. 'Come on,' she says. 'There's a good boy.' I start forward unsteadily, half expecting her to move towards me. She doesn't, and I make it all the way on my own. Triumph and elation, the adrenalin rush. I now think I was learning a simple lesson: either I could be a cripple, dependent on other people to wheel me around, or I could become an active, upright, paid-up member of the human race. But in order to do so, I had to take risks.

I was ten the next time I got that high. It happened in the old Finchley Road swimming baths, which have since been demolished. Up until that time, swimming baths were forbidden territory for me. The doctors said the chlorine in the water was bad for the fragile skin on my still troublesome ankle. But then, the doctors said everything was bad for my ankle and, anyway this was 1940, the war was on, and there was no nanny to keep me in line. So when the school went swimming, I went along with them. I splashed around in the shallow end, learning how to swim, but all that really interested me was the high board at the far end of the pool. There was one man using it who knew what he was doing – swallow dives, somersaults, deadman's dives, back flips, the whole bag of tricks – and I couldn't take my eyes off him. It was the most graceful thing I had ever seen.

The school's swimming instructor was an ex-drill sergeant, small and muscle-bound, with tattooed arms. When I asked him to teach me how to dive, he told me to sit on the pool's edge, put my hands above my head and roll forwards, pushing myself off with my feet. I practised that manoeuvre until the hour was up. The next visit, a week later, he got me standing upright and diving off the edge. The instructor was a martinet and every time I surfaced he looked at me with distaste: 'Point your toes!' Don't look down, look up!' 'Keep your legs straight!' 'Point your bloody toes, I said!' The next week, I went up onto the high board. It was a fixed board, covered with coconut matting, and its front edge bent slightly downward. It seemed outrageously high as I stood there, trying to work up my courage. Gradually, the echoing voices disappeared and I felt as if I were cocooned in silence. I waved my arms vaguely in the way I'd been taught, tried to look up, not down, and launched myself into space. For a brief moment, I was flying. When I hit the water, I crumpled ignominiously, and my legs were all over the place. The instructor looked at me with contempt and shook his head. But even he could not diminish my elation. That's what they mean by 'free as a bird', I thought.

The London blitz began a couple of months later. For a ten-year-old child, to whom the idea of death is meaningless, the bombs falling nightly, the anti-aircraft guns pounding away on Primrose Hill, the smashed-up houses I explored with my friends and, above all, the brilliant aerial ballet acted out above our heads during the Battle of Britain were sources of endless excitement, not fear. My disorganised parents delayed sending me off to boarding school until 1943, long after the blitz was over. By that time, I was well and truly hooked on the adrenalin high. When I found rock-climbing, I was already an addict looking for a fix.

'Life is impoverished,' Freud wrote, 'it loses in interest, when the highest stake in the game of living, life itself, may not be risked.' Later, when my days as a wild man were over and I had begun to kick my adrenalin habit, risk came to mean different things. Character, for example. I once spent a night out on an overhanging cliff-face, during which it became more or less obvious to me that my companion and I were going to freeze to death. We had taken certain risks (we thought they were calculated; in fact, they were stupid), and then got caught in a snowstorm. When the snow stopped, the temperature plummeted, and there was nothing to do but sit it out on a minuscule ledge – each of us had one buttock on, one buttock off – and hope we would make it through to the morning.

Silence is one of the attractions of the mountains – a total silence you find only above the timber-line, where nothing moves but the wind. But not on this occasion. The lower six hundred feet of the route had been up a steadily overhanging wall; the last thousand feet followed a crack that was partly overhanging and never less than vertical. Because the rock on the summit had been warmer than that of the north face we were on, the snow had melted above and turned the crack into a waterfall. Our bivouac ledge was protected from it by an overhang and, although we tried to stay awake (body temperature drops when you sleep), we kept nodding off, lulled by the sound of falling water.

At some dead point of the night, I woke feeling something was wrong. 'What's up?' I said. To my surprise, I found I was whispering. We sat still, listening. But there was nothing to hear. Finally, my companion said, 'The waterfall's frozen.' He, too, was whispering. It occurred to me that that was how freezing to death would be – numb and soundless. First the waterfall, then us. It was an idea I could have done without.

I suppose most people are worried about how they will behave under pressure. Certainly, I emerged from that night on the bare mountain with frost-bitten fingers and a greatly increased self-confidence. I no longer felt I had continually to justify myself, apologise and explain, I had learned that I was a survivor, that I didn't fall apart in a crisis, and that was a lesson that stood me in good stead later in other, very different risk situations: bad runs of cards at the poker table, bad runs of luck in my professional life.

At the time, however, the night out was just a part of being young, and being young meant being resilient and fit and lucky enough to get away with it. It also meant what Tom Wolfe called 'pushing the envelope'. When we got back to the hut the next morning, ravenous and swaying with exhaustion, we had reached the far, frayed ends of our tethers. But that, in itself, is something. To discover how much you can take, at what point you will or will not crack, is a useful piece of self-knowledge. Most young people want to test their limits – physically, intellectually, emotionally. Fighter pilot jocks do it one way, budding tycoons do it another, and artists do it another way still when they 'make it new'. It is a means of finding out what life has to offer or what kind of life you are capable of. It is a form of initiation rite. And the fact that it is sometimes deadly serious does not mean that it isn't also pleasurable.

On the contrary, it is the seriousness that makes it pleasurable. As every poker player knows, the best way to bring a dying game back to life is to raise the ante. Risk concentrates the mind, sharpens the senses and, in every way, makes life sweeter by putting it, however briefly, in doubt. The late Jack Straus, one of the world's greatest poker players and highest rollers – he once bet $100,000 on the outcome of a high school basketball game – was a pushover in what he considered 'small games', where the wins and losses were reckoned in four figures or thereabouts; but he was hard to beat in the big games. This was not because he was rich; his gambling habits away from the poker table and his casual generosity kept him permanently strapped. (He used to say, 'If they'd wanted you to hold on to money, they'd have made it with handles on.') It was because he wasn't interested: 'I wouldn't pay a ten-year old kid a dime an hour to sit in a low-stakes game and wait for the nuts,' he once told me. 'If there's no risk in losing, there's no high in winning. I have only a limited amount of time on this earth, and I want to live every second of it. That's why I'm willing to play anyone in the world for any amount. It doesn't matter who they are. Once they have a hundred or two thousand dollars' worth of chips in front of them, they all look the same to me. They look like dragons, and I want to slay them.' It was typical of Straus that, when he won the World Series of Poker, in 1982, he got less pleasure from the $520,000 prize money than from the fact that, on the first day, he had been down to his last $500, and had bluffed and outsmarted his way back from the dead. Like Hemingway, Straus's favourite proverb was, 'Better one day as a lion than a hundred years as a lamb.'

Risk activities – at the poker table, in the mountains, under the water, in the air, in caves – are all examples of what Jeremy Bentham called 'deep play'. And because Bentham was the father of utilitarianism, he profoundly disapproved of the concept. In deep play, he thought, the stakes are so high that it is irrational for anyone to engage in it at all, since the marginal utility of what you stand to win is grossly outweighed by the disutility of what you stand to lose. Straus, when he gambled, was willing to bet all he had – and no one can wager more than that. When my companion and I spent our cold night out, the gain was the dubious satisfaction of having climbed a difficult route in difficult conditions; what we stood to lose was our toes or our fingers or even our lives. Yet, however deep the play was, it was still play, and pleasure doesn't necessarily cease when things go wrong. On that occasion, I was particularly lucky because I was with Mo Anthoine, a brilliant climber and a marvellously funny, anarchic man, who seemed indestructible until brain cancer ambushed him a few years ago. While we perched on our ledge, waiting for the big chill, Mo behaved as if everything was perfectly normal. He kept the one-liners coming and the tone light. We swopped jokes, recited limericks, sang songs. In retrospect, it may have been the coldest night I have ever sat through, but I have spent far gloomier ones warm in bed with the wrong woman.

You burn out, of course, as you get older. I gave up diving early because my sinuses couldn't take it, sports cars went when the kids came, and, although I went on climbing until I was sixty-three, I made sure, latterly, that I was always on a top rope. I loved the exercise, but if I fell off the most I stood to lose was face. The poker games have got bigger, but you can blame that on inflation. I console myself with the thought that it was great while it lasted.

Not long ago, however, a friend took me flying in his old Tiger Moth biplane – a trim, elegant machine, with two open cockpits, one behind the other. To sit with your head in the open air, while the plane spins and rolls and loops and pirouettes, is the ultimate form of play. In every sense, it is a freedom from gravity – from the earth's heavy pull and from the responsibilities of everyday routine. Total freedom and also total happiness. Forget highboard diving, sports cars, poker, even climbing. None of them ever produced the pure rush of adrenalin – heart pounding, blood coursing sweetly through the veins – that I felt the first time I looped the loop in the Tiger Moth. At last, I truly understood what they meant by 'free as a bird'. Thank God, I thought, the bad old habits are still in place.

GQ magazine, 1992

People

Alfred Brendel

ON A MILD AND shining summer day in London five years ago, I was walking on Hampstead Heath with Alfred Brendel, who is generally reckoned to be the world's greatest living classical pianist. Two pretty girls approached us, deep in conversation. When they had passed, I said, 'What I hate about getting old is not that they don't respond any more; they don't even *see* me.' Brendel looked embarrassed. 'Actually, that is not a problem I have,' he replied. I had known Brendel for a decade by then, and that was the first time he had ever indicated, even obliquely, that he might be famous.

Despite his classical tastes, Brendel is an anarchic spirit, so fame is not something he cares much about. In December of 1993, he was elected an Honorary Bencher of the Middle Temple of the Inns of Court in London – an honour British lawyers bestow only on very few and very distinguished outsiders. Brendel began his speech of thanks by listing all the reasons why he should *not* have been chosen and why, in fact, he should never have made it at all as a famous musician:

I did not come from a musical, or intellectual, family. I am not Eastern European. I am not, as far as I know, Jewish. I have not been a child prodigy. I do not have a photographic memory, neither do I play faster than other people. I am not a good sight-reader. I need eight hours' sleep. I do not cancel concerts on principle, only when I am really sick. My career was so slow and gradual that I feel something is either wrong with *me* or with almost anybody else in the profession. Literature – reading and writing – as well as looking at art, have taken up quite a bit of my time. When and how I should have learnt all those pieces that I have played, beside being a less than perfect husband and father, I am at a loss to explain.

Brendel, of course, is a subtle man with a sly sense of humour, and he knew better than anyone that his apparent disqualifications were precisely the reasons why he was being honoured. He is especially venerated in England, where he now lives, because he does not fit the stereotype of the great performer. He is not noticeably temperamental and is curiously lacking in self-importance on stage. 'I love the way he just comes in and gets on with it,' one of his admirers said. 'He gives you austerity, not showmanship.' He also has many interests outside the closed world of music. He is astonishingly well-read in two languages – German and English – and in a highly intellectual, Central European way: philosophy and criticism and art history, as well as fiction and poetry. He himself writes well about music, contributes to the *New York Review of Books* and has published two collections of essays. He has an idiosyncratic collection of art – tribal, ancient and modern – and a passion for Dada and kitsch. As the same admirer said, 'Everything about him is Jewish, except him.'

Brendel lives in Hampstead, an area full of Jewish intellectuals, like Central Park West, and appears very much at home there. He is tall and bespectacled, with a high forehead, untidy thinning hair, a witty and benign expression, and a trace of what Nora Ephron has called 'the white man's overbite'. Away from the concert platform, he dresses conservatively, in sports jacket, cord trousers, crew-neck sweater: more like a university professor than a famous musician. Even his beautiful wife, Reni (Irene), doesn't fit the bill; she is independent, energetic and highly intelligent, a great reader, like him, but also a keen horsewoman, and passionately involved in their three children. In short, she is anything but a maestro's handmaiden.

As for Brendel, he is exceptional among musicians for the self-lessness with which he plays. He has a wonderful grasp of the structure of each piece, of the way it develops emotionally as well as intellec-tually, of where it comes from and where it is heading, and this makes his playing strangely inward, as though he were following the composer's own train of thought and enabling the audience to share in the act of creation. He clearly believes that the true purpose of a performance is to make the audience marvel at the composition, not at him. 'He doesn't get in the way of the music,' the pianist Imogen Cooper said. 'The music is just there and he is literally the transparent vessel for it. He knows what he is doing with every single note, of course, but when he's on form none of this can be noticed.' Brendel's friend, Sir Isaiah Berlin, who loves music but cannot read a score, said,

'There are two kinds of musician. The virtuosi love playing. That's what virtuosity is: you use the music for some kind of self-exhibitionism. When Shura Cherkassky was asked why he played so fast, he answered, "Because I can." The musicians I admire – Schnabel, Toscanini, the Busch Quartet – have a vision of the music they play, not of the playing of it. That is the world to which Brendel belongs. He is totally dedicated to the people he's playing. He takes great trouble with the score in order to get at what he regards is the truth. He studies the composers, he understands them, he enters their skins and tries to enter into the frame of mind in which these notes follow in this particular structure and that beginning leads to this end.'

Brendel himself wrote music when he was young. 'I am not proud of my own works and they are tucked away,' he told me. 'But they informed my musical outlook. I'm still trying to look at the works I play from the composer's point of view. I want to find out how the minds of certain composers work, and how it is that a great composer can express everything.'

Composing wasn't the only thing Brendel did in his youth. 'I was a genius in those days, like everyone else of seventeen. I composed, I painted, I wrote poetry.' Now he is sixty-five he is ironical about his early talents and pretensions and proud of what he didn't have: he was not a child prodigy, he did not win first prize at the Busoni Competition for piano-playing, but came fourth, winning the Bolzano prize, in a year in which no first prize was awarded. Shortly before that – he was seventeen and a Graz art gallery was showing his watercolours and gouaches – he had given his first public recital. Even then, his tastes were sternly highbrow. 'He likes the modernist tradition and complicated thought,' Isaiah Berlin said. 'He's a genuine intellectual who reads people like Diderot, Stendhal and Musil, but doesn't read Dickens much.' In musical terms, that means that Brendel has always been interested in the march of music – its progress from Beethoven to Wagner to Schoenberg and beyond – and in his youth he was particularly fascinated by the more intellectual aspects of music, like the fugue, where, he said, 'one can hear a number of voices and, at the same time, control them individually, with one's fingers.' His first recital stated these preferences loud and clear. It was called 'The Fugue in Piano Literature', and it included Bach, Brahms and Liszt, and a sonata of his own with a double fugue ('of course'); all the encores were fugues. 'That was noticed,' he said, and the Bolzano award, soon after, launched his career.

In a world full of child prodigies, this qualified as a delayed start, although Brendel now sees that as an advantage: 'I was lucky in not having a sensational early career,' he said. 'My particular talent needed to come on slowly.' His acceptance by the public was slow for another reason, too, which was that his subtle performances were at odds with some outlandish stage mannerisms: 'I didn't communicate well at first. I pulled unbelievable faces, I flailed my arms around all over the place, and sometimes my glasses flew off. Then I saw myself on television and realized that the way I looked was not the way I played. I also realized that there could be a harmony between the two. So, as I practised, I placed a mirror to one side of the piano to give me an indirect impression of what I was doing. That way, I gradually learned how to coordinate what I looked like with what the music expressed. I'm still fairly expressive, but now I play in big halls, I've calmed down and the audience has got used to me.'

Stage fright, however, was never a major problem for Brendel, perhaps because he was a much-loved only child who could do no wrong and who learned how to perform very young. He was born in Moravia, in 1931, the son of a master builder who soon turned entrepreneur, moving to Yugoslavia when Brendel was two, to run a hotel on the Adriatic island of Krk: 'The hotel had a record-player which I operated for the guests. The records were of operetta arias and I'd sing along with them, thinking, I can do that, too. It was my introduction to music as an art.' After a couple of years, the family moved to Zagreb, where his father managed a cinema and it was there that the young Brendel made his first appearance on stage: he played the lead part – a general, with sabre and fez – in a children's play staged in the Zagreb opera house. His parents were not particularly interested in music, but both of them had taken piano lessons when they were children – it was the done thing – and he still remembers them sitting side-by-side at the keyboard, playing simple four-handed arrangements: his father forcefully, with his face twitching, his mother straight-backed, pecking nervously at the keys. (It is an almost silent image, he says; the volume having been mercifully turned down.) So when he was six he, too, began piano lessons and his mother sat dutifully beside him while he practised.

'My piano talent wasn't evident until I was about eleven, then I more or less took off by myself,' he said. 'My mother and father were inseparable but they were not intellectuals or aesthetically minded,' he said. 'So apart from the loving atmosphere at home and the security that gave me at a certain age, what I have to thank them for most is the fact that I had to find things out for myself.' One teacher strengthened his outer fingers, another told him he was not relaxed enough, but after his first public recital he worked mostly on his own. He made tapes of his playing, and later there were recordings, and these, he says helped him develop: 'They made me listen to myself properly, they kept me in touch with my own playing, and once you can do that, some functions of the teacher become redundant,' he said. 'Having to do things for myself became a habit, which I think has served me well. Not having teachers meant I was listening to conductors and singers – Bruno Walter, Furtwängler, Klemperer and the young Dietrich Fischer-Diskau. They showed me that piano playing was a matter of turning the piano into an orchestra or a singing voice, and only rarely just of letting the instrument speak for itself.'

Brendel worked alone not because he was arrogant but because for him music was like his painting and his poetry: each was a separate world, with its own reasons and its own rewards, in which he could also find out about himself. 'He needn't have been a pianist,' Isaiah Berlin said. 'He could have been a painter or a writer; he'd have been a success as either. He chose music because it said more to him.'

Fourth or not, the Bolzano award decided for him what his career should be, but a crucial influence on his development was the pianist Edwin Fischer. Brendel first attended Fischer's master-classes in 1949, and what he learned there had more to do with an attitude to music than with technique. 'When Fischer sat down and played, he was an example of what a performer can achieve,' he told me. 'He never boosted his own ego; he was always humble in the face of a composer. In his classes, the focus was never on him or the student who was playing; it was on the composer, the compositions, and how you can illuminate them.' Imogen Cooper was herself profoundly influenced by what she learned from Brendel. 'I was twenty – going on twelve – when I first heard him play in public,' she told me. 'I went up to him and said, "I must work with you. Otherwise, I shall die." He said, "Better that you should live." So I got a bursary and went to study with him in Vienna.' Cooper thinks that Fischer's influence on Brendel was as crucial as Brendel's was on her. 'Once you know how to master the instrument, which is a big task, it's all to do with your inner world,' she said. 'That, ultimately, is where the talent lies. The key teacher is the one who puts you onto a certain wavelength when you are ready for it.' It is as though Fischer introduced the

young Brendel not to a career but to a moral and aesthetic universe –
the inner worlds of Mozart, Beethoven and Schubert – and Brendel
then dedicated his life to exploring it.

The seeds of Brendel's special approach to both music and life had
been sown even before he started to learn the piano. When the family
moved to Zagreb, in 1935, Brendel acquired his own little gramophone and a taste for Berlin pop songs. These, he thinks, changed his
life: 'My mother, who was a very serious person, told me the words of
one of these nonsense songs and this influenced my development,
though she didn't realise it at the time and wouldn't have told me
them if she had. The song went like this: "I tear out one of my
eyelashes, and I stab you, then I take a lipstick and paint you red. If you
are still angry at me, I've got an idea: I'll order scrambled eggs and
splash you with spinach." The lyrics sort of came out of her against her
better nature. She'd giggle and say, "Isn't that silly?" I was very little at
the time but I think it was the beginning of my love of inspired
nonsense. There was always this element of absurdity around, which I
now value highly. At school, I sang Croatian songs without understanding Croatian and I learned three alphabets at once – Latin, High
German, Cyrillic. It did something to me, something subversive. It
helped counteract all those dismal Nazis surrounding me, those blue-
eyed believers who listened to the radio when Hitler spoke, and
watched the Nazi propaganda films, the anti-Jewish films, the German
profundity films, which I saw at my father's cinema.'

A taste for absurdity was a way of surviving the war years. (His
father was called up late, but only for clerical work, and the teenage
Brendel was sent to dig trenches, but en route was frostbitten,
hospitalized, and then rescued by his determined mother.) Yet the
subversiveness ran deeper than that. The way Brendel tells it, his
progress as an artist – which was slow and serious and involved a great
deal of musicological study as well as the dedication and hard labour
necessary in acquiring a difficult skill – was always accompanied by a
kind of antic opposite: a fizzing, anarchic wit and a sense of absurdity.
The first questionnaire he filled in about his life – it was from a
Swedish newspaper – set the tone: Favourite authors? Shakespeare and
Edward Gorey. Favourite painters? Leonardo and Edward Gorey.

This antic disposition shows itself both in his idiosyncratic taste –
Romanesque churches, Baroque architecture, Dada, nonsense verse,
Gorey and Gary Larson – and in his playing. His Darwin lecture at
Cambridge, in 1984, 'Must Classical Music Be Entirely Serious?', was

suitably scholarly and illuminating for the solemn occasion, but it was also a wonderful comic performance. Brendel had a piano on stage and each time he dazzlingly illustrated a point he mimicked the music he played with startled looks and rapt smiles. He has a totally original talent for bringing out the wit in unexpected composers, especially Beethoven. He once finished a London performance of the Op. 14, No.2 sonata with an elegant, airy flourish which provoked a burst of laughter along with the applause. 'I'm not hooked on humour but I'm delighted by it,' he said. 'It makes life more liveable and loveable.'

His own life is arranged accordingly. The Brendels have two houses, one in London, the other in Dorset, and both have benefited from Reni Brendel's gift for making homes that are at once beautiful, comfortable and unconventional. Their London house is a grey-brick Victorian mansion near Hampstead Heath. Or rather, it is two Victorian mansions knocked into one; they bought the adjoining house when it came on the market in case new owners objected to Brendel's practising. (Many would have paid for the privilege of hearing it; the political commentator Hugo Young, whose garden abuts on the Brendels', says he often just sits out there listening when he should be working.) Neighbours are not a problem at Plush, the site of their country house, for it is hidden away in deepest Hardy country, where villages have names like Piddletrenthide. Plush itself is a scattered handful of cottages and a thatched pub that serves excellent food. The Brendels' house is on a rise, with a duck pond at its base, a view over the village, and noble trees all around. The building is Georgian – a wide, deep square – with mid-nineteenth-century additions which somehow add to the character. The Brendels have built on a simple wing for a swimming pool, because swimming is good for Brendel's overworked muscles. (He swims twice a day when he is at Plush – after breakfast and before dinner – always on his back, serenely, as though listening to music in his head.)

The new wing fits in well, but there are small details that make the Plush house different from other English country houses. The front door, for example, is flanked by two moonstruck wooden rams from Thailand, painted black and white, their eyes, nostrils and mouths highlighted in red, while in the flagstoned entry hall stand a pair of large wooden horses; one is laughing, the other smiling, and both have an in-turned, witty expression much like the one that Brendel often assumes when he is playing. The walls, too, are hung with the kinds of objects he likes to have around him wherever he settles: tribal art, oriental dolls, and Dadaesque curiosities: a lithograph of a ritual native dance, the warriors circling on all fours, each with a feather sticking up from his rump; a drawing of two people walking away from each other but with their heads enclosed in one box (Brendel calls it 'Marriage'); a framed Snoopy cartoon; big semi-abstract paintings of what might be rusting industrial decay. By some act of grace, Reni Brendel has made all this, and her own Swedish Biedermeier furniture, blend in with the deep sofas, striped wallpaper and pale, flowered curtains.

Brendel devotes a lot of his spare time to looking at pictures and, last October, when I was at Plush, he talked enthusiastically about a big exhibition he had seen in Paris of the Dada artist Kurt Schwitters. When I got back to London, I mentioned this to the writer on art David Sylvester, who often tours galleries with Brendel. Sylvester said, 'Schwitters is an exquisite artist; his pictures are great acts of redemption of the rejected. Yet I think it's interesting that the greatest living exponent of the classical repertoire should have this passion for Dada. As a musician, he is the one person, above all, who thinks his performances through. You would imagine that his favourite artist would be someone like Cézanne, who is at once classical and existential. Maybe Dada is Brendel's id.'

Brendel himself does not see it this way. What he loves in Dada is its playfulness. 'It's a graceful balancing act that opposes everything, including itself. The Dadaists used to say, "Whoever is against Dada is a Dadaist," ' he said. 'It appeals to me because it's liberating. I also collected kitsch and for me that was an important occupation. It shaped my sense of morals in art. I'm interested in prodigies because I've always been steeped in the other, rational side. I have a great need to learn what the norm is by dealing with what is *not* the norm – with the grotesque and the fantastic. But not when I'm playing. Art gives a sense of order, life is basically chaotic, and there's a tension between them. A sense of order comes from chaos and contains a bit of it, but it's the sense of order that's important in a work of art. For the performer, it's an order that is in flux, there are always variations on it, and within the framework of the composition, you can move relatively freely. You have to keep within those confines, but at the same time you also have to be aware of all the latent possibilities that give a work its special character – its atmosphere, its moods, its contrasts. A work of art is like a person; it has more than one soul in its breast.'

Perhaps Brendel's love of playfulness and absurdity helps keep him sane in his insanely demanding profession. So does his flair for sending himself up. On the door of his studio in London is an enamelled notice: 'Kirche. Kein Eingang,' and he once told me, 'If I ever had to write my autobiography I'd make the whole thing up.' He also said he would never hang a serious portrait of himself in his house, but he treasures a little statue of himself as a centaur, complete with spectacles, and in full concert gear. One of the many pleasures of his company is that you never know where the next sly joke is coming from. One snowy mid-winter afternoon I was walking with him on Hampstead Heath. It was about four o'clock and what was left of the grey light was beginning to fade. Brendel wore galoshes over his polished black shoes and was bundled up against the weather in a long navy blue overcoat, a beret and a woollen scarf. The pond at the Vale of Health was frozen and boys were skimming stones over the ice. Halfway along the path beside it, Brendel stopped in mid-stride and held up one finger: 'Listen,' he said. The stones were making a curious, pinging, twanging note on the ice. He smiled sweetly and said, 'Messiaen.'

Because I am a neighbour of Brendel in London, he sometimes invites me around, before recitals, to listen while he runs through the programme. It probably helps that, like Isaiah Berlin, I love music but cannot read a score, though, even if I could, comment is not what Brendel is after. Joseph Conrad once gave his wife the manuscript of a new novel, saying, 'I don't want criticism; I just want praise.' Brendel disdains gush and he assuredly doesn't need my praise. What I assume he wants is a sympathetic and attentive presence in the room, a sounding-board, not for vanity or reassurance, but simply to complete the artistic circle. Literature and painting are two-way communications – the poem needs a reader, the painting needs someone to look at it. But music is a three-way exchange – from the score to the interpreter to the listener – and the art of performance depends on the relationship between the musician and the audience. In 1974, Brendel wrote, 'In the concert hall, each motionless listener is part of the performance. The concentration of the player charges the electric tension in the auditorium and returns to him magnified.' These days, he is less optimistic about audiences: 'The public sometimes thinks an artist is a television set: something comes out, nothing goes back,' he said. 'They don't realize that if they can hear me, then I can hear them – their coughs, the electronic pings from their wristwatches, even the squeaking of their shoes.' He also said, 'I like the fact that "listen" is an anagram of "silent". Silence is not something that is there before the music begins and after it stops. It is the essence of the music itself, the vital ingredient that makes it possible for the music to exist at all. It's wonderful when the audience is part of this productive silence.' That, I think, is what he needs from me in these private sessions: stillness and attention.

Brendel has two pianos in his studio and when he first began asking me around, in 1981, he would place my chair off to one side where I could see him play. It was like watching a conduit under too much pressure: the music seemed to flow through him, from head to fingers to piano, and he was twisted and racked by the pressure of it. His neck distended, a muscle twitched in his cheek, he pursed his mouth, bit his underlip, then smiled at some particular sweetness. Occasionally, he made little grunting noises or sang sotto voce. In the small room, the sound was intense and reverberating, at times almost choking. Sometimes, halfway through, Reni brought up tea and she and I gossiped for a few minutes while Brendel stood fretting pianissimo, not wanting his concentration disturbed. Immediately she left, he sat down again at the piano, head back, eyes closed a moment, neck and cheeks tensed. Then he was playing again – those marvellous, disciplined cascades of sound.

When the Brendels took over the London house next door, he moved his studio to a smaller, different-shaped room and now he sits me immediately in front of the instruments. From there, I cannot properly see him and the effect is strange. Listening alone to a good hi-fi is sometimes better than being in a noisy audience in a concert hall. You miss the artist's presence and the sense of occasion but you hear the music more purely without being distracted by the man with a cough, the woman who rustles her programme, the kid who can't sit still. Because Brendel has the extraordinary gift for projecting himself into the heads of the composers he plays and playing as though he himself were thinking out the music for the first time, sitting right in front of the piano while this is happening makes you part of the process. In the small room the sound of the piano is huge. It is like being inside the music, hearing it breathe, exploring its structure as it unfolds around you.

'When I'm with Brendel, I know I'm in the presence of a man of genius,' Isaiah Berlin said. 'He is a genius because each time he plays a work it is new and fresh, whereas with lesser musicians, it's *da capo*.

When David Oistrakh played Tchaikovsky's Violin Concerto, it was lovely, it was delicious. Then he did it again and it was exactly the same. And very agreeable, too. With Brendel, there are no mechanisms at all, no question of "I know how to do this", then off he goes, playing wonderfully. That's why he looks so tormented when he plays. He doesn't enjoy it. It's a dedicated sacrifice on an altar, an exalted experience. That's why it makes a profound impact on anyone sensitive to the inwardness of music.'

Those private sessions with Brendel made it clear to me how much a performance cost him. After one of them, when he was soaked with sweat and looked more than usually drained, I asked, inanely, how he remembered it all. He answered, 'Memory is not a problem. What matters is the musculature.' His body, for him, is an instrument that he must care for and respect like his piano – except that he has at least three pianos and only one body. Last summer, Brendel spent a month in Provence without playing a note – the first time in decades, he said, that he had kept away from the piano for so long – and when he got back to London and began playing again he complained that his little finger was bruised. I must have failed to register an appropriate degree of dismay, because he added, 'The little finger has to withstand a lot.' He cocked the finger as if to play a note and a great ridge of muscle rose up along the side of his palm. His musculature, I realized, is as specialized as an athlete's.

The four-week rest had been ordered by a famous orthopaedist in Munich (Boris Becker is one of his patients), whom Brendel consults because he has recently been having trouble with vertebrae of the neck. Although the doctor has alleviated the pain with injections and massage, there are certain notoriously demanding works which Brendel feels he should not play again: the concertos of Brahms and Liszt, Schubert's 'Wanderer Fantasy', Beethoven's 'Hammerklavier'. Brendel shrugs the problem off, but he has begun to pace himself carefully: 'I'm getting older and I feel the stress more,' he said. 'Many of my colleagues have never taken a vacation in their lives, and I can understand that. When you are on a high level of tension you have to be very clever about winding down without getting sick or having circulation problems. You have to come down slowly, then you have to come back up again, and this can be painful when you start playing.'

Brendel himself has always insisted on two or three months each year without professional engagements, so that he can stay at home and read and think and be with his family. Home, however, means a house big enough for everyone to have privacy, which Brendel is addicted to. 'I love being on my own, but unfortunately I lack the necessary qualifications,' he said. 'I never learned to drive or cook; I'm not good at practical things. Maybe that's because my father was a master builder. If ever anything went wrong he was there to fix it immediately.' Despite his impracticality, Brendel is intensely focussed and self-contained as an artist. 'He has an extraordinary sense of timing,' Reni Brendel said. 'Not just of each movement but of every aspect of the performance: the breath and life of a piece, the time it takes to rehearse, the time he needs to practise. When he tours now, I don't go with him as much as I used to. The anonymity of hotel life and the rituals he creates for himself leave him free to concentrate. I provide a home life, full of energy and children, for him to come back to.'

Even so, Brendel is finicky about the details of his life. 'All my hang-ups have to do with my constitution and my professional life,' he said. 'I have to find out how to live comfortably in order to do what I'm doing. I intensely dislike open doors: I want to avoid draughts, I don't want the room I'm working in to smell of cooking.' 'Everything in his life is very structured,' Imogen Cooper said. 'The fringes on the rug have to be just so. He's terribly careful about what he eats and drinks and how his stomach reacts, and he's abnormally sensitive to noise. Barking dogs and noisy hotel rooms upset him almost beyond measure. I think his nerves are closer to the surface than other people's, although it's hard to know how much of this is ultra-sensitivity and how much a controlling mechanism which he uses to function to his ultimate capabilities. But he's got it down to a fine art and that's all that matters. And he's not at all grandiose or arrogant. He's relaxed in himself, a sweetie, really.'

Isaiah Berlin agrees, although he puts it differently: 'He is a person of absolute moral integrity and somehow he conveys that as a human being. Some people have social charm and others have sexual charm; Brendel has moral charm, a certain moral purity which conveys itself in a way that is enchanting. Reni has it, too; her moral taste is absolutely incorruptible. The Brendels' is an honourable household.'

In Brendel, however, moral charm is coupled with a kind of aesthetic ruthlessness. The first twenty minutes of the first lesson Imogen Cooper had from Brendel, back in 1969, was spent on the opening chord of the slow movement of a Schubert sonata. 'He stood with his back to me, saying, 'There's not enough thumb of the right hand,' 'There's too much bass,' 'It sounds heavy; it should sound ethereal.' I thought I'd never get it right,' she said. 'Then I did. He turned round and said, "Thank you. Let's go on to the next bar." He was never effusive in his praise and he didn't give much encouragement, but I knew instinctively, from the amount of time he was spending on me, that he thought I was OK. You have to be strong but, provided you're on his wavelength musically, you never forget it. He's not a natural teacher; he's not interested in your development; he's interested in imparting his vision of the music and letting you make something of it. His attitude is, "This is the way I see it. Take it or leave it." '

Last November, in Munich, I watched Brendel in action with the Austrian pianist Till Fellner, one of a few young musicians he keeps in touch with. Fellner is a quiet young man, tall and slender and polite, with dark eyes and short dark hair. He is 23 years old but looks younger, although he has been playing in public since he was six. The session took place in the apartment of one of Brendel's friends and the hostess had set out tea and biscuits on a table between two sofas near the piano. Brendel ignored them. He and I settled at a table in the far corner of the room while Fellner sat straight down at the piano and began to play a Schubert sonata [D845]. Brendel listened intently, following the score and making notes on it from time to time. He nodded, moved his fingers at certain tricky passages, and once he held up his hand like a traffic cop. He did not look at the young pianist or at me. At the end of the first movement, he said, 'Very nice,' in a business-like way, then got down to details. He sat down at the piano, played a passage, then Fellner took his place and played. Brendel said, 'Very nice, but maybe a little freer.' He sang a phrase and Fellner played it again and then again, while Brendel walked around behind him, head down, listening. At one point, he shook himself – a shake that started at his head and exited through his fingertips – like a man trying to break free. There was nothing of the master-and-the-pupil in their exchanges. They treated each other as equals and both were unselfconsciously absorbed in the music, unaware of anything beyond the intricacies of the score. The hostess came in for a moment, followed by her shambling Saint Bernard dog, but neither pianist seemed to notice her, and at no point did they look at me. After the second movement, when Fellner went off to the bathroom, Brendel said, 'He's the best of the younger pianists.' And that was all he said.

The previous evening, Brendel had played Beethoven's last three sonatas in the bleak Herkulessaal of the Residenz. The good burghers of Munich were older, better dressed and more sedate than the London audiences, but no less rapt. As usual, he just came in and got on with it without fuss. The muscles of his jaws worked, sometimes his head went back and he seemed to close his eyes, and at moments of great tenderness he smiled his strange, lost smile. But because the hall was big and I couldn't see his hands from where I sat, the music just seemed to happen, almost without his intervention. It did not cease even when he adjusted his spectacles with his left hand. This was the fifth time I had been present when Brendel played the last three Beethoven sonatas – three times before at public concerts in London, and once in his studio – but I had never heard him play them so exquisitely and with such understanding.

One of the most important lessons Brendel taught Imogen Cooper was that there is a tension that goes all the way through a piece of music and never lets up: 'He used to talk about the long silver cord that one pulls on,' she said. 'He'd crouch down beside the piano and say, "Go on, pull, pull." Sometimes there's a little kink in the cord, but it never sags. There's always a force irresistibly pulling it from the first note to the last. He used to say, "You've got to get the audience from the first note." I'd say you've got to get them from the moment you come through the door. How you command the space between the door and the piano makes the audience listen in a certain way. They listen with their eyes as well as their ears.'

That night in Munich, they seemed to be listening with their whole beings. Brendel says performing is a risky business and the concert pianist who wants to make a work new each time he plays it must live dangerously. 'As a performer, I have become aware of the paradox of my profession,' he said. 'You have to be in control and, at the same time, lose yourself completely. You have to think and feel in advance what you want to do and, simultaneously, to listen to what you *are* doing and react to that. You have to play to satisfy yourself and also play so that the people in the back row will get the message.' In other words, the concert platform is where his two worlds of intellectual control and inspired nonsense intersect.

Brendel thinks Beethoven's last piano sonata, Op. 111, is 'a premeditated conclusion, a last word leading into silence forever.' That evening, the trills with which the sonata ends had never sounded more beautiful or unearthly or final. Perhaps the end was especially poignant because Brendel, like Beethoven, was also saying farewell.

His troublesome neck might prevent him playing the 'Hammerkla-vier' again, so this might be the last time he would perform the complete cycle of Beethoven sonatas in Munich, and a complete cycle, he thinks, has a special impact on the audience: 'They grow together and become a group; there's the impression of a journey undertaken together and a goal achieved.' But there is no simple way of explaining the impact of that extraordinary performance and the depths he seemed to be exploring. ' "Depth" is an odd word,' Isaiah Berlin said. 'It's a metaphor but you can't translate it into other terms. Depth means penetrating into something very basic in oneself, and touching it, and feeling an electric shock.'

'One doesn't stop learning,' Brendel had said a month earlier, at Plush. 'I've learned how to control certain silences. They depend not just on what you play but on how you look. After the last chord of Op. 111, I don't move, I don't take my hands away from the keyboard, because directly I stir they applaud. Each time I play the Beethoven cycle the silence gets longer because I know how to relate to it, I know how to sit still.'

That night in Munich, Brendel sat still for a very long time and the applause, when it finally began, was slow to build, as though the audience were coming out from under a spell. Once it got going, however, it seemed like it would never stop. I was sitting at the end of a row and Reni, who had been a couple of rows behind me, came and crouched by my side as the applause thundered on and on. 'I'm glad you heard that,' she said.

The New Yorker, 1996

Philip Roth

PHILIP ROTH HAS HAD all the grandest prizes available to an American writer, some of them more than once, and he has been to the White House to have the National Medal of Arts pinned on him by President Clinton, but the honour that seems to have pleased him most is the forthcoming multi-volume edition of his collected works in the Library of America. This officially establishes him as an American classic, along with Melville, Hawthorne, James, Fitzgerald and Faulkner, and so far only two other writers – Saul Bellow and Eudora Welty – have been immortalised in this way during their lifetimes.

When the Library of America broke the news to him on his birthday, last March, the editors might have assumed they more or less knew the scale of their undertaking. He had, after all, just turned 71 and had recently finished his 23rd book. If so, I think they have underestimated the man. For the last decade, at an age when most writers are beginning to lose interest, happy to settle back to enjoy their reputations and repeat their old tricks, Roth has produced a series of books more powerful and accomplished than any he has written before. And he shows no signs of slowing down.

'Even now, he doesn't relent,' said Aaron Ascher, Roth's old friend and editor of six of his books. 'This is a seventy-something-year-old writer who is still going uphill and keeps getting better. He has back problems which give him great pain, yet he's always working. He works all the time and never stops, even in his worst periods. He said of this new book, "Writing has got harder than ever before; it's really tough." But he knew what he wanted and he did it. I'm not an easy mark, I've read too many books, but I don't know anyone like him – and not just for his talent and inventiveness.'

Like Ascher, and for similar reasons, I too am not an easy mark and, although I have known Roth for 45 years, his relentless dedication to the craft of fiction still astonishes me. We first met in 1959 when a Guggenheim fellowship took him to Rome and he stopped off in London on his way south. At that point, he had published just one book – a collection of stories called *Goodbye, Columbus* – but it had already established his reputation with the serious critics, won him a National Book Award and made him famous – or infamous – enough to be denounced by rabbis from their pulpits. We became friends from the start because both of us, back then, were edgy young men with failing marriages and a nose for trouble, who believed, as literary folk did back in the high-minded '50s, that literature was the most honourable of all callings and were baffled when life didn't work out as books had led us to expect.

In appearance, Roth seems to have changed less than most of us over the years. His face is lined now, his mouth has tightened and his springy hair has turned grey, but he still looks like an athelete – tall and lean, with broad shoulders, a small head and a nose like a hatchet. As it happens, sports have never much interested him, baseball apart, yet until recently, when surgery on his back and arthritis in the shoulder laid him low, he worked out and swam regularly, though always, it seemed, for a purpose – not for the animal pleasure of physical exercise, but to stay fit for the long hours he puts in on his work. He works standing up, paces around while he's thinking and has said he walks half a mile for every page he writes. Even now, when his joints are beginning to creak and fail, energy still comes off him like a heat haze, but it is all driven by the intellect. It comes out as argument, mimicry, wild comic riffs on whatever happens to turn up in the conversation. His brain is always switched on, his concentration is fierce, and the sharp black eyes under their thick brows miss nothing. Like all novelists, odd situations, physical detail, other people's quirks and whatever breaks the boring flow of routine living are raw material for Roth and his watchfulness is unrelenting. The pleasure of his company is immense, but you need to be at your best not to disappoint him.

He has always believed in the separation of life and art, literally as well as metaphorically. In Connecticut, his studio is back in the trees away from the house; thirty years ago, when he was spending half the year in London, he lived in Fulham and worked in a little flat in Kensington; in New York, there were two apartments on the Upper West Side, one for living in, a studio for work; when he lost interest in New York and moved more or less full-time to Connecticut, he kept the studio and that is where we met to talk.

The apartment is on the twelfth floor, a single large room with a kitchen area, a little bathroom and a glass wall looking south across Manhattan's gothic landscape of peaks and canyons, stone, concrete, steel and glass, with conical black water tanks sprouting like mushrooms from every roof, and the Empire State Building, with a wisp of cloud around its top, on the horizon.

The lectern at which Roth works is at right angles to the view, presumably to avoid distraction. Above it is a sketch of an open book, with an indecipherable text that might be in Hebrew, by his friend, the late Philip Guston. There is not much else by way of decoration: a bed with a neat white counterpane against the wall opposite the lectern, an easy chair in the centre of the room, with a graceful standing lamp beside it, all of it leather and steel and glass, discreetly modern. (There used to be a Nordic-Trak exercise machine, but that was years ago.) It is a place strictly for work, spare and chaste, a monk's cell with a great view.

This seems to fit Roth very well. Years ago, in London, we were fantasising about what we would like to have been if we lived our lives again. 'A parish priest', he said, 'swishing around in a cassock and hearing confessions.' He may have missed out on the cassock – he dresses soberly, neutrally, as though not to be noticed – and celibacy has never been his style, but in other ways his life is as stern, self-sufficient and dedicated as any priest's: he works long hours, eats sparingly, drinks hardly at all and goes to bed early. As for confessions: not only is he a great listener, he is also free to make up any sin he fancies in his books, unburdened by the problem of forgiveness.

All this austerity and discipline sets Roth apart from most writers, who usually make some pretence at living a normally cluttered life, but maybe he needs to live cautiously in order to take great risks in his work. It is possible, Camus once remarked, to live a life of wild adventure without ever leaving your desk. Even so, Roth's monkish routine is at odds with what he once called his 'reputation as a crazed penis' bestowed on him by *Portnoy's Complaint*. When *Portnoy* was published in 1969, it seemed to epitomise the anarchic spirit of the decade. Maybe it did, but the author himself was a product of the '50s, the last generation of well-behaved, sternly educated children who did more or less what they were told, believed in high culture and high principles and lived in the nuclear shadow of the cold war until their orderly world was blown apart by birth control pills and psychedelic drugs. *Portnoy* was considered outrageous when it appeared, but the real outrage was Roth's and he was outraged because he couldn't help being a good boy however much he yearned to be bad.

Like most Jewish families, Roth's was close-knit, affectionate and tempestuous. His father, Herman, was a passionate New Dealer, a forceful, indignant man, who worked for Metropolitan Life Insurance Company and rose to be a district manager – which was as high as a Jew could go before Congress passed the Fair Employment Act after World War II. He and his wife Bess were children of immigrants from Eastern Europe and they lived in the largely Jewish Weequahic section of Newark. In those days, before it was burnt down in the 1966 race riots, Newark was the commercial capital of New Jersey, a prosperous industrial town – breweries, leather goods, small manufacturing companies and large department stores – a city of half a million people, the largest in the state but small enough for workers to be able to walk to work. The neighbourhood schools were good and Roth was a straight-A's student. He graduated *magna cum laude* from Bucknell, an idyllic little college in Lewisberg, Pennsylvania, got his MA from the University of Chicago, did a spell in the army, was invalided out with a spinal injury, returned to Chicago to start a Ph.D and teach freshman English, then dropped out after one term. Ascher first heard of him when his sister, a student at Chicago, wrote to tell him she had sublet an apartment from 'a guy called Philip Roth. He says he's a writer.'

It was a long time, however, before Roth began to write about the world he was brought up in. Neither of his devoted, sensible parents seem to have had much in common with the comic nightmares who tormented Portnoy and they only began to figure large in their son's work after they died. *The Plot Against America* is, in a way, his memorial to them. When Roth was working on it he told his friend David Plante, the novelist, that he was 'writing about his parents in their prime, when their life was at its full and they were dealing with it'. Though the book turned out to be about a lot of other things as well, the portrait, according to Aaron Ascher, is strong and accurate: 'Herman was fiercely what he was – a marvellous, naïve man who loved his children and was perplexed by them. In this new book, Philip puts him in these terrible situations and he reacts exactly as he would have done in real life.'

Roth told me the idea for the terrible situation occurred to him when he read in Arthur Schlesinger's autobiography that the right wing of the Republican party had thought of nominating Charles Lindbergh, the famous aviator, anti-semite and friend of Hitler, to run for the presidency against FDR in 1940:

'I wrote in the margin, "What if they had?" Then I began thinking about other what-ifs, like what if Hitler hadn't lost? All this was

happening when I was a little child – I was born in 1933 – but it was
quite vivid to me because the great outside world came into the house
through the radio and through my father's reactions to it. So it began
to make sense as a novel. One of the reasons I could never write about
what our family life was really like was because my parents were good,
hard-working, responsible people and that's boring for a novelist.
What I discovered inadvertently was that if you put pressure on these
decent people, then you've got a story.'

Putting pressure on people and facts and his own experience is one of
the many solutions Roth has come up with for the problem he has
devoted his life to: how to transform life into art. The list of his other books
that faces the title page of each new work is not arranged chronologically
but by different narrators he has created to say his say: Zuckerman Books,
Roth Books, Kepesh Books, Miscellany, Other Books. I asked him, not
altogether jokingly, if this was because writing is such a boring profession
that he has to invent other narrators in order to have someone to talk to. As
I should have guessed, Roth was having none of that:

'I have to have something to do that engages me totally. Without
that, life is hell for me. I can't be idle and I don't know what to do
other than write. If I were afflicted with some illness that left me
otherwise OK but stopped me writing, I'd go out of my mind. I don't
really have other interests. My interest is in solving the problems
presented by writing a book. That's what stops my brain spinning like
a car wheel in the snow, obsessing about nothing. Some people do
crossword puzzles to satisfy their need to keep the mind engaged. For
me, the absolutely demanding mental test is the desire to get it right.
The crude cliché is that the writer is solving the problem of his life in
his books. Not at all. What he's doing is taking something that
interests him in life and then solving the problem of the book – which
is, How do you write about this? The engagement is with the problem
that the book raises, not with the problems you borrow from living.
Those aren't solved, they are forgotten in the gigantic problem of
finding a way of writing about them.'

His solutions to the problem have taken many forms as well as a
large cast of narrators. *Deception*, for instance, is written entirely in
dialogue, like a stage play. *Operation Shylock* is a find-the-Roth shell-
game, with a false Philip pretending to be the true one until neither is
quite sure who is who. The technical problem of *The Plot Against
America* was less tricky but equally hard to solve: although it is a Roth
book, the Roth who narrates it is aged seven:

'Prior to that, I'd had these rich brains telling the story and now I was going to have to look over the shoulder of a child. I never wrote *What Maisie Knew* and this was *What Little Philip Knew*. How do I do that without putting on a straightjacket? The answer turned out to be quite simple: if you have one child in the centre of the book, you have a problem, but it goes away when he is a child among children. So once I discovered the other children to act as foils for him I was in the clear. Then I had a child's perspective, but the book is no longer told by a child; it's told by an adult remembering his family when he was a child.'

Roth's artistic strategies for solving the problems each story presents are endlessly inventive, yet there is nothing high-flown about his attitude to them. Aesthetic theories and experiment don't interest him and when he talks about getting a story right he does so, like any craftsman, with a practical understanding of the materials he uses and techniques needed to get the job done properly. This fits precisely with the way he writes. In *The Ghost Writer*, the ageing famous writer, E.I. Lonoff, tells 23-year-old Nathan Zuckerman, the most disabused of Roth's stand-ins, that he 'has the most compelling voice I've encountered in years, certainly for someone starting out . . . I don't mean style . . . I mean voice: something that begins at around the back of the knees and reaches well above the head.' Voice in this sense is the vehicle by which a writer expresses his aliveness and Roth himself is all voice. Style, in the formal, flowery sense, bores him; he has, he once wrote, 'a resistance to plaintive metaphor and poeticised analogy.' His prose is immaculate yet curiously plain and unostentatious, at once unselfconscious and unmistakably his own, and it seems to come to him as naturally as breathing. Reading him, it's always the story that's in your face, never the style.

Though Roth is all voice, the voices of his different narrators are often, to my ear, hard to tell apart. So why the different disguises? One answer seems to be that his hard-edged, witty voice sounds so natural that the lazy reader might suppose he is listening to confession rather than reading a work of fiction. And this, to Roth, is an insult to all the labour he puts into his craft. It also links him with the cult of celebrity and that is something he has fought against throughout his career.

'One dreams of the goddess Fame,' wrote Peter De Vries, 'and winds up with the bitch Publicity.' Roth first encountered the bitch when *Goodbye, Columbus* provoked rabbis to denounce him as 'a self-hating Jew', and he responded by writing *Letting Go*, the most restrained of his novels, as if to show that he was indeed as serious and worthy as authors were expected to be back in the '50s. Being a good boy, however, did not sit easily either with his wild comic inventiveness or with the troubles he was having in a difficult first marriage. When he finally yoked comedy and rage together to produce *Portnoy's Complaint* the serious writer came face-to-face with the bitch Publicity and did not like what he saw.

'In 1969, I wrote *Portnoy*. Not only did I write it – that was easy – I also became the author of *Portnoy's Complaint* and what I faced publicly was the trivialisation of everything.'

Instead of being read as someone playing brilliant games with reality in the tradition of Kafka and Gogol, he got scandal, outrage and bestseller celebrity in its most crummy form. According to Ascher, 'the attacks were horrible and disheartening, especially from the Jews. He had to cope with the nightmare of a smash hit. It made him angry and defensive, so he closed up. But maybe it did him good. The set-back of great success changed and improved him as a writer. Without it, he'd have been different.'

Roth's immediate response was to refuse all public appearances and retreat to Yaddo, the writers' colony near Saratoga Springs, in upstate New York. Hiding himself away was easy, but disguising that distinctive, compelling voice of his was a trickier problem. His solution was ventriloquism, narrators with everyday lives not unlike his, but who see them differently and transform them into something else: unbridled, tough-talking Nathan Zuckerman who sniffs out every weakness and forgives no one; studious David Kepesh, a professor to whom outlandish things happen when he lets himself go, but who loves literature as much as he loves women; a character called Philip Roth whose relationship to the author is a source of mystery for both of them. Roth remarked to me, a propos President Bush, that born-again Christianity is the ignorant man's version of the intellectual life. Similarly, reading fiction as though it were true confessions is the ignorant man's aesthetics and Roth has made a mockery of it in many ways. The eulogist at Zuckerman's funeral in *The Counterlife* puts it pompously but well:

> What people envy in the novelist . . . is the gift for theatrical self-transformation, the way they are able to loosen and make ambiguous their connection to a real life through the imposition of talent. The exhibitionism of the superior artist is connected to his imagination; fiction is for him at once playful hypothesis and

serious supposition, an imaginative form of enquiry – everything that exhibitionism is not . . . Contrary to the general belief, it is the *distance* between the writer's life and his novel that is the most intriguing aspect of his imagination.

In life as in art: a puffed-up academic at a New York dinner party once tried to show his disdain for the famous author by pretending to mistake him for Herman Wouk and taking him to task for the structural weakness of *Marjorie Morningstar*. Roth, of course, was too smart to be indignant; he just played right along with the game and became Wouk for the rest of the evening. He had forgotten all about the incident, but when I reminded him of it he responded with the words of Mickey Sabbath, his wildest hero, to his mistress's recollection of some bygone outrage: 'Sounds like me.' Then he added, 'I got that rhythm from a scene in *Ulysses*. When Bloom is watching Gertie by the seaside he slips his hand into his pocket and Joyce says, "At it again." It's one of those phrases that just capture things. I think I use "At it again" in every book. It's not a homage. It's straight theft.'

Roth's most effective escape from New York celebrity was Czechoslovakia and its writers. He stumbled across them inadvertently when he was on a holiday tour of Europe and stopped over in Prague to pay homage to Kafka. This was in 1972, three years after both the nightmare success of *Portnoy* and the far greater nightmare that followed the Prague Spring. Through his Czech translator he met the blacklisted writers who cleaned windows and stoked boilers for a living while they wrote books they knew would never be published in their homeland. Their troubles put his into perspective:

'They made me very conscious of the difference between the private ludicracy of being a writer in America and the harsh ludicrousness of being a writer in Eastern Europe. These men and women were drowning in history. They were working under tremendous pressure and the pressure was new to me – and news to me, too. They were suffering for what I did freely and I felt great affection for them. People like Milan Kundera, Ludvík Vaculík and Ivan Klíma were utterly different from me, but I felt an allegiance to them; we were all members of the same guild.'

Back in New York, Roth immersed himself in the literature from behind the Iron Curtain. He went every week to a little college on Staten Island to attend Antonin Liehm's classes on Czech culture and learned about Polish fiction from Joanna Rostropowicz, the wife of his friend, Blair Clark. He also put his American reputation to good use by editing a series of eastern European fiction for Penguin. It was not just a rich subject for him, it was also an escape from his 'ridiculous fame':

'My life in New York after *Portnoy* was lived in the Czech exile community – listening, listening, listening. I ate every night in Czech restaurants in Yorkville, talked to whoever wanted to talk to me and left all this *Portnoy* crap behind. That was idiotic, this was not idiotic. I didn't want the New York gossip and the exiles could tell me something. I lived up in Connecticut, where Philip Guston was my friend, and had my East European world in New York, and those were the things that saved me. I think that's why Hemingway lived in Key West; he liked to be in a world that had nothing to do with what he did all day. Fame is a worthless distraction.'

Roth's annual two-week visits to Prague continued until 1977, when he was denied an entry visa, and they seemed to bring about a change in his focus as a writer. By then, he was spending half the year in London, but he left in 1989 to be with his father in his final illness and never went back. It was, he says, a huge relief to be home:

'I used to walk around New York saying under my breath, "I'm back! I'm back!" I felt like Rip Van Winkle waking up with a long beard and discovering there'd been a revolution and the British were gone! Being home, being free in my personal life brought a great revival of energy. I felt renewed.'

While he was rediscovering America, Roth immersed himself in the modern classics – Dreiser, Sherwood Anderson, Thomas Wolfe, Faulkner – and they reminded him of what American novelists do best:

'The great American writers are regionalists. It's in the American grain. Think of Faulkner in Mississippi or Updike and the town in Pennsylvania he calls Brewer. It's there on the page, brick by brick. What are these places like? Who lives there? What are the forces determining their lives? For American writers in the twentieth century, the impingement of place is almost everything. It had always been a subject that interested me – even *Goodbye, Columbus* is about a boy from one place meeting a girl from another, and they carry their places with them, and their places determine their destiny – but I hadn't yet discovered my own place, that town across the river called Newark, and it didn't have any power for me until it was destroyed in the riots of 1966. Before, it was too pleasant and my family was too decent to write about. Only when the place had been burned down and the families I knew had been exiled did it become a fit subject for enquiry.'

The energy released by his return to America culminated in his great, subversive outburst of comic outrage and exasperation, *Sabbath's Theatre*. The book reads, to me, like *Portnoy's Complaint* retold by a sixty-year-old man raging not about sex, but against the injustice and ludicrousness of death, and it was a turning point. Having vented his rage at the prospect of death, and while he still had time, he set about writing a series of novels about what it was like to live in the United States in the second half of the twentieth century. After his experience in eastern Europe, he now saw the place more sharply through the lens of history.

Back in the '50s, when Roth was starting out and literature was considered the noblest of all vocations, the best writers responded in an intensely inward way to whatever was going on in the big outside. All that changed, Roth thinks, when Kennedy was assassinated in 1963:

'It was an event so stunning that our historical receptors were activated. The stuff that's happened in the last forty years – the Vietnam war, the social revolution of the '60s, the Republican backlash of the '80s and '90s – have been so powerfully determining that men and women of intelligence and literary sensibility feel that the strongest thing in their lives is what has happened to us collectively: the new freedoms that came in the '60s, the testing of the old conventions, the prosperity. That's what Updike is writing about in his two best books, *Rabbit is Rich* and *Rabbit at Rest*, and Bellow in *Mr. Sammler's Planet* and *The Dean's December*. They may not be Bellow's greatest novels, but what matters is his struggle to deal with the immediate present. And that's what I, too, was struggling with in the three novels that followed *Sabbath*. In all these books, people prepare for life in a certain way and have certain expectations of the difficulties that come with those lives, then they get blindsided by the present moment; history comes in at them in ways for which there is no preparation. In *American Pastoral*, Swede Levov, the independent private man, gets blindsided by the public world; in *I Married a Communist*, Ira Ringold, the public man, gets blindsided by what happens to him in his private life; in *The Human Stain*, Coleman Silk who, because of the colour of his skin, has been unburdened by the problem of race, suddenly says the word "spooks" and unleashes the current moment. Literally current; I'd finished with Ira in 1998 and was wondering "What else?" Then I thought, "It's all around you! It's staring you in the face! You don't have to go back to the past. Now you can write about the moral environment you're living in." I kept hearing about college teachers losing their jobs, and everywhere there was an atmosphere of persecution, like the one Hawthorne wrote about, that manifested itself most extravagantly in the crazy impeachment of President Clinton.

' "History is a very sudden thing," is how I put it in *American Pastoral*. I'm talking about the historical fire at the centre and how the smoke from that fire reaches into your house. That's what happens in *The Plot Against America*, but there it's invented history exposing an invented present. A fascist becomes president, the Jews suddenly become outsiders and this little boy thinks, "I'm an American kid from an American family in an American school. What's all this about?" You've got to remember that America is different from Europe. The schools Americanised kids; they saluted the flag each morning, it was a single-language education and parents wanted them to speak English; "Don't speak like me," they used to say. So the first generation that spoke English without an accent was American. That was it. My father and his brothers never doubted that for a moment. Also, the Jews secularised themselves here with enormous energy because at first no rabbis came; they stayed behind in the shtetls – those little theocracies run by the richest man and the rabbi – where they had authority. Over here, they lost their power. I was brought up in a Jewish neighbourhood and never saw a skullcap, a beard, sidelocks – ever, ever, ever – because the mission was to live here, not there. There was no *there*. If you asked your grandmother where she came from, she'd say, "Don't worry about it. I forgot already." The Irish, Greeks and Italians who had a longing for the old country could always make some money and go back, but the Jews who came here cut themselves off. And because there was nowhere to go back to they took to America in an extraordinary way. To them, this was Zion. So in this new book, when overnight they become aliens in their own country, the blow is enormous.'

Roth and I talked together for two days and, as usual with old men, we ended up talking about age and the humiliations that attend it. Recently, he told me, he'd called a writer we both know:

'He answered the phone with a voice so old, so dead, so out of it that I couldn't talk. I just started to cry and had to hang up. When I called back I said, "Sorry, I'm very emotional right now." He said, "Yes, I can hear that." But he didn't remember it later. I think about Hemingway and Faulkner and how it ended for them – tragically, not peacefully in their sleep. Faulkner drank himself to death. Hemingway had had many accidents, his body was banged to bits, the booze had saturated him and he couldn't write; he had nothing to live for any more, so he shot himself. The demise of great talents and great imaginations like theirs breaks your heart. These are lives of torment, both of them. I'm not a romantic about writing, I don't want a tormented life and, by and large, I haven't had one. But these guys . . . I can't stand to think about how they ended.'

'And now it's beginning to happen to us.'

'Who knew what it would be like? There may be a biological blinder about age that's built-in. You are not supposed to understand until you get there. Just as an animal doesn't know about death, the human animal doesn't know about age. When I wrote that book about my father in old age, *Patrimony*, I thought I knew what I was talking about, but I didn't really. In this new book I've brought him back in his virility, both my parents in their full flower, because that's what they need to contend with what happens – their full force, which was very real. The flow of energy in our house was extraordinary.'

It was also the atmosphere in which Roth's own special talents began to flourish. When he was a teenager and his older brother Sandy was an art student in Brooklyn, they would meet up with their friends most weekends at the Roth house in Newark:

'My mother loved it. Eight or ten boys, a very mixed bag, but one thing they had in common was tremendous humour. Some of them I still know and they remember roaring with laughter in our house – laughing and eating and laughing. This was in 1948. My father had just been promoted, my grandparents were still alive, no one was sick and the energy was terrific. It was a wonderful period, a great explosion of camaraderie. There was rivalry to some degree, but it was all around talk. Our subject was the comedy of being between fifteen and twenty – comedy located in sex and frustration – lots of longing, little activity. It was raucous but not obscene because they were in our house and there were rules to obey. I think that was the incubator for everything.'

Maybe it still is, in a ghostly way. According to David Plante, 'Roth often visits his parents' grave in New Jersey. He stands at their graveside and weeps. Then he begins to talk to them and they answer him back. So he starts joking with them, they have these funny, bantering conversations and he goes away feeling better.'

Torquil Norman

TORQUIL NORMAN, FOUNDER AND chairman of the board of Bluebird Toys, which is one of Britain's largest toy manufacturers, looks, appropriately, like the friendly giant in a children's story. He is enormously tall – six foot seven inches – but does his best to disguise his height with an amiable stoop. His grey hair is untidy; his head seems too small for the rest of him; his face is squeezed up around a prominent nose. He dislikes formality of any kind – particularly suits and ties and tight collars – and he has a knack for finding common ground with unlikely people and putting them at their ease. This gives him a curious classlessness, which, combined with his taste for pleasure and adventure, make him seem like a throwback to an earlier style of English gentleman – more daring, charming and carefree than the lean and hungry entrepreneurs of Margaret Thatcher's decade.

Norman's taste for adventure takes a specific form: flying. He has been flying in light airplanes about as long as he can remember. His father, who held one of the first pilots' licenses issued in Britain, flew him to Switzerland in his three-seater Leopard Moth in 1934, when Torquil (his mother was Irish and the name is Gaelic) was one year old. One of Torquil's two older brothers, Desmond, who is equally obsessed with flying (and, in partnership with John Britten, eventually designed and produced one of England's most successful airplanes, the Britten-Norman Islander), took him flying and taught him the rudiments while Torquil was still a schoolboy at Eton. Torquil left Eton in a blaze of glory: he was Captain of Boats and President of Pop, the school's most exclusive club, whose members wore check trousers and fancy waistcoats under their morning coats, and moved in an aura more glamorous and powerful than that of the Queen and the Prime Minister combined. He celebrated leaving school by getting his pilot's licence at the minimum legal age, eighteen, and flying his housemaster, Hubert Hartley, to Gibraltar. Hartley was a benign and distinctly absent-minded gentleman, which was just as well, since Torquil at that time had only about forty hours' solo flying experience and the aeroplane, a Leopard Moth he had bought for £400, was not in good shape. 'It was an act of great faith on Hubert's part,' he told me, 'and bravery beyond the call of duty.'

Torquil still owns a Leopard Moth, although his current one is far more air-worthy than his first. One of the reasons he is devoted to the marque is that it reminds him of his father, Sir Henry Nigel St. Valery Norman, who looms large in Torquil's life as a romantic figure: he was gifted, quixotic and remarkably courageous, and he died when Torquil was still a child. Sir Nigel had studied architecture at Cambridge and combined his profession and his love of flying by getting into airport construction at the start. In 1919, he built London's first airport, in what were then the rolling green meadows of Heston, just west of town. The old hangars are still standing, but everything else has gone: the control tower, the Propeller Bar, the floral clock that was visible from the air. The M4 motorway now runs straight down what was once the main runway.

Sir Nigel also started an air charter business, Airwork, that is now part of British Airways. When the Second World War broke out, he went into the RAF as a Wing Commander and used his experience with Airwork to help start up the Airborne Services. He organized the air transport and Lieutenant General Frederick 'Boy' Browning, the husband of Daphne Du Maurier, provided the troops. Although parachuting was not Sir Nigel's brief, it was an aerial thrill he had never experienced and he felt, characteristically, that he couldn't ask his men to jump if he hadn't jumped himself. He suffered, however, from a chronically bad hip, which made it impossible for him to land on hard ground. He jumped anyway, into Lake Windermere, and nearly drowned. It was the kind of daredevil gesture his youngest son has since found irresistible. In 1943, Sir Nigel was posted to North Africa as chief operations officer to Sir Arthur Tedder, who was the commander of the Mediterranean Allied Air Command, but the passenger plane carrying him from England had an engine failure on take-off. True to form, Sir Nigel went forward to help the pilot. When the plane crashed, nose first, the passengers escaped, but he and the pilot were killed. Torquil was ten at the time, and he had not seen his father since 1940, because he had been evacuated to America.

Between the wars, Sir Nigel had commanded the famous 601

Squadron, the Auxiliary Air Force Squadron of the County of London, based at Hendon. The 601 Squadron, the flying equivalent of Eton's Pop, was an intensely social club renowned for its wild parties and outrageous behaviour. Its members managed to make even their drab RAF uniforms flamboyant – they wore jackets with red linings, and bright-red socks – and they took pride in paying no attention to military discipline. In due course, all three of Sir Nigel's sons joined 601. Mark, the eldest, seconded himself to it from the Coldstream Guards; Desmond joined after National Service in the RAF; Torquil joined after a post-war stint in the Fleet Air Arm. 'It was the most wonderful flying club in the world,' Torquil told me. 'Every weekend we'd get together and fly Meteors around, burning up two hundred gallons of gas in twenty minutes and having a terrific time. Each summer, we went to camp in Malta for two weeks' non-stop flying and drinking. Our casual attitude gave regular RAF officers the fits, and they were constantly reporting us to the Air Ministry. Not that that had the slightest effect on us. Eventually, though, their complaints turned us into an important economy measure, and the government packed us in. But it was great while it lasted.'

In 1951, when Torquil finished at Eton, young men leaving school were still being conscripted into the National Service, which usually meant two years of boredom behind a desk in a Quonset hut in the middle of nowhere. Torquil, whose threshold of boredom is low, wangled his way into the Fleet Air Arm and trained as a naval pilot. Doing that presented certain problems since Torquil, fully grown, was three inches taller than the maximum permitted for a fighter pilot. The first day on parade, the commander at the Lee-on-Solent base camp stopped in front of him and asked how tall he was.

'Six foot two and a half inches, sir.'

'That's bloody stupid, for a start. I'm six foot three and you're at least four inches taller than I am. Petty Officer, take this man away and measure him.'

So they marched Torquil off – left-right, left-right – to the gymnasium, but when the tape came out Torquil, who was wearing regulation naval bell-bottom trousers, bent his knees and measured six foot two and a half. 'Why not put that down at six three and a half?' he suggested mildly. And that was the last he heard of it.

After Norman got his wings, he was posted to Lossiemouth, in Scotland. There he flew the Seafire, the naval version of the Spitfire. It was a beautiful plane, he says, but it had its problems: 'It had a twenty-three-hundred-horsepower engine on an airframe about the size of a Comanche, which gets by nicely with 180 to 250 hp. It flew like a bullet. You could lift off that plane and go straight up vertically. But the torque was so great that you had to be careful with the throttle. They changed the right-hand tyre every fifty flights, but the left tyre had to be changed after ten take-offs because the pressure of torque on the wheel stripped the tread.' Flying Seafires also presented a problem peculiar to Torquil. The first time he went up in one he complained, in his diffident way, that it was a bit odd that such a sophisticated fighter should be without an artificial horizon. It wasn't, but because of his height he had been sitting with his head pressed up near the canopy, and the instrument was obscured by the gunsight. After that, he learned to squeeze down in the seat whenever he flew blind through the clouds.

Torquil's training as a Navy fighter pilot almost ended with a bang. He had been transferred from Lossiemouth to Culdrose, in Cornwall, where he learned to fly the Sea Fury, the naval version of the Tempest, before joining HMS *Illustrious* at sea to complete his stint of deck landings. In those days, landing on an aircraft carrier was even trickier than it is now. The flight decks ran straight up and down the ship (now they are angled), with barriers and rows of parked planes at the forward end. In addition, piston-engined planes have drawbacks that jet pilots have never had to contemplate. The pilot of a jet sits up front and can see where he is going. He also lands with the throttle open and does not close it until the aircraft has been stopped by the arrester wires, so if something goes wrong he still has flying speed; he can fly on around for a second try. The Sea Fury, in contrast, was a big, wide plane with a huge radial engine up front, which made it impossible to see the carrier in the final approach. The pilot had to come in blind, relying entirely on the signals of the batman, who stood on a raised platform over the sea and waved instructions with two little paddles: speed up, slow down. 'Brilliant people,' Torquil said. 'They could judge your speed to within a couple of knots simply by the attitude of the plane.' Another problem was that the Sea Fury could not be landed unless it was fully stalled – no longer flying – so there were no second chances if you got it wrong. And the engine torque was so great that if you opened the throttle too quickly the plane flopped over on its back.

Naval planes have hooks under their fuselages or tails which are lowered on landing to catch the arrester wires on the deck. As Torquil was boosted off the catapult on his final, qualifying flight, his hook dropped and then banged up against the underside of the plane so hard that the spring that held it in place for landing was broken, and the hook was left hanging down. The flight controllers ordered him to fly past slowly to let them inspect the damage, and then told him to fly around for a while to burn off some fuel. When he finally came in to land, the hook hit the deck and bounced straight up again without catching a wire. The plane went clear over the first barrier. 'I dimly saw the planes parked in front of me and didn't know what to do,' Torquil said. 'I had a terrific urge to open the throttle, but a friend had done that, flipped his plane over, and gone into the sea, so I was very clear that it would be a mistake. All I could do was push the nose forward.' The left wheel caught in the second barrier and spun the plane over on its end. It landed nose down, flattening the propeller boss, and then flopped right way up onto the deck, its undercarriage broken off, sliding backwards toward the parked planes. The engine broke away, the fuel lines ruptured, the fuel exploded. But because the plane was sliding backward there was a thirty-knot wind coming over Torquil's shoulders, blowing the flames away from him. When he leaped out of the cockpit and raced upwind, he was passed by the flight-deck officer, racing in the opposite direction in order to climb into the cockpit to shut off the fuel and turn off all the other switches: 'All the things I was too scared to do, because I thought the plane was about to explode,' Torquil said. 'I was really ashamed of being so uncool.'

The medical officer walked Torquil around for half an hour to make sure he was all right. He was more than all right: he was high as a kite, cocky, laughing at everything, and behaving as if the whole episode had been one great joke. So they gave him an hour to calm down, and sent him up again, in another plane. By that time, the weather had changed. It was cold and grey, the sea had risen, the carrier was pitching violently, and the light was failing. 'In order to react properly in complicated situations, you are supposed to be relaxed,' Torquil said. 'I have to say I was as tense as a spring when I came in to land. It was a miracle I got that bloody plane on the deck in one piece. Coming downwind, with the carrier going up and down in the grey sea, I began to realize the situation had a down side to it.'

He was not censured for the accident, and he qualified without a bad mark on his record. A couple of months later, his two-year National Service was over and he went up to Trinity College,

Cambridge, to read economics and law, but by then his addiction to flying was irreversible. 'I was hugely privileged to be doing things the way they had been done all through the war, and to be doing them in those incredible aircraft,' he said. 'It was my two years in the Fleet Air Arm that really got me excited about flying.'

Torquil had kept his old Leopard Moth while he was doing his National Service. While he was posted to Lossiemouth, he flew it down to London most weekends, usually in the company of one of the local WRENS (Women's Royal Naval Service). It was an offer, apparently, that few of them could refuse. He also had the plane while he was up at Cambridge, and spent his weekends with the wild bunch at 601 Squadron. He took a year out on an exchange scholarship at Harvard, and earned his holiday money by ferrying a Piper Tri-Pacer out to the West Coast. At the end of the Harvard year, he went to Alaska. His great-great-great uncle was Sir Alexander Mackenzie, the first man to cross the North American continent north of Mexico, and the discoverer of the Mackenzie River, in northwestern Canada. Torquil's plan was to follow Mackenzie's route by car, bus and boat, but he ran out of money and spent three months logging and laying pipeline. His final year at Cambridge seemed like an anticlimax, but at least he got a Blue for rowing in one of the years when the Light Blues won a Boat Race. ('I don't think he'd have *let* them lose,' his wife, Anne, told me.) And every weekend when the weather was halfway decent there was flying, in his Leopard Moth or in 601's Meteors. The point was, no matter how hard he was working, to keep the lines open to that special sense of freedom, physical release, elation and camaraderie which is shared by the flying fraternity.

Torquil kept to the same pattern during the next five years, while he was working in the international department of J.P. Morgan in New York. When he arrived in America, the first thing he did was buy himself an old Cessna 180, and he kept it for two years. Then, because his brother Desmond had links with Piper agents, he started to buy their demonstrator models – aeroplanes like the Piper Comanche, which were fast and had a long enough range for him to fly to Virginia for a weekend's golf or to the West Indies for a spot of sun. 'One of my nicest memories is of flying back to New York on a Sunday night after a smashing weekend,' he said. 'There are huge radio masts south of Tetaboro Airport, in New Jersey, that broadcast a station called WINS. Its slogan is, "You give us twenty minutes and we'll give you the world." The masts go up two hundred feet and are so powerful that you can switch the radio compass on to them from five hundred miles out, and navigation then becomes history. You get the news and your direction simultaneously. It was the greatest pleasure to be able to fly like that when you were tired out and had had a lovely time.' He also discovered that he could fly the Pipers back to England during the summer and sell them at sufficient profit to pay for his holiday.

In 1959, Torquil met the American parachuting ace Jacques Istel, who had opened a parachuting-and-skydiving centre in Orange, Massachusetts. So Torquil, feeling that, on principle, he should explore whatever pleasures the sky has to offer, took up parachuting. Istel had bought an old farmhouse which he called the Inn at Orange. The name was misleading; it was just a big bunkhouse filled with kids who came to jump; but the atmosphere was wonderful. The Inn had an airstrip but there were no lights on it. The first time Torquil went there, on a Friday evening after work, he reckoned he could fly to Worcester and then follow the road lights almost to the airstrip. The only problem was how to land. He called Istel before he took off and told him to park the car at the end of the runway, so that he could land into the headlights. It was a good idea in theory, but in practice the glare made it impossible for him to tell how high off the ground he was. All he could do was put the plane into a gentle descent and wait until he hit something. Luckily, it was the runway. After that, they developed a safer technique: Istel would park at the downwind end of the runway, headlights blazing, and Torquil would land over the top of the car. The car would then follow him down the airstrip.

Torquil took to parachuting and skydiving as effortlessly as he had taken to flying. In those days, training was less formal and regulated than it is now. He did a morning's practice and jumped off a high table to show he could land, then went straight up and did static-line jumps – those in which the parachutist's rip cord is fixed to the plane and is pulled automatically at the critical moment. After that, it was free-fall or bust. For a few weeks, he held the national baton-passing record: he passed a baton in free-fall on his fourteenth jump. It seemed a perfect way to round off a week's banking: first the night flight to Orange and the tricky landing on an unlit airstrip, then two days of pumping adrenalin in one of the riskiest and most liberating activities ever invented, then the night flight back to the city and his job at Morgan.

There was an English girl at Orange, but for a while Torquil never managed to meet her. Her name was Anne Montagu, and she was not the kind of young woman you would associate with free-fall parachuting. She had brown hair, startled dark eyes, a lovely smile and a tentative manner. She had also trained as a painter at the Slade School in its great days, when William Coldstream and Lucian Freud were around. Why, exactly, she was skydiving at the Inn at Orange was not clear except that, like many upper-class English, she had an eccentric, wild streak that occasionally demanded expression. 'It was a confused period of my life,' she said. 'I wanted to do something entirely out of myself – something that was up to me alone – to find out if I really cared about anything.' In those days, however, the wild streak did not include her compatriots. 'I heard about this Englishman who was as brilliant at skydiving as he was at everything else, and I made a point of not being there when he was around,' she said. No sooner did Torquil manage to meet her than she moved out to Hemet, California, where Istel had started a second parachuting school. It was some months before Torquil caught up with her again, and she succumbed to the temptation of being flown around the United States and the Caribbean by this guy who was brilliant at everything. 'He asked me where I wanted to go,' Anne said. 'I'd driven across the States and I'd studied the map but I could never find the Shenandoah River, which I felt strongly about because of the song and the lovely name. When I said, "The Shenandoah," he just turned the plane around and pointed it in the right direction. He knew exactly where it was. It was dark when we got there. There was a marvelous moon and the great sweep of the river. Well, this is it, I thought.'

Anne and Torquil were married in 1961, and that same year he left J.P. Morgan in New York and returned to England for good. He and Anne flew home before the wedding in his Piper Comanche – a harrowing journey, via Bermuda and Lisbon, with bad weather and minimum visibility all the way. They eventually landed in England, not at one of the London airports but at Eastleigh, in Hampshire, because Torquil wanted to introduce his bride-to-be to his mother, who was living in nearby Salisbury. As they were climbing unsteadily out of the cockpit, a customs officer pedalled up on his bicycle. He was wearing a club blazer and white flannels, and was clearly furious at having been dragged away from his cricket match. He immediately embargoed the airplane, and Torquil had to leave an expensive wristwatch as surety before he and Anne were allowed off the airfield.

There was not a lot of flying for the next few years. Torquil worked in London for the merchant bankers Philip Hill, Higginson, Erlangers, and he and Anne began what within seven years became a family of five children – three boys, two girls – all of them, like their father, very tall indeed. Occasionally, he got to fly the bank's airplane, but that was not enough to keep in practice, and eventually he let his pilot's license lapse.

It took Torquil four and a half years at Philip Hill to discover he was not cut out to be a banker. It was not just that he did not like wearing a suit and eating business lunches. He also lacked the instinctive pusillanimity that seemed necessary to the banking temperament. 'Investment bankers have a very low attention span,' he said. 'If a project isn't going to make a lot of money for them in a short time, or if there are significant risks, then they are very tentative about getting involved. I discovered I had too much sympathy for the people we refused to lend money to because they actually needed it.' He also discovered that the side of banking he enjoyed most was learning about how people ran their businesses. He and another wild man, Ken Bates, had started a venture-capital company, Batehill, which put money into small businesses, took a share of the equity, and tried to help the companies succeed. Two years later, when Philip Hill merged with M. Samuel to become Hill Samuel, which is now one of the major merchant banks, Torquil, who has no taste for mergers and the infighting that goes with them, quit and became general manager of Mineral Separations, a large industrial holding company, with the job of clearing up the smaller subsidiary companies that were not doing well. By 1969, he had sold most of them off and among those left was Berwick's Toy Company. He bought that one from Mineral Separations with the help of a merchant bank, and proceeded to build it up until it was one of the largest toy companies in Britain, with a turnover, in 1979, of sixteen million pounds.

Initially, his main concern had been to make the company efficient and profitable, but gradually the toys themselves began to interest him more and more. He found he had a flair for knowing what children want. 'Kids love detail,' he said. 'And that's something I can bring to the party, because I love detail, too. And I love coming up with copy that will amuse children. I suppose I have a very low mental age.'

Torquil's friends put it differently. 'The length of time he has worked in the industry and the level he's worked at have given him an extraordinary understanding of which products and ideas are acceptable,' said Tom Charnock, who is the former managing director of Bluebird Toys and has worked with Torquil for more than a decade. 'Despite his size, he's able to scale down to the vision a very young child will have of your product. We, as adults, look at a toy and think, That looks pretty good. But Torquil has the ability to imagine he's a four-year-old and he's seeing it at eye-level. What we see is, say, a small garage, but to a little child it's a tall building and he's looking at it from underneath. An adult, looking down on it, would make sure the roof tiles looked good, but Torquil, seeing it from underneath, thinks, It's got to have rafters here, decorations there. He gets more satisfaction in seeing the product in the hands of children than in the profitability.'

In September of 1979, however, having turned the company around and made it into a major force in the market, he had a serious policy disagreement with a colleague on the board of what was by then called Berwick Timco. Although Torquil hates company politics and had left his career in banking rather than be dragged into them, this disagreement was so profound that he resigned, and mounted an attack to buy the company back. An extraordinary general meeting was called, and he defended his record from the floor. He put his case so eloquently that when the vote came he lost by a mere two percent, even though the whole board was united against him. 'The united board frightened the shareholders,' Anne said. 'They'd never heard of one guy being right and the whole board wrong.'

The result, for Torquil, was a mid-life crisis in the most literal sense: at the age of forty-six, he found himself out of a job, with relatively little money, and five children to educate. 'I spent two months moping around the house and having my portrait painted by Anne,' he said. Anne herself doesn't see it quite that way. In the portrait, Torquil is a dark, brooding figure sprawled disconsolately in an armchair, a book in his lap, his long legs stretched out in front of him. It is a sombre painting done in bold brush-strokes – blues and grays and greens, the impasto so thick that it seems almost as though the artist were modelling in paint. She has caught the depression as well as the man, and it is a painting with which she is, rightly, very pleased.

Self-pity is not a vice that Torquil feels drawn to, and he is not a person who likes losing. 'He took an awful knock at Berwick Timco,' said Joe Brewer, a major figure in the British toy trade. 'The vote would have killed a lesser man. But he picked himself up, dusted himself off and started again.' Another colleague, Bill Dowle, who buys toys for Woolworth's in Britain, called the Berwick Timco vote 'the making of Torquil and also the making of Bluebird Toys.'

What happened was in fact quite simple: Torquil got the idea for a toy. It was a little playhouse in the shape of a teapot, with teacup armchairs, a teacup motor car, tea-chest tables, and a white dog called Sugarlump. When you turned the lid, the rooms swung around inside, and when you lifted the lid like an umbrella there were places to stow the figures. Its name was the Big Yellow Teapot. 'What he had done was reinvent the doll's house,' Bill Dowle said.

Torquil made a model of the toy and then could not bear the idea of licensing it for someone else to manufacture. What the hell, he thought. *Per ardua ad astra*, as they say in the R.A.F. – I'll start my own company. But to do that he needed more than one product (the Big Yellow Teapot turned out to be one of the most successful toys ever made in England, and is still sold, a decade later). So he looked around for gaps in the market. This was the time when, thanks to economies at the Ministry of Education, school lunches, which had once been free to everyone, were becoming expensive. Suddenly, there was a new social split in schools between rich kids, whose parents could afford to pay for hot lunches, and poor kids, who had to make do with sandwiches in a plastic bag. Torquil's idea was for junior lunchboxes, bright-coloured, decorated with the children's favorite characters – Mickey Mouse, Mr. Men, My Little Pony – and with their own special plastic flasks inside. Lo and behold, hot lunches no longer seemed such a big deal, and the kids with the zippy lunchboxes had a social edge. The market turned out to be just about unlimited; his company still makes hundreds of thousands of lunchboxes every year.

Having sorted out his ideas, Torquil called Tom Charnock, who was then working for Peter Pan Playthings, a Berwick Timco subsidiary in Peterborough. They arranged to meet in the windswept car park of the Comet Inn, near the old De Havilland factory in Hatfield. As Charnock described it, it was a classic Torquil occasion: 'He opened up the back of his car, lifted some blankets and sheets, and there were these wonderful model toys. They were made of cardboard and bits of plastic and clay modelling materials. It was quite a variety. When we got to the lunchboxes, I said, "The British don't use them. The Americans do, the Europeans do, but we don't." He said, "Well, that's the size of the market," and I thought, That's the scale of the guy. Because other people aren't doing something doesn't mean the idea should be ignored. Quite the contrary – it should be examined. That was really the statement he was making to me. When I told him the products looked terrific, he said, "OK, would you like a job?" "Where's the factory?" I said. "We don't have one of those," he said. "We'll have to shop around for one." He made it sound like going to the local supermarket to buy a can of beans. I said, "What about really boring things, like salary?" "I can't pay you what you're being paid now," he said. "Terrific," I said. "How about a car?" "Haven't you got one at home we could use?" he said. "Where's the office going to be?" I said. "Haven't you got a spare bedroom?" he said. "Hang on, Torquil," I said. "It needs a certain leap of the imagination to take all this in." "It'll all come good in the end," he said. And I replied, "What the hell, it's worth it." So there I was, at the end of an hour and a half, throwing up a decent career, a decent salary and decent prospects to go to no factory, no office, no this, no that, no the other. It was an interesting situation. My wife and kids thought I was deranged.'

The problem was how to finance the new company when all that Torquil had in the bank was a gigantic overdraft. His one asset was the family house – a rambling, rather shabby Edwardian mansion with a swimming pool at the far end of an overgrown garden. The house was on Avenue Road, St. John's Wood – an expensive address, close to Regent's Park. Anne had never much liked the neighbourhood: the shops were distant and expensive, and there was little sense of community, because most of the neighbours were foreign diplomats. So when a property company offered a huge sum to tear down the house and build a luxury-apartment block, Torquil accepted it. The proceeds from the sale paid off his overdraft and provided some of the initial capital for the new company. His merchant-banker friends put together the rest, and in January of 1981 Bluebird Toys opened, in a small rented factory in Swindon, seventy miles west of London.

The beginning of the 1980s was a low point for the British economy. 'We were the paupers of the world,' Tom Charnock said. 'People were wondering when they were going to bury England and call it quits, then maybe start off again on another island, somewhere else. The toy industry went through a particularly bad time. Five or six major companies went to the wall, and the share of toys made in Britain slipped from about two thirds of the British market to less than a quarter. Torquil saw this huge negative – high unemployment, market-share decline – as an opportunity. His attitude was: If we start a business in a depression, when things get better it's going to be easier to be successful. When I mentioned this to my wife, she said, "What happens if you're not successful?" She was right, of course. Torquil tends to focus on the potential benefits, rather than harp on the negatives.'

Most other business men agreed with Jenny Charnock. 'Torquil's opening a factory in Swindon was considered suicidal at a time when almost everything manufactured – particularly if it was small and plastic – was imported from the Far East,' said Irwin Steinhouse, a London property developer who knows the Normans. 'We gave him our admiration and our sympathy in advance. We reckoned it was the act of a remarkably courageous man – like flying old airplanes, only more so.'

'He's a patriot,' Anne Norman said. 'He wanted to help the British economy get going again – to employ people at a time of mass unemployment. He feels a responsibility for his advantages. He also wanted to show the people at Berwick Timco that he could do it – that he had been right all along. He felt their treatment of him was a slur on his name, and he wanted to clear it.'

Torquil's colleagues in the toy industry did what they could to help. 'I'd kept them amused all summer with my great battle with the board of Berwick Timco, so they were very sympathetic,' he said. 'Toy-making is a nice business. The products are fun and, because it's a fashion industry, there's a lot going on all the time. It's also a small industry and people rarely leave it, because you make friends and they help you out.' In its first year of business, despite the huge expenses of opening a factory, tooling it up, buying a computer, and drumming up customers for its new line of toys, Bluebird astonished its bankers by losing a mere eighteen thousand pounds on a turnover of a million and a quarter. It has since reocated its Swindon premises twice and now occupies a factory and offices that measure a quarter of a million square feet. The company also has a factory of 115,000 square feet in Peterborough, in the East Midlands, and a third factory, of 300,000 square feet – on seven acres – at Merthyr Tydfil, in South Wales. It now directly employs twelve hundred people in all, and gives work to about the same number through its suppliers, toolmakers and plastic converters. In 1989, its sales were thirty-nine million pounds, and its profits were two million two hundred thousand pounds.

Meanwhile, Berwick Timco, which had made a profit of a million and a half pounds in the year Torquil left them, 'got into a muddle,' as he put it, and went into receivership. 'Neither Torquil nor I took pleasure in seeing them go to the wall,' said Tom Charnock. 'There were a lot of good people in the company, and just a few very influential guys who had taken their eyes off how the business needed to be. But perhaps the reason I wasn't too picky about details when we started Bluebird was that I understood Torquil had something to prove. And if you've got something to prove you'll either prove it or fail abysmally. Torquil desperately wanted to demonstrate to investors and bankers that the Norman name was sound, that he was financially capable, and that he could put a business together. I think those motives had a lot to do with moving us forward in the early years. But by the time we floated Bluebird as a public company, in the mid-80s, that pressure had become history, because we had demonstrated sales up from zilch to eight, nine, ten, eleven million, with a fourteen-percent return on sales, pretax. From there on, we were marching forward, and Torquil didn't have anything to prove any more.' In 1986, Bluebird, already a major force in the British toy industry, bought Peter Pan Playthings from the failed Berwick Timco group, and two years later they added Merit Toys, another Berwick Timco subsidiary – a gesture that appealed to Torquil's finely honed sense of poetic justice.

In Bluebird's first years, Torquil, up to his neck in debt, worked flat out to make the company a success. But even though he was both the chairman and the chief executive, the aspect of the job that appealed to him most was making decisions about the products: what they should look like, how they fitted together, how they worked. Once the company became big, that seemed to him the most important element in its continuing success. 'It all becomes easier if you've got something everyone wants to buy,' he said. 'It's relatively easy to take on good accountants, production people and salesmen, but it's extraordinarily hard to find good products. After all, it's a small, idiot industry, so who wants to design toys?' He did, for one. In due course, he stopped being an executive and took on the combined role of chairman and product-development manager, and Bluebird became the only British toy company to spend large sums of money on design and development. Now the ideas come mostly from him, but he also talks to designers and inventors and visits toy fairs all over the world, trying to work out which areas of the market have been neglected. He has a talented team of technicians, who advise him on what is possible in terms of engineering and the shapes that can be obtained from injection-molding tools. As a result of his feeling for children – for what they want and what they respond to – and, above all, his passion for detail, his company has led the way in miniaturization. For 1990, for instance, there was a range of tiny dolls in immaculate detail – with their own desks and cars and kitchen tables – designed as rings, all small enough to be worn on a child's finger. Torquil has also done what he can to reinvent toy soldiers, restoring them to something like they used to be when he was young: not twelve-inch-high Action Men, the macho equivalents of dolls, but little inch-and-a-half figures similar to the soldiers children used to arrange, by the regiment, across the nursery floor. The figures have moustaches and bulging muscles; the vehicles have guns that fire, hatches that open and shut, bombs that drop. Torquil's New Model Army is called M.A.N.T.A. Force, and its enemies are Mad Karnock's Evil Karnoids. There are already twenty million M.A.N.T.A. men and Karnoids in the world, and in a couple of years, Bluebird predicts, they will outnumber the population of Great Britain. The company has also produced an even smaller-scale army, called Zero Hour, whose slogan is, 'When the Brave Must Fight to Save the World.' 'They're going to have to fight bloody hard,' said Torquil, 'because they're only three quarters of an inch high.'

While the Norman children were growing up and their father was transforming himself into a captain of industry, there was no time for flying. So Torquil consoled himself with the Bus. In its way, the Bus was the ultimate toy, designed by Torquil to carry him, Anne, their five children and their friends. He drew up the plans, bought a chassis, had the coachwork built by Plaxton, a specialist firm in Scarborough, and then drove the completed shell to Southend-on-Sea, where a team of carpenters, electricians and upholsterers fitted it out as lovingly as if it had been one of the Royal Family's Rolls Royces.

The Bus had three main compartments. There was a master bedroom at the back, with a seven-foot bed, cupboards, drawers and a basin. In the centre were five bunks, four running across the Bus; the fifth ran longitudinally and had an electronically controlled toilet beneath it, which slid in and out on rails. Up front was a kitchen with a table that seated ten and could be lowered hydraulically to become an enormous bed. One of four rows of seats could be lifted up and swung over, depending on whether you were eating or driving. Each bed or bunk had its own reading light, and there was a hi-fi system with speakers in every compartment. On top of the Bus was a twenty-foot-long roof rack with a boat on it. In the trunk was a motor bike.

Twice a year the family took off on the cross-Channel ferries for the continent – Easter in Brittany, summer further afield – with no hotel bills and no worries about where they would sleep at night. They would stop at little beaches, go boating and fishing, and build enormous sandcastles. Then, after supper, Torquil, who gets by without much sleep, would drive off again into the night, with the kids sitting up front in their pajamas. (There were holders along the dashboard for their cups of cocoa.) They would wander off to bed, one by one, and wake next morning to a different beach. The summer of the Fischer–Spassky chess marathon, 1972, Torquil and Anne would take a chess set and putter off on the motor bike to a nearby cafe, where they would spend hours drinking wine and replaying the Reykjavik games from the newspaper accounts. And each year, when the motor racing circus arrived in England for the British Grand Prix, Torquil would drive the Bus down to Brand's Hatch, where the family camped for the three days of practice and racing. They bolted chairs to the roof and had their own grandstand for the race. At night, they wandered around the pits, watching the Ferrari mechanics change engines and throw spanners to each other, and listening to them sing *Rigoletto* – 'the whole magic,' Torquil called it. And the Bus itself was a continuing magical experience, created by Torquil to give his children a taste of childhood perfection. The children are grown-up now, but they still talk about it as a major influence in their lives.

The Normans kept the Bus for eleven years, and finally sold it, in 1975, to a drag-racer named Ron Picardo; he dolled it up with coloured lights, put a trailer on the back for his dragsters, and used it to take his family around the country to watch him race. In 1989, the Bus was resurrected as another Bluebird best-seller: the Big Red Fun Bus, a London double-decker kitted out with living-room, bedroom, kitchen, a garden on the roof, and a cast of seven, including a monkey, a hedgehog and a hen.

All this time, the flying bug was still working away in Torquil's system. Finally, in 1985, when Bluebird went public and the family fortunes were securely reestablished, Anne bought him an old De Havilland Tiger Moth. 'He was always buying me these wonderful presents and I could never find anything good enough to give him in return,' she said. 'Once he bought me a jukebox – bright blue and in full working order – but the biggest present he ever gave me was a canal barge. It was a secret. He arranged for it to be brought down from Rugby to London, and one morning it just appeared in the canal at Regent's Park. It was a marvelous gesture, but it was also a kind of disaster. The children were all small, and I had a room where I painted, and there was just no space in my life for it. I couldn't make it into a studio, because it rocked and was too small for my canvases. People threw stones at it; we'd go down and repair it, but there was nothing we could do to stop them. It was just awful. It was like having another child, but one I couldn't look after and had to let die. It came so near being destroyed by vandals that in the end we had to sell it. But it had a sort of afterlife: someone kept chickens in it at Maidenhead. It was the only one of Torquil's brilliant presents that went wrong – a wonderful surprise, but just too much. I bought him the Tiger Moth because I wanted, just once, to give him something really great.'

His Tiger Moth is like the airplanes I used to make out of balsa wood and paper in my childhood: a little biplane with two open cockpits, one behind the other, a deep-blue fuselage, white wings and tail plane, and struts of polished wood – every detail bright and clean and perfect. The first time I saw it, in September of 1986, Torquil was keeping it just north of London, at the Panshanger airfield, not far from the old De Havilland factory. (The factory is now part of British Aerospace.) Panshanger is about as rudimentary as an airfield can get before it reverts to arable land. It has a clubhouse with a coffee machine, a radio which usually functions only at weekends, three hangars – one big, two small – and a pump for fuelling airplanes. Torquil's hangar was away from all this, on the far side of the field, in a little doorless shell of corrugated iron, big enough, at a pinch, to hold three light aircraft.

The Tiger Moth is small and light and delicate-looking, as airplanes were supposed to be before they became just another form of cramped and impersonal mass transport in which you know you are airborne only if you are lucky enough to be sitting by a window. When Torquil removed the chocks from its wheels, it was light enough for the two of us to manoeuvre it easily out of the hangar – you lifted it by its tail strut and pushed – but because it was made of wood and canvas it had to be handled with care. There were special places to put your feet when you climbed into the cockpit, and special places not to hold on to. We put on our gear: a zip-up flying suit for him, an extra sweater and jacket for me, and leather flying helmets and goggles for both of us – just like Snoopy and the Red Baron. The engine started sweetly at the first swing of the propeller. We strapped ourselves in, Torquil behind, I in front. The seat harness was a four-point con-

traption made of three-inch khaki webbing. At the start, it felt
uncomfortable to be held so rigidly in place; later, when we were
flying upside down, I was glad of it.

We taxied out onto the runway, Torquil revved the engine to a
pleasant roar, the plane moved forward, the tail lifted, and in less than
a hundred yards we were airborne. The instruments on the dashboard
were minimal – an airspeed indicator, a rev-counter, an altimeter, a
turn-and-bank indicator, an oil pressure gauge and a compass – ageing
black dials with yellowish needles and figures. The joystick in my
hands and the rudder control pedals were linked to those in the rear
cockpit, so I could follow what Torquil was doing to control the
plane. My head was out in the air, the wind was in my face, the sun
shone peacefully.

We climbed to a thousand feet and levelled off. Flying at this low
level is like being on an invisible seam between the earth and the sky
and, paradoxically, you can feel the height more acutely than when
you are at a greater altitude. All the details below were intensely sharp:
the harvest neatly stooked in the fields, cars on the roads, a man
walking his dog across a field, a child waving to us from his back
garden, a grand Palladian mansion with a bright blue swimming pool
on its lawn, and, farther off, the office blocks of Hemel Hempstead
and St. Albans glinting in the sun.

Torquil pulled back gently on the joystick. At three thousand feet
we flew suddenly into cloud. One moment the clouds were above
us, looking as solid as rock; the next we were moving through them
at ninety miles an hour – great, softly streaming masses, as beautiful
as a girl's hair. Then, just as suddenly, we were out again in the
sunlight.

The intercom was an old fashioned air tube into the headphones of
my helmet. Torquil's voice came in above the noise of the engine:
'Feel like some aerobatics? Nothing fancy.'

I nodded vigorously.

'Loop,' said the cheerful voice in my ear.

Torquil dipped the nose, then pulled back hard on the joystick. My
mouth dropped open with the g-force and my stomach dropped with
it. The sun, which had been obscured by the upper wing, came into
view. Then the pressure on my stomach eased and we were moving
downward fast. There was a blur of blue and green and yellow, which
cleared slowly. I looked up and saw the fields, with their bales of hay
in tidy rows, right in front of my face, yet in no way did I feel upside

down. Then, still slowly, the sky was back where it should be, and the horizon was steady.

'OK?'

'Terrific.'

'Right ho, then. Let's try a spin.'

Again the plane dipped and climbed, my mouth dropped open, my stomach lurched. At the top of the curve – this time I was ready for it and could see the earth clearly above my head – the engine stopped and the plane seemed to hang motionless. There was a violent movement of the rudder pedals, and suddenly we were falling like a sycamore leaf, round and round, the landscape and sky spinning faster and faster, and in utter silence, until the plane steadied, the engine burst into life again, and the world reassembled itself.

There was a third manoeuvre, a barrel-roll, during which, I learned later, the airplane spirals like a corkscrew. But I could not make that out at the time because my stomach was rolling faster than the barrel and my mouth had dropped open so wide I thought it would unhinge itself. All I saw was a spinning vortex of sky and ground.

'Sorry about that,' Torquil said over the intercom. 'Bit untidy.'

The loop, the spin and the barrel-roll are formal procedures – three of a large repertoire of aerobatic manoeuvres – with set rules and criteria for performance. You get it right or you do it shoddily or, worse still, you foul up. But essentially, they are all variations on a single theme: play. And what distinguishes this particular style of play from landbound equivalents is that it is in three dimensions. When Torquil put the Tiger Moth into a steeply banked turn, it felt as if the airplane had poised one wing tip on an invisible pinnacle, then pirouetted around it. It was dancing in three dimensions, playing in space, and the effect it produced was one of total freedom.

On my first visit to Panshanger, there was a little Cessna 180 in Torquil's private hangar, along with the Tiger Moth. When I went back a few months later, there was a third plane inside: an old De Havilland Leopard Moth, a high-winged monoplane with an enclosed cabin that seats three – the pilot up front, two passengers behind him. The Leopard Moth was just back from being rebuilt and, like the Tiger Moth, every detail was shining and perfect. The cabin, in particular, was a marvel of old-fashioned craftsmanship – cloth head lining, polished woodwork, seats padded in red leather – like the inside of a vintage car. 'The design of light aeroplanes hasn't advanced much in the last fifty years,' Torquil said. 'The Leopard Moth does everything a modern plane would do, and at about the same speed. It'll fly me to Bordeaux in comfort at 115 miles an hour. And it has the added advantage of folding wings, so it's easy to store. That's one of its pleasures. The other is its construction. All the Moths were designed at a time when they didn't have an excess of power in the engine and they didn't have these modern materials like titanium and carbon fibre. So they made aircraft out of materials they understood: high grade Irish linen, nice wood like ash, tubular steel welded up for the engine bearers. In the Leopard Moth, the shock absorbers are rubber pads under compression, and the fuselage is plywood and fabric. There's nothing complicated about it. The materials suited what they were trying to do. It's a question of craftsmanship, not high tech.'

It was raining that day when Torquil collected me at nine a.m., but the weather people had predicted clear skies by ten. We hung around, listening to the rain hammering on the hangar's corrugated iron roof, while Torquil lovingly, and unnecessarily, rubbed a cloth over the Moths' immaculate paintwork and tinkered with the engines. It was still raining at midday when the pubs opened, and it cleared only when we drove into London, several pints to the bad, at two o'clock.

This disappointment seemed to convince Torquil that he had let me down, so he called a couple of weeks later and offered me a quick spin up to Norfolk in the Tiger Moth for a rally of old airplanes. One of the pleasures of flying in an open cockpit in England in early summer is that you don't have to stop to smell the flowers; they come to you. At two hundred feet on a warm day, great clouds of perfume envelop you as you go: mayflower from the hedges that bound each little field, wafts of pine-scent from the intermittent patches of plantation. At Felthorpe, there were rows of old airplanes lined up outside the clubhouse, all of them brightly painted and beautifully turned out. Each time a new plane arrived – planes were coming in from all over the country – people waved, greeted one another, then wandered up to admire the machinery and talk shop. It was like being a member of an exclusive club, except that the qualifications for joining had nothing to do with class; all you needed was a passion for flying old aircraft. And, unlike most English clubs, this one invited the wife and kids to come along and share the fun. Most of them were crowded around a barbecue that was smoking away outside the clubhouse. We flew back to London stuffed with charcoal-broiled hamburgers and sausages, and there were no aerobatics that day.

The peak production time for the toy industry runs from June until mid-November, in order to get goods into the shops during the buildup for Christmas. From November to June, there is a series of toy fairs – in Harrogate, Paris, London, Milan, Nuremberg, New York, Valencia, Tokyo – at which the manufacturers show their products, push new lines and do business with agents and buyers. Toy fairs are Aladdin's caves of everything a child could ever wish for, from tinsel for the Christmas tree to hand-carved, Georgian-style rocking-horses, with detachable leather saddles and tack, that retail for more than two thousand pounds. The only peculiarity of the occasions is that there are never any children around. The places swarm with soberly dressed business men and women making deals or sitting solemnly, head to head, trying out the latest games.

Torquil is President of the British Toy and Hobby Manufacturers Association, and so a major figure at the London Toy Fair, which takes place at the end of January each year. In 1990, the main story going the rounds of the fair concerned a typical Norman escapade. He had taken a friend for a quick spin in the Cessna to Clacton-on-Sea, on the Essex coast. The Cessna needed an airing, he said, and, more important, Clacton has a fish-and-chip shop where the chips are distinctly superior and the fish comes straight from the sea. He mentioned the jaunt, in passing, to a financial correspondent of *The Times*, who printed the story in the 'City Diary,' where it was picked up by the tabloid press and a couple of local radio stations. A number of the bigger players in the toy industry went around the London fair with clippings of the tabloid report and whipped them out of their pockets without provocation, with the sole purpose of embarrassing Torquil.

Partly, it was good clean fun, but it was also a gesture of affection. Quite simply, his colleagues in the trade are proud of him. 'Torquil *is* the British toy industry,' said Ken Lewis, a director of Woolworth's. Joe Brewer said, 'He's enormously knowledgeable about products, and brilliant at developing ideas. He's also the greatest contact man I know. He knows everybody, and everybody knows him. When someone says "toys," everybody thinks of Torquil.' Bill Dowle said, 'He's a great ambassador for the toy business. He has enriched the world.' Even Tom Charnock, who is not given to superlatives, agrees. 'You don't have to be very good to be highly regarded in the toy industry,' he said. 'It's an insular business, sometimes downright incestuous. You have grandfather, father and son all working in the same company. That doesn't really make for innovation. Torquil functions on a different level from the others. He spent a considerable time in merchant banking; he speaks two or three European languages; he has legal training, and his whole educational level is far above the general norm; he is a brilliant sportsman and he flies old airplanes. Back in the Elizabethan days, he'd have been out there sailing the ships, finding us new lands to the west, taking on the Spaniards on the high seas.' In other words, the Clacton jaunt was just another of those larger-than-life gestures his colleagues routinely expect from Torquil, like a champagne lunch he gave at another fish-and-chip shop the day after Ava Gardner died. He and his friends ate deep-fried cod and drank Moët & Chandon to wish his favorite film star well in the great Hollywood in the sky.

The Nuremberg Toy Fair, the major event in the toy-makers' calendar, takes place in early February, ten days after the London fair. The night before the 1990 Nuremberg fair opened, England was swept by storms, and flights from Heathrow were delayed, so Torquil staged another of his impromptu parties. Duty-free champagne, jugs of orange juice, and pint mugs full of ice made Buck's Fizz; smoked salmon sandwiches from the cafeteria – all thick-sliced bread and very little salmon – provided the food. Within ten minutes, a dozen gloomy toy traders were having a great time. By the time the flight was called, fifty minutes late, we had got through a bottle of champagne apiece, though, according to H.M. Customs regulations, no bottles of alcohol are supposed to be opened until the purchasers have left the country. But the duty-free receipts are stapled to the plastic bags the bottles come in, so if you put the empties back in the bags and throw the lot into the rubbish bins there is no trace of your crime. 'I think we've found a chink in the security,' Torquil said.

The party continued on the plane and then in the hotel in Nuremberg, where bratwurst, sauerkraut and beer had been ordered by telex in advance. When I left it, at two a.m., Torquil was still going strong, and when I got down to breakfast the next morning, at 7.30, he was there before me, his meal already finished. For the next four days, he patrolled the fair, doing deals and looking for new ideas. But even Torquil, with his apparently limitless energy, restricted the number of pavilions he visited. The London Toy Fair fills both floors of Earls Court, a vast, hangar-like exhibition hall between Kensington and Hammersmith, but its whole spread could be hidden away in one corner of the Nuremberg Fair, which consists of thirteen huge pavilions built in the '50s and '60s to restore Nuremberg to the position it had occupied before the Second World War as the world centre of the toy industry. 'If you walked all the aisles, you'd cover more than twenty miles,' I was told. And that was without detours.

Torquil's first appointment of the day was with Abe Mohr, a tough-looking Israeli with a greying Velázquez beard, a lined face and sharp grey eyes. Mohr, who looks as if he were on permanent reserve duty with an elite commando regiment, is an agent for the band of eccentrics who spend their lives inventing toys. At the fair, he had rented a windowless cubby hole with a table, chairs, a coffee machine, and, at the back, a large cupboard, its shelves piled with cardboard boxes of varying sizes. He had two people to help him – a silent elderly woman with a benign smile, and his wife, who was lean and fit and handsome, like him, and looked as if she were a member of the same regiment. Torquil had come with John Hanwell, the young development manager from the Merit Toys division of Bluebird. The older woman hovered by the shelves; the rest of us settled around the table.

'I'm giving you first choice,' Mohr said. 'The pick of our market research.'

Torquil looked embarrassed. 'Actually, we don't do market research,' he said. 'We work on hunches.'

The older woman handed Mohr a big box marked 'Foot Tops.' The tops were small and plastic, and Torquil seemed unimpressed.

Mohr shrugged. 'OK, so the box is huge, the merchandise is small.'

'I was thinking of marketing a game called Royalty,' Torquil said. 'A big box with nothing in it except a piece of paper saying the royalty goes to Abe.'

Mohr opened another box and said, 'Are you looking for bubbles?'

'I love bubbles.'

Mohr took out an elaborate yellow gun and filled it with liquid soap. When he pulled the trigger, the soap dribbled out of the end of the muzzle and there were no bubbles.

'Don't you feel a slight sense of disappointment?' Torquil asked.

'We have one that works with foam,' Mohr said. 'I'll show it to you in New York.'

The boxes kept coming: the Sound Car, whose sound was not impressive; Body Bell, which comes on a belt and dances when you dance; Musical Squares; Willy the Weight-Lifter; Wiggle 'n' Giggle; Whatchamacallit.

'That name is my one contribution to the toy industry,' Torquil said. 'I invented it twenty years ago.'

'It's still selling, and now I've got the rights,' Mohr said.

More toys: Crazy Airplane, Zebra and Lions, Cat in the Fishshop, Dachshund and Fleas. We played the Ice-Floe Game, Top Hat, and Jumping Monkeys. Torquil and Mohr got involved in a keen game of Tricky Tac Toe, which entailed putting magnetic butterflies onto magnetic flowers; if you put them on the wrong way, they jumped off. When Mohr won, Torquil gave him a sour look and said, 'Whatever happened to customer relations?'

All the time, Torquil and John Hanwell were taking notes on the toys that interested them. At the end of the meeting, Torquil flipped through the notes and summarized them into a tape-recorder for transcription back at the head office in Swindon. Mohr and Hanwell arranged further talks for the following week in New York. 'I won't be able to make that,' Torquil said. 'My diary is full.'

Then Torquil disappeared into the packed aisles like a long-distance swimmer into the sea. I sighted him occasionally, looming above the crowd, always deep in conversation with some seemingly diminutive colleague, and he appeared at some of the spontaneous lunch parties the British contingent held each day at one of the fair's five restaurants. Otherwise, there was no way of keeping up with him. I gave up each day by about four o'clock, went back to the hotel and slept for two hours, while Torquil went on with his ten-hour tour of duty. 'He's meeting people, cementing relationships,' Bill Dowle said when I asked him what Torquil was doing. 'But mostly he's looking for ideas for 1992. He's one of the very few of us who go to the Tokyo Toy Fair. You can't buy anything in Japan any more, and it's hard to sell to them. He goes for ideas and for joint ventures.'

In the evenings, Torquil came straight from the fair to the cocktail parties that British agents were throwing for foreign buyers. Then we all moved on to dinner – Bavarian Chinese, Bavarian French, even plain Bavarian – followed by long sessions in Nuremberg's picturesque medieval pubs. It was more like an endurance test than a trade fair.

Torquil was also the prime mover behind the binge the British throw themselves each year at Nuremberg. Everybody comes – the buyers, the agents, the salesmen, the representatives of the big firms and the small – and what is remarkable about the evening is the friendliness, the apparent lack of rivalry, and people's willingness to drink too much and make fools of themselves without worrying about image or reputation. 'Compared with America, the British toy trade is a community, small and compact, like a village,' an agent named

Roslyn Verlinden said. 'You know everybody, you help each other out. And unless you're a proprietor the chances are you'll want to move to another firm at some stage, so it's natural to be friendly.' Bill Dowle put it more succinctly: 'Of course it's a friendly industry. What do you expect when the end product is a happy child?'

Between work and celebration, Torquil seemed to be putting in a twenty-hour day in Nuremberg, and at the end of it he and the rest of the crew flew on for more of the same at the New York Toy Fair. He travels light: one suit, a pile of shirts, an ancient sweater, and a bottle of Lea & Perrins Worcestershire Sauce, because, he says, you can't get Lea & Perrins in Europe, and the American makers have modified the taste and he doesn't approve of the result.

During the toy-fair season, Torquil's flying is mostly on hold, except for occasional sorties like the fish-and-chips run to Clacton. Then, as the days begin to lengthen and the temperature rises, the urge to fly reasserts itself. For Torquil, Panshanger has two things going for it: it is a short drive from his house in Camden Town, and it is near the old De Havilland factory. Its drawback is that his private hangar had no doors. Although the airfield is in a peaceful rural area, it was tempting fate to keep two restored classic airplanes sitting there unprotected, so by the summer of 1989 Torquil was using Panshanger only for the little Cessna 180 he had bought 'to get about in' while his Leopard Moth was being rebuilt. It was the same model that he had had when he was living in the States a quarter of a century earlier. 'A lovely plane,' he said. 'Fast, and perfect for getting in and out of small fields. Once I'd got it, I fell in love with it all over again. Then the Leopard Moth came back and I found myself a bit over-aeroplaned.'

To the outsider, the Cessna is just another light plane, with none of the coachbuilt, craftsmanly appeal of the two Moths. But it is quiet and comfortable, and the next time he offered me a spin in the Tiger Moth we first flew the Cessna, sedately and in shirtsleeves, to Swindon. Tom Charnock, who has caught the flying bug from Torquil, has a farm not far from the factory, and one of its fields has been turned into a landing strip. At its edge is a brand new hangar with sliding, lockable doors, in which the Leopard and Tiger Moths were then kept. We parked the Cessna; put on our Red Baron headgear, and took off in the Tiger Moth. It was the early morning of another sweet-smelling day, the mayflower in full bloom, the fields a tender new green. We flew over the Swindon factory, and I was suitably impressed. When the time came for aerobatics, Torquil pointed the plane northwest and shouted, 'Let's buzz the house!'

When Torquil was a child, his grandfather owned six hundred acres of Gloucestershire and a large country house. But the old man grew tetchy and alcoholic in his last years, and fell under the influence of his Russian secretary, to whom he eventually gave power of attorney. The secretary proceeded to rob the family blind. Although they took him to court and appealed the case right up to the House of Lords – the British equivalent of the Supreme Court – the grand family mansion was lost. The land that remained was divided among Torquil's mother and her three sons. It included a kind of time capsule of Old England – an ancient wood of oaks, ashes, sycamores and box trees, threaded with mossy rides and bounded along one edge by a little trout stream called the River Churn. Over the years, Torquil has bought out his brother Desmond's share and built himself a big house of honey-coloured Cotswold stone. The house is called Far Park, and it has a fine view of the wood and the folded landscape that surrounds it. The estate also has excellent shooting, but Anne Norman objects so fiercely to blood sports that the gamekeeper pretends that everything he shoots has died of natural causes. 'It's the only game estate in Britain where all the pheasants die of old age,' Bill Dowle said.

Because of his size, Torquil has difficulty finding houses that fit him. Ten years ago, when he sold the mansion on Avenue Road and moved to a Victorian terraced house in Camden Town, he had the basement excavated a couple of extra feet in order to provide a kitchen and dining-room he would feel comfortable in. At Far Park, he solved the problem by designing the house himself. The living-room is vast, with a pitched roof, like the roof of a church, supported by a great stone pillar of a chimney, and with a gallery halfway up one side large enough to house a three-quarter-size snooker table. All the doors are massive and oaken, and when I am there I have the impression that I have to reach up to open them, like Gulliver among the Brobdingnagians. This is a pity, because Torquil has a talent for putting people at their ease, and whenever I am with him he stoops more than is strictly necessary, to disguise the thirteen-inch difference in our height.

Torquil and Anne use Far Park irregularly, at best. 'I didn't see why we couldn't spend our holidays in the country with the kids,' Anne said. 'So we tried it once, and it was a disaster. Torquil spent the first week designing a rowing boat, which turned out to be not very stable. The second week, he just fell apart and watched television. He's not good at doing nothing.' He also has a peculiarly cavalier attitude toward possessions. The grand mansion in St. John's Wood 'had a swimming pool in its garden – a great rarity in London. The first time Tom Charnock visited the place, there were 'thirty or forty people going through the front garden and around the back,' he told me. 'People of every size, colour, race, creed, and denomination. I thought it was a meeting of the United Nations. When I got up to Torquil's office, at the back of the house, I looked out of the window, and the pool area was packed with people from one end to the other – kids swimming, mums sunning themselves. I said, 'Torquil, you've been invaded.'

'Oh no,' he said. 'One day a week, I open the pool to the neighbourhood. I tell them not to bring glasses and things like that, because it's dangerous for the children. But they don't leave much mess. What the heck, so there are a few crisp packets to pick up afterward. But they've all enjoyed themselves.'

It was the same at Far Park the first time Charnock went there: 'There must have been a hundred Boy Scouts swanning about the place. Ten sleeping bags in every room. Torquil said, "Sorry about the mess. We've got the Boy Scouts staying." "How do you mean?" I asked. And he said, "Oh, I let them have the house for two weeks every year." You just can't compete with a guy like that – with the generosity, the free and easy attitude to the things he owns. And, when you think about it – Boy Scouts, local kids – in both instances, he's looking after the younger generation. Maybe he uses them as a testing-ground for toys.'

'*You just can't compete with a guy like that*': everything Charnock said about Torquil seemed to contain that mixture of baffled affection, respect and exasperation. Yet Charnock is a notoriously tough business man, a brilliant manager and strategist, and Torquil relies on him heavily for Bluebird's remarkable growth in a competitive market. In return, Torquil and his appetite for life and risk have made Charnock a rich man, as Charnock himself is the first to admit. He also admits to an unfulfilled ambition of his own for Torquil: he wants to get him a knighthood. 'It goes with his patriotism, his buccaneering spirit, and the Biggles aeroplanes,' he said. It is not an ambition he is ever likely to fulfil, because Anne would never agree to her husband's accepting a title. Charnock takes this philosophically. 'Torquil has an ambition for me, too,' he said. 'He wants to make me a nicer man. But he won't succeed.'

Torquil's casually democratic style applies also to the organization and the running of his factories. In January, 1990, I had spent a day with him at Dragon Parc, an industrial estate on the edge of Merthyr Tydfil. Merthyr was a coal mining town, but the pits gradually closed in the 1980s, and it became a depressed area. When Bluebird opened, in 1989, there were thirty-five hundred applications for three hundred and fifty jobs. They interviewed every applicant and wrote polite letters to all of them, the successful and unsuccessful alike. The politeness paid off. When the unions arrived to organize the factory – South Wales is traditionally a strong union area – the work force rejected them, not for political reasons (Merthyr is a safe Labour seat) but because there seemed to be no function the unions could usefully serve. 'We practise Japanese-style management,' said Barry Gunter, the managing director of the Welsh factory. 'We have meetings twice a week between workers and management, and any problem that comes up we deal with straight away.'

Torquil added, 'We haven't gone as far as Honda, where the managing director does calisthenics every morning with the staff. And we don't disapprove of unions. We simply think that if we are doing our job properly the unions won't have much to do.'

A tour of Dragon Parc with Torquil is a peculiarly relaxed and chatty affair. The Bluebird factory is red brick, huge and modern, with three vast storage areas, all bigger than than the biggest hangar at Panshanger. The assembly area is equally large and staffed mostly by women, who have nimbler fingers than men and so are more adept at putting together intricate plastic toys. Torquil seemed to know all of the women by name. He asked after their families or flirted with the unmarried ones, leaving them flushed with pleasure.

According to Tom Charnock, that is standard Torquil procedure: 'He'd wander into the plant at Swindon and say, "Good morning, I'm just going to have a . . ." He wouldn't finish the sentence. What he meant was that he was going to scull around the place, say hullo to everybody and chat them up. Then, for the rest of the week, whenever I saw, say, the secretary from five offices down the corridor, she would say, "Wasn't that wonderful, Torquil asking me about my youngster? How did he know he's still got a cold?" And I'd think,

Goddamn it, he's too much for me. But the truth is, he's genuinely interested in people.'

The same democratic principles apply to the works' annual Christmas parties. The British tradition is to have separate bashes for office and factory workers, with the management mingling hardly at all. But not at Bluebird. 'We don't differentiate,' Charnock said. 'There is no set table seating. I could be sitting with the company accountant or with one of the guys from the dispatch bay. When we threw the first Christmas party at Merthyr Tydfil, Torquil and I went down with our wives, and all the girls there brought their husbands. You have to appreciate that these are ex-miners, Welsh rugger players, tough guys by any standard, with handshakes that could crush rock. Torquil and I were at the bar with them, whacking back pints of beer. I have to say, I excelled myself: I have never drunk so many pints in my life, and I was still standing at the end of it! I reckon I got a five-out-of-ten score from the local boys. They thought, At least he's trying. It seemed to me an ordinary kind of Bluebird party – we met people, we chatted, and it went well. But a week later, I got letters from a couple of the girls who work there, asking me to thank Torquil for coming down, and saying that neither they nor their husbands had ever before had the opportunity to be with the bosses, either when they were in the mines or at any other factory they had worked in. The next time I was there, I made a point of meeting the ladies. I told them, "This is silly. We do it all the time." They replied, "In Wales, it's unheard of." That struck me as odd, since there are a lot of Japanese companies in the area. It made me wonder whether we're doing it right or wrong.'

Since Torquil became president of the British Toy and Hobby Manufacturers' Association, he has applied the same principle to the much more formal occasion of the association's annual dinner. He has done away with the presidential high table and most of the pre-arranged seating plans. Guests now sit where and with whom they want. Contrary to all expectations, everyone seems to prefer it that way. Nobody wants to return to the old hierarchical fashion and, even when Torquil's term of office expires, the revolution, like those in Eastern Europe, seems to be here to stay.

The Sunday we flew over Far Park, a selection of the now grown-up Norman children were weekending there, along with assorted girlfriends and boyfriends, and when we buzzed the house they came running out in their pajamas, waving and shouting. Torquil looped the loop, did a particularly dizzy spin, and pirouetted the Tiger Moth on a point a hundred or so feet above the lawn. Then everybody waved again, and we flew back to Swindon.

'What do you bet we got the buggers out of bed?' Torquil shouted through the air tube.

As we flew back to London in the Cessna, he told me about the latest addition to his private fleet, a DH 90 Dragonfly. The Dragonfly was the Learjet of the 1930s, a machine that Torquil has always loved: 'not that I knew anything about them, I just loved the way they looked.' The pretty face, however, went with a nasty temperament. The Dragonfly is famous for being one of the few airplanes De Havilland got wrong. Although it flew sweetly once it was airborne, it was a monster on the ground. Its fuselage was too wide and its tail plane was too small – a combination which gave it a tendency to ground loop, or veer sharply to one side, on take-off and landing. Because of this quirk, only one Dragonfly is still flying; all the rest have been written off. At the time Torquil bought his, it was a pile of matchwood outside a hangar in Louisville, Kentucky. It had got that way on a demonstration flight when it swung on take-off and the pilot, who may have known very little about its peculiarities, had driven it, with both throttles wide open, into an eight-foot ditch. When Torquil heard about the wreck, he hated the idea of its remains becoming a set of spare parts for the one Dragonfly still intact. Besides, having had the Leopard Moth rebuilt, he knew all about the British craftsmen who were devoted to bringing old airplanes back to life and would understand the intricacies of the Dragonfly's double-diagonal plywood construction. It was a temptation he could not resist.

Just how Torquil intends to fly four classic planes during weekend breaks in his hard-driven life as a captain of industry he does not say. Yet collecting old planes doesn't interest him, he swears; it is just an adjunct to his one true passion – flying. 'I'm not unique in this,' he said. 'Anyone who has ever been sufficiently involved in flying to go solo and get his license finds it's a passion he can never get over. There is no end to the pleasure flying gives me. My planes go in and out of fields and farm strips. The other day, for instance, I flew from Panshanger to Northumberland to see a friend. A nightmare journey to drive, but in the Cessna it took me a mere hour and forty minutes, and I landed in a field just a mile from my friend's house. There I was, transported to a totally different world. It's like magic. You can go places, see different things, have some adventures, and all the time there are these little technical problems you have to solve. You kid yourself there's an element of skill involved, but it's like everything else: once you know how to do it, it gets a lot easier. Still, there are always moments when you are actually required to exercise a margin of skill. That's what makes the whole package irresistible.

'Because it happens in three dimensions, it attacks every one of your senses. Flying above cloud or in it or very low or at night – whatever you're doing, your senses are being bombarded with stimuli. Military aircraft, of course, are the ultimate turn-on, because they do everything on the biggest scale. In a Meteor, you could do five or six hundred miles an hour; it was so powerful that you could point it straight up and go to twenty thousand feet. And, because it was so strong, you could do what you wanted with it. In the Fleet Air Arm and the 601 Squadron, we used to have these wonderful tail chases. The idea was to try to get on the other bloke's tail while preventing him from getting on yours. You'd go straight up, then stall or pull over, and if he came past, you knew you'd got him. The whole sky was your playground. You were trying to outwit the other bloke and go to the limit of what your body could stand before you blacked out. Because the plane was unbreakable, it was your skill and your physical thresholds that were being tested.

'Of course, I'm too old for that sort of stuff now, and anyway you can't play those tricks in a Tiger Moth if you want to keep it in one piece. The aerobatics I do now are a hundred percent safe. It's not risk that turns me on; it's the skill involved in doing a manoeuvre nicely instead of clumsily. There's no danger involved in flying an aeroplane in unlikely positions. Rolling, spinning, being upside down is simply fun, pure hedonism. However prosaic life may be, however hard I'm working, and however boring the drudgery, I can climb into the Tiger Moth and the sheer thrill of it puts everything in perspective. Dancing on a cloud: that's what I do when I'm up there, and that's how I feel when I land.'

The New Yorker, 1990

Pastimes

Exploration

The Worst Journey in the World

IN THE SECOND HALF of this century, the great unknown for explorers has been space. But the exploration of space is a highly technical project and, forty years after it began, we still don't know much about it back on earth because NASA has yet to find room on a spacecraft for anyone who is able to put his experience into words. The astronauts have videoed fragments of life in space and Hollywood has glamorized it, but *The Right Stuff*, Tom Wolfe's imaginative re-creation of what it *might* have been like, is as near as we get to the thing itself. We still don't know how it really feels to be blasted off beyond the pull of gravity, or how you live weightless and apparently in slow-motion while the capsule circles at an insane speed in that huge darkness; we don't even properly know what our planet looks like from out there in space. The astronauts are too busy with their scientific chores to bother with anything else. Even if they knew how it was done, writing is not their brief. As they report it, life in space sounds not much different from a spell in a Best Western motel in Topeka, Kansas.

Antarctica, which was the great unknown at the beginning of this century, has been lucky in comparison. Scott justified his two expeditions, and helped finance them, as scientific research. He even shortened the odds against his own survival by refusing to dump the thirty pounds of rocks he and his companions were dragging from the South Pole. 'We travelled for Science,' Apsley Cherry-Garrard wrote in *The Worst Journey in the World*. He insisted that the race for the Pole was a minor consideration and denied the charge that Amundsen, who beat them to it, 'was perfectly right in refusing to allow science to use up the forces of his men, or to interfere for a moment with his single business of getting to the Pole and back again. No doubt he was; but we were not out for a single business: we were out for everything

we could add to the world's store of knowledge about the Antarctic.'
A large proportion of the men who joined Scott's second Polar
expedition in 1910 were scientists, but in those days education was less
specialized than it is now and all of them had had the classics beaten
into them at school. They knew Shakespeare and Milton and the
other great English poets as well as Latin and Greek, and, along with
their technical books, the authors they took with them included
Dickens, Thackeray, Charlotte Bronte, Hardy, Tennyson, Browning,
Charles Darwin and historians like Napier and Herbert Paul. Not only
did they love reading, they put a high price on clear, expository prose
and kept journals even in the most appalling conditions.

Cherry-Garrard was not a scientist, although he was officially listed
as 'assistant zoologist' to Dr. Wilson, the expedition's Chief of
Scientific Staff. He had read Classics and Modern History at Oxford
and his colleagues joked that Scott had taken him on because he knew
a lot of Latin and Greek. Cherry-Garrard himself couldn't believe his
luck. The doctors in London had wanted to turn him down because
he was so near-sighted that, he said, 'I could only see people across the
road as vague blobs walking.' He was also the baby of the party: he was
twenty-four when the *Terra Nova* sailed from Cardiff and the cabin he
shared with two other juniors was called 'the Nursery.' But he was
strong, fit, cheerful and willing, and he had something to prove. His
father, an army general who married late and died while Cherry-
Garrard was still at Oxford, was described by Field Marshal Lord
Wolseley as 'the bravest man I have ever seen.' His son made no secret
of being often scared, but the trials he endured and the style in which
he endured them would have put his father to shame.

What Scott wasn't to know when he picked Bill Wilson's myopic
young friend was that he was taking on an extraordinarily gifted writer.
Cherry-Garrard took nine years to complete *The Worst Journey* and in
that time he became friends not just with like-minded adventurers such
as Mallory of Everest and Lawrence of Arabia, but also with some of the
country's most illustrious authors: Shaw, Galsworthy, Barrie, Wells and
Arnold Bennett. Maybe they or their example egged him on, but I
doubt it. He writes better than any of them and the gift was there from
the start. This, for example, is how he describes the Midwinter Night
celebrations at Cape Evans in his diary:

A hard night: clear, with a blue sky so deep that it looks black: the
stars are steel points: the glaciers burnished silver. The snow rings

and thuds to your footfall. The ice is cracking to the falling temperature and the tide crack groans as the water rises. And over all, wave upon wave, fold upon fold, there hangs the curtain of the aurora. As you watch, it fades away, and then quite suddenly a great beam flashes up and rushes to the zenith, an arch of palest green and orange, a tail of flaming gold. Again it falls, fading away into great searchlight beams which rise behind the smoking crater of Mount Erebus. And again the spiritual veil is drawn –

> Here at the roaring loom of Time I ply
> And weave for God the garment thou seest him by.

Inside the hut are orgies. We are very merry – and indeed why not? The sun turns to come back to us tonight, and such a day comes only once a year . . .

Titus [Oates] got three things which pleased him immensely, a sponge, a whistle, and a pop-gun which went off when he pressed the butt. For the rest of the evening he went round asking whether you were sweating. 'No.' 'Yes, you are,' he said, and wiped your face with the sponge. 'If you want to please me very much you will fall down when I shoot you,' he said to me, and then he went round shooting everybody. At intervals he blew the whistle . . . As we turned in he said, 'Cherry, are you responsible for your actions?' and when I said Yes, he blew loudly on his whistle, and the last thing I remembered was that he woke up Meares to ask him whether he was fancy free.

It was a magnificent bust.

This is perfect prose: lucid, vivid, bone-simple, and full of feeling, both for the beauty of the scene and the silliness of his friends; a perfect balance of precision and pleasure. The two lines of Goethe's translated verse seem, in comparison, pale and inflated. Cherry-Garrard may even have sensed this because there are almost no literary allusions in the finished narrative, although he loved poetry and relied on it to keep him going when things were bad.

Scott's heroic death ensured him a place in British history, and the fact that he died a good loser, having been beaten to the Pole by the business-like Amundsen, made his immortality doubly secure. That story is told in Scott's journal, which formed the basis of the book *Scott's Last Expedition*. It is a sad and powerful document, but Cherry-

Garrard gave Scott and his companions a different kind of immortality by making them the occasion for a literary masterpiece. *The Worst Journey* is to travel writing what *War and Peace* is to the novel or Herzen's *Memoirs* are to autobiography: the book by which all the rest are measured.

Apart from his natural talent and love of clear language, it may be that Cherry-Garrard wrote as well as he did because he made the same demands on himself as a writer as he had as a member of the expedition. He had been through something extraordinary and he did not wish to falsify the experience. He did not go all the way to the Pole; at the top of the Beardmore Glacier, Scott had to decide between him and Oates for the final push and he chose Oates – a great disappointment for the younger man, but a blessing for litera-ture. Cherry-Garrard tells that story in his book, but 'the worst journey' itself was different and, although no one died on it, even grimmer. Scott called it 'the hardest journey ever made.'

It started from the expedition's base at Cape Evans on June 27, 1911, ended on August 1, exactly three months before Scott went for the Pole, and it involved just three people: Bill Wilson, 'Birdie' Bowers and Cherry-Garrard. Needless to say, it was made in the name of science: Wilson wanted to collect the eggs of the Emperor penguin in the hope that the embryology of that primitive creature might shed some light on the link between birds and reptiles. During Scott's first Antarctic expedition, ten years earlier, Wilson had discovered one of the Emperors' breeding grounds at Cape Crozier, but that was in the spring and by then the chicks were already hatched. And this was the problem: the Emperor penguin lays its eggs in June and July, the middle of Antarctic winter, and no one had ever sledged at that dead season. It was, Cherry-Garrard wrote, 'the weirdest bird's-nesting expedition that has ever been or ever will be.'

There were two things against it: darkness and cold. The sun had gone below the horizon months earlier and the explorers' only light was that of the moon or, when the moon was down and there were no clouds, of the stars. This was in 1911, so of course they had no electric torches. To read the compass they used matches, which mostly wouldn't strike, and sometimes they lit a candle: 'we carried a naked lighted candle back with us when we went to find our second sledge. It was the weirdest kind of procession, three frozen men and a little pool of light. Generally we steered by Jupiter, and I never see him now without recalling his friendship in those days.' In practical terms,

Cherry-Garrard was less bothered by the darkness than his companions; it was too cold to wear glasses and, without them, he was so
myopic that he could scarcely see beyond the end of his nose, even in
daylight. Even so, the darkness was claustrophobic and frustrating; it
weighed on them and made even the simplest chores difficult and
slow.

And the cold was deadly. At times, the temperature went down
below −77° Fahrenheit, one hundred and ten degrees of frost, and
most of the time it was in the −50s and −60s: 'I know that if it was only
−40° when we camped for the night we considered quite seriously
that we were going to have a warm one.' −40° is where Fahrenheit
and Centigrade meet. Their protective clothing was primitive – wool
and flannel and badly stitched fur – and their reindeer-skin sleeping-
bags were useless. Sleeping, in fact, was a greater trial than sledging:

> The temperature was −66° when we camped, and we were
> already pretty badly iced up . . . For me it was a very bad night:
> a succession of shivering fits which I was quite unable to stop, and
> which took possession of my body for many minutes at a time
> until I thought my back would break, such was the strain placed
> upon it. They talk of chattering teeth: but when your body
> chatters you may call yourself cold. I can only compare the strain
> to that which I have been unfortunate enough to see in a case of
> lock-jaw . . . The minimum temperature that night as taken
> under the sledge was −69°; and as taken on the sledge was −
> 75°. That is a hundred and seven degrees of frost.

They realized very soon 'that the only good time of the twenty-four
hours was breakfast, for then with reasonable luck we need not get
into our sleeping-bags again for another seventeen hours,' though
even breakfast had its problems: 'it was very difficult to splinter bits off
the butter.'

Sledging was a nightmare to be endured, but at least it was work, a
task to keep them going. The conditions were far too harsh for the dogs
or ponies – the expedition members always treated their animals more
tenderly than themselves – so they put on harnesses and used man-
power to haul the gear – 757lbs. of it, almost 253lbs. a man. Since this
was too heavy and bulky for one sledge, they packed it onto two and
toggled them together. But the terrain was terrible – ice ridges, chaotic
areas of pressure, 'sastrugi' – snow furrows that looked as if they had

been ploughed by giants – and crevasses everywhere. The snow was so cold that it had crystallized into hard particles that wouldn't melt under the pressure of the sledges' wooden runners; it was like dragging them through sand. To haul both sledges together was impossible, so they dragged one a mile, then plodded back and hauled the other. That meant they marched three miles for every mile they advanced. On a good day they made three and a half miles and walked ten. The distance from Cape Evans to Cape Crozier is 67 miles.

Cold and darkness and exhaustion made a nightmare even of the straightforward task of following their own footprints back to the second sledge:

These holes became to our tired brains not depressions but elevations: hummocks over which we stepped, raising our feet painfully and draggingly. And then we remembered, and said what fools we were, and for a while we compelled ourselves to walk through these phantom hills. But it was no lasting good, and as the days passed we realised that we must suffer this absurdity, for we could not do anything else. But of course it took it out of us.

'It took it out of us.' The remorseless grind of hauling was made worse by frostbite and the frostbite was made worse still when the liquid in their blistered hands froze solid. Their sweat froze before it had a chance to evaporate through their clothing and formed a layer of snow and ice against their skins, their breath froze and turned their balaclavas into helmets of thick sheet ice, their sleeping-bags froze while they were in them, and when they got out of them in the morning they had to plug the mouths of the bags with gear in order to create a frozen hole which they could push into at night.

The cold was so fierce and its effects so sudden that even the comparative warmth of the tent created problems, and leaving it after breakfast required a strategy all its own. Cherry-Garrard discovered this early on:

Once outside, I raised my head to look round and found I could not move it back. My clothing had frozen hard as I stood – perhaps fifteen seconds. For four hours I had to pull with my head stuck up, and from that time we took care to bend down into a pulling position before being frozen in.

It sounds almost comical, which is how Cherry-Garrard preferred it; his clean, spare prose made heroics impossible. Yet he never pretends that what he and his companions went through was ever less than dreadful:

> Through all these days, and those which were to follow, the worst I suppose in their dark severity that men have ever come through alive, no single hasty or angry word passed their lips. When, later, we were sure, so far as we can be sure of anything, that we must die, they were cheerful, and as I can judge their songs and cheery words were quite unforced. Nor were they ever flurried, though always as quick as the conditions would allow in moments of emergency . . .
>
> There are those who write of Polar Expeditions as though the whole thing was as easy as possible. They are trusting, I suspect, in a public who will say, 'What a fine fellow this is! We know what horrors he has endured, yet see how little he makes of all his difficulties and hardships.' Others have gone to the opposite extreme. I do not know that there is any use in trying to make a −18° temperature appear formidable to an uninitiated reader by calling it fifty degrees of frost. I want to do neither of these things. I am not going to pretend that this was anything but a ghastly journey, made bearable and even pleasant to look back upon by the companions who have gone. At the same time I have no wish to make it appear more horrible than it actually was: the reader need not fear that I am trying to exaggerate.

Cherry-Garrard is talking about a new style of exploration: not of unknown country – Wilson had been to Cape Crozier before – but of the limits of human endurance. When Bowers suffered agonizing cramps or the stove spat a lump of boiling blubber into Wilson's eye or the liquid froze in blisters on Cherry-Garrard's fingers, each of them suffered terribly and suffered for each other's suffering, but they never complained out loud. This reticence has nothing to do with what psychobabblers call 'denial.' It was simply part of the pact that kept them going. As Cherry-Garrard describes it, courage, or whatever it was that got them through their ordeal, was largely a matter of patience and determination; they just went on doing what had to be done. It was also a question of manners; they forbore to intrude on each other's suffering out of sheer politeness.

Despite the cold, they never quite lost their explorer's sense of how strange and beautiful this unknown place could sometimes be:

> there was one halt when we just lay on our backs and gazed up into the sky, where, so the others said, there was blazing the most wonderful aurora they had ever seen. I did not see it, being so near-sighted and unable to wear spectacles owing to the cold. The aurora was always before us as we travelled east, more beautiful than any seen by previous expeditions wintering in McMurdo Sound, where Erebus must have hidden the most brilliant displays. Now most of the sky was covered with swinging, swaying curtains which met in a great whirl overhead: lemon yellow, green and orange.

Interludes like this were rare, but they helped keep the three men going.

It took them three weeks to reach Cape Crozier where they built a makeshift igloo out of canvas and snow and boulders, and found the Emperor penguins and stole some eggs. Then, as though they had not already suffered enough, real disaster struck:

> Cirrus cloud was moving across the face of the stars from the north, it looked rather hazy and thick to the south, but it is always difficult to judge weather in the dark. There was little wind and the temperature was in the minus twenties. We felt no particular uneasiness. Our tent was well dug in, and was also held down by rocks and the heavy tank off the sledge which were placed on the skirting as additional security. We felt that no power on earth could move the thick walls of our igloo, nor drag the canvas roof from the middle of the embankment into which it was packed and lashed.

> 'Things must improve,' said Bill.

> I do not know what time it was when I woke up. It was calm, with that absolute silence which can be so soothing or so terrible as circumstances dictate. Then there came a sob of wind, and all was still again. Ten minutes and it was blowing as though the world was having a fit of hysterics. The earth was torn in pieces: the indescribable fury and roar of it all cannot be imagined.

> 'Bill, Bill, the tent has gone,' was the next I remember . . .

Bowers logged the wind as Gale Force 11, but Bowers tended to underestimate and Cherry-Garrard was certain it was Force 12, a full hurricane. Either way, it blew without let-up from Saturday morning until sometime on Monday. First, it blew away their tent, then it blew down the igloo. They huddled in their useless sleeping-bags, unable to cook and with only the drifting snow to protect them, assuming that 'the tent had been taken up into the air and dropped somewhere in [the] sea well on the way to New Zealand,' and that their only option was to behave as well as they could until they froze to death: 'we lay and thought, and sometimes we sang.'

The tent had indeed been sucked up into the air but, miraculously, it had dropped intact, poles and all, a few hundred yards from where they lay. When they found it, 'we were so thankful we said nothing. . . . If that tent went again we were going with it. We made our way back up the slope with it, carrying it solemnly and reverently, as though it were something not quite of the earth.' The tent did not go again and they made it back to Cape Evans, despite the cold, with three of the five stolen eggs intact. More importantly for Cherry-Garrard, they kept their image of themselves intact:

We did not forget the Please and Thank You, which means much in such circumstances, and all the little links with decent civilisation which we could still keep going. I'll swear there was still a grace about us when we staggered in. And we kept our tempers – even with God.

Two years later, Cherry-Garrard took the precious eggs to the Natural History Museum in London for the zoologists to examine. By then, Wilson and Bowers were dead (they and Scott were found lying side-by-side in their tent, arms peacefully folded on their chests, straight and separate, polite to the last, stopped in their tracks by a two-week blizzard, eleven miles short of their supply depot) and Cherry-Garrard himself was still trying to come to terms with what he had gone through. What followed was bad social farce. The museum officials were not interested in the eggs that had almost cost three lives and they treated the brave explorer with disdain, as though he were a messenger-boy. When the outraged Cherry-Garrard refused to leave without a receipt for the eggs, he was made to kick his heels in the corridor outside some functionary's office while the great man attended to more urgent matters. And when he went back later with Captain Scott's sister, the museum denied all knowledge of the eggs.

Cherry-Garrard plays the scenes as a comedy of manners: good manners against bad manners, gentlemen against petty officials, men of action against pen-pushers. But it went deeper than that. The museum functionaries, with their self-importance and petty-mindedness, were the England he had gone south to escape from. And that, of course, is one of the attractions of places that are blank on the map: you go to get away. Mallory's famous reason for wanting to climb Everest – 'Because it's there' – was only half the story. The other half was 'Because you're here' – where 'you' included the town, the job, the hierarchies, the wife, the kids, the dog and, above all, the kind of person who would ask such a stupid question in the first place.

Hardship was a price you paid for getting away and also part of the lure, since hardship was what Cherry-Garrard's generation had been trained for. This is different from the early days of exploration when so much of the globe was still unknown to European travellers. In his account of 'The Discovery and Conquest of Mexico,' Bernal Diaz does not bother to mention how terrible it must have been to sweat in heavy armour through the tropical forests between the Gulf and Mexico City; there was too much strangeness to report and the prizes were too great; empire and riches were worth a little discomfort. At the turn of this century, however, the British Empire was already in place and one of the main purposes of British education was to train the right kind of people to administer it. Whence the bleakness, discomfort and harsh discipline of the Public School system. Cherry-Garrard had been very unhappy at Winchester, but after four years there even the Antarctic must have seemed like Claridge's. Arrogance and snobbery may have been unfortunate by-products of a Public School education, but the point of it all was fortitude.

The embodiment of this ideal was Capt. Oates, 'a brave man and an English gentleman' Scott called him, who laid down his life for his friends. But Oates's generation was wiped out in World War I and their concept of good behaviour went with them. Hemingway's cult of 'grace under pressure' was altogether more glamorous and self-regarding. Its icon was the matador, alone in the bull-ring but surrounded by an adoring audience. There is no audience in truly unforgiving places like the poles or the high mountains (it was, after all, the late Victorians who invented Alpine climbing as a sport) and that is part of their allure: no audiences, but also no excuses: if you didn't behave well you didn't survive, and no one would know except your companions.

The Worst Journey in the World is the great literary testimony to fortitude. But it is also a great book because it is full of life and appetite. Cherry-Garrard, being young and fresh out of England, was wide open to everything that was on offer: to the beauty of the desolate landscape and the charm of the creatures in it, particularly the penguins and seals; to the excitement of it all and the risk; to the pleasures of friendship and the even more complicated pleasure of undergoing an ordeal as terrible as the Winter Journey and coming out of it alive. It was the only book he wrote and after it his life went downhill. He gradually became obsessed with what he might have done to save his companions – in fact, he could have done nothing more than he did – and was eventually hospitalized with what sounds like a paranoid breakdown. But that was all later. The book itself is clear and vivid and full of a kind of tenderness for the life he led down there and the people he was with. It is also curiously self-effacing. Cherry-Garrard could never quite believe his luck in having been picked by Scott, despite his youth and lack of qualifications, so he never quite lost his sense of gratitude for having been there. It is the only literary masterpiece I know that is motivated by modesty.

New York Review of Books, 1997

The Ulysses Factor

When I was a little chap I had a passion for maps. I would look for hours at South America, or Africa, or Australia, and lose myself in all the glories of exploration. At that time there were many blank spaces on the earth, and when I saw one that looked particularly inviting on a map (but they all look that) I would put my finger on it and say, 'When I grow up I will go there.' The North Pole was one of those places, I remember. Well, I haven't been there yet, and shall not try now. The glamour's off.

The atlas has always figured large in the daydreams of adventurous children; this one is Conrad's narrator, Marlow, easing himself into the nightmare of 'The Heart of Darkness'. A century later, the blank spaces on the map have all been filled in and it's not the explorers who set out for South America, Africa and Australia but kids in their gap year between high school and college, while modern Marlows in knee-pants fantasize about space travel.

The glamour of the North Pole was only briefly off when Conrad was writing his story in the 1890s – perhaps because of the ungentlemanly bickering between rival expeditions – and it was on again within a decade. In the opening years of the twentieth century, the great vision of a commercial link between Europe and China through the Northwest Passage had turned out to be a delusion, but the race for the North and South Poles was as much a patriotic obsession as the space race was fifty years later. Now the polar regions are glamorous and mysterious again, even though they have been crossed, re-crossed, mapped in detail, and even partially colonized. Seven different nations maintain research stations around the edge of Antarctica, there is a permanent American base at the South Pole itself, and regular cruise ships take tourists to the tip of the Antarctic Peninsular to admire the penguins. At the opposite end of the world, the Arctic is ringed with Early Warning systems and they are drilling for oil not far from where would-be discoverers of the Northwest Passage perished.

Even so, the frozen wastes have reasserted their hold on the public imagination. Publishers' lists regularly feature books with 'white' or 'ice' in their titles, and recently one of them, Dr. Jerri Nielsen's *Ice Bound*, even made it onto the best-seller list.[1] In part, this may have been provoked by our anxiety about global warming: the ice-caps are melting and the survival of the creatures they support, such as polar bears and Emperor penguins, is becoming steadily more chancy. Social conscience and moral uplift, however, are not usually what readers of polar literature have uppermost in their minds. When imagination is involved, remoteness and adventure will always win out against righteous causes. In his general introduction to the excellent Modern Library Exploration Series, which is gradually reissuing out-of-print classics of the genre, the editor John Krakauer quotes Paul Zweig:

> The oldest, most widespread stories in the world are adventure stories, about human heroes who venture into the myth-countries at the risk of their lives, and bring back tales of the world beyond men . . . It could be argued . . . that the narrative art itself arose from the need to tell an adventure; that man risking his life in perilous encounters constitutes the original definition of what is worth talking about.[2]

Adventure is a great palliative for restlessness, even for those whose adventures are all in the head: 'Comes over one an absolute necessity to move', wrote D.H. Lawrence in the opening sentence of *Sea and Sardinia*, back in 1921, when even Sardinia seemed wild and unvisited. Lawrence, of course, was no explorer, but he was chronically footloose,

1 Dr. Neilsen developed breast cancer during her winter at the South Pole. Since she was the station's only doctor she had to perform biopsies on herself and administer her own chemotherapy. She is an exceptionally brave and resolute woman, but her chatty narrative, full of details about her failed marriage and alienated children, lets her down. Human interest seems oddly out of place at the South Pole, where inhuman disinterest reigns.
2 The more recent additions to the series include the first English translation of *The Mountains of My Life* by the great Italian climber Walter Bonatti, and David Roberts's sly and well-researched *Great Exploration Hoaxes*, which casts doubt on, among others, the polar heroes Peary and Byrd. They have also issued the first English translation of Valerian Albanov's *In the Land of White Death*, a wonderfully lively, almost tender account of disaster in the Siberian Arctic, and the subsequent endless journey on foot to safety, which only two survived. Albanov, who died in 1919, must have been an unusually gifted writer because this version reads exceptionally well, despite being a translation of a French translation of a German translation of the original Russian.

forever packing his bags and leaving without provocation, wandering the globe in search of some ideal place to settle and never finding it. The rest of us, less driven as well as less gifted, stay home and read, imagining the unimaginable with our feet up, safe and warm and comforted by the knowledge that, should we decide to light out for the territory, there will always be a jet to fly us there and a travel agent to organize the details.

The polar regions are different: they are an unfailing source of peril, frozen deserts as hostile, hard to get to, and hard to survive in as the vertical deserts of the high mountain ranges, and they hold our imagination now just as firmly as they held the Romantics' two centuries ago. At that time, when they were unexplored and barely even charted, they represented nature at its most sublime. When the American explorer Charles Wilkes probed the coast of Antarctica, around 1840, he drew on Gothick romance and Coleridge's 'Kubla Khan' to describe the marvels he had seen:

> Some of the bergs were of magnificent dimensions, one-third of a mile in length, and from one hundred and fifty to two hundred feet in height, with sides perfectly smooth, as though they had been chiselled. Others, again, exhibited lofty arches of many-coloured tints, leading into deep caverns, open to the swell of the sea, which rushing in, produced loud and distant thunderings. The flight of birds passing in and out of these caverns, recalled the recollection of ruined abbeys, castles, and caves, while here and there a bold projecting bluff, crowned with pinnacles and turrets, resembled some Gothick keep. A little farther onwards would be seen a vast fissure, as if some powerful force had rent in twain these mighty masses. Every noise on board, even our own voices, reverberated from the massive and pure white walls. These tabular bergs are like masses of beautiful alabaster: a verbal description of them can do little to convey the reality to the imagination of one who has not been among them.

This wild and untouched landscape was the ideal Romantic inspiration and the perfect setting for Romantic fantasies. The Ancient Mariner's fateful albatross appears out of the polar fog. So does Dr. Frankenstein, who is rescued while sledding across the ice in pursuit of his monster, and tells his improbable story to the captain of a ship northbound out of Archangel towards the pole. As far as the Romantics were concerned, the polar wastes were as far as they could get from the bewigged and powdered polite society of the Augustan age, and sublime enough to justify their wildest imaginings.

Though sublimity is no longer what we are after, we have our own modern version of Augustan constriction. In place of wigs and corsets and elaborately codified manners, we are suffocated by comfort. We live in climate-controlled environments with labour-saving devices, where travel is effort-free and everything from sex to Singapore noodles is instantly available at the end of a telephone or the click of a mouse. Even exercise has become an optional, after-hours, and often expensive recreational activity, something to do in the gym or the pool or on the golf course. Thomas Hardy's heroes and heroines walked, uncomplainingly and as a matter of course, distances that nowadays only professional athletes would contemplate. In these cosseted circumstances, privation and danger acquire a glamour all their own. Hence, perhaps, the cult of 'the right stuff' and the popularity of extreme sports, like sky-diving and bungee-jumping. Hence, too, the fascination of the polar wastes: although airplanes and radio have made them less inaccessible than they were, they are among the few places left that are utterly without comfort and where nothing can be taken for granted.

This has always been one of their greatest attractions. Explorers are driven by the unappeasable need to peer over the next horizon, 'To sail beyond the sunset, and the baths/ Of all the western stars,' which the English biographer J.R.L. Anderson, with Tennyson in mind, called 'the Ulysses factor.' For most of them, hardship is the price they pay, more or less willingly, for their curiosity and ambition, but even the intrepid Captain Cook was appalled by Antarctica:

> I, who had ambition not only to go farther than anyone had been before, but as far as it was possible for man to go, was not sorry at meeting with interruption; as it, in some measure, relieved us; at least, shortened the dangers and hardships inseparable from the navigation of the southern polar regions.

Cook had every reason to be scared; the little wooden three-master in which he was circumnavigating the globe was not built to withstand pressure from the polar ice-pack. Even so, he went back three more times, and each time was thwarted by the ring of ice that encircles the Antarctic continent. Finally, he gave up:

> The risque one runs in exploring a coast, in these unknown and icy seas, is so very great, that I can be bold enough to say that no man will ever venture farther than I have done; and that the lands which may lie to the South will never be explored. Thick fogs, snow storms,

intense cold, and every other thing that can render navigation dangerous, must be encountered; and these difficulties are greatly heightened, by the inexpressibly horrid aspect of the country; a country doomed by Nature never once to feel the warmth of the sun's rays, but to lie buried in everlasting snow and ice.

The implacable hostility that defeated Captain Cook was precisely what drove later polar explorers on. For them, hardship was an end in itself. The great Norwegian explorer Roald Amundsen wrote in his autobiography that his childhood inspiration had been the adventures and tragic fate of Sir John Franklin, who disappeared mysteriously in search of the Northwest Passage: They 'thrilled me as nothing I had ever read before. What appealed to me most was the sufferings that Sir John and his men had to endure. A strange ambition burned within me, to endure the same privations . . . I decided to be an explorer.'

Amundsen was the twentieth century's most successful explorer: he was the first man to find a way through the Northwest Passage (it took him four years, from 1903 to 1906, and at the end he declared it useless); in 1912, he was the first to reach the South Pole; in 1926, he and two companions made the first traverse of the north polar ocean, which – given the squabbling between rival claimants – probably made him the uncontested first discoverer of the North Pole, even though he travelled in an Italian dirigible, not on foot.

Yet privation figures hardly at all in Amundsen's narratives. On the contrary, the strangest thing about his account of his journey to the South Pole is its cheerfulness. It seems never to have occurred to him that he might fail. Being Norwegians, he and his companions had been brought up to cope with snow and ice. Extreme cold did not bother them, they knew how to ski and dog-sledge, and they took the dangers so much for granted that even their bad moments, which were many, became a source of pleasure. For example, when the runner of one of their sledges partially tipped into a crevasse and their team's photographer took his time setting up his bulky camera to immortalize the scene, Amundsen comments:

I mention this little incident just to show how one can grow accustomed to anything in this world. There were these two – Wisting and Hassel – lying over a yawning, bottomless abyss, and having their photograph taken; neither of them gave a thought for the serious side of the situation. To judge from the laughter and jokes we heard, one would have thought their position was something quite different.

More important, Amundsen's planning, timing and preparation were faultless. Every detail was worked out in advance in order to ensure that everyone, including the dogs, would be as protected and well-fed as possible. This, for instance, is how Amundsen describes the typical end of a gruelling day over difficult ice: they set up their tent ('It looks cosy enough'), then lash into their three-course evening meal: first soup, then pemmican, then

> The cups are carefully scraped, and the enjoyment of bread and water begins. It is easy to see, too, that it is an enjoyment – greater, to judge by the pleasure on their faces, than the most skilfully devised menu could afford. They positively caress the biscuits before they eat them. And the water – ice-cold water they all call for – this also disappears in great quantities, and procures, I feel certain from their expression, a far greater pleasure and satisfaction than the finest wine that was ever produced. The Primus hums softly during the whole meal, and the temperature in the tent is quite pleasant.

Amundsen was writing in the after-glow of a great triumph – he had planted the Norwegian flag at the pole and brought his whole party safely home. Although the journey was in no way as easy as he makes it sound, by the end of it the Norwegian team had actually gained weight.

It was a remarkable achievement, but that is not why people go to – or read about – the frozen wastes. On the contrary, most of the books are records of failures. Shackleton's great epic *South* is about surviving a disaster and in Apsley Cherry-Garrard's masterpiece, *The Worst Journey in the World*, three men struggled through weeks of the coldest weather anyone has ever endured, before them or since, in order to collect a few penguin eggs which the scientists back home didn't want. The true spirit of polar exploration was summed up by Captain Scott when he arrived at the South Pole a month after the Norwegians and found their flag fluttering over the tent Amundsen had named 'Polheim': 'Great God! This is an awful place.' Within a few weeks he and his comrades were frozen to death, three of them trapped in a blizzard only a few miles from their supply depot.

Heroic failure – the cult of the good loser – is a very British specialty and maybe that is why polar exploration, in the nineteenth century, became a national obsession. The poles were England's Moby Dick – an impossible quest, a killer fantasy that demanded sacrifice – although the man who got it all going, John Barrow, Second Secretary at the

Admiralty from 1804–1845, was in no way a visionary. In *Barrow's Boys*, a witty, sharply written and well-researched account of Barrow's long reign (he was 81 when he retired), Fergus Fleming calls him 'Britain's first true civil servant', 'a model of dullness' on the outside, but underneath ambitious, dogged, clever and manipulative. He made himself a minor reputation as a geographer, having served under diplomats in China and South Africa and written books about the countries, but he carved a major career out of exploration. Not that he himself went anywhere once his feet were securely under a desk in the Admiralty, but he had a passion for filling in blank spaces on the map – in Africa as well as at the two poles – and he had the resources to put his dreams into practice.

In fact, he could pick and choose from virtually the whole Royal Navy, which had become the largest fleet in the world during the Napoleonic Wars. When the wars ended, Fleming writes, 'the ships were laid up "in ordinary" and the seamen were simply thrown back onto the streets from which they had often been pressganged in the first place.' But the officers were career men, harder to dispose of, and their numbers gradually increased until there was 'one officer for every four men. But 90 percent of these officers had nothing to do . . . The average age of an Admiral was seventy-six. Below them on the list hundreds of grey-haired captains drew their half-pay with autumnal melancholy. In 1846, of 1,151 officers, only 172 were in full employment.' For Barrow, these ambitious, restless, under-used, bored men were an inexhaustible pool of talent. They would sail no matter how niggardly the sums Barrow gouged out of the Treasury, and being in the Royal Navy, with its tradition of 'rum, buggery and the lash,' they were inured to deprivation and brutality. At the same period, the great British Public Schools were developing a similar code of fortitude – without the rum. The result was a host of young men to whom hardship came so naturally that the implacable hostility of the polar regions seemed like light relief after what they had already endured while they were growing up.

The most successful of Barrow's boys was James Ross, who discovered the magnetic north pole, in 1831, and, ten years later, was the first to break through the guardian ice-pack into the Antarctic sea that now bears his name. (He also has an island, an ice-shelf and a rare seal named after him.) The others, in comparison, were failures. William Parry made three unsuccessful stabs at the Northwest Passage and one at the North Pole. John Ross, James's uncle, aborted his first attempt at the Northwest Passage and was ice-bound for four winters on his second. They were following Barrow's orders, but Barrow, Fleming writes, 'was never quite right. When he had a geographical opinion it was frequently the wrong one. And when he had no opinion he formed one on the wildest of conjectures suggested by others. Sometimes he hit the spot; more often he missed it.' And when the expeditions he sent out failed to validate his whimsical theories he savaged them anonymously in the *Quarterly Review*.

The most famous of Barrow's boys was Sir John Franklin, who led an overland expedition to explore the north coast of Canada between the mouths of the Mackenzie and Coppermine Rivers and, Barrow hoped, to link up with Parry's ships on their way through the Northwest Passage. As Fleming describes him, he was also the most improbable of explorers:

> John Franklin was a beefy genial giant who literally could not hurt a fly. He was formal, painfully shy and abnormally sensitive: to order, let alone witness, a flogging made him tremble from head to toe . . . He was brave, determined and would obey orders to the letter . . . The deciding factor, however, was Franklin's charm. Everyone who met him agreed that this was his outstanding characteristic – it was impossible not to like him . . . It can only have been Franklin's charm that won him the leadership of the 1819 Canadian expedition because he had nothing else to recommend him. Aged thirty-three, he was overweight and suffered from a poor circulation that left his fingers and toes cold even in an English summer. He was unfit and had no experience of land travel. He could not hunt, canoe or trek. Three meals a day were a must; he could not move without tea; and even when he could move he could manage no more than eight miles a day unless he was carried.

As it happened, Franklin walked many hundred miles during the three years he was away, although the overland expedition was an unqualified disaster: half the men starved to death, the others survived by eating lichen – they called it *tripes de roche* in fond remembrance of French gastronomy – then they ate their shoes, and some of them finished by eating each other. On his return to England, Franklin found himself famous; he was 'the man who ate his boots.' Twenty years later, in 1845, he sailed back to the Arctic on another futile attempt to discover the Northwest Passage and disappeared completely. His formidable wife refused to believe he was dead and it took another nine years to find traces of the doomed expedition. Meanwhile, rescue missions set out regularly, though not always in the most likely directions. 'In later years,' Fleming writes, 'when a man said he was going to look for Franklin – whose legend was perpetuated for the purpose – it was understood that he was trying for the North Pole.'

One of the most curious aspects of the early expeditions is the sheer inappropriateness of their gear. Cold weather clothing was primitive and, as naval officers, they felt themselves so superior to the native Inuits that they learned almost nothing about survival from them. Eventually, the more savvy explorers took to wearing fur outer garments, but a pigheaded few stuck to cocked hats and brass buttons, reluctant to relinquish the insignia of rank:

> Kennedy and Bellot conducted their explorations in conditions of disparate harmony: Kennedy soldiering on in his thick furs while Bellot hopped about in a nice ensemble of salmon-pink tunic and tall sea-boots, showing with each bound just a hint of white leggings.

The naval belief in doing everything the hard way explains a lot about Britain's heroic failures and eventually contributed to the death of Captain Scott and his companions. Even before Barrow had sent out his first expedition to the Arctic, he could have learned how to do it successfully from William Scorseby, a self-taught but extraordinarily shrewd scientist and inventor, who was also the most successful whaler in Britain. He had fished in Baffin Bay for years and understood the strange movements of the Arctic Ocean, he knew the Greenland coast and the people who lived there and what was needed to survive in extreme cold. He also knew how to travel in it – with dogs and light sledges, as the Inuit did. But there were no British officers who knew how to handle dog-teams, and anyway Scorseby wasn't a Navy man. (Barrow scuttled his proposals for the Northwest Passage – Scorseby thought it possible but pointless – then published them anonymously as his own.)

The Royal Navy had no sledge-dogs, but they had plenty of enlisted men who, unlike dogs, did what they were told and needed to be protected by their betters from idleness. Hence the British tradition of man-hauling. Scott took Mongolian ponies to the Antarctic, but the conditions were too harsh for them and most ended up in the cooking-pot. While Amundsen's party cruised to the South Pole behind their dog-teams, Scott's men harnessed up Royal Navy-style and dragged their ponderous, over-loaded sledges themselves, imagining unrelenting hard labour and bone-weary exhaustion were badges of honour.

Maybe they were and maybe that, finally, is why people go to these places. As Charles Neider wrote on his first flight to McMurdo Sound, in 1969, 'You and your fellow passengers sit in two rows on red canvas seats, facing each other across a fence of strapped-down seabags, and wonder what Antarctica will be like and what you will be like in it.' What you will often be, according to the early explorers, is bored. When James Ross battened down for another Arctic winter, he wrote:

> The prison door was shut upon us . . . Amid all its brilliancy, this land, the land of ice and snow, has ever been, and ever will be a dull, dreary, heart-sinking, monotonous waste, under the influence of which the very mind is paralysed, ceasing to care or think . . . it is but the view of uniformity and silence and death . . . where nothing moves and nothing changes, but all is forever the same, cheerless, cold and still.

This is boredom of a special kind, however — a kind that kills unless you pay attention — and that, too, is part of its attraction, especially to the British. They didn't go because they knew about snow and ice — snowfalls are as rare as heat-waves in England — they went because they knew about hardship and suffering and valued fortitude — that famous stiff upper lip — above everything else. This kind of bravery has nothing to do with the chest-thumping Darwinism of Robert Service — 'This is the Law of the Yukon, that only the Strong shall thrive; / That surely the Weak shall perish, and only the Fit survive' — and it has everything to do with putting one foot monotonously in front of the other, with refusing to complain, and preserving as best you can good manners in unmannerly situations. During the nightmare winter expedition that became *The Worst Journey in the World*, Apsley Cherry-Garrard wrote mildly:

> We were quite intelligent people, and we must all have known that we were not going to see the penguins and that it was folly to go forward. And yet with quiet perservance, in perfect friendship, almost with gentleness those two men led on. I just did what I was told . . . I wrote that night: 'There is something after all rather good in doing something never done before.' Things were looking up, you see.

Cherry-Garrad's style of resigned, low-key, almost docile courage died, more or less, with the hosts of young men who were slaughtered like cattle during World War I. In those days they called it 'moral fibre' and it was impossible to thrive in the polar regions without it. For some, I suspect, it was – and is – also something very like depression, some quirk of nature or nurture that convinces them that the world is an unremittingly stern and hostile place and bleakness is their natural environment. People who think that way are never altogether easy with a comfortable, undemanding life, not because of the comforts but because they feel they are getting away with something, as though they were confidence tricksters creating a tough image they don't deserve. Everyone else is taken in, but they know better, so they call their own bluff by going to harsh, unforgiving places where every sham, sooner or later, will be exposed.

Those who organize polar expeditions always have grand scientific excuses when they are looking for funds, but for the explorers themselves the final point of the exercise is survival. In 1913, the Canadian naval ship *Karluk* set out towards the North Pole, was trapped in the ice off the north-east coast of Alaska, and drifted helplessly west for five months until she broke up off Wrangel Island in Siberia. The captain and an Inuit hunter went for help and eventually organized a rescue, but only twelve of the twenty-five on board survived. Jennifer Niven ends *The Ice Master*, her vivid account of the disaster, with a triumphant letter home by one of the lucky ones:

> The one thing I wish this letter to do for me is to show you I am alive, and how much I am alive. Just think of it all of you – I am alive. And more than alive – I am *living*. None of you know what life is, nor will you ever know until you come as near losing it as we were.

Years ago, *Punch*, which used to be the prime source of British humor, published a cartoon of two explorers in what was then called 'darkest Africa.' One of them is saying, 'I came here to forget, but I can't remember what.' For polar explorers the answer was always clear: they went to the worst places in the world in order to come back alive.

Flying

Saint-Exupéry

1

Powered flight was the first great technological achievement of this technological century, and it developed at an astonishing pace. In 1976, just seventy three years after the Wright brothers' first stuttering flights at Kitty Hawk, Concorde went into commercial service, carrying whoever could afford the fare – tycoons, grannies, babes-in-arms – across great distances at supersonic speeds. More important, the passengers thought nothing of it. In the space of a single lifetime, flight had changed from an impossibly dangerous adventure, strictly for heroes and a very few heroines, to a commonplace routine.

That routine has now become so commonplace that it has made rail travel seem romantic again. To move from city center to city center in a comfortable seat, with plenty of space to move around in and a picture-window view of the passing scene, now seems infinitely preferable to the pychopathology of everyday flight: the frantic race to a distant airport, the queues, the delays, the ill-temper, the cramped journey with nothing to look at except the back of the seat in front of you or, at best, the video screen fixed to it; then, on arrival, the whole tedious process in reverse, with the added grief of mislaid luggage. Flying has become just another tribulation we endure in the name of impatience.

That is not how it appeared at the start. The crowds who came to watch the first aviators coax their flimsy contraptions into the air felt they were in on a second creation. In the ancient world it was taken for granted that the gods could fly (it was just another aspect of their divinity), and in biblical heaven, of course, angels had wings (how else could they get around up there?). But the wings themselves were a source of great wonder:

And when they went, I heard the noise of their wings, like the noise of great waters, as the voice of the Almighty, the voice of speech, as the noise of an host: when they stood, they let down their wings.

That is the prophet Ezekiel contemplating God's seraphim. This is the young Franz Kafka, in 1909, watching Blériot fly:

One sees his straight upper body over the wings, his legs are deeply planted as if they were a part of the machinery. The sun is sinking, and under the baldachin of the grandstands, it throws its light on the soaring wings. Devotedly everyone looks up at him; there is no room in anybody's heart for anyone else. He flies a small circle and then appears almost directly above us. And everyone looks with outstretched neck as the monoplane falters, is controlled by Blériot, and even climbs. What is happening? Here above us, there is a man twenty meters above the earth, imprisoned in a wooden frame, and defending himself against an invisible danger which he has taken on of his own free will. But we are standing below, pushed away, without existence, and looking at this man.

Ezekiel was imagining the wonders of heaven, Kafka was simply describing what he saw. What they both have in common is a kind of modesty, the modesty of artists faced with material so extraordinary that it makes them insignificant.

Robert Wohl quotes Kafka's 'The Airplanes at Brescia' in *A Passion for Wings*. He says that Kafka had gone to the air show deeply depressed, hoping to stimulate his imagination, and he wrote about it because his friend, Max Brod, had challenged him to a contest to see which of them could come up with the better description. But Kafka was just one of many creative people who was fired up by the new science of aviation. Wohl is a cultural historian and the thesis behind his erudite, shrewd and beautifully illustrated book is that, for artists, aviation was an imaginative turning-point, deeply implicated in the Modernist avant-garde movement. The crowds who flocked to watch the first aviators in action were not just after thrills. They were also moved by the strangeness of the enterprise, the bravery of the fliers, the plain miracle of powered flight in machines that were heavier than air. Those daring young men in their cockeyed machines, cobbled

together from wood and linen and wire, somehow embodied the
aspirations of the new century. According to Wohl:

Marinetti's first Futurist manifesto was published in the direct
aftermath of Wilbur Wright's triumphant flights in France. His
1909 play, *Poupées électriques*, was dedicated to Wright 'who
knew how to raise our migrating hearts higher than the captivat-.
ing mouths of women.' Pablo Picasso, Georges Braque, and
Robert and Sonia Delaunay were among the many artists, poets,
and intellectuals who made their way to Issy-les-Moulineaux, a
field on the outskirts of Paris, to watch with astonished and
admiring eyes the early airplanes fly. As Le Corbusier, a student
in Paris at this time, was later to put it, modernists believed that
the airplane was 'the vanguard of the conquering armies of the
New Age.'

Aviation belonged to the new century in part because the
engineering that went into flying machines was utterly different
from that of the Industrial Revolution. Nineteenth-century engineering revolved around the steam engine. It was about weight and
brute power – beautifully machined heavy steel, burnished bronze,
polished copper pipes, ornamental cast-iron – everything built, with
no expense spared, to withstand great pressures and last any number
of lifetimes. Airplane construction is the opposite of all that; it is
about lightness. The Wright brothers started out making bicycles,
which were all the rage at the turn of the century (Wohl calls the
bicycle '*la petite reine* of fin-de-siècle France'). They knew about
thin-wall steel tubes, wire-spoked wheels, chain drives and whatever
else it took to construct efficient machines that weighed as little as
possible. In effect, they were practical engineers at the cheap end of
the market, but they happened to be fascinated by flight. 'When not
soaring or working on the gliders,' Wohl writes, 'Wilbur [Wright]
spent his time studying the flight of vultures, eagles, ospreys, and
hawks, trying to discover the secret of their ability to maneuver with
their wings in unstable air. To those who later asked him how he
learned to fly, he loved to reply, through his scarcely opened lips:
"Like a bird."'

This is the point at which engineering intersects with the imagination, with mankind's ancient dream of freeing himself from gravity.
Until the first fliers got to work, the body was earthbound but it

enclosed a soul that flew – in meditation, in poetry, and, as Andrew
Marvell showed, sometimes spectacularly in both:

> Casting the Bodies Vest aside,
> My Soul into the boughs does glide:
> There like a Bird it sits, and sings,
> Then whets, and combs its silver Wings;
> And, till prepar'd for longer flight,
> Waves in its Plumes the various Light.

At the beginning of this century, the new light engineering that
allowed man to fly seemed to the uninitiated a kind of poetry. Wohl
quotes a writer in the *Atlantic Monthly*, in 1913, who claimed that
'Machinery is our new art form' and praised 'the engineers whose
poetry is too deep to look poetic' and whose gifts 'have swung their
souls free . . . like gods.' The French were particularly susceptible to
this style of hyperbole. François Peyrey, one of Wilbur Wright's most
eloquent admirers, called him a poet and compared him to one of
'those monks of Asia Minor who live perched on the tops of
inaccessible mountain peaks. The soul of Wilbur Wright is just as
high and faraway.' Wrong, says Wohl. Wright was, in fact, 'deeply
middle-class and unheroic', but the French were obsessed with the
glamour of flight, so they pretended not to notice his limitations.

Wohl has trawled the backwaters of the first literature of flight – and
seems to have had a great time doing so – but what he comes up with
is mostly rhetoric, doom and triumphalism: a turgid epic by Edmond
Rostand, author of *Cyrano de Bergerac*, glorifying a new race of airborne heroes; H.G. Wells's *The War in the Air*, in which a fleet of
German zeppelins destroys New York; the works of Emile Driant, a
disaffected army officer and disciple of Jules Verne, who foresaw the
military uses of airplanes and wrote boys' adventure stories in which
perfidious orientals and blackamoors are outwitted and overawed by
magnificent white men in their flying machines. (That colonial myth
survived a long time and was immortalized in a *New Yorker* cartoon in
which a cannibal warrior, festooned in bones, is saying to his king,
'There's a guy just landed in a Sikorski S-61 who claims he's a god or
something.')

Further upmarket, the rhetoric was turgid in a different way. Kafka
had seen D'Annunzio strutting among the gentry at the air show at
Brescia but, unlike Kafka, D'Annunzio managed to hitch a ride with

one of the fliers. This prompted an outpouring of enthusiasm for this new arena for heroes, and a novel, *Forse che sí forse che no*, (Perhaps Yes, Perhaps No), in which the aviator is seen as a new form of superman, a 'celestial helmsman,' 'the messenger of a vaster life,' scornful of the poor folk down there on earth, and of women and foreigners in particular. Although the novel's purple prose and operatic carry-on seem absurd now, it was vastly successful at the time and was greeted as an 'incomparable poem in prose about our modernity.'

Aviation, in fact, seem to have inspired the Italians to a particularly ferocious style of heroic modernism that would have baffled practical men like the Wright brothers and Blériot. Marinetti was as besotted by flying as D'Annunzio, but chiefly as a brand-new god-like means of destruction, starting with – who else? – his literary enemies, then proceeding to his other pet aversions – romantic love, monogamy, the Pope, the 'vast clamour of messy women' who can't understand the grandeur and necessity of war – and ending with a wild slaughter of Italy's current arch-enemy, the Austrians.

Maybe this frantic note had something to do with the new cult of speed, which had begun with the automobile, then literally took off with the first powered flights; but it sounds like a failure of literary imagination. The truth is, in the early days writers responded to aviation in the tritest ways – as a new heroism, a new mythology, a new freedom, a new apocalypse – in other words, as a new source of bombast into which to channel the fierce nationalism and war-fever of the period. Apart from a few journalists, only Kafka seemed content to report scrupulously what he saw and so, strictly by implication, to convey the strangeness of what was happening. It was left to the painters to explore the aesthetic possibilities of flight.

Robert Delaunay had a passion for wings and was a regular pilgrim to air shows, but what fascinated him, says Wohl, 'was not so much the airplane as an object or the new view it offered of the world but the inspiration it provided to experiment with form, color, and light: not the machine as such but the symbol of modernity.' In the notes he made on his famous composition of blazing suns and revolving propellers, *L'Hommage à Blériot*, Delaunay wrote: 'Simultaneous solar disk. Forms. Creation of the constructive disk. Solar fireworks. Depth and life of the sun. Constructive mobility of the solar spectrum: birth, flame, flight of airplanes.' The point was not to paint flight but to make flight painterly.

The Russian Suprematist Malevich took that process one stage further – into pure abstraction. 'The airplane was not contrived in order to carry business letters from Berlin to Moscow,' he wrote, 'but rather in obedience to the irresistible drive of this yearning for speed to take on external form.' But the external form of speed is streamlining, the smoothing down and eventual elimination of detail in the process itself. In the same way, representation dropped steadily away from Malevich's paintings, like the earth dropping away from a climbing airplane. Somewhere behind the crosses and intermeshed oblong blocks of colour in his late paintings are the outlines of aircraft, but they are purged of detail, reduced to their essence, purified by mental flight. 'Our century is a huge boulder aimed with all its weight into space,' he wrote. But for Malevich in his studio, the goal he was aiming at was the clarity and remoteness of inner space.

2

There is a crucial difference between the imaginative apprehension of flying, and all it symbolizes, and the actual experience of flight. D'Annunzio and Marinetti went up but only as day-trippers, so all they got was the adrenalin rush. Hence their vainglory, their inflated prose, their muscle-flexing delusions of power, their contempt for the poor creeps left below. The people who really flew didn't write about it. They were either plane-makers, like the Wright brothers or Blériot or De Havilland, absorbed in the technical problems of flight, or they were rich young sportsmen – the fast cars and polo gang – who took up flying for 'the fun of it' (which was the title Amelia Earhart later gave her memoirs). When the Great War came that sportsmanship survived as a kind of latter-day chivalry. The aces who did battle in the sky somehow redeemed the monotonous slaughter in the mud below. The infantry resented them, but the high command and the public loved them, and they gave journalists something stirring to write about. (An uncle of mine had flown Sopwith Camel fighter planes on the western front – in those days, in itself a considerable achievement for a man called Levy – and the glamour of it clung to him until he died forty years later.) Chivalry plus the magic of flight were a powerful concoction. Yeats did justice to this 'lonely impulse of delight' in his beautiful poem 'An Irish Airman Foresees His Death,' but readers who wanted to understand the real experience of flying – what it felt like to be up there in the open cockpit of a fragile, unreliable plane, with very few instruments and no radio – had to wait until 1931, when Antoine de Saint-Exupéry published *Night Flight*.

Saint-Exupéry had the same aristocratic background as the other early sportsman-fliers but no money to go with it. To judge from Stacy Schiff's subtle, sensitive, and extraordinarily fair-minded biography, this was just one of his many contradictions. As a small child, he wrote poetry – reams of it – yet he was good with his hands and fascinated by machines. At school, he was both a literary star and an gifted mathematician, yet he couldn't pass exams. He was pathologically disorganized and absent-minded, yet he managed to master the precise and difficult art of flying. He was, at his best, a modest man with a talent for understatement, yet he also had a Gallic weakness for abstraction and rhetoric. He was a writer who hated the literary life and the literary crowd and yearned continually for action. He adored his wife and was compulsively unfaithful to her (as she was to him). He was aviation's first and greatest writer, yet he became internationally famous through a winsome, saccharine fairy story, *Le Petit Prince*. Above all, he was a spoiled *fils à maman* who became a national hero, 'an indulged, profligate son,' Schiff calls him, 'who would make a near-religious appeal for the stoic, responsible life.'

His father had died when Antoine was three and his mother, Marie, struggled for the rest of her life – not least to support her feckless elder son in his expensive habits (he always lodged cheap, in a state of chronic chaos, but he had a taste for good restaurants and lordly gestures). Marie, Schiff writes, 'was a devoted mother who would remain unceasingly compassionate, attentive, giving, and pious, all qualities her elder son would put to the test.' He was the surrogate man in a house full of women (his young brother died at the age of fifteen), the undisputed leader of a gang of siblings and local kids, dazzling them with card tricks, beating them at chess, expecting and getting praise on-demand for his dreadful verse, and, despite his snub-nosed, owlish face and shambling presence – a cross, says Schiff, between Wallace Shawn and the young Orson Welles – effortlessly charming the whole world. He left, a friend said, 'permanent wounds in the hearts of those who saw him smile, even once.' It added up to one of those magical childhoods which are hard to recover from. Later, when years of flying the Sahara to South America route had transformed him from aristocratic Saint-Exupéry to plebeian Saint-Ex, he wrote to his mother saying, 'I am not sure I have lived since my childhood.'

He arrived at school in Le Mans in 1909, one year too late to see Wilbur Wright's first flights at nearby Hunaudières. But flying was already the national craze, and Saint-Ex was bitten seriously enough to haunt an airfield near the family home during the holidays. At the age of twelve and despite his mother's veto, he managed to con a ride from one of the pilots. At that point, his obsession began in earnest, although it was another ten years before he got his pilot's license – ten wasted years during which he failed his exams to *les grands écoles*, failed his exams for the navy, and frittered time away expensively in Paris, pretending to study architecture. He finally learned to fly – privately, of course; *maman* paid – while doing his national service as a mechanic in the air force, but even then his vocation still eluded him. He pushed a pen as a bookkeeper in Paris, he worked as a travelling salesman for a truck company, and the only flying he did was when he took paying customers up for brief tourist circuits at Le Bourget.

Then, in 1926, he landed a job with the company that eventually became Aéropostale, flying the mail, first from Toulouse to Alicante, then extending gradually south down the western edge of Africa, to Casablanca and Dakar and on, by the shortest Atlantic crossing, to South America – Buenos Aires, Rio, Santiago, Asuncion and Patagonia. For Saint-Ex, joining Aéropostale was like coming home – to a home, finally, with men in it. The spoiled mother's boy took to privation, danger and solitude like a duck to water. Nothing fazed him: crash-landings in the desert, night flights with no landmarks and a useless compass, a hurricane in Patagonia that tossed his plane around like a pingpong ball, months virtually on his own in a wooden shack – with a plank bed, a wind-up gramophone and a deck of cards – as chief of 'the most desolate airstrip in the world,' at Cape Juby, in the western Sahara. The grimmer things got, the more he seemed to thrive. His life was full of disasters, but he took his innumerable plane crashes and injuries in his stride. What brought him down was civilization and its discontents: the machinations of the literary world in pre-war Paris and of the French exiles in wartime New York; his various doomed love affairs; his constant shortage of money; above all, his dreadful marriage to his Salvadorean wife, Consuela, who was small and helpless and beautiful, but also a pathological liar and self-dramatizer, as compulsively unpunctual and quarrelsome as she was unfaithful, and elusive to the point of giddiness. Lewis Galantière, Saint-Ex's translator, called her 'Surrealism made flesh.'

Saint-Ex was more famous for his crashes than for his flying, and for a simple reason: compared to his colleagues, he was a lousy pilot – absent-minded, easily distracted, and so indifferent to risk as to be foolhardy. Describing a night flight across the Libyan desert which ended in a particularly spectactular disaster, he wrote, 'I am navigating. I have on my side only the stars.' It sounds wonderful but it was true only because he had screwed up; he hadn't bothered to take a radio. 'What he demonstrated,' Schiff writes, 'amounted less to grace than insouciance under pressure.'

He also demonstrated an aristocratic disdain for technical detail. In 1943, to escape his miserable exile in New York, he wangled his way back into active service with a French squadron flying Lockheed P-38s under the overall command of the Americans. By then, he was so broken by his numerous injuries that he had to be helped into the cockpit and was unable to bend down and tie his own shoelaces. He was also unable to read the altimeter; when ordered to fly at 2,000 meters (6,500 feet) he blithely went up to 20,000 feet – without oxygen. He blamed the plane, of course, dismissing the state-of-the-art P-38 as 'a sort of flying torpedo that has nothing whatever to do with flying and, with all its screens and buttons, makes of its pilot a sort of chief accountant.' Even the sympathetic Schiff calls him 'the world's greatest Luddite aviator' and he drove his American superiors wild. When he crashed a P-38 on a training flight – he forgot to pump the hydraulic brakes before landing – he was outraged by the Americans' outrage. 'Sir, I want to die for France,' he announced to the commanding officer. 'I don't give a damn if you die for France or not,' the American colonel replied, 'but you're not going to do so in one of our airplanes.'

The colonel was wrong. Despite his objections, Saint-Ex went on flying reconnaissance missions, often not over the areas he had been assigned, reading as he flew, scribbling notes to himself, oblivious to enemy aircraft and gunfire, 'trafficking,' says Schiff, 'in miracles.' On July 31st, 1944, one month after his forty-fourth birthday, he ran out of miracles. He took off from Corsica for a mission over Lyons and was never seen again. He may have been shot down, he may have made one idiot mistake too many, or he may simply have been so weary and depressed that he no longer cared what happened to him and so didn't bother to attend to the tedious technical routines necessary for survival. Whatever the reason, his plane vanished and no traces of it were ever found.

Yet it was precisely his limitations as a pilot that made his books so convincing. He came to flying from writing, not vice versa, and he wrote about it wonderfully because it was a skill he had acquired by hard work. A natural flier would have simply got on with the job without noticing what was involved, whereas Saint-Ex was constantly aware of the details: the sound of the engine, the shifting stresses on the wings, the way the stars appear and vanish on cloudy nights, the moonlight like 'polar snow.' The cockpits of the planes he flew were regularly littered with balled-up scraps of paper covered with notes and sketches which, even on test-flights, usually had little to do with the technical behavior of the aircraft. But they had everything to do with the experience of flight, with what it felt like up there, what he saw, what he thought about. *Wind, Sand and Stars* and *Flight to Arras* are the great books of aviation because the narrative is embedded in detail.

Flight to Arras, for example, describes a pointless reconnaissance mission during the fall of France in 1940, which Saint-Ex was too old, too battered and far too famous ever to have undertaken. Because of all that, he was open to everything – to the beauty of the evening and the fading landscape, of the tracer bullets arching towards him and the anti-aircraft shells exploding all around. The whole world takes on a terrible poignancy and clarity, as though he were seeing it all for the last time – which he surely must have thought he was. He has too much to do to think about death, yet he thinks a great deal about his delectable childhood. Although the book dribbles away into a maundering soliloquy on the meaning of life – rhetoric and senti-mentality were always his fatal Cleopatras – his description of the mission itself is incomparable.

There was something else keeping Saint-Ex paradoxically down to earth when he wrote about flying: his constant awareness of the shadowy presence of the company he kept professionally, as a pilot. He was uneasy around other writers and distrusted literature as an end in itself. 'One needs to live in order to write,' he said. 'One needs to have something to say.' He also wrote in a letter, 'Café society never taught me anything. I like people who have been tied more closely to life by the need to eat, to feed their children, and to survive until the end of the month. They are wiser.' A character in *Southern Mail*, eavesdropping on a group of pilots, puts it more tersely: *'Ils font un métier. J'aime ces hommes.'* ('They're doing a job. I like these men.') Saint-Ex's fellow fliers at Aéropostale had the most demanding of jobs to do and they didn't give a damn about literature. (Most of them objected to his early books, and those who didn't were embarrassed by them.) Their disabused view of his – to them – moonlighting second job as a writer kept him in check. Although he sounded off about the meaning of life, he was scrupulously modest on the subject of bravery. According to the philosopher Merleau-Ponty, Saint-Ex was a man who found himself 'to the extent to which he runs into danger.' That was also true of his prose. He knew that heroism exists only in the eye of the beholder, the outsider, and courage is simply a matter of getting on with what has to be done and attending to details in difficult situations. Hence the vividness of his best writing, its solidity and precision. Language, he said, was like 'a sophisticated machine, very scientific, where one word too many – like a grain of sand or the slightest clumsiness, like an incorrect maneuver – could result in a crash.' He watched himself as a writer because he knew that out there, beyond the literary world and his admiring readership, was another audience whose good opinion he passionately desired, an audience of fliers like himself, who really understood what was at stake and would not be fobbed off with histrionics. So he tried to write as unfussily and as naturally as they flew, to write as he would like to have flown – without crashing. He wrote about what he knew and he happened to have lived an adventurous life, but his canonization as a national hero would have struck him as absurd. Although he liked coping with dangerous situations, danger itself was no more important to him than his hopes of winning the national lottery: 'like a broken heart, it keeps you busy.' What mattered most to him was that he had a *métier*, and he wanted to get it right.

New York Review of Books, 1995

High Flier

CAMUS ONCE SAID — I think he was writing about Nietzsche — that it is possible to spend a life of wild excitement without ever leaving your desk. The life of the mind, he meant, can be as risky and challenging as any heroic enterprise. Beckett in his room, listening to his voices, taking it all down, following the black thread of his depression wherever it led, purifying it, refining it over and over again, was as heroic in his persistence as Shackleton and his companions rowing their open boat across the Scott Sea from Elephant Island to South Georgia.

Well, maybe. But that isn't how it usually feels. The writer at his desk is more like a lighthouse keeper than an explorer, bored and isolated and pining for distraction. The literary world may seem appealing from the outside and some of its gaudier practitioners may treat it as though it were a subdivision of show biz — all public readings and parties and sounding off on talk shows — but in reality it is just another sedentary, middle-class profession, like psychoanalysis but far more lonely. At least the analyst gets to see patients, whereas most writers I know sit on their own and wish they were somewhere else. That, in fact, is what they write about: their fantasies of what life might be like in a world where the things people do have real consequences and the mistakes they make can't be caught in the next draft; they have to be paid for on the nail. From the writer's side of the plate glass window, it is hard to imagine that anyone out there would ever want to get in.

James Salter turned to writing after years in one of the most exacting and exclusive of all adventurous professions. He was an Air Force fighter pilot, one of the stars Tom Wolfe wrote about so vividly in *The Right Stuff*, a fighter jock right at the top of the pyramid. He had flown with men who later became famous as astronauts,

Grisson and Aldrin and White; he had shot down enemy planes over Korea, and, although Salter himself is a modest man and never spells it out, he seems to have been the lead pilot in the Air Force's aerobatics team. At the age of thirty-two, when he was still a hot-shot flier at the peak of his career, a lieutenant colonel with years to go before he would be shunted off to a desk job in Washington, he resigned his commission and settled down to write for a living.

It took a brave man to sacrifice a brilliant career doing something he loved for the chancy life of a writer. Even so, I have to confess that I find his decision baffling, if only for childish reasons. I was a kid in London when the Battle of Britain was being fought and fighter pilots – Churchill's few to whom so much was owed by so many – were every schoolboy's heroes. Most of them were young men fresh out of school, only a few years older than we were, but with their reticence and casual gallantry, their leather flying jackets and white silk scarves, they seemed unimaginably glamorous, and the deadly aerial ballet they performed above our heads each day – Spitfires and Hurricanes versus Messerschmidts and Heinkels – was the most exciting show on earth. I yearned to do what they were doing more than I have ever yearned for anything. Luckily for me, the war ended before I was called up and the yearning faded, but in that embarrassing corner of my heart where the inextinguishable schoolboy lives on I am still convinced that flying a fighter plane is the most desirable of all possible activities. To give up all that excitement and glamour for the solitary life of a writer seems to me incomprehensible.

As Salter describes it, the decision was equally incomprehensible to him and *Burning the Days* is, among other things, his attempt to solve the mystery. For years, the challenge and exhilaration and companionship of flying gave him everything he wanted, so the idea of quitting came to him out of the blue, as unexpectedly as one of the MIGs he had fought over the Yalu River. All it took was a casual remark by an acquaintance and suddenly his whole life was unravelling:

A few months earlier, Spry, who had graduated a few classes after me and was in group operations, had told me he was resigning. Almost at that instant – he had somehow given me the freedom, hurled the first stone – I made the decision. It was far from decisive, I had perhaps waited too long, but there was still the idea that had never left me, of being a writer and from the great heap of days making something lasting.

The Air Force – I ate and drank it, went in whatever weather on whatever day, talked its endless talk, climbed onto the wing to fuel the ship myself, fell into the wet sand of its beaches with sweaty others and was bitten by its flies, ignored wavering instruments, slept in dreary places, rendered it my heart. I had given up the life into which I had been born and taken up another and was about to leave that, too, only with far greater difficulty . . .

I was thirty-two years old and had been in uniform since I was seventeen. As I walked into the Pentagon I felt I was walking to my death.

The wording makes it clear that, even forty years on, Salter is still uneasy with his decision. He says he turned writer with the idea of 'from the great heap of days making something lasting.' Yet, like the autobiography itself, the chapter in which he makes his choice is called 'Burning the Days,' as though what he had really done was reduce to ashes everything he had previously been and believed in.

So why did he do it? Kenneth Littauer, Salter's literary first agent, had also risen young to the rank of lieutenant colonel, but he quit the army, he said, because 'There was no one to talk to.' That does not seem to have been one of Salter's problems. He enjoyed the company of his fellow pilots, their shop talk and swagger and wild partying, almost as much as he enjoyed flying and for a time was content to keep his writing apart: 'late at night, back from a restaurant, back from the bar, I sat writing. I had three lives, one during the day, one at night, and the last in a drawer in my room in a small book of notes.' When the small book of notes became a novel it was time to change his life. He wasn't a loner, although loneliness – 'a lonely impulse of delight,' Yeats called it – was one of the pleasures of flying. But he was a very private man, and true privacy was something the Air Force could never provide.

Salter is private even when he is writing the story of his life. *Burning the Days*, in fact, is extraordinary for the things he doesn't mention, beginning with his real name. It was Horowitz but because his first novel, *The Hunters*, was written when he was a serving officer he was obliged to publish it under a pseudonym and the pseudonym stuck. He also doesn't mention that *The Hunters* was sold to Hollywood and made into a film starring Robert Mitchum. He says very little about his first marriage and nothing about his second, though he is not at all reticent about his many casual love affairs along the way.

The truth is, facts don't much interest him, although the facts are intriguing. His father was an engineer turned property speculator, a powerful, stylish, rather distant figure whose speculations, in the end, went badly wrong. But between the wars the family was still comfortably off and rising, and Salter's childhood on the Upper East Side was sheltered and conventional. His mother was a lady who lunched, 'handsome and haughty'; his father's 'suits and shoes came from De Pinna, and mistresses from women who worked in the office or the garment district'; Salter went to summer camps, where he learned to box, and to the best private schools, where he read Dickens and Byron and Kipling. He planned to go on to Stanford but his father had graduated first in his class from West Point so, as a favour to him, Salter entered there too, and was accepted.

He went to West Point to please his aloof father and all he found there was his father's inner world writ large: 'It was a place of bleak emotions, a great orphanage, chill in its appearance, rigid in its demands. There was occasional kindness but little love.' Salter writes brilliantly about his first year as a 'plebe' – the endless drills and parades, the utter lack of privacy, the brute authoritarianism, the senseless orders that had to be obeyed because, for soldiers, orders are orders, however senseless:

> Demands, many of them incomprehensible, rained down. Always at rigid attention, hair freshly cropped, chin withdrawn and trembling, barked at by unseen voices, we stood or ran like insects from one place to another . . . It is the sounds I remember, the iron orchestra, the feet on the stairways, the clanging bells, the shouting, cries of *Yes, No, I do not know, sir!*, the clatter of sixty or seventy rifle butts as they came down on the pavement at nearly the same time. Life was anxious minutes, running everywhere, scrambling to formations.

Being a Jew called Horowitz can't have made his difficult life any easier, though he doesn't mention it because Jewishness was not something he had been brought up to think important. His family was non-religious, more or less assimilated and long-established in America. All Salter says is that he resented having to go to Friday evening services and soon dropped them in favour of Sunday chapel. He was indifferent to both religions, though his own religious difference probably meant a good deal to his fellow-cadets in the 1940s and must

have added to his general misery. During his first year, Salter loathed
the whole mindless bullying show but, knowing that his elegant,
unloving father had flourished at West Point before him, he refused to
be beaten and yearned secretly to succeed:

> At the same time, kindled in me was another urge, the urge to
> manhood. I did not recognise it as such because I had rejected its
> form. *Try to be one of us*, they had said, and I had not been able to. It
> was this that was haunting me, though I would not admit it. I
> struggled against everything, it now seems clear, because I wanted
> to belong.

In the end, his manhood was proved and he accepted the whole West
Point code: duty, honour, country, and also comradeship and self-
reliance. By the time he graduated, in 1944, the sheltered, bookish
New York boy had disappeared forever. He was one of them; the
army had become his life.

It turned out to be a very good life indeed. No one, not even Saint-
Exupéry, has written better about the thrill and pleasure of flying.
This, for example, is Salter learning to fly, sensing for the first time the
wild freedom of what he beautifully calls 'unstructured air:'

> Early flights, the instructor in the rear cockpit, the bumpy taxiing
> on the grass, turning into the wind, tail swinging around, dust
> blowing, and then the abrupt, wild sound of the engine. The
> ground was speeding by, the wheels skipping, and suddenly we
> were rising in the din to see the blue tree line beyond the field
> boundary and, below, the curved roofs of the hangars falling away.
> Now fields appeared, swimming out in all directions. The earth
> became limitless, the horizon, unseen before, rose to fill the world
> and we were aloft in unstructured air.

And this is his first experience in an F-86, flying as wingman to a
veteran of the Korean war:

> He rolled over and, power on, headed straight down. I didn't
> know what he intended or was even doing. I fell into close trail,
> hanging there grimly as if he were watching. The airspeed went to
> the red line; thousands of feet were spinning off the altimeter. The
> controls grew stiff, the stick could be moved only with great effort

as we went through rolls and steep turns at speeds so great I could feel my heart being forced down from my chest.

We burst through the overcast and into the narrow strip of sky beneath. We were well over five hundred knots at about fifteen hundred feet. It was almost impossible to stay in position in the turns. I had both hands on the stick. All the time we were dropping lower. We were not moving, it seemed. We were fixed, quivering, fatally close.

Five hundred feet, three hundred, still lower, in what seemed deathly silence except for an incandescent, steady roar, in solitude, slamming every moment against invisible waves of air. He was leading us into the unknown. My flying suit was soaked, the sweat ran down my face. A pure pale halo formed in back of his canopy and remained there, streaming like smoke. I began to realise what it was about. Never looking at me, absorbed by the instruments in front of him and by something in his thoughts, sometimes watching the world of dark forest that swept beneath us, hills and frozen lakes, he was gauging my desire to belong. It was a baptism.

Nothing Salter has written matches the intensity and precision of his descriptions of flying. I think they are what he will be remembered for. 'It had been a great voyage,' he says of his time in the USAF, 'the voyage, probably, of my life.' Everything that followed was an anti-climax.

His father died, broken, broke and chronically depressed. One year later, Salter resigned his commission. Having vindicated himself by his father's unforgiving standards, he set out to prove himself in literature. Some writers, like Salter's friend John Masters, author of *Bhowani Junction*, lead adventurous lives as soldiers, then settle down and write adventure stories. Salter was more ambitious. In Auden's words, 'Perfection, of a kind, was what he was after'; Salter says 'I wanted . . . to achieve the *assoluta*.' Stirring yarns didn't interest him; he wanted to transmute adventure into high art, like Conrad and Malraux, and it shows in his prose.

Irwin Shaw, who became an improbable father-figure to Salter, put his finger on the problem: 'The difficulty, he had told me at one point, was that I was a lyric and he a narrative writer. "Lyric" seemed a word he was uncomfortable with. It seemed to mean something like callow.' No one could seriously accuse Salter of being callow but I see what he means. Shaw was a story-teller who wielded prose like a blunt instrument; Salter is a high-stylist whose prose is sophisticated and self-conscious to the point of mannerism and he is simply not interested in telling stories. All his novels are short, full of telling insights and passages of dazzling description, yet somehow they lack a narrative thread and drain away into the sand. Even the story of his life – especially his life after West Point and the Air Force – is told in fragments, as though held together only by a sensibility, not by a man who suffered and was there.

While Salter was in Europe with the USAF after World War II, he lived the grand life of the imperial occupying army, dining at the best restaurants, staying at the best hotels, with money to burn and all the girls he could ever want. Along the way, he developed a passion for France and all things French. (His erotic epic, *A Sport and a Pastime*, is as much a love-letter to provincial France as it is to the young object of his desires.) He also fell under the spell of New Wave writers like Marguerite Duras and their oblique, detached take on the art of the novel. His own temperament was too romantic – too high-flown in every sense – for him to follow them all the way but he loved their attention to detail and aesthetic strictness.

Details, in fact, are what interest him most – details woven together to create mood and atmosphere:

She was from Marseille, skin pale and shining like fruitwood. Her dress was cut low, her breasts smooth and perfectly separated. We danced like a couple, as if we had come there together. She was pressed against me. The black tile pillars slid before my eyes, the mirrors, the trio at the floorside table, and a girl with short black hair, the gold of a wedding band on her finger. They were the *haut monde*, come for titillation.

Canadian pilots are entering. The band is playing something I would like to remember. Far away it seems, unmourned, are all the other nights, the unattainable women, nurses, admirals' daughters, the colonel's wife that time unsteadily playing blackjack. 'Just give me a little bitty one,' she pleaded, 'don't give it to me unless it's little.' It was dealt. A jack. She stared at it, looked at her hole card, stared again. Her handsome, slurred face. 'All right,' she announced, 'twenty-one.' But it was not. The dealer took the money.

The morning light of Africa is brilliant and flat. The empty street, the silence. How was it? they want to know.

The effect is of a kind of pointillism in words, at once pure and tricky, full of allusions and reverberations and, sometimes, unnatural inversions, glowing but static, a prose that leads back onto itself, perfection for perfection's sake.

When Salter is writing about his military life none of that seems to matter because he is still in the grip of what he went through and the intensity of his experiences carries him through. The combination of intensity and chiselled prose, in fact, is what makes the first half of his book unique. But his life after flying was far less interesting. His novels didn't sell well, so while he laboured over them he kept afloat by writing film scripts, drifting between Los Angeles and Rome, with diversions to Paris and London. One of his scripts was the excellent *Downhill Racer*, for Robert Redford, but most of them came to nothing, though they paid his expenses lavishly and he continued to live the rich imperial life, courtesy of the movie business.

The second half of *Burning the Days* contains many clever sketches of the stars and fixers and whores who make up the demimonde of Hollywood and *cinecittà*. Salter is sharp-eyed and always generous in his friendship, but movie and literary gossip is thin stuff compared with what has gone before and Salter himself seems to know it. The most moving passage in his story of his life as a civilian – his 'counterlife,' he calls it, 'a life of freedom, style, and art, or the semblance of art' – is his description of the Apollo 11 moonshot in July, 1969. He watched it on television in the St. Regis Hotel, in the company of his nubile Italian mistress, who had flown from Rome to meet him. While the two of them were fiercely making love, his friend and fellow-pilot Buzz Aldrin was on his way to the moon, along with Neil Armstrong, to step onto its surface and into history. Watching the blast-off, Salter feels first the 'confusion and panic' of someone who has been left behind, then 'hollow, as if I had lost everything.'

> I have never forgotten that night or its anguish. Pleasure and inconsequence on one hand, immeasurable deeds on the other. I lay awake for a long time thinking of what I had become.

Aldrin was achieving the celebrity of the hero, the celebrity Salter had once yearned for and might also have achieved if he had stuck to flying, but which he knew no book of his would ever bring him.

As though to emphasize that he has betrayed his own stern code, he follows the scene immediately with a sketch of a rich Italian scriptwriter in Hollywood. He is a man who seems to have everything: 'the grand house, the Rolls Royce in the covered driveway, the gardens', and a graceful Swedish girlfriend to go with them. Not so, says a mutual friend, 'He's an artist *manqué*. He thinks he's wasted his talent on movies, which he detests. Actually, he's never written any good movies – they're all trash except for one . . . He's the saddest man I know.'

Unlike the Italian, Salter has written several impressive books and *Burning the Days*, the one in which he tries to make sense of his life, is his best and most compelling. It is his moonshot, though whether or not it makes up for not walking on the moon only he can say.

New York Review of Books, 1998

Poker

The Education of a Poker Player

WHEN I FIRST PLAYED poker I believed, as all beginners do, that it was a game of chance, rather like *chemin de fer*, where you gambled money on the turn of a card. Perhaps that was why the game appealed to me: for the risk and the obscure sense of machismo that goes with risk-taking. To gamble more than I could decently afford, blindly, like a dare, seemed a rather dashing thing to do. It proved what was otherwise not altogether apparent: that I was one of the boys, that I didn't care. But it was also a misapprehension that cost me a good deal, both in money and in self-esteem. I lost regularly and was lucky only in that the people I played with in those days were as innocent and inexperienced and self-deluding as I was.

One summer, however, a young American appeared in our game. He was a pale, sweating youth, grossly overweight. His eyes were small and close-set, his podgy face was freckled, his crew-cut carroty. In comparison to our fast-talking, rather literary group, he seemed hopelessly inept and dull. A hick, clearly, with no small talk at all and even less charm. But he cleaned us out effortlessly, twice running, until the man who had brought him was told to withdraw the invitation.

He handled the cards like a professional, crisply and deftly, and at the time all of us suspected him of cheating. I realise now that he was simply playing the classical game as it should be played, 'by the book', while the rest of us were gambling wildly, unable to believe that hands which had started well wouldn't necessarily finish that way, or that we did not have some secret, special claim to the money we had already so optimistically contributed to the pot.

Soon after that, a friend lent me Herbert O. Yardley's *The Education of a Poker Player*, and I began to understand what the game is about. Not luck but calculation, memory, patience, skill in reckoning the odds and percentages and, above all, observation: the ability to recognise and interpret the small fidgets and quirks, the hesitations, the voice's faint changes in timbre, which indicate tension or confidence.

I read Yardley through twice; first incredulous that anyone could play the game so conservatively, then appalled by my own previous naivety and optimism. Then I went back to the game and tried to apply what I had learned. For two years after that I played 'by the book' – that is, by Yardley, whom I re-read solemnly, ritually, each week before the game. And for two years, with a couple of minor and very mild exceptions, I did not lose.

It was, even in retrospect, a good time. My bank manager smiled at me whenever we met and asked no questions – or rather, he stopped asking questions – and the reviews I wrote weekly began to seem more pointless than ever. They became merely a way of filling in the days before I sat down at the poker table at eight o'clock each Friday evening. Why bother at all, I began to wonder, if it is this easy to make a modest living? But mercifully, before I had time to follow that train of thought through to its end, the call came, as it sometimes did in those days, to an American university, and by the time I returned the group had scattered. The games I graduated to were altogether subtler and sterner. Everybody knew 'the book' and the percentages, and most had read Yardley. Although there were no more easy pickings, the pleasure of playing the game skilfully with other skilful players was finally sharper, even when I lost, than the simple, ego-boosting satisfaction of taking money off mugs.

And that, in the end, is what it is all about. Terence Reece, who played bridge for England, has said that in terms of skill there is nothing to choose between bridge and poker. Yet, before the Gaming Act of 1960, it was illegal to play poker in any British card club because whichever weird bureaucracy controls these matters had officially classified it, along with bingo, craps and roulette, as a game of chance. I suppose the civil servants were confused, as they often are, not by the reality of the game, but by its appearance. Poker *looks* like gambling – and at a low level of skill it is gambling – because it must be played for money. The chips are as much instruments of the game as the cards. The way you bet or check or raise tells the other players about the nature of the cards you purport to hold.

To take a very simple example: the game is five-card stud, pot-limit, and three players are left after the last (fourth) open card has been dealt. One has an ace exposed, the next a jack, the third a king. No pairs are showing. Everything therefore depends on the hidden cards in the hole. The player with the open ace has taken the lead in betting only in the first round, when the rules of the game forced him to. After that, he has checked and the player with the exposed jack has made all the running, while those with the ace and the king have just seen the bets, each feigning uncertainty. When the last round begins there is £10 in the pot. As usual, the ace checks and the player with the jack immediately bets £10. Since the others have not visibly improved, he expects them to fold. Instead, the player holding the king sees the £10 and re-raises the pot, now £30. Then the man with the ace sees that £40 bet and raises again.

What he is saying with his re-raise is that he has his ace paired in the hole and so cannot be beaten. This is, of course, precisely what the player with the king had also implied when he raised the jack's bet. He had been encouraged to do so because the ace, like him, had feigned weakness earlier in the hand by leaving the betting to the jack. That is, the two players with powerful hands had *not* bet in order to disguise their strength, then they had both raised in order assert it. In other words, money has – and is – its own language in poker. The way you use it supplements or qualifies the information your opponents glean from your cards.[1]

Perhaps it is this combination of cards and money and beady-eyed skill in handling both that makes poker such a peculiarly American game. Given the chance, the Irish and the Chinese will gamble on anything. But although there are famous exceptions, that does not necessarily make them good poker players. On the contrary, to bet on horses, dogs or raindrops sliding down the window-pane is, at best, a romantic weakness. You have to believe in your luck, in your special relationship with fate, in the possibility that you are somehow chosen and blessed. Against all the evidence, you have to be an optimist.

Poker, however, is not about luck. It is about winning and the disciplines necessary for this: calculation, patience, insight, deception, ruthlessness. It embodies, in short, all the elements of that Social

1 If the player with the ace really has a second ace in the hole, he will want to tempt the others to call him. So he is less likely to raise the whole pot – £100 – than an amount that will seem to offer the others reasonable odds – say, £40 or £50. But this in itself is as much an opportunity for bluff as the maximum raise would be. Similarly, a £100 bet might be interpreted as a sign of weakness, an attempt to buy the pot. That, however, should be no temptation to the player holding the pair of jacks who, at that moment, has only invested about £12 in the pot.

Darwinism – the doctrine of the survival of the socially and economic-
ally fittest – which is the reality behind the American dream. 'The
game exemplifies,' said Walter Matthau, 'the worst aspects of capitalism that have made our country so great.'[2] To put it another way,
the American dream – as it is purveyed in political and advertising
rhetoric – is the bluff by which Americans are persuaded to accept the
altogether harsher, less forgiving realities of the lives most of them
lead.

Yardley vividly illustrates this Social Darwinism in the early part of
his book when he is describing his youthful apprenticeship in the
game in his small Indiana home town at the turn of the century:

> I saw the big Swede, Bones Alverson, a poor weather-beaten corn
> farmer, bet the last of his farm against a tent show, only to die three
> minutes later, his cards clutched in his hands – a winner.
>
> I saw Jake Moses, a travelling shoe salesman, bet ten trunks of
> shoes. I saw a bank teller trapped with marked money he had
> stolen from the bank; a postmaster go to jail for shortages at the
> post office.
>
> Horses, cattle, hogs, wagons, buggies, farming implements,
> grain, sawmills – all sold to play poker. New owners showed
> up at the sawmills, feed and grocery stores.

Yardley's stories are dramatic, simple and loving, like the folk tales
collected by the Brothers Grimm. And in a way, this is what they are:
the mythology of America on the move, the winners winning, the
losers going under.

Each story illustrates a particular form of the game – draw, stud and
some of their variations – and includes Yardley's peculiarly stringent
rules for winning. These rules themselves illustrate another aspect of
the cynical reality beneath the American dream. The classical game
Yardley advocates is not only conservative, it is also deeply pessimistic.
'I do not believe in luck –' he says, 'only in the immutable law of
averages.' In his style of poker there is no room for play in any of the
frivolous senses of the word. Frivolity is, quite simply, too expensive.
What his advice amounts to is, Assume the worst, believe no one and
make your move only when you are certain that you are either
unbeatable or have, at worst, exceptionally good odds in your favour.

2 Quoted by David Spanier in his entertaining and instructive book, *Total Poker*, London,
1977.

This is an ironclad system when playing against weak players who do not understand the odds or the endless finesses possible. Against strong players, who know 'the book' and have the necessary discipline, it may be less immediately effective, since they will recognise your tactics and simply fold when you bet. That, however, is not Yardley's business. He was a purist writing for embryo purists, concerned only with the rules and values of classical poker.

'Classical' may seem an inflated word for a rather shady pastime. Yet it is wholly appropriate, for there is a kind of strict beauty in the game when it is played in this way – every detail accounted for, every nuance recognised. The excitement has nothing to do with the passive, masochistic thrill of roulette; it is closer to the tension of chess, the most purely intellectual of all games. At a certain shared level of skill, poker, like chess, is a psychological combat. It depends finally on your insight into your opponent's state of mind and how it will affect his willingness to call or raise or fold. Is he depressed or riding high? What is his financial position, off the table as well as at it? What are his vanities, his fears? At its best, poker is a contest of wills and personalities, one end of which is power. You want to be able to predict, even to dictate, how the other players will respond to each of your moves.

This interplay between the personalities around a poker table, and the combination of cynicism and insight necessary to win, is where the real fascination of the game lies. Perhaps this is why Yardley's book continued to hold me, even after I had assimilated his advice and had a working knowledge of the percentages. When I first picked it up, I was ignorant not only in the ways of poker. I also had the deep ignorance which often goes with excessive education. I had been through the most high-minded academic mill: a monastic public school, Oxford, Princeton, Harvard. I had read a vast number of books and written a couple of my own. Yet, in practice, I was naive to a degree which still, years later, makes me blush. I had a marriage I could not handle, a childish desire to be loved by the whole world, and an equally childish conviction that everything would turn out all right in the end. When it didn't I was – simply and profoundly – outraged. I had lived my life as I played poker, recklessly and optimistically, with all my cards open on the table and nothing in reserve. I had also assumed that everybody else was doing the same.

I was wrong, of course, and it was about the time I began to realise this that I first read Yardley. Read: 'You should study your own weaknesses as well as those of your opponents. Keep a poker face. Keep silent. Don't gripe when you lose a hand or gloat over a winning one.' Read, above all: 'A card player should learn that once the money is in the pot it isn't his any longer. His judgement should not be influenced by this. He should instead say to himself, "Do the odds favour my playing regardless of the money I have already contributed?"' What applied so cogently to money in a poker pot applied equally to the feelings I had invested my disastrous personal affairs: 'Do the odds favour my playing regardless of what I have already contributed?' I knew the answer. The only puzzle was why I should have discovered it not in Shakespeare or Donne or Eliot or Lawrence or any of my other literary heroes, but in a funny, vivid, utterly unliterary book by an American cryptographer and intelligence agent. It seemed absurd, disproportionate to the efforts I had made. But it was the beginning of my real education and I sometimes wonder if that was what Yardley, too, was implying in his title. In the end, what he is describing is not so much a game of cards as a style of life.

Introduction to Herbert O. Yardley, *The Education of a Poker Player*, 1979

No Limit

WHEN POKER PLAYERS GET together they don't talk about the hands they have won. They talk, instead, about 'bad beats,' the hands they should have won but didn't, because the cards were freakish or, more often, because some other player made a stupid call. Bad-beat stories are long-winded and bad-tempered, and their punchline is always roughly the same: 'I mean, what was the schmuck doing in the hand anyway with a pair of lousy deuces?' Bad beats haunt you like bad dreams. You brood about them, you complain about them, you play them over in your head again and again. And this is how it should be, because while it is happening a truly bad beat feels like a waking nightmare.

This is a poker story, so it starts with a bad beat. The setting is Binion's Horseshoe Casino, in Las Vegas, during the World Series of Poker; the event is the World Championship; the game is Texas Hold 'em, $10,000 buy-in, no-limit. (In Texas Hold 'em, each player is dealt two cards face-down, 'in the hole.' The two players to the left of the dealer are forced to bet 'blind' – before they see their cards. The other players either call the blind bet or raise it or fold. Then three communal cards, called the 'flop,' are dealt face-up in the centre of the table, and there is another round of betting, although this time the players may check. Then two more communal cards – known as 'Fourth Street' or 'the turn,' and 'Fifth Street' or 'the river' – are dealt face-up, one at a time, with a round of betting after each. The five cards in the centre are common to all the players, who use them in combination with their hole cards to make the strongest possible hands.)

Like most nightmares, this one begins sweetly. I am playing with great discipline, my stack of chips is building nicely, I am in control. Then the scene darkens and the horrors start. I am in the dealer's position – 'on the button,' the classic position in which to make a bet in the hope of stealing whatever money is already in the pot. I cup my hands around my hole cards and peer at them: two aces, the strongest starting hand in the game. I raise, but modestly, as though I were 'on the steal.' To my delight, an early caller who has a lot of chips in front of him re-raises. This is what I was hoping for. 'Raise,' I say. I put my hands behind my stacks of chips and move them all into the pot. (In no-limit poker you can bet as much as you want whenever you want as long as the money's on the table.) My opponent thinks for a long time; he looks at me; he looks at the mass of chips in the middle of the table; he studies his cards. I have more chips than he does; if he calls the bet and loses, he will be out of the tournament. Finally, he shrugs and pushes all his chips forward. The pot is huge and whoever wins it will be the tournament's chip leader. Since there can be no more betting, the tournament coordinator asks us to turn over our cards for the benefit of the TV cameras. When the other player sees my aces, he shakes his head despondently, turns over an unsuited king and queen, and rises from his seat, ready to make a humiliated exit. I settle back smugly, unable to believe my luck. The dealer pauses dramatically, thumps the table with his fist, and deals the flop: king, king, deuce of different suits, giving my opponent three kings. Another pause, another thump, another card: seven. Only a third ace will save me now. But the last card is a jack, and from being one of the tournament leaders I am now down there at the bottom, scrabbling to stay alive. A few hands later, I am out.

The nightmare really happened, though not at Binion's, and not even at a poker table. It happened on my computer, at home in London, while I was warming up on a video game of the World Series, two days before I left for Vegas. I took it as a good omen: bad beats like that tend not to come in pairs.

This year, the World Series of Poker, which takes place annually at Binion's Horseshoe, and runs from mid-April to mid-May, celebrated its silver anniversary. It is the Wimbledon of poker tournaments, the most popular, the most prestigious, and the longest running. It began in 1970, when Benny Binion invited a handful of his poker-playing cronies – some were professionals and some were amateurs, but all of them high-rollers and most were Texans – to get together at the Horseshoe in order to compete against each other in various forms of poker at stakes only they would contemplate. When all the games were over, they voted democratically for who should be nominated the champion of champions. The man they elected was Johnny Moss, who celebrated his eighty-seventh birthday during this year's tournament, and is still competing. How much money Moss won during that first unofficial tournament is not recorded, but the Binions commemorated his victory by giving him a massive silver cup with his name engraved on it.

Since that first tournament, the event has grown exponentially. By 1990, the entry to the main event – the $10,000 no-limit Texas Hold 'em World Championship – was approaching the magic number of two hundred. Two hundred buy-ins meant two million dollars to be distributed in prize money – about forty percent to the winner, the rest according to finishing place. The Binions, who understand what makes gamblers tick, stopped fussing with percentages, and guaranteed the world champion one million dollars, as well as the 14-karat-gold bracelet with his or her name on it that is also given to the winner of each of the subsidiary events. For the silver anniversary, Jack Binion, who has been president of the Horseshoe since 1964, added a further attraction: the champion would win his weight in silver as well as his million dollars, and anyone who made it into the money in the minor events would receive a commemorative silver bar.

Like the World Series, the Horseshoe Casino itself has grown enormously in recent years. When I first went there, in 1981, it was a shabby little place, dark and narrow, and in terms of decor it had nothing to offer at all. It was also overpoweringly noisy, for the simple reason that it was always packed. If you wanted action – real action with no upper limits on the bets you made – forget the ritzy palaces on the Strip; the Horseshoe was the place to go. Las Vegas itself has changed since then and is no longer the gambling town it used to be. A decade ago, the town was a Disneyland for the middle-aged, where you could live out your fantasies of the good life for as long as your money lasted. Now it's just another Disneyland for children, with gambling on the side – a collection of theme parks with pirate shows, mediaeval tourneys, exploding volcanoes, wild west shows, talking statues, and whatever else it takes to amuse the kids. But even back in its unreconstructed period, the hotels on the Strip had pretentions to glamour – slave girls to serve you drinks at Caesar's, trapeze artists swinging around above your head when you gambled at Circus, Circus, arcades of pricey shops, tennis courts, golf courses. At the Horseshoe, however, what you saw was what you got: gambling without frills but also without limits.

Somehow, the Binions had worked out the right formula for

serious gamblers. It helped that Benny Binion had been boss of gambling in Dallas until 1946 when, as he dourly put it, 'my sheriff got beat in the election' and he had to leave town in a hurry. The Dallas connection guaranteed him the loyalty of the high-rolling Texans after he moved to Las Vegas. Supporting Benny was the patriotic thing to do, and anyway the Binions were their sort of folk. The Binions responded by providing their sort of outsize gambling action, along with the best steaks and the hottest chili in town. Yet even the loyalest Texans drew the line at staying in the handful of pokey rooms above the casino. They gambled at the Horseshoe but stayed across the road at the Golden Nugget, particularly after Steve Wynne refurbished the place from top to bottom, put in a huge pool, and made the hotel as luxurious as anything on the Strip.

The Binions eventually solved the accommodation problem by buying the casino next door, a great, echoing barn of a place called the Mint, which was nearly always deserted, and had just two things to recommend it, both of them on its roof: a small swimming pool – the only one downtown in the early '80s – and a huge illuminated clock (also the only one downtown, then and now, in a city where time has been officially banished in case it interferes with business). The Mint had a lot of rooms, none of them particularly luxurious, but considerably more comfortable than the flophouse above the Horseshoe. The Binions did almost nothing to tart the place up or improve the amenities; there is still no comfortable bar to schmooze in during breaks from the action, no saunas, jacuzzis or any of the other keep-fit facilities that casinos on the Strip lay on as a matter of course. They simply knocked down the wall between the two casinos, removed the giant illuminated 'M' from the clock, put a horseshoe in its place, and called the whole block Binion's Horseshoe. And that was all it took. Overnight, the dismal, empty spaces of the Mint were jampacked with gamblers, whooping it up and having a great time.

During the World Series, the crowds reach saturation point as hundreds of poker players fly in from all over the world. Most are amateurs and they come from every corner of the United States, from Great Britain, Ireland, Germany, France and Italy, from Scandinavia, Australia, Costa Rica. This year there was even a twenty-one-strong deputation from New Caledonia, a tiny group of islands in the south Pacific; they spoke French and most of them seemed to know only four words of English: bet, check, raise and fold. The players come in all shapes and sizes, although the predominant size is extra-large. (When one 350-pounder left the table I was playing at, a wag called out, 'Two seats here, floorman.') The out-of-towners are there primarily to compete in the tournaments, which cover most current forms of poker and vary in expense from the $1,000-buy-in Women's Seven Card Stud to the $10,000-buy-in World Championship. The Las Vegas professionals play in the tournaments, too, but simply as a courtesy to Jack Binion and because their status as champions requires it. Their real business is in the side games that go on day and night, non-stop, while the World Series is in progress.

These cash games are listed in a kind of shorthand on a roster at the back of the tournament area. The smallest is 'PLH 1–2–5' – pot-limit hold 'em, in which the compulsory blind bets are $1, $2, and $5, and the buy-in is $500; from there, the size of the games climbs steadily toward the stratosphere. The biggest game of all is off in a corner on Table 61, where ex-champions like Doyle Brunson, Johnny Chan and Stu Ungar hold court. According to the board, the game on Table 61 is '2/7 NL, 100 ante, 200–400' – that is, deuce-to-the-seven razz, a particularly brutal form of lowball, in which each player antes one hundred dollars before every hand, the two players to the left of the dealer are forced to bet two hundred and four hundred dollars blind, and there is no limit to the size of the subsequent bets. The buy-in for that game is $25,000, but no one usually sits down with so little. One night during my stay, someone at the table won a single pot of nearly $100,000.

In other words, the World Series is not just the foremost poker tournament; it is also a hustlers' convention, a brief season, like the run-up to Christmas on Fifth Avenue, when the professionals reckon to make enough money to set themselves up for the year ahead. The economy of poker works in the same ruthlessly Darwinian way as that of the corporate world: bigger fish eat smaller fish, and so on ad infinitum. The local champs beat their local games, bring their winnings to Vegas, and lose them to the professionals.

The first time I watched the World Series, in 1981, I was bug-eyed with wonder, like a visitor from Mars. And indeed, there was a great deal to wonder at, starting with the giant sums of money involved. Back then, there were no cheap ways of entering a tournament and the players in the World Championship event were truly the elect, the highest of high-rolling amateurs – oil men, real estate brokers, movie moguls, investment bankers, rich doctors and lawyers, a few gangsters, and a handful of tough and classy women – to whom ten grand meant more or less nothing and who were playing purely for the pleasure of sitting down with the best poker players in the world. As for the top professionals, money was not their problem; if they were temporarily short there were always big-time gamblers to stake them in return for a slice of their winnings.

Over the years, the World Series acquired a great deal of glamour in the poker world and inspired a large number of imitations. But one major problem remained: how to attract all those good players who were out there yearning to get in, but who were never going to build up enough money for a stake. In 1984, someone had the smart idea of organizing 'satellites' – competitions for the competitions – in which ten players would ante up a thousand dollars each and play a freeze-out, winner take all. But even a thousand dollars is a substantial sum to invest in a nine-to-one shot, and it was still beyond the range of many hopefuls. The next step was super-satellites – multitable events in which each player paid $220 for two hundred chips and, during the first hour, could rebuy additional stacks of two hundred for $200 a throw. If enough people entered – and they entered by the hundreds – there would be sufficient money to guarantee everyone at the final table an entry to the main event. There are now satellites for all the events. At the Horseshoe, they start a few days before the beginning of the World Series, but for months before that they had been running in casinos across America and around the world. The World Series is no longer the exclusive preserve of the top professionals and the million-aires; it has been democratized.

Like all poker players, I have dreamed of playing in the World Championship. This year, I got my chance. I had been training for it for fifteen months, playing in tournaments once or twice a week in London. Although I often reached the final table and occasionally won an event, I knew that in Vegas they marched to a different tune. I would be like a good club tennis player with a wild card entry to Wimbledon: the game played by the top players has no relation to the game played by the likes of me; it just looks the same. But at least I could try not to make a fool of myself. I would pace myself, get used to the pressures, work out some strategies for survival.

The basic strategy was to stay sane in an insane environment, which meant getting in shape both mentally and physically. The physical part was straightforward: first, get over the jet lag (I arrived almost two weeks before the main event), then establish a routine in which poker was only one part: regular meals, plenty of sleep, and twenty laps of the pool each morning before breakfast. The mental training was harder. The first step was to create an orderly space within the ambient lunacy, a space that contained books to read, a computer to work on, and television news to remind myself that there was a world elsewhere.

A key part of that private space was the little balcony outside the picture windows of my room. From up there on the twenty-second floor of the Horseshoe, the view was spectacular: out across the railroad tracks and the ring road to the blue mountains circling the horizon, down onto the crowds on Fremont Street and the maze of pipes, steel walkways and air ducts on the casino roofs. At night, the mountains disappeared and the town became a blaze of lights: rivers of coloured neon cascading down the fronts of the buildings and reflecting in the opaque glass of the Golden Nugget's tower block, a sea of smaller lights stretching out across the desert, and, up above, the winking lights of hovering choppers and planes coming and going from the airport. Even from high up, it was never quiet out on the balcony; the air-conditioning plants kept up a steady roar, and every few minutes the giant cowboy above the entrance of the Pioneer Club down on Fremont saluted the passers-by and repeated, in a tinny voice, 'Howdy, pardner. Welcome to Las Vegas.' (Benny Binion cheered when 'Amarillo Slim' Preston, the famous poker player, blasted the cowboy with a shotgun from his window in the Horseshoe because the voice kept him awake.) Despite the noise, room 2208 was a fine and private place to retreat to and I spent a good deal of time there. Then, when I was good and ready, I would go downstairs and play cards.

Poker is a game of many skills: you need card sense, psychological insight, a good memory, controlled aggression, enough mathematical know-how to work out the odds as each hand develops, and what poker players call a leather ass – i.e., patience. Above all, you need the arcane skill called money management: the ability to control your bankroll and understand the long-term implications of each bet (how to avoid the casual five-dollar call that ends up in a five-hundred dollar disaster), so that you don't go broke during a session. All good players have these skills, but the pros have them to a far greater degree than the amateurs. Another difference between the two groups, however, is not often mentioned: somewhere along the road, the pros have lost their sense of urgency. For them, their lives are one long poker game, which began when they turned professional and will end – if it ever ends –

when they retire or die. Mostly, they reckon to win, but sometimes they lose, and when they do they shrug and leave the table and come back the next day or the next week, knowing the game will always be there. Amateurs are less philosophical: because they usually play no more than once or twice a week, they want to cram as much action as they can into the limited time at their disposal, so they stay too long at the table and play until they can't think straight.

In order to survive in Vegas, you must divest yourself of the sense of urgency. Day or night, the game you want is always in progress, and you must treat it as the professionals do: when nothing is going right, when you sit for hours folding unplayable hands, or, worse, when every time you are dealt two kings someone else has a pair of aces, you must learn to get up from the table, swallow your losses, and come back another time. Quitting when you are ahead is easy; to cut your losses and run takes far greater discipline.

One morning I had breakfast with Mickey Finn, an American professional who plays mostly in Europe. Finn is an affable man, but that morning he looked grim. 'I'm running bad,' he said. 'I've dropped ten big ones since I arrived.' 'Now what?' I asked. His face brightened. 'I've drawn a line under it and I'm starting over,' he said. 'I feel much better.'

Finn has played a lot of cards in Vegas and he understands the pressures. Many of the British contingent this year were newcomers to the scene who got off the plane, took a taxi to Binion's and were promptly swallowed alive. Normally, the poker room at the Horse-shoe is buried away in a far corner of the casino, but during the World Series a large area in front of the reception desk is cleared of slot machines and becomes the tournament poker pit. As a result, you are already engulfed in the action even before you have checked in. Right behind you is a sea of intent faces; the dealers are deftly flicking out the cards, summoning cocktail waitresses, announcing vacant seats; the voices on the intercom deliver messages; and faintly, beneath it all, is a rattling sound, like surf on shingle, as the players riffle their stacks of chips up and down and in and out, waiting for a playable hand. All this is music to the poker addict's ear, the sweet music of action, and for some of the London mob it was irresistible. They arrived with bucket-shop excursion flight tickets they couldn't change, went straight to the tables without bothering to unpack their bags, got caught up in the fever, and blew all their money. Forty-eight hours later, they were huddled together, penniless, up on the pool deck, waiting for their flights home and too broke to eat even at Binion's coffee shop, which is famous for its two-dollar steak dinners. 'Be a pal,' they would mutter. 'Nick us a couple of bananas from the buffet.' But at least the sunshine was free and they went home with great tans.

Others, less innocent, had come with bigger bankrolls, prepared for battle, and had then been destroyed. Fat Alex, for example, is a regular winner in the big games at the London casinos. At the Horseshoe, he was wandering around dazed, like a man who has been mugged. He had been in town for three weeks, he told me, and had dropped £40,000 ($60,000). When I commiserated with him, his Arab melancholy overflowed. He squeezed my hand gratefully, then ambled off, shaking his head. When I saw him again a couple of days later, he had lost another £10,000. But back in London all he said was, 'It was worth it. I had a wonderful time.'

Fat Alex was not necessarily playing badly; he had simply been mesmerized by the flood tide of money that washes around the place during the World Series. The hundred-dollar bill is the unit of currency at Binion's. No smaller denomination 'plays' at the poker tables if you want to back up your stacks of chips with cash, and no smaller denomination has any meaning, except to tip the waitresses or buy a sandwich.

This illusion is fed spectacularly by the professional poker players. They walk around in cheap nylon bomber jackets and soiled tee shirts. If you saw them on the street you would give them a buck. Then they fish about in the pockets of their tattered jeans and pull out enough money to support an average family for a year – inch-thick wads of $100 bills, held together by rubber bands. All of it is legal tender, but none of it is for buying things. Money to the professionals is like a toolbox to a mechanic – it is what they work with, the instrument they need to ply their trade. It has no reality for them, except in the intricate calculations of a poker game; but that is a reality they understand down to the last tiny nuance. All the amateurs can see, however, are huge sums that seem to be casually up for grabs. The sight bewitches them and they blow off their own resources scrambling for the illusory pot of gold.

According to a journalist friend who specializes in these matters, there is also a great deal of another kind of money washing around during the World Series – funny money, mostly from drugs and guns. The safety deposit boxes at the cashiers' cage are stuffed with bills, he said; maybe as much as fifty million. And washing around with it are agents of the IRS, the DEA and other law-enforcement agencies, most of whom he claimed to recognize. That, too, adds to the intoxication for people from the straight world, with families and mortgages and routine jobs.

In other words, for four weeks each year, Binion's is the craziest place on earth, and it takes enormous self-control simply to stay sane.

Even the language spoken at the tables is calculatedly unreal. Whatever the size of the game, the general rule is: Never call a buck a buck. Over at Table 61, when someone bets 'a dime' he means a thousand dollars, and even in the small games they divide by one hundred. Treating money like small change somehow adds to the pleasure. When the dealer says, 'Your nickel,' the player on the big blind obediently pushes forward a five-dollar chip. The first player to act says, 'A quarter to go,' and throws in a green twenty-five. An elderly man wearing a white Stetson and a white cavalry shirt flicks a $100 bill into the pot and says, 'Make it a dollar straight.' The dealer thumps the table and deals three spades into the center. Without hesitating, the man who had originally bet the quarter now bets $250. The man in the white Stetson looks at him, looks at the exposed cards, shrugs, and throws his cards face-up into the center: an ace and king of hearts. 'Right string, wrong yo-yo,' he barks. But the very next deal he comes out raising again before the flop. 'Don't mess with him,' another player says as he folds his hand. 'He's hotter than a polar bear in the Mojave Desert.' Three players call, however, then fold docilely when white Stetson bets $500 after the flop. 'It's like picking fresh grapes', someone says admiringly. 'The bigger they are, the easier it is.' White Stetson beams, and when a harassed floorman bustles over with chips to replenish the dealer's tray, he says, 'How about a smile, Jimmy?' 'Haven't got time,' the floorman replies.

The atmosphere is curiously festive, and disdain for money is part of the festivity. Large sums are changing hands, yet the poker tables buzz with the pleasure and excitement and good humour that come when people get together to do something they love doing and do well. When someone wins a hand because another player checked when he should have bet, the winner scoops in the chips and says, wonderingly, 'Only in America can a guy get a free card and make money. Only in America.'

Another element of the festivity is the food. All day and every day, Jack Binion lays on a lavish banquet for the players, starting with the mother of all breakfasts: all the juices, all the fruits, and every hot dish you ever dreamed of and were afraid to ask for all at once. There is a chef to cook your eggs just so, another chef to carve your ham, another hovering in case of emergency, and teams of white-jacketed waiters to top up the hot-plates of hash, sausage, bacon, pork chops, and French toast. Dinner is on the same scale: mountains of oysters and crab legs and shrimp, great roasts of beef and turkey, giant bowls of salad, rows of hot-plates full of chops, chicken legs, fish and vegetables, and racks of rich desserts. The abundance contributes to the unreality; at the buffet I saw a man piling blackberries and raspberries onto a plateful of beef and potatoes; a willowy old lady takes five chocolate eclairs, pauses, considers, then takes a sixth. It is all part of the holiday atmosphere; in food, as in poker, anything goes.

The revels end abruptly when you sit down to play a tournament. There are twenty-one open events in the World Series, and each of them is like the last chance saloon: the atmosphere is gloomy, the faces are tense and unsmiling, and 'the general chitchat,' in P.G. Wodehouse's words, is 'pretty well down-and-out.' The reason is simple: if you make a mistake or suffer a bad beat in a cash game, you can always reach into your pocket and pull out more money, but if you make a mistake in a tournament you are out. (In two of the events, Deuce to Seven Draw and the biggest of the Omaha tournaments – Omaha being a four-card variant of hold 'em – rebuys are permitted during the first three hours of play if, at any time, you have fewer chips than you started with; but that is not an option open to everyone, because the original stakes in those events are five thousand and-two-and-a-half thousand dollars respectively.)

For players like me, there is another cause for alarm, and it has to do with pride. The tournament events are our chance to sit down with the champions on equal terms – or, rather, on equal financial terms at the start. 'We're ambitious amateurs, and we don't want to be humiliated,' said my friend Julian Studley, a New Yorker who plays regularly and successfully in the big tournaments. 'The great players don't have that problem. They'll go for the brilliant, do-or-die move, and if it doesn't come off and they get eliminated, so what? It doesn't bother them. We are different. We want to stick around because our egos are very much affected by being able to say we were still there on the second day of play or past the dinner break, or whenever it was. Even if we have no chance of winning the championship, we want to hang in. It's a real mistake to give up hope and think, This is my last shot. Your last shot is your last chip. Every time someone is eliminated, it's a benefit to you. The point is to survive.'

Johnny Chan said much the same, but from a different point of view. Chan is small and trim and compact, with a heart-shaped face and unnervingly sharp eyes. He won the World Championship twice, in 1987 and 1988, and this year he became the first player to bring his total earnings in the World Series to more than two million dollars – to $2,038,544, to be precise. Chan tends to talk in imperatives, a style which goes with his commanding presence, and he reacts to amateurs like a great white shark reacts to blood: 'No-limit is a game to trap people,' he told me one afternoon when he was taking a break from the monster game at Table 61. 'When you find a weak player, try to get everyone else out. Now it's between you and the weak player. Now you need to trap him, make him lose something. You don't have a hand – who cares? Bluff him out. He's weak. Make a play. When you sit down, you look around the table and see how many weak players there are. Who is the weakest? That's the one you go for. You try to avoid the good players until you get to the final table. That's what you've got to do to win.'

'Sometimes weak players get lucky and fluke their way through,' I said hopefully.

'It happens. If the best players won every time it would be very boring. There would be no tournament. Everybody has the opportunity to win. If I have two aces and a weak player has two queens, and at the end he catches a queen, what am I going to do? So he wins the money, OK?'

'But suppose it was the other way around: you have the queens, he has the aces?'

'That happens, too. But I try not to go broke with two queens. That's the difference between the good player and the weak player. If you don't have the nuts you shouldn't put all your money in.'

When Studley talked about not giving up hope, he made me understand how hopeless my position was at this level of poker. Chan's staccato commands deepened my gloom. So did Artie Cobb, but after I talked to him one evening over dinner in the Sombrero Room, at least I began to understand the measure of the difference between the small fry and the great whites. Cobb has ginger hair, a big belly, a mournful face, and a taste for funny hats (this year's creation was a cardboard fish). He is a talented poker player, who has won three tournaments in the World Series, but he is not up there with the champions, and has thought deeply about why this is so. 'There are a lot of fine players out there, but the great player always has that little edge on them,' he said. 'The player who is not great has tendencies he always falls into when he has a good hand, a mediocre hand, or a weak hand. The great players can spot them easily. They read the table like a walking computer. They understand when they have to gamble more and when they have to gamble less. The average player doesn't always understand that. When the game starts, everyone has the same number of chips. The favorites are favorites because they know what they have to do to win the tournament. They can't stay idle and hope they're going to double-up their stack along the way. They try to increase it a little bit at every limit, sometimes even with marginal hands most people don't want to play, like an ace with a doubtful kicker.' (A kicker is the 'side,' or subsidiary, card to a more powerful card.) 'I remember an extraordinary hand played by Stu Ungar and Doyle Brunson. Both of them had ace-queen in the hole, and Gabe Kaplan, the actor, was there with king-jack. The flop was ace, ace, king. Stuey made a small bet on the flop and the others called. The next card was a three. Stuey came out betting, Gabe folded, and Doyle just moved all-in. It was a huge bet, and if Stuey called and won, Doyle would have been out of the tournament. Each of them knew the other had an ace, so it was down to the kicker. An amateur might have thought an ace was good enough or that Doyle would only move all – in with a full house – with ace-king or ace-trey in the hole. But somehow Stuey sensed that Doyle was making a play. He thought a long time, and if he had had less than ace-queen he might have folded. It was possible that Doyle had ace-jack, but that was unlikely, knowing how well he plays. So Stuey figured they must have the same hand, ace-queen. He called, and they split the pot. And that's a mind-set only great players get into. That's the deep part of the game which the average player has no concept of.'

I played in three events in the World Series – the $1,500-buy-in Texas hold 'em (pot limit), the $2,500-buy-in Texas hold 'em (no limit), and the $10,000-buy-in World Championship itself – and each was grimmer than the last. That made good sense to me, since the prize money shared out among the finalists grew steadily more serious in each event: $370,500 in the $1,500 tournament, $550,000 in the $2,500 game, and a staggering $2,680,000 in the World Championship. It also made sense that I played less freely as the grandeur of the occasion increased. But while the World Series was in progress, I was also playing in cash games, and what didn't make sense was how my play in them was like a mirror image of the way I played in the tournaments. Hold 'em is, among other things, a game of calculated agression: if your cards are good enough for you to call a bet, they are good enough to raise with. According to Don Williams, a small, bearded, fast-talking and successful professional, 'When you're betting, you've got two chances of winning: you can take the pot there and then, or you can have the best hand. When you're calling a bet, you've only got one chance: you've got to have the best hand. But you don't win tournaments just by showing the best hand.' I followed his advice in the cash games and did very well; whenever I had bet before the flop I bet again after it, if the other players checked, even when the exposed cards had not helped my hand. More often than not, the original callers meekly folded and I took the money. But I only played in the modest pot-limit cash games, with other amateurs and small-time professionals. The heavy hitters were busy elsewhere.

Even so, the tournaments started encouragingly for me. The morning after I arrived in Vegas, I played three $165 satellites for a place in the $1,500-pot-limit Texas hold 'em event, and won the third. By the time the last satellite finished, the tournament was beginning (forty-five minutes late), so I had no time to brood. There wasn't even much to brood about. I've played for those stakes before, so the money didn't scare me. Nor did the players; although most of the poker stars were playing, none of them came to the tables I was at. And if they had, I would probably not have noticed; I was in the no-man's-land of jet lag compounded by a fitful night's sleep, and was playing on automatic pilot. That was OK, too, because pot-limit hold 'em, where you may never bet more than is already in the pot, is the type of poker I play most of back home in London. It is my game, and to prove it I'd waltzed through a satellite to get there. In other words, Las Vegas hadn't yet got to me. By the time the game was about four hours old and around eighty of the original two hundred and forty seven starters were left, I had tripled my original stack and was beginning to think that maybe I might make it to the final table. At that point, hubris struck, I made a foolish mistake, and was gone ten minutes later. I blamed it on jet lag.

I also got into the $2,500 (no-limit) hold 'em event through a satellite − or rather, by surviving in a number of satellites until only two or three players were left, and then dividing the spoils. (Satellites are played with special tournament chips which have no value outside the game; the winner is also paid in special grey chips, similar to the casino's one-dollar chips, though even more battered and unprepossessing; each is worth $500.) It took me just over a week of intermittent satellite play to rustle up enough chips for the $2,500 event; by that time I was fully tuned in to Vegas, its hierarchies, its insane values, and to the seriousness of what I was getting into.

The event was played on the last Friday of the World Series and was a dress rehearsal for the big one, which was scheduled to begin on the following Monday. There were two hundred and twenty entries, including most of the stars, and enough prize money to solve all my problems. I responded to the occasion by playing the kind of poker I used to play in my ignorant youth when I imagined the game had something to do with gambling. In no limit hold 'em, where any mistake can be terminal, this was lunacy, but it was brought on by dumb luck. As soon as the game began, I was bombarded with good cards – with big pairs, with aces and high kickers of the same suit – until I began to think I could do no wrong. Psychoanalysts call this state of mind 'mania'; the poker pros describe it more vividly: 'He wanted to give his money away,' they say, 'but the cards wouldn't let him.' I walked on water for less than an hour, then made two disgraceful calls, and sank ignominiously. I scuttered back upstairs with my head down, in case I met anyone I knew. Even when the door of my room was locked behind me, I was too ashamed to brush my hair, because it meant seeing my face in the mirror.

The weekend before the World Championship, Binion's Horse-shoe was like a pressure-cooker with the heat turned up beneath it. The casino was packed with gawping spectators, the poker pits swarmed with TV crews, with self-important people flashing press cards and asking dumb questions, with players short of funds working the crowd, trying to hustle deals. In the cash games tempers frayed: one player threw his cards at the dealer after a bad beat; a white-bearded old man started a shouting match with a thin-lipped Greek thirty years his junior, invited him outside to settle the matter, then marched off, muttering obscenities. There was a final feeding frenzy in the $1,000 satellites. People were buying in, losing, buying in again, as though a thousand dollars truly were no more than a dime, and the aggression was insufferable; the players moved their chips around brutally, as if their manhood depended on it. Behind them, a group of professionals lounged against the rail like hawks in a tree, waiting to pick off an easy satellite to save themselves the ten-grand entry fee on Monday. The air-conditioning seemed unable to cope, the voices on the intercom never let up, the sheer predatoriness was battering. I ground back some money and pride in a cash game and went to bed early.

The morning of the big day was chilly and overcast. A brisk wind was blowing and I had the pool to myself. Around 12.30, I wandered down to the casino. Although crowds were gathering around the tournament area and journalists bustled about, the frenzy of the last few days was over. The players stood around in little groups, talking in subdued voices, eyeing the opposition. Off to one side, Jack McClelland, the tournament coordinator, sat at a table drawing the seat numbers and droning them out on the intercom. The big board behind him had space for two hundred and forty names, but that was not enough. Because of the satellites and the fact that this was the silver anniversary of the World Series, two hundred and sixty-eight hopefuls, a record, had signed up for the World Championship. The sight of my own name, at No. 182, up there with all those champions whom I have watched for years, from a safe distance, should have been exhilarating. Instead, it filled me with gloom.

There were formalities to go through before the action started: a tribute to the late Telly Savalas, who competed twelve times in the big event; 'Gentleman' Jack Keller, the 1984 World Champion, was inducted into the Poker Hall of Fame; Jack Binion made a brief opening speech. Then we all dispersed to our appointed seats. Mine was Seat 1 at Table 56; at $10,000, it was the most expensive seat I had ever sat on. Next to me was Billy Baxter, a famous high-roller and one of the great deuce-to-the-seven players. Jack Keller was in Seat 6. Ken Flaton, another expert, was in Seat 8. As I watched them amble up, I remembered the old proverb, 'Beware of what you want; you may get it.'

Finally, the chatter subsided, and Jack McClelland gave the starting orders: 'Dealers, shuffle up and deal.' On the television screens around the room, President Clinton was holding a news conference; he seemed to be in good form, relaxed and lively, but the sound was off.

In 1993, Mick Cooke, an Englishman I know, had made it to the final table. 'In the early stages, I came in with nothing lower than a pair of jacks,' he said later. Two jacks are strong enough to call with and easy to throw away. A pair of queens is a trickier hand to play; I was dealt them four times – twice in the first fifteen minutes – and in the end they were my undoing. But my first mistake occurred an hour or so into the game. I was dealt an eight and seven of diamonds when I was in the big blind. There were two or three callers, but no raise. The dealer thumped the table, burned (discarded) the top card and dealt six, nine, ten. The seven and eight in my hand gave me a straight. It was an almost perfect flop, except that the exposed nine and ten were both hearts. I checked, in the hope of trapping someone, and a young woman called Barbara Samuelson came out betting. She was tall and rangy, with a mannish figure, a small face and large hands, and her style of play was fearlesss and aggressive. I should have moved all-in immediately, in order to shut her out, but greed overcame me; I wanted more of her chips. So I raised a paltry thousand, and she called. The next card was bad for me: the queen of hearts, making a possible flush and a higher straight. When I checked, she checked. The last card was a king, and this time she bet strongly. I should have folded – any good player would have folded – but I was in love with my puny straight, so I made a crying call. She had a pair of jacks in the hole and had made a higher straight than mine. (Samuelson eventually placed tenth, the highest-ever finish by a woman in this event.)

At least I wasn't the only one making mistakes. Within two hours, three former World Champions had gone. 'Gentleman' Jack Keller slow-played a pair of aces, moved all-in when a king and a ten flopped, and was called instantly by Billy Baxter, who had king-ten in the hole. Minutes later, Stu Ungar, who won the title in 1980 and '81, stalked past, looking furious. Phil Hellmuth, Jr., winner in 1989, followed. 'I had two aces, but I ran into a pair of tens,' he said. Billy Baxter watched them go. 'I'll tell you one thing,' he said contentedly. 'They sure knocked some whales out of this already.'

Baxter promptly got into a raising battle with a friend of his who had moved into Keller's seat. When it ended, both had all their chips in the center and both had pairs of aces. Much jocular relief on both sides.

At 3.45 there was a ten-minute break. As we settled again around the table, Baxter and his pal were chatting together about hold 'em. 'Not my pond,' Baxter was saying.

'Hell, man, you just busted a guy in the Hall of Fame.'

'That just shows you I'm not long for this world.'

For the next hour and a half, my chips bled away in antes while I folded unplayable hands. Then, for the fourth time, I was dealt two queens. I bet a thousand, and Baxter instantly reraised another thousand. Maybe I should have moved all-in to shut him out. But he had position over me and massive firepower. So I just called. The flop was king, seven, deuce. When I checked and he bet two thousand, I knew what his hole-cards were: an ace and a king; with anything stronger, he would have checked to trap me; with less, he would have checked for fear of being trapped. My only hope was to catch one of the two queens remaining in the deck or to bluff him. I suppose I should have folded there and then, and kept my last two grand for a better spot. But the antes were eating me up, and that pair of queens in my hand seemed like a mountain after the cards I'd been seeing. I thought and thought, then called, hoping my long pause might have puzzled him. The next card was another deuce. That was my chance. I pushed in what was left of my stack and said, 'Come on, Billy, let's gamble.' He looked at me slit-eyed and hesitated. 'You got a deuce?' he said. And for a moment I thought I'd bluffed him out. But the pot was large and the bet was small, so he called. The last card was a jack. Without waiting, he turned over the ace-king I knew he had.

When Adlai Stevenson lost to Eisenhower in 1952, he said that he was too old to cry, but it hurt too much to laugh. I understood how he felt. I had been preparing for this day for fifteen months, and when it came I blew it. I had made the classic mistake of a newcomer to the big league: I played what the pros call 'tight-weak' – afraid to bet without the stone-cold nuts, and easily scared out. But at this level players can smell your fear, and they run all over you. I couldn't even complain about bad beats. On the contrary, I knew justice had been done. I am a good pot-limit player, but in pot-limit you can make a big enough bet to bluff an opponent out without putting your whole stack in jeopardy. No-limit is different. You get very few chances and the smallest mistake can destroy you. I had failed to take the chances I'd been offered, and ended by making a big mistake.

The first person I saw when I left the table was Nic Szeremeta, an Englishman who knows all the odds. 'At least you were beaten with the best hand,' he said consolingly. 'Two queens are a fifty-five to forty-five favorite over ace-king offsuit.'

A few minutes later, as though to prove his point, I watched a replay of the identical hand on an adjacent table: someone bet with ace-king offsuit, then called a massive all-in reraise by a guy holding a pair of queens. But this time the first card to be flopped was a queen, giving the raiser three queens and making him chip-leader of the tournament at that point.

At breakfast the next morning, I saw Herb Bronstein, who was considered a strong contender for the title. He, too, looked stricken.

'Yeah, I'm an also-ran,' he said. 'You wait a whole year for your chance and then it's gone.'

'I've been waiting all my life,' I answered.

When I called my wife in London with the news, she burst into tears.

The World Championship is a four-day event and, like the other also-rans, I could not bring myself to watch it with any interest until the last day, when the field had been reduced to six and show biz took over. The final table was set up, as though for a prizefight, in a fenced-off square, its entrances blocked by security guards. Around the table was a cordon sanitaire for the television crews and press photographers. Behind it, and flanked by two big TV screens, was a dias where the players were interviewed as they were eliminated from the game. Hanging all around were banners inscribed 'World Series Of Poker / Binion's Horseshoe / Silver Anniversary'. There were two blocks of reserved seats – one for the players, the other for the press – but no matter how close you sat all you could see was a slumped back, a profile, a foot tapping secretly below the table. The things that really mattered – the cards, the facial expressions, the size of the bets and the manner in which they were made, the dealers' deft, eloquent fingers as they handled the cards – could only be seen on the TV monitors.

In best prizefight style, there was a weigh-in before the start, so that the winner's weight in silver would be ready at the end. By 10.25 the ceremonies were over. For the last time, Jack McClelland called, 'Shuffle up and deal,' and the cards were spun out. Within two and a half hours, three finalists had been eliminated, two of them when they moved all-in against players holding ace-queen, and a queen came on the flop. Each time I thought, Where were you when I needed you?

Then the action froze. The chip-leader was Hugh Vincent, a scrawny, chainsmoking, bespectacled amateur, with a goatee beard, a cheap white buttoned shirt, and a blue cap. He had begun the day with almost a million and a half dollars in chips – more than half the money in play – and he used his muscle to harry the other players, pushing his luck, living on the edge, playing brilliantly by the seat of his pants. Close behind him was Russ Hamilton, a Las Vegas professional. He weighed three hundred and thirty pounds, and when he climbed on the scales before the start, they ran out of silver ingots. He had pale hair, a ghost of a beard, and sharp, calculating eyes, piercing blue, above fat cheeks; his clothes were pale blue to match his eyes. At the table, he was a thoughtful and forbidding presence, biding his time, making no mistakes. He sat for what seemed hours without stirring; only his eyes moved, missing nothing. A long way behind came John Spadavecchia, a Miami businessman who looked as if he had just walked out of a Scorsese movie: a creased face with a lot of mileage on it, dark hair, dark patterned shirt, gold watch, gold bracelet, gold ring.

The 1994 World Series had already broken all sorts of records, including the total number of entrants into all the events (3,832) and the total prize money distributed ($9,969,500). In the World Championship event, more records went: it had the largest entry (268), the highest-placed woman player (Barbara Samuelson), the largest single pot ($1,980,000), and, in the closing stages, the biggest-ever blind bets ($25,000 and $50,000). The other record broken was the three-handed marathon that ended the game: more than five hours passed without a player being eliminated, while Spadavecchia tried to claw his way back to level terms and Vincent leaked his money away, little by little, to Hamilton.

Spadavecchia went, finally, at 6.25. Five minutes later, Hamilton was dealt the hand that had been my undoing – a pair of queens. But this time a third queen appear on the flop, and he trapped Vincent into the largest pot in the history of the event. Ten minutes later, it was over. Russ Hamilton had the title, one million dollars, $28,512 in silver ingots, the winner's gold bracelet, and the honor of having his picture up on the wall of the poker room along with all the other greats.

That evening, I had dinner with the English writer, Anthony Holden, an old friend and fierce poker player. Afterwards, we wandered back to the tournament area to find a game. But there was no tournament area. The tables had gone, the players had gone. All that was left was a cleaning man wearily vacuuming an empty stretch of leaf-patterned carpet. It looked desolate.

We stood there for a while in silence. Then I said, 'Why do they always get the queen when they need it and we don't?'

'That's the mystery of life and poker,' Tony said. 'I guess the answer is they invented the game, so they deserve it.'

The New Yorker, 1994

Eric Drache: Poker Player

IN LAS VEGAS, THE professional poker players are mostly dour, scruffily dressed men, many of them from Texas, who will give you the precise odds on any proposition, but tend to run out of small talk when the subject drifts away from gambling. If you use the word culture, they don't reach for their revolvers, they just say 'Liberace.' They leave Vegas rarely, but only to travel to other gambling centres, like Reno or Gardena, or to the big private games in Los Angeles, Houston and Dallas.

Eric Drache is the odd man out among them. He is sophisticated and cosmopolitan, with a taste for fine wines and good food, and he loves to travel in the grand style (in London he invariably stays at Claridge's). His English wife – a colonel's daughter from Crediton, in Devon – is a Phi Beta Kappa graduate of Columbia, who is currently doing post-graduate work in psychology at Berkeley. Drache himself looks more like an Ivy League professor than a Vegas gambler. He dresses sedately, usually in a tweed sports jacket or a blazer, and he almost always wears a tie. He has the kind of haircut the Beatles sported back in the early '60s, when they were still nice young boys: a neatly trimmed pudding bowl thatch, covering his ears. It makes him look younger than he is, although, considering the ground he has covered and the sums of money he has gone through, he is still pretty young.

Drache – pronounced Drake – was born in Brooklyn in 1943, brought up in Carlstadt, New Jersey, and has been gambling for as long as he can remember. He began with marbles and baseball cards: 'We used to flip them, and the first one to get ten heads would win all the cards on the floor – maybe eighty cards. Then you'd trade them for other things; they were a form of currency.' From flipping baseball cards, he moved, aged around ten, to penny poker, playing the game as though it were a shoot-out, with no reference to the other people's cards: 'What I regret most about my misspent youth is all those years I wasted because there was no one around to tell me that poker was a game of skill. I used to play against open aces without a pair in my hand, without a three-flush. I just played. I lost my allowance every single week for years. I had one thing going for me: I was always a good creative financier; I borrowed from people, but I always managed to pay them back. I had a part-time job in high school, which basically financed my gambling.'

He won a chemistry scholarship to Rutgers, but dropped out just before the end; he was at the race track for a double-header the day of his final examinations. The army drafted him, turned him into a Military Policeman and sent him to Vietnam, an experience he consistently downplays: 'I was stationed in an air-conditioned hotel in Cholon, attached to the Pot Limit 7-Card Stud Division. In theory, I was with the 716th MPs, but I played pot limit 7-stud as my assignment.' It was around that time that he read Herbert O. Yardley's *The Education of a Poker Player* and his life, like that of many players before and since, was transformed: 'It broke poker down into an area that was my strong suit – mathematics. It showed me that if you have three clubs and don't catch one on the turn, you're about a 9–1 underdog to make a flush. It made me realise that poker is a game of skill.' From being a consistent loser, he became a consistent winner. He claims, like Richard Nixon, never to have had a losing day of poker while he was in the services.

Back in New Jersey, he began to play in all the private games he could find. Only when he noticed the same faces turning up regularly at different games, did he begin to realise that poker had its professionals – or rather, players who imagined they were professionals: 'There are a lot of people out there right now who think they play for a living but are afraid to keep records. Playing for someone else's living is what they're doing. Somebody makes a living when they play, but it is not necessarily them.'

Drache, however, kept records and was doing just fine. So, to keep the revenue coming, he started his own game, where he could play and also have money coming in from the rake-off of each pot. His mother approved, oddly enough, on the grounds that poker, being a game of skill, was more respectable and controllable than playing the horses. Since he held the game in Carlstadt, on his own turf, he reckoned he had no need to pay anyone for permission to run it. The local hoodlums thought otherwise and tipped off the police. One night during a game, there was heavy knocking at the door: 'The dumb girl who lived in the next apartment thought I had friends over to see me, so she pushed the buzzer. Like, all of a sudden, aged twenty-three, I had eleven friends who wore suits and black shoes!' Drache was arrested, sentenced to six months in jail, and fined $2000. But he turned even that to his advantage: 'My probation officer was a very fair guy, so I paid off the fine early, and used him as a credit reference. Amco, Household Finance and Bergen County Prosecutor's Office were my references. My mother thought I was crazy.'

He went on winning at the poker table in bigger and bigger games, until he gradually came to the conclusion that, in all New York and New Jersey, there weren't games high enough to satisfy him. An attorney friend, who was losing heavily at baccarat, agreed to stake him to play in Las Vegas. But, at the last moment, the lawyer was found to have been embezzling clients' money and his funds were frozen. So Drache borrowed $600 and flew to Vegas on his own. He started in the small games and moved steadily up. Within three months, he had won $70,000. Within two years, he had lost $750,000. He won it back, lost, won, and has been on the see-saw ever since. Apart from short visits, he never went back East.

If you ask him when he arrived in Vegas, he answers vaguely, 'Probably somewhere in 1970 or '71. But the dates don't mean anything and I've no way of measuring time. I mean, what do I know whether it was '70 or '71? What difference does it make? It's all one long poker game.'

In the course of that 17-year game, Drache has become Mr. Poker in Vegas. He runs and shares in the profits from the Golden Nugget's Poker Room, the busiest and most pleasant in town, and he organises Vegas's two most successful annual tournaments – the World Series of Poker at Binion's Horseshoe in May and the Golden Nugget's Grand Prix in December. He also gives advice to anyone who needs it on how to run poker tournaments in other parts of the globe – in London, Dublin, Wolverhampton, Marrakesh, Malta and the Isle of Man. Because he is charming, funny, easy-going, and knows how to handle people, he is the man all the serious poker players turn to when they have a problem. He carries a mobile telephone with him wherever he goes, and talks into it constantly. The last time I had dinner with him at the Nugget, the mobile phone was beside him on the table, but switched off, and nobody was supposed to know where he was. Even so, he was called away to the restaurant's telephone for apparent emergencies five times in two hours.

The next evening, he was playing poker over the road at Binion's Horseshoe. For the one month a year when the Horseshoe Poker Room is open – during the World Series – the side games in the evenings, after the tournament is over for the day, are the biggest you can find anywhere. Drache and four other players were warming up for the serious action in a stud game in which the antes were $100, the first two bets $400, the last three $800. As well as a mass of black $100 chips, Drache had in front of him an envelope containing $20,000 in $100 bills. Every so often, he racked the chips, counted them down quickly, and looked at his watch. He owed someone a hundred thousand, he explained, and had promised to pay him at midnight. 'I've got thirty-eight so far,' he said. 'Four hours to go.' He turned to Steve Zee, a spectrally thin New Yorker, who has a bald head and a Charlie Chan moustache. 'If I ever went to Gamblers Anonymous, I'd have to tone down my testimony,' Drache said. 'There's no way they would believe the figures – the wins and losses, the amounts of money I've borrowed and lent. I'm not kidding. It doesn't sound realistic even to me.' 'I went to GA once,' Zee said. 'There was this guy who wanted to give up all gambling, except college basketball and gin.'

Someone came up to Drache while he was playing a hand and asked him to arrange a free meal in the steak restaurant. Someone else wanted to borrow money. Jack Binion, who runs the casino, came and whispered urgently in his ear: the FBI were in the room, he said, looking for a suspect. Drache answered politely, made jokes, greeted passers-by, arbitrated a problem at an adjacent table, and eyed every girl who passed, at the same time as he looked at his cards, bet, raised and folded in his crazily expensive game.

As it happened, he was 'on a rush', hitting miracle hand after hand. Finally, he was dealt three exposed fours. Stu Ungar, who won the World Series two years running while still in his twenties, was showing two aces. When Drache was dealt his third four, Ungar threw his cards at the dealer and stalked off. 'That's the trouble with being a player and running a poker room,' said Drache philosophically. 'You take your friend's money, then you're supposed to ban him for bad behaviour.'

Minutes later, Steve Zee went broke, and a young Thai player decided he had had enough. The game broke up temporarily, but one hour later it had started again, with the stakes upped to $800 and $1600. Drache paid off his man at midnight, as arranged.

A poker game, traditionally, is not an occasion where people talk much. You can get through hours of fascinating play with a bare handful of phrases: 'Check', 'Raise', 'Fold', 'Take it'. Yet poker rooms are curiously unquiet places. Behind the relentless voice of the casino telephone operator on the intercom – 'Telephone call for Mr. Green, Mr. Danny Green' – is a persistent susurration, a continual fast clicking noise, rising and falling, sometimes loud, sometimes murmuring, like the song of the cicadas in the Mediterranean summer. It is the sound of gamblers playing with their chips, running them through their fingers, separating them into two columns, then squeezing them upward and inward so that the columns run together like water. It is a knack that takes a lot of practice, a token of countless hours of boredom at the tables. But it is also an oddly rousing background noise, and it is part of the gambling fever that takes over during a tournament. The poker rooms at the Horseshoe and the Nugget are jam-packed, and the gamblers sit behind mountains of chips, as well as wads of $100 bills, which are held together by rubber bands in packets of $5000. At the best of times, Vegas induces in you a belief that $100 won't buy a loaf of bread. During the tournaments, a kind of delirium takes hold, in which money loses all meaning and relevance outside the game in progress.

Drache has spent the last seventeen years coping with that fever. 'The trick is to look on chips as units,' he said. 'It doesn't matter whether it costs you $500 a bet or $5, the odds remain the same. So it's a question of money management. You don't want to risk your entire bankroll in one game, so you play a little lower. My problem is that I want to play at all times in games where my life could change dramatically in one week. Unfortunately, it has changed sometimes – the wrong way. I guess I have too much gamble in me.'

An example of what Drache means by a big game. Years ago, his wife, Jane, called him in the middle of a game to say she'd been in a car accident. The conversation went like this:

Eric: 'Are you hurt?'
Jane: 'No.'
Eric: 'Is anyone else hurt?'
Jane: 'No.'
Eric: 'That's all right then.'

Jane: 'But I've done fifteen hundred dollars' worth of damage to
the side of the car.'

Eric: 'Then call the insurance.'

Jane: 'But fifteen hundred dollars' damage to our beautiful Jaguar!'

Eric: 'Honey, I'm stuck four beautiful Jaguars at this moment. Call
the insurance.'

The swings in fortune that have marked Drache's career are now
part of the Vegas folk lore. The first time I met up with him again in
the May of 1988, he was as welcoming as ever, but slightly distrait.
'I'm in the middle of borrowing $750,000 off a guy I met four days
ago,' he explained. 'Don't laugh. I reckon I've got an even money
chance.'

Gambling Times once ranked Drache seventh best 7-stud player in
the world, but qualified its praise by saying that he had a problem: he
always played with the top six. Yet poker, he says, 'has been very
good to me.' His problem has not been with winning, but with the
boredom of playing in high-stakes games when vast sums are
washing around the table and none of them are coming his way:
'You get in a rut where nothing is happening for you, you're not
catching any cards. Then you've a choice either of playing badly – in
which case you've no chance of winning – or of getting up and
shooting craps. Of course, there's a third choice, which is neither of
the above, and that is you should just quit. The one quality every
poker player looks for is complete independence. You can play
when you want, quit when you want. The only person you have to
deal with – and it's the toughest one – is yourself. Sometimes, I can't
tell myself to quit, because once you get tired you're not a rational
person. It's tough to say, "Am I still earning?" The only way to do it
is to say, "If I lose back ten bets I'm going to quit, because I'll assume
I'm tired, even though I don't feel tired." The few times I've done
that, I've never regretted it and gone back into the game. I've even
quit games where there were drunks throwing their money away.
But I knew I was as drunk as they were because I was tired – not
drunk from alcohol, but punchdrunk from playing all those hours.
The difference between the top players is not a matter of skill but of
self-control, of minimising your losses when you're tired or playing
unlucky. There are players that win nine times and lose once, and
they're still losers, because they throw it all away on the last day, or
three days, when they can't stop. If I'd had an ejection-seat that

would have just pushed me out of games when I was tired, it would have been very profitable.'

Instead, he developed a taste for sports betting and craps that, at one period, destroyed all his poker winnings. He never stayed long at the craps table – usually no more than ten minutes – but he always bet the maximum, and he got through a fortune. At the end of a poker game in which he had won comfortably, a fellow-professional asked him if he were getting even at last. Drache laughed. 'If I was playing simultaneously in all the high-stakes poker games in the world, and winning in each of them, I still couldn't get even,' he replied. I once mentioned to him the rumour that he was two million dollars to the bad. 'That's exaggerated,' he said modestly. 'It was four-and-a-half million, and I'll never do it again!' Then he added, 'Most players have some sort of leak that destroys the money they make at poker.'

His debts, however, have never altered his way of life. 'I've been preparing to be rich for many, many years,' he said. 'I've learned how to spend money.' That means limos instead of taxis, and private jets to the big private games in Los Angeles. 'If there were four of us going to the same game, we'd hire a jet that charged $300 an hour waiting-time, so that if the game broke up at four in the morning we didn't have to wait three hours for a flight home. In that LA game, you could expect to win or lose $50,000. So if four people put up five or six hundred dollars a piece for a plane, you're talking about one percent of your expected win or loss.'

I asked why amateurs, however wealthy, would want to sit down with professionals like himself. 'They don't realise they're amateurs,' he said. 'Anyway, what is the definition of an amateur in poker? You're either a winner or a loser. A guy may be a winner in a certain game, so he wants to move up a grade. It's the Peter principle: you never know when you've reached your level of competence or incompetence until you've tried it. And it's exciting for them to sit down and play in a high-stakes game against the best players in the world. It's very rare that you can compete with the best in something and not look ridiculous. But you can do that in poker, because there's an element of luck involved. Amateurs are always going to remember the one hand when they had aces and the world champion had kings, but they were unlucky and got outdrawn. They forget about all the hands the professional bluffed them out of. What other event could you do that in? You couldn't bowl or shoot pool against the best in the world, and in any kind of physical sport you'd not only look embarrassed, you'd probably be injured in the first minute.'

And how, I asked, do the professionals handle the amateurs, so that they come away from a game wanting to play again?

'My goal is to make people feel it's very classy to lose,' Drache said. 'It means that they're obviously very wealthy or, if not, that they handle themselves well. Of course, when I lose, everybody at the table is sad, because I owe them all money. At one point in my career, I had eleven safety-deposit boxes and zero money. There was nothing in the boxes except rubber bands. I agree with Errol Flynn: 'If I died with money in the bank I'd consider myself a failure.' Sometimes people ask me why I play in such high-stakes games. I say that I wouldn't if I were a multi-millionaire; I'd be travelling around the world. But I don't know what I'd do if I didn't play poker for a living. I'd like to deal with people, but there would have to be an element of risk. I couldn't function if I knew I had a guaranteed income – no more, no less. I need the possibility of really dramatic risk. Maybe I'd be an attorney. I like the idea of fencing with the other attorney and manipulating the jury. But I guess the risk would be for my client, not for me. I once played poker all night with an attorney, who was due in court in the morning to defend someone in a murder trial. He had all the defence papers in a briefcase under the poker table! His client got life, without the possibility of parole. He was guilty, of course, but what chance did the poor guy have?

'All in all, I guess I'll stick to poker. Playing in the big games here in Vegas gives you confidence, because you deal with the best in the world. You have to put your money where your mouth is. Also, you get immediate gratification: you win the pot, it gets pushed to you straight away; you don't have to wait for them to send you a cheque in the mail. And there are no prejudices. Poker reduces everyone to a simple level. Degrees, languages, education, colour, none of that means a thing. All that matters is the amount of chips in front of you. You cannot find a more open-minded group of people than poker players.'

You also cannot find a group of people who reduce everything quite so readily to terms they understand. All of them have an unshakable conviction that every situation can be broken down into odds and percentages – even though it may not be necessary to act on them. This, for example, is Drache on the poker players' attitude to the risk of catching Aids: 'If you're heterosexual it's a long shot – about

1000–1 – and the general rule for a long shot to become an even-money chance is to multiply the odds by 0.69. For practical purposes, we round that out to 0.7. That means that, if a girl's got Aids, you've got to go to bed with her 700 times to have a fifty-fifty chance of catching it. Well, there's no one in the whole wide world a poker player is going to sleep with 700 times!'

On June 21, 1988, Drache flew out to the coast to see his clever wife graduate with two master's degrees at once. That evening, he breezed into the poker room at the Golden Nugget, looking exceptionally elegant in a Dunhill blazer and a Conway shirt, and sat down at a $300–$600 limit game at the back of the room. I was playing $10–$20 Hold 'em at an adjacent table. When I went to bed at three a.m., his game was still going strong. 'Let's have dinner tomorrow night,' he said.

At midday, when I went back to the 10–20 game, Drache was still playing. 'Same game?' I asked.

'I don't have two Dunhill blazers,' he replied.

Six hours later I caught his eye. 'Let's make that breakfast, not dinner,' he called. 'I'm stuck.'

Later, he disappeared from the game and returned after an hour – showered, shaved, and sleekly dressed in a beige sports jacket and a silk tie. Everyone else at the table was wearing a tee shirt.

When I went to bed at four a.m. the next morning, his game was still going strong. We never had breakfast and, when I left the casino to catch the afternoon flight back to New York, Drache was still playing.

Interview, 1988

The World's Best Poker Player

1

According to Alexis de Tocqueville, belief in luck was one of the fundamental characteristics that separated the closed hierarchical societies of Europe from the wide-open democracy of the new world, where class-distinctions were fluid and the possibility of going from log cabin to White House wasn't a foolish dream: 'Those who live in the midst of democratic fluctuations,' he wrote, 'have always before their eyes the image of chance, and they end by liking all undertakings in which chance plays a part.'

Tocqueville was writing when poker was still a crude riverboat gambling game, but as it spread north up the Mississippi, then west with the gold rush and cowboys – stud poker got its name from horses – it gradually developed into a pastime that seemed to embody the frontier spirit. Like pioneering, poker thrived on great expectations and self-reliance, on risk-taking and opportunism as well as the willingness to fold a losing hand and move on. By the turn of the century it had become the national game, as intrinsic to the American psyche as chess is to the Russian, cricket to the English and motor-racing to the Italian. 'The game,' said Walter Matthau, 'exemplifies the worst aspects of capitalism that have made our country so great.' Poker, he meant, is social Darwinism in its purest, most brutal form: the weak go under and the fittest survive through calculation, insight, self-control, deception, plus an unwavering determination never to give a sucker an even break.

In 1960, John Scarne, one of the great authorities on gambling, reckoned that poker was played regularly by at least forty-seven million Americans. But despite its popularity, there was always something shady about the game, as though it had never quite freed itself from its crooked origins. Old poker, as it was first played early in the 19th century in the casinos of New Orleans and on the Mississippi steamboats, was a game for four people, played with a twenty-card deck; each player was dealt five cards, bet or folded them, according to their value, then showed down their hands. Because there was no draw to upset the distribution of the cards, it was an ideal game for cardsharps who knew how to fix the deck, deal seconds, and mark cards. By mid-century the game had been adapted to a fifty-two card deck, but the cheaters didn't go away; they simply adjusted their skills to the challenge and their continuing presence in illegal backroom games – or the threat of it – darkened the reputation of the game. Even in the legal poker rooms of Las Vegas, there was no guarantee that all games were straight until the mob lost control of the casinos and the new corporate owners realized there was more profit in honesty than in cheating.

'Is poker a game of chance?' someone asks W.C. Fields in *My Little Chickadee*. 'Not the way I play it,' he replies. Fields is an old-style cardsharp and he dresses the part – top hat, white gloves, dingy frock coat. These days professional poker players prefer bomber jackets and baseball caps, but on the question of chance they and Fields would agree: all of them work on the principle that poker, like chess, is a game of skill and the better player will always win in the long run. (What they don't mention is that the short run, even for the best players, can sometimes last longer than they could ever imagine.) Like artists, the professionals see themselves as free spirits, loners who operate outside the system, without bosses to answer to or timetables that they haven't chosen for themselves, and they thrive, some of them spectacularly, simply by virtue of their natural talents. Most have photographic memories and all of them – even old-timers like Puggy Pearson and the late Johnny Moss, whose schooling ended at third grade – are blessed with two gifts: a flair for mathematics that enables them to calculate the odds precisely at each turn of the cards, and an instinct for 'reading' other players – for sniffing out the vanities and fears that make them vulnerable, and for figuring out the cards they are holding. It is a formidable combination that would probably guarantee success in the straight world, yet until very recently, when poker became an international craze, even the finest players seemed uneasy about the social status of their chosen profession.

2

The most conspicuous exception was Stuey Ungar, who is generally reckoned to have been the most gifted card player of all time. In *One of a Kind*, his biographers, Nolan Dalla and Peter Alson, make it clear that Ungar was never bothered by the opinion of the straight world for the simple reason that he had very little contact with it. His father was an illegal bookie and loan-shark who owned a Lower East Side bar called Fox's Corner on Second Avenue and 7th Street. Because he had all the right connections, the place was popular with gangsters, so Stuey, who went there with his older sister Judith every day after school from first grade on, spent what passed for his childhood hanging around wise-guys, absorbing their wit and wisdom, and acquiring their bad habits along with their patter. As he told Nolan Dalla,

> I always tried to make excuses to hustle up to the bar where all the guys were talking. I wanted to see what was going on. The first thing I can remember, the first conscious memory that I have, was learning how to work the soda gun. I musta drunk ten Cokes a day trying to weasel my way up to the bar to hear their conversations. I just wanted to be part of it.

Stuey was hyper-active and extremely smart, a fiercely competitive little kid who loved taking risks, but he was also undersized, skinny and fragile, so he got his kicks from indoor games, starting with checkers and Monopoly with his sister, then graduating swiftly to cards – always for money, since gambling was what everyone did at Fox's Corner. School bored him but he had a talent for numbers and by sixth grade he was keeping the books for his illiterate father. Like most bookies, Ungar Senior didn't gamble, but his wife had a passion for cards, which she played very badly, while her small son looked on and tried to tell her what to do. 'From the time I was seven,' Stuey told Dalla,

> I was watching my mother play poker and gin; I was helping my father out, balancing his books. I mean, before I could tie my fucking shoelaces, I could handicap a horse.

If his father had lived he might have kept the boy in school, but he died *in flagrante* with one of his many mistresses when Stuey was fourteen, leaving him to his feckless mother. Her son may have taught her cards, but she taught him nothing in return; it was another twenty-five years before he learned even elementary table manners from the exasperated wife of a friend. He dropped out of school, got hired as a dealer in an illegal card club, and began to make serious money playing gin rummy.

The previous year, when the family celebrated his bar mitzvah at the Americana Hotel, there were, he told Dalla, 'so many wiseguys there, the feds wanted to subpoena my bar mitzvah album.' After the death of his father, the wiseguys became his family. Dalla and Alson are understandably reticent about Ungar's connections to the mob, but the implication is that they were steady and deep. He was virtually adopted by a foot soldier in the Genovese crime family, an ex-con called Victor Romano, who ran a group of card clubs in midtown Manhattan. Romano may have felt sorry for the boy, but he also saw him as a source of income. Stuey, at fourteen, played gin rummy so well that he was already destroying all the best players on the East Coast; by the time he was sixteen, he was so good that no one would take him on, so he was forced to concentrate on poker. But he was also an addicted gambler who had no use for money except for gambling; he earned fortunes playing gin, then immediately blew them away at the racetrack. From Romano's point of view, that made him a precious asset to be nurtured and saved from harm:

> Stuey was invited to a sit-down with the boss of bosses, the Mafia captain Gus Frasca. Victor [Romano] thought it was important to make his relationship with Stuey official, so that everyone would understand the Kid belonged to him. The meeting with Frasca . . . lasted no more than five minutes, but when Frasca shook Stuey's hand it was as if the king's sword had been touched to the shoulders of a young knight.
>
> 'I'm a made man,' Stuey bragged to everyone after the meeting. He loved his association with organized crime. Being connected carried enormous stature in the gambling underworld, and it was a virtual guarantee of personal protection.

For Stuey, being connected was like a grant from some grand foundation: it gave him status as well as protection. For the gangsters, it was simply a no-lose proposition: they staked him to play cards, took a percentage of his winnings, and then took another hefty cut from the bookies to whom he promptly lost the rest. That, presumably, is what his biographers mean when they call him 'a stake horse for the mob':

Ungar's nickname among the mobsters was 'Meyer,' as in Meyer Lansky; in poker circles, in deference to his fearlessness, he was known as 'the Kamikaze Kid.' But his gifts as a card player were so uncanny that he has also been called 'the Mozart of poker.' The poker-playing novelist James McManus wrote about Ungar in *Positively Fifth Street*, his fascinating account of how he became the only literary man ever to make it to the final table of the World Series of Poker in Las Vegas – he finished in sixth place, walking away with a quarter of a million dollars. 'Brutally precise in assaulting big pots,' McManus writes admiringly, 'Ungar's near-suicidal black magic with chips mesmerized countless opponents into folding superior hands to him.' McManus is fascinated by the headlong nature of Ungar's genius and how similar it was to the 'impossible, even deranged leaps of insight that seem to be a common denominator dividing ordinary artists from the biggest of the big boys and girls.' He makes a persuasive case that, in his reckless and defiant use of his remarkable skills, Ungar can be compared to Sylvia Plath.

Dalla and Alson's biography is full of examples of Ungar's uncanny gift for reading his opponents' cards. In one cash game, for instance, he called a bet of $32,000 with a mere nine and ten of different suits in his hand because he somehow knew – correctly – that his opponent was holding nothing better than four and five or five and six. As the hand evolved card by card and bet by bet, there was a weird logic to Ungar's call, but we see this only with hindsight, because we know the concealed cards of each players. In the heat of the action, with $32,000 at stake, analysis of that order has less to do with logic than with creative imagination – that is, with the intuitive certainty with which artists know what they know. If he had got it wrong, the call would have seemed suicidal, but he made it his business not to get things like that wrong. Even so, the sheer arrogance and daring of the move stops your heart. I'm sure Sylvia Plath would have approved.

Ungar's ability to read his opponents was otherworldly, but he had no idea of how to deal with them away from the table. Other professionals who make their living in the biggest games are proficient in charm as well as cards, but Stuey had been reared by thugs and he had no charm. 'He was an obnoxious winner and a poor sport,' his biographers write, 'a taunter and a braggart,' who had no 'under-standing of the art of the hustle. Once he started playing, his competitive instincts took over and overwhelmed common sense. His mission wasn't to win money – it was to destroy people and be the best ever. As a result, he . . . scared away potential opponents.'

Ungar was brought up streetwise, but the streets were all he knew and he behaved accordingly: he threw tantrums at the table, tore up cards that offended him, swore at the dealers and sometimes spat at them. Not only did he spend most of his life without learning how to handle a knife and fork, he also ran through millions of dollars without ever having a bank account or a credit card. The first time he won the World Series, in 1980, only a few months after he started playing Hold 'em, he was unable to collect his winnings immediately because he had no Social Security card. When he won the title again the following year, he appeared on the *Merv Griffin Show*, for which he was paid $300, plus a further $100 for the rerun. 'Just think,' he said proudly, 'in my whole life, those were the only paychecks I ever received.'

Sixteen years later, Ungar won the title a third time – the only player ever to have done so – but by then his life was in shreds. In New York, after his father died, his mother had become addicted to painkillers and his sister to heroin, but Stuey stuck with his addiction to non-stop action: when the card games bored him he threw his money away at the racetrack or betting sports with the bookies. He could brilliantly calculate the odds involved in playing fifty-two cards, but the odds on flesh-and-blood horses and football players are harder to predict. When his debts made New York too hot for him, he moved to Las Vegas where the action never stops and the crowd he mixed with bet on everything – just to make it more interesting. But gambling is legal in Nevada, so perhaps it lacked some of the thrill it had back east and, in place of an inner life, he needed some other stimulant. So he started taking drugs – not casually, for relaxation, but in the same headlong, suicidal way in which he gambled – and by the time he made his great comeback to win the World Series for a record third time, in 1997, they had almost destroyed him. According to his biographers, he looked and smelled like a hobo and had snorted so much cocaine that one side of his nose had caved in like a punctured tyre. He was also broke and had difficulty persuading anyone to stake him for the $10,000 entry fee.

That third title won him a million dollars. Half of it went to the man who backed him, the rest was gone within months, most of it on crack and coke, and the following year he was too far gone even to try to defend his title. Six months later he was found dead in a seedy hotel in downtown Las Vegas; a porno movie was running on the television and there was vomit on the floor. During his lifetime, Ungar is reckoned to have won thirty million dollars at cards, but 'the cheapest commodity in his life was always money' and he died broke. To help out his long-neglected widow and daughter, his high-rolling pals took up a collection at his funeral.

3

Ungar's self-destructiveness was dreadful, but the waste that went with it was worse: aside from the millions he casually threw away, he had an IQ of 185 and he used it only for gambling. Naturally, he enjoyed his fearsome reputation and the titles he had won, and he wanted them on record – if only to give his daughter something to be proud of. *One of a Kind* started as a series of interviews with Nolan Dalla, which Ungar intended to become an 'as-told-to' autobiography. He loved fame, but he had no idea of how famous he might have become if he had lived a few years longer.

Poker may be America's national game and its second most popular after-dark activity, but until recently high-stakes poker was a small world where all the best players knew each other – if not personally, at least by name. It's still a small world at the top but now, thanks to television, the rest of the world knows who's who in it. *World Poker Tour* is the Travel Channel's highest-rated show; it is also that rarest of television marvels, a show with an audience that grows with each rerun. Poker is now the rock and roll of the dot com world, played on the internet by millions of hopefuls every hour of the day and night, all over the globe. When Ungar won his second World Series title, in 1981, there were 75 contestants and his prize money was $375,000. Last year 5,618 players anteed up $10,000 each and the winner, an unknown Australian called Joe Hachem, finished up with $7,500,000, the largest prize in the history of any game or sport.

There are plenty of young internet players who win their way into televised tournaments. Most of them wear their baseball caps back-to-front, a website's brand name on their shirts and, like Ungar, they have a talent for mathematics and a restricted view of culture: Stuey's reading stopped at the sports pages; the new kids were brought up on comic books, Tolkien, and Dungeons & Dragons. Some of them make a good living from cards but few, as yet, belong to the true poker elite. The highest rollers are a tight-knit group, presided over by two of the greatest living players, Doyle Brunson and Chip Reese. Their base is the high-stakes section of the Bellagio Casino's poker room in Las Vegas, and what happens there – who wins and how much – is strictly confidential.

Five years ago, however, confused rumors of a gigantic game began to circulate: a billionaire banker from Dallas had come to the Bellagio wanting to play as high as the professionals cared to make it. Previously, the biggest game spread there had been for limits of $4,000–$8,000 (i.e., the players would bet in units of $4,000 in the first two rounds of betting, then $8,000 in the second two rounds). The banker, Andy Beal, preferred $10,000–$20,000 limit, and wanted to go higher. The pros eventually obliged, reckoning Beal to be just another rich fish waiting to be landed. They started playing him in February 2001 and went on intermittently, whenever Beal had time to spare, until May 2004. By then, the stakes had been raised to an astonishing $100,000–$200,000, making it the biggest game in history. Michael Craig's *The Professor, the Banker, and the Suicide King* is a fascinating account of what happened.

Professional poker players are notoriously reticent about their wins and losses, so Craig, a lawyer who loves poker, must be an exceptionally sympathetic listener to have got them to talk about the marathon so freely and in such detail since the sums involved were so enormous as to seem unreal. High-stakes poker players have always inhabited an alternative universe in which money has no meaning except as a way of keeping score, and what you do with your chips – when and how you bet or check or raise – is simply a form of communication. The goods and pleasures those chips could buy in the real world are of no interest to the high-rollers until they get up from the table. When Andy Beal came to town, however, the stakes became so high that the real world reappeared in their calculations and they began to fear for what Doyle Brunson calls 'the poker economy.'

On his first visit, Beal left the Bellagio $100,000 ahead, which the pros took as a good sign, indicating that he had got lucky and would be back. They figured correctly, but underestimated their man. Beal wasn't just a brilliant businessman who had gone from fixing broken TV sets to owning his own bank; he was also, among other achievements, a self-taught mathematician who had worked on Fermat's Last

Theorem. When he turned to poker he wanted to start at the top and beat the best players at their own game:

> Andy knew he would never be able to match them for experi-
> ence and instinct. On the other hand, he felt he could match –
> and maybe exceed – their ability to work out the right play based
> on the odds with the brute force of his intellect and determina-
> tion.

Back home in Dallas after his first trip to Vegas, he wrote his own program in BASIC, ran millions of hands through a computer, studied the results and practised constantly, in the belief that he could beat the pros by perfect calculation of the odds and unwaveringly correct play. And because the top players have extraordinary powers of observation and could pick up 'tells' about the cards he held and how he might play them from the smallest clues – from the way he breathed, the tone of his voice, the look in his eyes, or the throb of a vein in his neck – he also concluded that he must eliminate all traces of personality. The next time he sat down with the pros at the Bellagio he wore wraparound dark glasses and earphones clapped to his head to keep out the small talk. He must have looked like some robot from an alien planet, but people who play poker at this level are like the finest intelligence agents; they know practically all there is to know about disguise, duplicity and betrayal.

Beal's one true advantage was his wealth and he could only make that count if he played them heads-up, one-to-one, and raised the stakes so high that his opponents were out of their 'comfort zone.' Comfort zone is a curious concept for people used to playing for hundreds of thousands of dollars, but Craig has a telling example of what it means. In one of the later games, when Beal's opponent left the table to go to the bathroom, his place was taken by Lyle Berman, the venture capitalist who founded the World Poker Tour: 'Berman played four hands, two of which he immediately threw away, forfeiting the blinds. He lost $900,000.'

No one had ever wanted to play so high before and, though the pros were sure they could beat him, Beal owned a bank and they were only able to take him on by pooling their resources and playing him as a team, each in turn. That was how Beal wanted it but, with hindsight, it was a mistake. It is hard enough for an amateur to go heads-up with the world's best poker players, but to take them on in sequence, each of them starting fresh while he was tiring, was a reckless decision that gave them an extra edge.

He also played too long. One of the many talents that goes to make a professional poker player is the ability to concentrate for hours on end, then quit when his or her concentration begins to falter. Amateurs, even gifted amateurs like Beal, get too caught up in the game to know they are tired, so they lose their focus, persuade themselves it is only a momentary lapse, then start throwing their money away. Beal was a formidably disciplined player, but Vegas was not his hometown and he never slept well there; that, too, gave the pros an extra edge.

Just how much they won in the end Craig doesn't say – several millions, for sure, though not as much as some of them claimed and nothing like enough to disturb Beal's comfort zone. But it wasn't easy for them and there were times when Beal did so well that he had them running scared. In one day, Craig reports, he won nearly $12 million, half of it from the great Chip Reese. No other amateur had done that before or is ever likely to do it again. Beal's battle with the pros may have cost him a lot of money, but in the real world, where Goliath always beats David, he finished up looking like a winner.

New York Review of Books, 2006

Gambling

High Rollers

IN THE SPACE OF a couple of crazy years, the brothers Frederick and Steven Barthelme, respected writers though by no means in the big time, managed to blow more than a quarter of a million dollars in the Mississippi gambling boats. *Double Down* is their account of how this happened, what led up to it and spurred them on, and how it ended in tears when, as a final insult, the casino which had taken their money charged them with conspiracy to cheat.

It is a gripping and bewildering story, although its real subject is not so much their fatal addiction to gambling as, in every sense, their inheritance. The small fortune they destroyed came to them after the death of their troublesome father and they are more interested in him than in what they did to his money. In the end, their book is a memorial to their parents; the gambling is a colòrful extra, a narrative thread, a symptom of some larger upset, an excuse.

Like most addicts, the brothers began innocuously. Both of them were night-owls and occasionally, instead of going to the movies or settling down to write, they used to drive the seventy miles from Hattiesburg, Mississippi, where they taught creative writing, to the casinos around Gulfport. Sometimes they went with their partners or a colleague, more often they went on their own. They played the slots, goofed around at the blackjack tables, won a little, lost a little, then drove back to their sober university routines. It was just another night out, fun and noise and dazzle, and a chance to rub shoulders with the kind of people they never met on campus – ordinary folk with boring jobs and no interest at all in books or ideas or whatever else went to make the small change of academic and literary life. Hattiesburg is a placid, relatively affluent little town, 'clean and bright,' they say, 'and the people were friendly.' The casinos were another world.

Back in the 1830s, when cotton prices were high, the gambling

boats that plied the Mississippi from New Orleans to St. Louis were
kitted out as floating palaces for the benefit of plantation owners flush
with money and determined to have themselves some fun, no matter
how much it cost them. The boats were also crowded with professional gamblers and cardsharps – Clark Gable figures with diamond
stick-pins, gold watch chains, embroidered vests – equally determined
to help themselves to the easy money on offer. All that romance is
long gone. These days the professionals wear tracksuits and baseball
caps and there is nothing palatial about the modern gambling boats.
They don't even go anywhere; they are simply top-heavy, neon-
strung barges – 'Wal-Mart[s] with a high flashing-light content,' the
Barthelmes call them – moored to concrete pillars a few feet off a
particularly dreary stretch of the delta coast: 'The beaches had never
been much good. The sand had been sucked out of Mississippi Sound
and spread alongside Highway 90 like something in the bottom of an
aquarium. It looked wrong, like a bad hairpiece. The water was the
color of pot roast.' The casinos were as frowsy as the landscape:
'paddle-boat quaint: cheap tux shirts, black bow ties, red cartoon
suspenders . . . The architecture . . . [was] Disneyesque: pirate ships
and mock cowboy saloons slathered in happy neon.'

For the brothers, the awfulness was part of the casinos' charm. In joints
like these the usual rules didn't apply; they could do whatever they wanted
for as long as their money lasted. Or, as they say in Vegas, the casinos have a
golden rule: the man who has the gold makes the rules. Unluckily for the
Barthelmes, they got lucky on their first visit: they played the slots, hit a
couple of jack-pots and walked away with the casino's money. It was only
a few hundred dollars, but that wasn't the point. The point was it was so
easy: eleven hundred dollars they hadn't sweated for by writing or
teaching, eleven hundred dollars that had simply happened to them
while they were having fun. Later, they discovered that 'this was typical,
that it happened just this way for a lot of people who went to casinos. You
win something sizeable, and thereafter gambling takes up residence in
your imagination.' But by then they were hooked.

Free money is a beguiling illusion. Gamblers who play only games of
chance over which they have little or no control – roulette, baccarat,
craps, slots, even blackjack – are kept going by the dream of some *deus ex*
(slot)-*machina* who will transform their dingy lives with a shower of gold.
They tend to be superstitious, to favour certain clothes, finger lucky
charms and believe in the power of thought to influence the fall of the
cards or the spinning roulette ball. Above all, they believe in their luck,

though the ones who survive temper their belief with caution. They know that the casinos make their unseemly profits out of one simple certainty: nobody stays lucky. The house's edge – the 1 to 16 percent permanently in its favour – will always eat up the gamblers in the long run. So if the wise get lucky, they play their rush, then quit while they are ahead.

Professional gamblers are another breed entirely. They know about runs of luck and how to use them, but they believe in percentages, logic, calculation, in the immutable laws of probability and, even more, in their own skill. Most of them play poker and avoid casino games, although some of the professionals have what they call a 'leak': having sat for hours at the poker table watching every move and calculating every bet, they will wander over to a craps game and throw their winnings away. But usually that is simply a release of tension after the iron discipline of high-stakes poker.

The professionals who gamble for a living are compulsive winners in much the same way as the Barthelme brothers, like all the other gamblers who keep the casinos in business, are compulsive losers. But they have one thing in common: an utter disregard for the reality of money. In the gambling world money ceases to be something you need to lead a life – to pay the rent or the dentist's bill, to buy food and drink and clothes. It becomes, instead, just a way of keeping score. The professionals carry around doorstop wads of $100 bills and regard them as tools of their trade. As a token of their disdain for the usual ways of the world, they omit the zeroes when they bet, then divide by ten. Depending on the size of the game, a 'nickel' is $5, $50 or $500; a 'dime' is $10, $100 or $1,000. And nobody even notices because money, in casinos, doesn't look like money. Instead of a green treasury bill validated by a president's face, it is a little coloured disc stamped with a number and the name of the casino. A New York gambler who went by the name of 'Big Julie' once remarked sagely, 'The guy who invented gambling was bright, but the guy who invented the chip was a genius.' The chip is like a conjurer's sleight of hand that turns an egg into a billiard ball, a necessity of life into a plaything, reality into illusion.

This blasé attitude suited the brothers just fine. They had learned to feign indifference at their parents' knees. For the Barthelmes feigning indifference was both a sport and a code of honor:

For us is was a family thing, helped you get by in the family. Lots of fast folk in the family, people who were always thinking, always ahead of you, so what we practised was making everything look like nothing, smoothing stuff out, taking things in stride. Do otherwise and you were vulnerable, at risk, somebody was sure to make a joke at your expense . . . But that wasn't the end of it. Rationality was prized, but so was intensity. Feeling was admired and given broad authority, but any *display* of feeling tended to get mocked . . . We cared a great deal about things, because that was what you were supposed to do, but caring made us vulnerable, both inside the family, which was pretty much a non-stop you-blinked game played by seven people, and in the outside world as well. Appearing to be blasé – indifferent, relaxed, casual, un-concerned – was essential protective coloration disguising this vulnerability.

There were five Barthelme children – a sister, who became a public relations executive, and four brothers, all of them writers. Donald, the most famous, died of cancer in 1989; Peter writes mystery novels; Frederick (Rick) has published eleven works of fiction, and Steven a book of short stories. Rick and Steve were the youngest, a family within the exclusive family, joined to the others by what they call 'fierce tribal solidarity', but sharply aware that they belonged to a secondary, junior branch. This drew them together and made them mutually supportive. They taught at the same university, gambled together, went broke together, and have now written this book together so seamlessly that it is impossible to tell stylistically where one leaves off and the other starts.

The father of this talented, edgy brood was an avant-garde architect in Houston, successful and respected, but an outsider by temperament, imperious, impatient and hard to please – 'a decent man,' they write, 'but troubled and not at all accessible.' The mother, whom they adored, was an architect in a different way: 'The family was something she invented, shaped, guided, and protected as parent, pal, co-con-spirator, nurturer, teacher, dresser, role model.' She was also the mediator between the children and their difficult father, and after she died at the age of 87, in 1995, their father became more exasperating and inaccessible than ever, and the children more or less gave up on him. He died sixteen months later, aged 89, leaving them with a load of guilt as well as a load of money.

Rick's and Steve's gambling had already intensified after the death of their mother; it had become wilder, more reckless, as though their grief made them beyond caring. Guilt and rage complicated their grief for their father and, to exorcise him, they set about throwing his money away. In true Barthelme style, however, they had no intention of being outsmarted. They bought shelfloads of books on blackjack and slot machines, studied the strategies, the percentages, the arcane skills of money management and card-counting, then forgot all about them directly they sat down to play. Or rather, since haughtiness is also a family failing they admit to, they disdained to apply whatever gambling sense they had acquired:

> The whole business of counting cards was the antithesis of our motive in playing blackjack. It wasn't much *fun* counting cards. It was hard work. You had to concentrate and watch everything with headachy eyes. It was impossible to count and still joke with the dealers and pit bosses, bet crazily, and generally have a high old time.

What they are talking about is style. Part of that style was their father's 'anarchic arrogance' and 'tenacity that boggles the mind,' and they applied it at the gaming tables: 'Winning is better than losing, but neither one is the goal of gambling, which is *playing*. Losing never feels like the worst part of gambling. Quitting often does.' For them, unfortunately, quitting nearly always meant going broke, not quitting while they were ahead – one year, Steve won $132,000 on the slots, but still ended up a loser – so their doggedness was also a cover for a feverish, suicidal addiction. This is not a problem for them. The brothers are subtle, sophisticated men who have thought a lot about their addiction and its multiple causes. They have been to Gamblers Anonymous, read the literature, studied their own complex motives, and they talk about them knowingly, almost affectionately, in much the same way as they talk about the pleasures of gambling. That, too, is part of the family style:

> As card-carrying Barthelmes we believed two things, although neither provided adequate emotional cover: first, that we could 'understand' things and thus tame them, and second, that words, adroitly deployed, were a bullfighter's cape – they allowed you to step aside and avoid the horns of a threatening experience. It helped to have something smart to say, though that wasn't

essential, since it wasn't the quality of the thought that was the key, just that the thought was always there, between you and *it*.

One of the *its* that thought and feigned indifference protected them from was their comfortable middle-class life as university teachers:

> It was an aesthetic thing . . . Everywhere around us were writers and artists and professors, hard at work at what Ishmael Reed describes as 'all wearing the same hat' . . . What we didn't like about the academy was the falseness: conservative people presenting themselves in Che Guevara suits, digging hard for career advantage while settling hearty congratulations all around for assigning radical authors to their students to read, thus threatening the established order.

For many comfortably-off people, one of the lures of gambling is its seamy side: it is a way of rubbing shoulders with gangsters without getting hurt. Not so for the brothers. Gambling, they write, gave them 'the opportunity to behave bizarrely, just like – we imagined – ordinary, everyday people. We didn't think we were wild and crazy; we thought gambling made us regular guys.'

I suspect it also made them think (or remember) they were writers, rather than 'two boys from a middle-class family with a work ethic and a belief in doing things well', who had ended up more or less where they began – doing 'awfully sweet work, in our awfully sweet lives'. For them as writers, being middle-class was a hindrance because it meant being able to 'buy yourself out of the threatening and the immediate, which is the very stuff that the best writers deal with. Teaching was clearly a kind of betrayal. 'As college professors we were automatically in an out-of-harm's-way subculture'. Now their father's money had ensured that they could leave their jobs, devote the rest of their lives to their art, yet still be out of harm's way, untroubled by what C.K. Ogden famously called 'Hand-to-Mouth Disease,' the occupational hazard of writers. Having been schooled in dissatisfaction and arrogance meant that there was only one way out of their quandary. Family honor required that they should throw their inheritance away.

In the end, they came to see the advantages of a comfortable, settled life, and had learned a little humility: 'Daily life, the whole sad self of it, now meant something to us . . . Our perspectives changed. We cared more about things we used to make fun of; we had a greater distaste for the easy puffing of folks trying day after day to make themselves important, and at the same time we found them a bit more in our hearts.' Before this change could occur, they had first to see what 'real' life, as they had imagined it, really looked like. That illumination came when they were banned from their favorite casino for cheating, booked, indicted, threatened with trial and publicly humiliated. The case was eventually dropped – an article in the *New York Times Magazine* made it sound as if it had less to do with the Barthelmes than with a squabble between a dealer and a casino supervisor – but not before the brothers had been put through the wringer: first, interrogation in a concrete, windowless room hidden inside the casino car park, followed by hours in the belly of the police station with other felons, then months waiting to be brought to court and trying to talk common sense to lawyers. Their super-ego was no longer their pig-headed, hard-to-please father; it was a meat-faced thug in a uniform and he scared them out of their wits.

Although it was a harrowing experience, they describe it without ever losing their casual, ironic, cooler-than-thou tone of voice. The whole book, in fact, is a wonderfully seductive performance – witty, self-aware, at once full of subtle feeling and implacably knowing – a triumph of style over temporary insanity. I suspect this is what confused the casino bosses and persuaded them to ban two high rollers who were consistently hosing the establishment with money. To the men in Armani suits who ran the joint it seemed inconceivable that anyone could play so whimsically and incompetently for such high stakes. There had to be some ulterior motive, some arcane scam they were setting up in order to make a killing. The bosses didn't understand that incompetence and whimsicality are sometimes part of the writer's baggage, a professional deformation, more artistically interesting to those who suffer from it than the patience, dead reckoning and discipline it takes to play properly. I once asked a poker professional how he and his colleagues persuaded any amateurs, no matter how rich, to play cards with them when they knew they couldn't win. He answered simply, 'I try to make them feel it's stylish to lose.' The Barthelme brothers turned stylish losing into an art. It cost them a small fortune, but at least they salvaged a stylish book from their disaster.

New York Review of Books, 2000

Learning from Las Vegas

FIFTEEN YEARS AGO, WHEN I first began going regularly to Las Vegas, the town was strictly for adults. Sometimes you would see stunned waifs wandering around Glitter Gulch downtown or asleep on the carpeted sidewalk outside the Golden Nugget while their parents blew their week's wages inside, but there was only one casino that made any pretense of catering to children. That was Circus Circus, which offered them a mezzanine crammed with carnival sideshows and video games, and a view of the casino, with trapeze artists swinging around over the heads of the gamblers below. The place seemed to have been designed as a gambling-aversion cure by an unusually sadistic behaviorist. It was bewildering, batteringly noisy, and circular, a new level of Dante's hell. My small daughter was taken there once by the mother of another girl she had met at the swimming pool of a neighboring casino. The mother gave the kids ten dollars each and went off to play blackjack. When the money ran out they went down to find her. Since it was an offense for a minor to enter the gambling area, the girls – both nine years old, and with long blond hair like Tenniel's Alice – were promptly arrested by a security guard.

It was outrageous, of course, but it seemed oddly appropriate. In 1980, when the mob was still all over town, Las Vegas was a Wonderland in which even Alice could be arrested for a misdemeanor. That was one of its attractions. Back then, Nevada was the only state in the union where gambling was legal, and its gaming tables were the only places where people from the straight world could rub shoulders with gangsters and not get into trouble. The wiseguys were as much a part of the town's non-stop pageant as the cascades of neon.

Not any more. Modern Vegas has been redesigned for the benefit of children, with pirate battles, jousting knights, and exploding volcanoes. It has become just another Disneyland, a family theme park with gambling on the side to keep the adults happy. Even the gambling is childish. Back in the 1980s, the center of the casinos was the 'table games' – blackjack, roulette, baccarat, craps, poker – games that involve some social exchange with other people – players, dealers, croupiers – and varying degrees of skill. (Poker, at its highest level, is as sophisticated as chess, and even roulette players have to make choices.) There were acres of slot machines, of course, and armies of little old ladies, with Dixie cups full of quarters, grinding away at them. But the real action was at the tables and, for non-professionals at least, action was what the gamblers were there for. Sometimes the players won, sometimes they lost, but the pleasure was in the game itself: the stir of excitement at each new deal or roll of the dice or spin of the wheel, the competitive urge to beat the other players or the dealer or the house.

Gradually, however, casinos have cut back the space allotted to table games and filled it with slot machines. Although I go to Vegas often, I don't consider myself a gambler; I never bet on anything I can't shuffle and the only game I play is poker. So for me, the gloomiest moment of the Vegas year occurs just after the end of the World Series of Poker at Binion's Horseshoe. The World Series is the oldest and most prestigious of all the tournaments, and players come from all over the globe to compete. For the three weeks the tournament lasts, the large space in front of the Horse-shoe's reception desk is filled with poker tables – dozens of them, all packed night and day, and with people lining up to play. The high-stakes side action before, during, and after the events of the Series itself is unceasing right up until the start of the main and final event, the $10,000 buy-in no-limit hold 'em tournament, which begins on a Monday and ends on Thursday. Two hours after it is finished and the new World Champion has been crowned, the poker tables have vanished, as though they had never been, and in their place are ranks of slot machines. It is business as usual again, even at family-owned Binion's Horseshoe, the Mecca of high rollers.

For the casino operators, slot machines have distinct advantages over table games: they cost a mere $5,000 each and, in the words of a gambling official, they 'show up every Monday and they don't go out on strike.' But compared to traditional forms of gambling, playing the slots is an autistic activity – mindless, solitary, and addictive – and its popularity is growing at a terrible speed. 'Between 1990 and 1992, table game betting at Nevada and Atlantic City casinos fell by about 15 percent, while slot machine revenues rose by nearly 40 percent,' writes Robert Goodman in *The Luck Business*, a sharp and informative survey of American gambling. 'Today's casinos are little more than theme-decorated warehouses . . . designed for mass consumption – the new "McGambling."'

Goodman is only passingly interested in Las Vegas; his subject is the Las Vegasing of America, the spread of what he calls 'fast-food,' 'convenience' gambling, available everywhere on demand. These days it is no longer even necessary to go to a casino to gamble. There are slot machines and lottery terminals in bars, restaurants, and stores, and because 'McGambling' is electronic, it will soon be available to anyone who has access to a computer:

> As recently as 1988, casino gambling was legal in only two states: Nevada and New Jersey. By 1994, six years later, casinos were either authorized or operating in twenty-three states and were proposed in many others. . . . Total yearly casino revenues nationally nearly doubled – from $8 billion to about $15 billion. . . . In the early 1990s revenues in the gambling industry were climbing about two and a half times faster than those in the nation's manufacturing industries. . . .
>
> By the beginning of 1995, legal gambling in the United States [including lotteries] was generating over $37 billion in yearly revenues – more than the total amount Bill Clinton promised to use during each of his first four years in office to help rebuild America's transportation system, create a national information network, develop the technology to clean up the environment, and convert the defense industry to a peacetime economy.

Goodman sees this explosion of legalized gambling as just the latest in a series of desperate attempts to find a magic bullet to cure ailing economies:

> In the 1950s and 1960s, it was called 'urban renewal' – cities were torn to shreds to eliminate slums and attract more business and more affluent residents. During the 1970s and 1980s, it became a game known as 'industrial recruitment' or 'smokestack chasing' – local and state governments pitted themselves against one another

in an effort to woo companies with tax breaks, subsidies, and promises of low wages and lax environmental standards.

Legalized gambling has worked no better than its predecessors and, like them, it creates more problems than it solves. The casino operators have prospered, of course, but of all the communities that have tried to strike it rich through legalized gambling, only the Indian tribes who opened casinos on their reservations have truly benefited. Exercising their rights to open casinos under a 1988 act of Congress, the Indian tribes had a distinct advantage over other hopefuls: they had very little to lose. Most were destitute and dependent on government handouts. The casinos brought in visitors with money to spend, and, because the tribes owned the casinos, the tribal councils could decide how the profits should be spent.

The Connecticut Pequots, for example, whom the Puritan settlers once called 'a stately warlike people' and then tried to exterminate, were virtually extinct by the end of World War II. Their two-thousand-acre reservation near Stonington had shrunk to 214 acres, and one family was living on it. Today the reservation is back to its original size and the Pequots are one of the most prosperous Native American tribes. They have their own police and fire service, a lavish community center, comfortable houses, and a number of thriving business enterprises. All of this has been financed by the Pequots' casino, Foxwoods, despite the fact that the building itself goes against the basic principle of casino design: i.e., include nothing that might distract the players from the serious business of losing money. In practice this means no clocks and no windows. The Pequot tribal elders, however, are proud of their reservation's pretty, wooded countryside and they insisted on windows. The Connecticut landscape is indeed charming, although whenever I've been there nobody has seemed to be paying much attention to it. Foxwoods is currently the most successful casino in the country (it grossed approximately $600 million in 1994) for the simple reason that it draws in customers from New York and all the major cities in New England. If you live in Boston or Providence or Hartford or New Haven and you want to gamble legally, there is simply nowhere else to go.

In other words, the tribal casinos have prospered for the same reason Las Vegas has become the fastest-growing city in the States. (In the early 1990s, Goodman says, nearly six thousand people were settling there every month and investors were pouring more than $2 billion a year into gambling-related projects alone.) You can gamble anywhere in Nevada, but Reno is also a cattle town and Carson City is the state capital. Las Vegas, in contrast, is strictly a one-product, purpose-built town. It sits there in the middle of the desert with its neon lights fizzing, and visitors flood in with the sole purpose of spending money. Looking after them and servicing the hotels – including thirteen of the twenty largest hotels in the world – gives work to a population of one million. Surprisingly few of the residents gamble much – they wouldn't survive if they did – but all of them need houses and stores and restaurants and automobiles, doctors, lawyers, and accountants. Goodman calls Nevada's gambling 'an export product,' and this is something Vegas shares with some of the Western tribal casinos. It is surrounded by a *cordon sanitaire* of desert; if you want to go there to gamble, you have to hustle some money, pack a bag, and travel.

The new gambling towns lack this geographical advantage. Casinos and riverboats have sprung up across the US during the last decade in the hope of attracting tourist dollars to help failing economies, but none of them was sufficiently remote. The tourists came, lost their money at the casinos, then drove straight home, ignoring the local shops and restaurants. Meanwhile, there was a sharp rise in 'impulse gambling' by local residents who dropped in to play the slots or the tables on their way home from work, thus wasting cash that might have been used for clothes or appliances or a meal out, and creating social problems – gambling addiction and crime – which had to be paid for by the community or the state.

Goodman is scathing about the economic illusions underlying 'McGambling': by legalizing gambling and promoting their own lotteries, state governments are encouraging what Goodman calls 'the pathology of hope' and helping to transform the most powerful industrial nation on earth into 'a scavenger economy.' One of the most serious effects of recent economic trends, he thinks, has been the collapse of confidence in the utility of work: 'In a 1960s survey, nearly 60 percent of Americans believed "hard work pays off." By the 1980s only one in three people considered this to be true.' As companies are streamlined and workers laid off, young people don't necessarily expect a long-term job; they take what they can get, and many have to become reconciled to the prospect of long periods of unemployment.

When work is no longer a reliable route to prosperity, a big kill in the lotteries or the slots becomes the one hope of escape from the economic trap. This has always been the lure of lotteries and one of the reasons why, since the sixteenth century, governments have used them when they were strapped for cash; they are an irresistible form of voluntary taxation on those who can least afford it. People with money to spare gamble for entertainment; the poor gamble to change their lives. Years ago, in London, a cheerful Cockney charlady who worked for a friend of mine told him that every week, for the whole of their married life, she and her husband had invested one pound in the football pools. My friend asked her if they had planned what they would do with the money if they ever won big. 'Of course,' she replied. 'We've known all along. We'll split it down the middle and live separate.' The dream of affluent separation had kept them together for forty years.

These days, Goodman writes, nobody seems immune to the pathology of hope:

> Speculation has now become as much a part of ordinary people's lives as their music and sports. Our doctors have become as knowledgeable about real estate syndicates and tax shelters as they are about identifying viral strains, our religious leaders are as likely to know about accelerated depreciation as they are the rituals of their faith. And now more and more people are becoming as skilled at doubling down at blackjack as they are in the techniques of their trades and professions.

It makes sense that the smart money will invest in the gambling industry, which produces 30 to 50 percent yearly profits, instead of in the average American business, which earns 5 to 8 percent. Even Lee Iacocca, America's most eminent captain of industry, is doing it. Soon after he rescued Chrysler from collapse, he wrote in his autobiography that within a few years the US economic arsenal was going to consist of little more than drive-in banks, hamburger joints, and video arcades. Ten years later, Iacocca has retired from industry and become a big player in the casino business.

Goodman is not opposed to gambling as a pastime – he does it himself, he says – but he is appalled by the prospect of Las Vegas as a blueprint for the future of the American economy. Playing the market is a form of gambling but at least it may finance business enterprises.

Playing the slots or lotteries is different; it is investing in a dream – the dream of something for nothing – and the only people guaranteed to make a profit are those who run the games. During the recession of the early 1980s, Iowa's farming and agricultural equipment industry suffered severely, its population loss was the highest in the country, and its unemployment rate rose to nearly 16 percent. To stop the rot, the state legalized riverboat gambling, although in a strictly controlled and limited way: 'We are beating our plowshares into amusement centers,' a riverboat owner announced grandly.

Just over one year later, he moved his boats downstream to Biloxi, Mississippi, where there were fewer restrictions, and Iowa was left with six hundred unemployed casino workers and a hefty bill for the public improvements they had made to accommodate the boats. In the words of another casino developer, 'The problem with this industry . . . is that it doesn't create anything. It offers entertainment and leisure, which is obviously of great value, but it doesn't create anything in the long run.'

It also has what public relations people call 'an image problem.' Until governments got into the act by organizing lotteries, gambling had always been associated with organized crime. Consequently, when gambling was legalized and promoted as healthy entertainment, the illegal operators were delighted. William Jahoda, who worked for one of the Chicago mafia families, told the Chicago Gaming Commission that 'any new form or expansion of legal gambling always increased our client base. Simply put, the stooges who approved Las Vegas nights, off-track betting, lotteries, etc. became our unwitting front men and silent partners.' This has been especially the case in Nevada since the state legalized gambling in 1931. The casinos in the original downtown Las Vegas were mostly run by West Coast underworld characters who had previously owned illegal clubs in Los Angeles and offshore gambling ships. They made money, of course, but not in a big way; although Los Angeles gamblers traveled to Vegas to play legally, the casinos in Glitter Gulch prospered most by catering to the workers on the Hoover Dam.

Modern Las Vegas was invented by an East Coast mobster, Bugsy Siegel, who had been sent to LA by the syndicate to take control of the racing wire to the West Coast. It was Siegel who had the bright idea of building a huge gambling palace out in the desert on the road into town, festooned with lights and impossible to miss. Siegel's Flamingo was built in 1945, financed by his associates back east. And although the casino defied the laws of probability by losing money consistently for two years, and Siegel himself was murdered in 1947, the idea was too good to waste. Casino followed casino and the road west out of town became the Strip, which now stretches for six miles into the Clark County desert. The Mormons, who governed Nevada, did what they could to keep out organized crime. But in the years following the repeal of Prohibition the mob had accumulated huge amounts of money and Vegas seemed the best possible place to invest it because it was flooded with that most desirable commodity for criminals, ready cash.

Nicholas Pileggi's latest mafia chronicle, *Casino*, is particularly eloquent about the money that washes daily through the casinos and finishes up in the counting rooms, the windowless inner sanctuaries from which even the casino owners are legally barred:

> Count room workers go about their tasks with the deadened glaze of people who must steel themselves against the dazzling daily experience of being immersed in the sight, smell, and touch of money. Tons of it. Stacks of it. Bundles of cash and boxes of coins so heavy that hydraulic lifts must be used to move the tonnage of loot around in the count room.
>
> There is such a daily fortune of stacked paper bills pouring into the count room that rather than being counted, the cash is assembled into various denominations and weighed. A million dollars in $100 bills weighs $20\frac{1}{2}$ pounds; a million in $20s, 102 pounds; and a million in $5 bills, 408 pounds.
>
> The coins are poured into specially made Toledo electronic coin-weighing scales manufactured by the Reliance Electric Company . . . that sort and count the coins. A million dollars in quarter slot machine winnings weighs twenty-one tons.

Every mug who buys a lottery ticket has a secret dream of his own counting room: quantities of cash so great that they must be weighed rather than counted, a fortune that would transform his dingy life overnight. In Vegas the dream is an everyday reality, though not for most players. According to Frank 'Lefty' Rosenthal, the principal witness in *Casino*, the philosophy of Las Vegas is simple: 'Give them a free drink and a dream, and they give you their wallets.'

Lefty Rosenthal is now living in retirement in a house next to a golf course in Boca Raton, which seems a fitting end for a bookmaker and professional gambler who spent his life studying form in racing and sports and working out the odds in obsessional detail. *Casino* is based in considerable part on Pileggi's talks with him. Anthony 'Tony the Ant' Spilotro, Rosenthal's friend from his Chicago childhood and the other main character in *Casino*, also ended in an appropriate way. Spilotro was a 'widow-maker,' a five-foot-five, 135-pound killer who terrified practically everyone he met, backed down to no one, and, in the words of an FBI agent, 'dared you to murder him.' In 1986, Spilotro and his brother Michael were savagely beaten to death and buried in an Indiana cornfield four miles from a farm owned by Joseph J. Aiuppa, ex-boss of the Chicago outfit.

For more than a decade, Rosenthal and Spilotro ran a large proportion of gambling in Las Vegas on behalf of the Chicago families. Both men had gone there when the heat back east became intolerable – Rosenthal in 1967, Spilotro in 1971 – and both brought their particular talents to bear on the scene. Rosenthal, the numbers man, set up the first legal casino sports gambling facilities and acted as the mob's eye-in-the-sky for the gambling operations; he ran the entertainment and even the catering with the same obsessional attention to detail – ten blueberries, no more, no less, to each muffin – as he organized the skimming of the casinos' profits. Spilotro was the enforcer who terrorized anyone who got out of line and took a percentage from the street operators, the bookies, shylocks, dope dealers, and pimps. 'In his first five years in Las Vegas,' Pileggi writes, 'there were more murders committed than in the previous twenty-five.' As a sideline, he brought in a team of stickup men and burglars from Chicago – they were called 'the hole-in-the-wall gang' – to break into houses and jewelry shops and pick up whatever loose cash was around.

So far as the bosses back in Chicago were concerned, Rosenthal and Spilotro were in town to look after the skim – the money illegally siphoned from the casinos' daily take. A number of the casinos had been financed by the mob-controlled Teamsters' Central States Pension Fund, and the investors, Pileggi says, 'wanted their dividends in cash to avoid FBI and IRS problems.' Skimming is a fine art, so Rosenthal brought in an artist, a wizard slot cheat called George Jay Vandermark, who managed to skim between seven and fifteen million dollars out of four casinos in less than three years. For the bosses, it was an ideal arrangement, but Rosenthal and Spilotro let their private lives and enormous egos get in the way of business, and the whole thing, literally, exploded in their faces.

If gambling is a victimless crime, then Rosenthal, unlike Spilotro, was not a criminal. But because he was a known associate of criminals and had a rap sheet for illegal bookmaking and attempted bribery, the Nevada Gaming Commission refused to license him as a 'key executive' to run a casino. A front man was needed, someone with no criminal record, no criminal associates, and preferably no under-standing whatever of criminal activities. The man Chicago picked was Allen Glick, a plump, balding, thirty-one-year-old minor league real-estate developer from San Diego. Glick had originally come to Las Vegas to buy a parking lot. He ended up as the nominal owner of four casinos, with a $62.7 million loan from the Teamsters' pension fund. In those days, the ownership of Vegas casinos was all done with mirrors – companies within companies within companies – but Glick himself was a one-man hall of mirrors. Pileggi quotes a homicide detective who interviewed Glick in his ostentatious, mirror-lined office: 'He was like a zombie. A nonperson. And the mirrors all around the room were reflecting the same nonperson. After a while I began to wonder which of these guys was the real Glick.' In other circumstances Glick would have been a buffoon, an uptight hustler besotted by the trappings of wealth – the company jets, the Olympic-size swimming pool at his California home, the Lamborghini in the garage. But, as Pileggi describes him, he was also transfixed by fear. Anyone who gave him grief was murdered by the mobsters – helpful, perhaps, but also a reminder of what might happen to him – and he himself had been summoned to Kansas City in the middle of the night to be threatened with death by the local mafia boss.

The scene in Kansas City is one of the strongest in Pileggi's *Casino*, and like most of the other scenes it is both fascinating and puzzling. The speaker is supposed to be Glick, yet the voice is utterly unlike the transcripts of Glick's various testimonies. The same is true of the principal narrator, Lefty Rosenthal, who also figures prominently in *The Black Book and the Mob*, an exhaustive sociological study of the 'Black Book,' the Nevada Gaming Commission's register of undesir-ables who were legally forbidden to enter casinos. Rosenthal fought long and hard against being listed in the Black Book, and in the extensive court transcripts he comes across as a powerful witness –

aggressive, fast on his feet, and clever – but grammatical and dramatic
he was not. In Pileggi's version, Rosenthal is like the rest of the cast, a
master storyteller with total recall for conversations that took place
long ago. Will the real Lefty Rosenthal please stand up?

As in his other books about the mob, Pileggi is writing about real
people whose lives and collected works figure in FBI files, court cases,
police and newspaper reports, as well as in the transcripts of the
McClellan Subcommittee on Gambling and Organized Crime. His
method is to let the characters speak for themselves, interweaving their
voices and shifting the focus with great skill to keep the narrative
moving. Pileggi has a fine ear for the rhythm and vitality of gang-
sterspeak – 'I'm driving with my heart in my mouth. I'm swallowing
muscle' – and the book reads wonderfully well provided you remember it is a combination of fact and dramatization, not journalism. The
author never says where or when the interviews took place and,
although he thanks a pageful of people for their help, there are probably
as many others who are quoted extensively and not acknowledged.

The result is a semi-documentary, with interviews recollected in
tranquility, edited and rearranged, real life reconstructed as a gangster
movie. And such a work, of course, has an advantage over fiction
because real life always outstrips the imagination. No one could have
invented a scene in which someone eats pasta while a vise is tightened
around a victim's head until his eyes pop out. But it happens in *Casino*.
Tony Spilotro worked the vise, while Chuckie Nicoletti watched and
ate, and Pileggi somehow makes it all sound terrifically macho, as if to
say, 'See how tough these guys were!'

In the movie of *Casino*, Scorsese keeps the head-squeezing but
omits the spaghetti-eater. But then, he also omits most of the other
details that give Pileggi's book its edge. Glick, who might have been a
richly comic figure, is edited down to a cipher, and Robert De Niro is
fatally miscast as Lefty. Rosenthal (now called Sam 'Ace' Rothstein)
was interesting because he was obsessional, calculating, and also
emotionally stupid. De Niro turns him into just another wiseguy,
hard as nails but good with numbers, and too arrogant to play local
politics. Joe Pesci does much the same with Nicky Santoro, the
character based on Spilotro. In *GoodFellas*, Pesci was terrifying because
he was bewildering; there was no telling when his amiability would tip
over into murderousness. He plays Spilotro on one note, without a
flicker of wit or appetite. His violence is terrible but monotonous.

First-rate directors usually do best when adapting second-rate books because first-rate books induce reverence and cramp their style. Robert Altman made a masterpiece, *M*A*S*H*, out of a negligible novel in the same year, 1970, when Mike Nichols was turning a masterpiece, *Catch-22*, into a grandiose flop. Pileggi is not comparable to Joseph Heller – or even to Elmore Leonard – but his book is well-paced, informed, and hard to put down. None of that survives in the movie, although he and the director wrote the script together. Scorsese's *Casino* is just another Las Vegas spectacular, as noisy and purposeless and, at three hours, as seemingly eternal as the kids' inferno at Circus Circus.

At their best, both Pileggi and Scorsese have a talent for making crime seem sexy, for making the psychopath's affectless violence look like casual wit. But the truth is that Spilotro was a cold-blooded murderer and Rosenthal, in his fastidious way, was a corporate thief. What they did may make for a lively read and an expensive movie, but a lot of people were casually murdered and fortunes were stolen. Shift the perspective just a little and you have a squalid story of greedy, egomaniacal thugs, and a great piece of propaganda for the anti-gambling lobby.

Scorsese's movie ends where *Running Scared*, John L. Smith's biography of the casino owner Steve Wynn, begins: with the dynamiting of the Dunes Hotel and Casino, once the shiniest of the mob's Las Vegas investments. The demolition, which took place in October 1993, was one of the greatest shows the town had ever seen. It was done to make way for yet another of Wynn's pleasure palaces – he already owned the Golden Nugget, the Mirage, and Treasure Island – but Smith sees it as a symbolic gesture: 'With a single command, and $1.5 million in explosives, Wynn will do in thirty seconds what his wiseguy predecessors failed to accomplish in two generations: erase from the skyline and the public's mind the memory of the old mobbed-up Las Vegas.'

Wynn was the right man to press the button because he presents himself as the acceptable face of gambling – immaculately dressed, barbered and smiling – the man who, almost single-handedly, has turned a huckster's paradise into a gangster-free zone.

Smith, who is a highly respected Las Vegas columnist and a fourth-generation Nevadan, is not impressed. For him, Steve Wynn's public image is as much an illusion as the disappearing elephant in the magic act of Siegfried and Roy. In private, the man portrayed by Smith has a vast ego, a short fuse, and dubious connections. The alleged connections – specifically, with the Genovese family – were too questionable for the British Gaming Board, who refused Wynn a license to open a casino in London. Smith himself never suggests that Wynn has had direct dealings with gangsters, but this is not true of some of Wynn's executives. It is naive to think the situation could have been otherwise since one of the duties of a casino executive is to attract high rollers. You don't have to be a mobster to love easy money – that is why people gamble – but mobsters tend to have unusual amounts of untaxed income to dispose of and casinos have traditionally made great laundromats for dirty cash. However strenuously regulated they may be, it is not their business to check the source of every $100 bill that is exchanged for chips.

Smith has been around Vegas too long to have any illusions about the purity of the operation. On the contrary, he admires old-time, casino-owning gamblers, like Moe Dalitz and Benny Binion, who had no pretentions about what they did. What Smith seems to dislike most about Wynn is his Mr. Clean façade, his pretensions to be the Walt Disney of Las Vegas who has transformed the sleazy old joint into a fun place for all the family. It seems a reasonable objection: 'We're not U.S. Steel,' a colleague of Wynn's said. 'And we never will be. We'll always be thought of as an industry on the edge of propitious behavior.' But Wynn is now the emperor of Las Vegas, and notoriously litigious. It took a brave man to question his clothes.

New York Review of Books, 1996

BOOKS

Poetry

Beyond the Gentility Principle

IN 1932 F. R. Leavis proclaimed that Eliot and Pound had between them brought about a significant reorientation of literature. Twenty years later he took most of it back again, blaming the anti-critical workings of the London literary circuit and the decay of an educated reading public. He may have been perfectly justified in crediting the metropolitan pundits with setting up so many false gods. But the relative failure of talent is another matter entirely. So is the manner in which so much of the talent that has arrived has been misused. The London old-boy circuit may often be stupid, conceited and parasitic but I don't believe that it is in a deliberate conspiracy against good work.

I once suggested* that the experimental techniques of Eliot and the rest never really took on in England because they were an essentially American concern: attempts to forge a distinctively American language for poetry. Certainly, since Eliot removed himself into another, remote sphere of influence by proclaiming himself 'Anglo-Catholic in religion, royalist in politics and classicist in literature', the whole movement of English verse has been to correct the balance experimentation had so unpredictably disturbed. Some time in the twenties Thomas Hardy remarked to Robert Graves that '*vers libre* could come to nothing in England. "All we can do is to write on the old themes in the old styles, but try to do a little better than those who went before us."' Since about 1930 the machinery of modern English poetry seems to have been controlled by a series of negative feed-backs designed to produce precisely the effect Hardy wanted.

The final justification of experimentalism lay, of course, beyond mere technique. The great moderns experimented not just to make it new formally, but to open poetry up to new areas of experience. The

---

* In *The Shaping Spirit* (London: Chatto and Windus, 1958).

kind of insights which had already been substantiated by the novelists – by Melville, Dostoevsky, Lawrence and even, at times, by Hardy himself – seemed about due to appear in poetry. The negative feed-backs came into action to stop this happening.

The literary historians perhaps would see the process differently. And the English scene is peculiarly amenable to literary history: it is savage with gang-warfare which, at a distance, can be dignified as disagreements between schools of verse. So maybe a little potted, though rather partial, literary history would be in place.

The thirties poets reacted against those of the twenties by asserting that they had no time to be difficult or inward or experimental; the political situation was too urgent. Auden gave them the go-ahead because he combined an extraordinary technical skill in traditional forms with an extraordinary feel for the most contemporary of con-temporary idiom. When he began it must really have looked as though he were about to do something quite new in English. In a poem like 'Sir, no man's enemy', for example, he used the new, difficult language of psychology with a concentration that was almost Shakespearian; or even in an unambitious piece like 'O lurcher-loving collier, black as night' he managed triumphantly to re-create a traditional lyric – its ancestor is 'O mistress mine, where art thou roaming' – in terms of the contemporary, unromantic, industrial scene. His trouble was that he was too skilful; he found both the art of verse and the art of success too easy. So he was able to channel his deep neurotic disturbances into light verse – much of it, admittedly, very fine – while his contemporary knowingness, his skill with references, with slang, with the time's immediate worries went into the production of a kind of social, occasional verse, mostly traditional in form, but highly up to date in idiom. His example encouraged a whole swarm of poetasters who believed, apparently, that to be modern was merely a matter of sounding modern; it had precious little to do with originality. (I would exclude from this Louis MacNeice, whose social-political verse was mostly more effective and certainly more deeply felt than Auden's own.) By the end of the thirties experimental verse was out and traditional forms, in a chic contem-porary guise, were back in. That was the first negative feed-back.

The reaction to Auden took the form of anti-intellectualism. He was thought to be too clever and not sufficiently emotional for the extreme circumstances of the forties. The war brought with it a taste for high, if obscure, rhetoric. The log-rolling thirties were followed by the drum-rolling forties. The new master, of course, was Dylan

Thomas. But Thomas was not only a fine rhetorician, he also, in his early poems, had something rather original to say. Admittedly, he was under constant pressure from the literary public relations officers to continue at all costs less with his poetry than with his act as the blindly inspired poet; which meant that his rhetoric eventually ran on when the reasons for it had faltered. But the talent was there, however self-destructive it eventually became. His followers, however, used his work as an excuse to kiss *all* meaning good-bye. All that mattered was that the verse should sound impressive. This was the second negative feed-back: a blockage against intelligence.

The third stage was yet another reaction: against wild, loose emotion. The name of the reaction was the Movement, and its anthology was Robert Conquest's *New Lines*. Of the nine poets to appear in this, six, at the time, were university teachers, two were librarians, and one was a civil servant. It was, in short, academic-administrative verse, polite, knowledgeable, efficient, polished, and, in its quiet way, even intelligent. What it had to offer positively was more difficult to describe. Even the editor found he could define it only in negatives:

It submits to no great systems of theoretical constructs nor agglomerations of unconscious commands. It is free from both mystical and logical compulsions and – like the modern philosophy – is empirical in attitude to all that comes. . . . On the more technical side . . . we see the refusal to abandon a rational structure and comprehensible language. . . . It will be seen at once that these poets do not have as much in common as they would if they were a group of doctrine-saddled writers forming a definite school complete with programme and rules. What they do have in common is, perhaps, at its lowest, little more than a negative determination to avoid bad principles.

Mr Conquest is, I think, exaggerating when he says that his poets have nothing very much in common. For example:

> Picture of lover or friend that is not either
> Like you or me who, to sustain our pose,
> Need wine and conversation, colour and light;
> In short, a past that no one now can share,
> No matter whose your future; calm and dry,
> In sex I do not dither more than either,
> Nor should I now swell to halloo the names

Of feelings that no one needs to remember:
The same few dismal properties, the same
Oppressive air of justified unease
Of our imaginations and our beds.
It seems the poet made a bad mistake.

Perhaps the logic seems a little tenuous? The shifts a little hard to follow? The content a little too fine-drawn? They should do. The piece is synthetic; it contains eight of the nine *New Lines* poets. I have omitted D. J. Enright since he rarely sticks to the metrical norms on which the rest insist. Otherwise I have not cheated in compiling the poem. I have taken the poets in the order in which they appear in the anthology, without using more than two lines from any one and without changing the punctuation except, in a minor way, between quotations. Yet though the poem may not be quite comprehensible, it is, I think, unified in tone. Wouldn't the impartial reader be hard put to know where one quotation ended and another began? Wouldn't he find a considerable similarity in the quality both of the language and of the experience? A kind of unity of flatness? The pieties of the Movement were as predictable as the politics of the thirties poets. They are summed up at the beginning of Philip Larkin's 'Church-going':

> *Hatless, I take off*
> *My cycle clips in awkward reverence.*

This, in concentrated form, is the image of the Welfare State Englishman of the late forties and early fifties: shabby and not concerned with his appearance; poor – he has a bike, not a car; gauche but full of agnostic piety; underfed, underpaid, overtaxed, hopeless, bored, wry. This is the third negative feed-back: an attempt to show that the poet is not a strange creature inspired; on the contrary, he is just like the man next door – in fact, he probably *is* the man next door.

Now, I am wholly in favour of restoring poetry to the realm of common sense. But there is always the delicate question of how common common sense should be. All three negative feed-backs work, in their different ways, to preserve the idea that life in England goes on much as it always has, give or take a few minor changes in the class system. The upper-middle class, or Tory, ideal – presented in its pure crystalline form by John Betjeman – may have given way to the predominantly lower-middle class, or Labour, ideal of the Movement and the Angries, but the concept of gentility still reigns supreme. And gentility is a belief that life is always more or less orderly, people always more or less polite, their emotions and habits more or less decent and more or less controllable; that God, in short, is more or less good.

It is a stance which is becoming increasingly precarious to maintain. That the English have succeeded so long owes a good deal to the fact that England is an island; it is, literally, insulated from the rest of the world. But since the First World War, that insulation has slowly broken down. Robert Graves's *Goodbye to All That*, for example, shows perfectly how powerless the orthodox defences ultimately became under extreme conditions. When the level of misery was normal the defences worked efficiently enough. His childhood at preparatory and public school meant loneliness, philistinism, lewdness, insensitivity and unhappiness. These were all to be expected, and Graves duly countered them in the orthodox ways: games, toughness, asexual love, wit, and a clipped, dry, you-can't-touch-me manner. He developed, in short, a stiff upper lip. This got him through the first two years of the war, then gradually it broke. The horror of the trenches was too great. What he saw and what he went through were beyond the bounds of anything his training had prepared him for. Physically he survived, but emotionally he could no longer properly cope. The result was a kind of shell-shock which, he himself says, stayed with him for ten years. And even then he had to exile himself from England and erect the elaborate barricade of White Goddesses and classicizing through which his genuine poetry has only slowly and painfully filtered.

In the same way, George Orwell felt he had to purge himself of his governing-class upbringing by deliberately plunging into the abjectest poverty and pain partly, at least, because what he saw in Burma gave the lie to the whole ethos in which he had been raised.

The only English writer who was able to face the more uncompromising forces at work in our time was D. H. Lawrence. And he was born in the working class and spent most of his life outside England; so he had almost nothing to do with middle-class gentility. 'In those days', he wrote, 'they were always telling me I had genius as though to console me for not having their own incomparable advantages.'

But these forces I have invoked are beyond mere shell-shock and class guilt. They are general and concern us all. What, I suggest, has happened in the last half century is that we are gradually being made to realize that all our lives, even those of the most genteel and en-islanded, are influenced profoundly by forces which have nothing to do with gentility, decency or politeness. Theologians would call these forces evil, psychoanalysts, perhaps, death instinct. Either way, they are the forces of disintegration which destroy the old standards of civilization. Their public faces are those of two world wars, of the concentration camps, of genocide and the threat of nuclear war.

I do not wish to over-dramatize the situation. War and cruelty have always existed, but those of the twentieth century are different in two ways. First, mass evil (for lack of a better term) has been magnified to match the scale of mass society. We no longer have local wars, we have world wars, which involve the civilians quite as deeply as the military. Where once, at worst, regiments of professional soldiers were wiped out, now whole cities go. Instead of the death of individuals, we have a mass extermination. Instead of individual torture and sadism, we have concentration camps run scientifically as death factories. The disintegration, to put it most mildly, has reached proportions which make it increasingly difficult to ignore. Once upon a time, the English could safely believe that Evil was something that happened on the Continent, or farther off, in the Empire, where soldiers were paid to take care of it. To believe this now requires at best an extraordinary single-mindedness, at worst stupidity.

The second, and specifically modern difference in our attitude to the problem is this: the forcible recognition of a mass evil outside us has developed precisely parallel with psychoanalysis; that is, with our recognition of the ways in which the same forces are at work within us. One of the self-therapeutic purposes, for example, of Bruno Buttelheim's secret psychoanalytic observations when he was in Dachau and Buchenwald was to educate himself into realizing how much of what went on around him expressed what went on inside himself. Another analyst has suggested that the guilt which seems to dog the refugees who escaped from Germany may in part be due to the fact that the Nazis fulfilled the deepest and most primitive drives of the refugees themselves, killing fathers, mothers, brothers, sisters and children. Be this as it may, it is hard to live in an age of psychoanalysis and feel oneself wholly detached from the dominant public savagery. In this way, at least, the makers of horror films are more in tune with contemporary anxiety than most of the English poets.

But as England was not affected by the concentration camps, so it has remained, on the whole, contemptuously impervious to psychoanalysis. Primitivism is only generally acknowledged in this country when it takes a peculiarly British form: the domestic sex murder. Then the gloating is public and universal. Had Freud been born in London instead of Vienna, he would probably have finished in criminology.

I am not suggesting that modern English poetry, to be really modern, must be concerned with psychoanalysis or with the concentration camps or with the hydrogen bomb or with any other of the modern horrors. I am not suggesting, in fact, that it *must* be anything. Poetry that feels it has to cope with predetermined subjects ceases to be poetry and becomes propaganda. I am, however, suggesting that it drop the pretence that life, give or take a few social distinctions, is the same as ever, that gentility, decency and all the other social totems will eventually muddle through.

What poetry needs, in brief, is a new seriousness. I would define this seriousness simply as the poet's ability and willingness to face the full range of his experience with his full intelligence and not to take the easy exits of either the conventional response or choking incoherence. Believe in it or not, psychoanalysis has left its mark on poetry. First, the writer can no longer deny with any assurance the fears and desires he does not wish to face; he knows obscurely that they are there, however skilfully he manages to elude them. Second, having acknowledged their existence, he is no longer absolved from the need to use all his intelligence and skill to make poetic sense of them. Since Freud, the late Romantic dichotomy between emotion and intelligence has become totally meaningless.

This position had, I think, already been partially assumed by T. S. Eliot when he wrote *The Waste Land*. The poem follows, with great precision and delicacy, the movement of a psyche, not just of a society, in the process of disintegration. Eliot's talk of classicism, like his use in the poem of literature and theology, was an elaborate and successful defence which forced impersonality on a deeply personal and painful subject. But during the later twenties and thirties in America, Eliot's technical achievements and the radical revaluation of literary tradition that went with them seemed so bewilderingly impressive that the urgently personal uses this technique was put to were overlooked. A whole school of criticism was developed to prove technically that there was no necessary or even significant connection between art and its roots in the artist's life. During the forties, however, when English poetry was at a nadir, there arose in the States a new generation of poets, the most important of whom were Robert Lowell and John Berryman. They had assimilated the lesson of Eliot and the critical thirties: they assumed that a poet, to earn his title, had to be very skilful, very original and very intelligent. But they were no longer concerned with Eliot's rearguard action against the late Romantics; they were, I mean, no longer adherents of the cult of rigid impersonality. So they were able to write poetry of immense skill and intelligence which coped openly with the quick of their experience, experience sometimes on the edge of disintegration and breakdown. Robert Lowell's latest book *Life Studies*, for example, is a large step forward in this new direction. It may contain no single poem as impressive as the 'Quaker Graveyard in Nantucket', but the total impact of the book as a whole is altogether more powerful. Where once Lowell tried to externalize his disturbances theologically in Catholicism and rhetorically in certain mannerisms of language and rhythm, he is now, I think, trying to cope with them nakedly, and without evasion.

But to walk naked is, of course, no guarantee of achievement in the arts – often the contrary. Several pieces in *Life Studies* fail for appearing more compulsively concerned with the processes of psychoanalysis than with those of poetry. Conversely, with their deliberate common sense and understatement, some of the Movement poets command, at their best, a self-contained strength and a concern for the discipline of verse which is vital if the art is to remain public. The question is the kind of success a style allows. Compare, for instance, Philip Larkin's 'At Grass' with Ted Hughes's 'A Dream of Horses':

AT GRASS

> The eye can hardly pick them out
> From the cold shade they shelter in,
> Till wind distresses tail and mane;
> Then one crops grass, and moves about
> – The other seeming to look on –
> And stands anonymous again.
>
> Yet fifteen years ago, perhaps
> Two dozen distances sufficed
> To fable them: faint afternoons
> Of Cups and Stakes and Handicaps,
> Whereby their names were artificed
> To inlay faded, classic Junes –
>
> Silks at the start: against the sky
> Numbers and parasols: outside,
> Squadrons of empty cars, and heat,
> And littered grass: then the long cry
> Hanging unhushed till it subside
> To stop-press columns on the street.

Do memories plague their ears like flies?
They shake their heads. Dusk brims the shadows.
Summer by summer, all stole away,
The starting-gates, the crowds and cries −
All but the unmolesting meadows.
Almanacked, their names live; they

Have slipped their names, and stand at ease,
Or gallop for what must be joy,
And not a fieldglass sees them home,
Or curious stop-watch prophesies:
Only the groom, and the groom's boy,
With bridles in the evening come.

Larkin's poem, elegant and unpretentious and rather beautiful in its gentle way, is a nostalgic re-creation of the Platonic idea of the English scene, part pastoral, part sporting. His horses are *social* creatures of fashionable race meetings and high style; emotionally, they belong to the world of the R.S.P.C.A. It is more skilful but less urgent than 'A Dream of Horses' by Ted Hughes:

We were born grooms, in stable-straw we sleep still,
All our wealth horse-dung and the combings of horses,
And all we can talk about is what horses ail.

Out of the night that gulfed beyond the palace-gate
There shook hooves and hooves and hooves of horses:
Our horses battered their stalls; their eyes jerked white.

And we ran out, mice in our pockets and straw in our hair,
Into darkness that was avalanching to horses
And a quake of hooves. Our lantern's little orange flare

Made a round mask of our each sleep-dazed face,
Bodiless, or else bodied by horses
That whinnied and bit and cannoned the world from its place.

The tall palace was so white, the moon was so round,
Everything else this plunging of horses
To the rim of our eyes that strove for the shapes of the sound.

We crouched at our lantern, our bodies drank the din,
And we longed for a death trampled by such horses
As every grain of the earth had hooves and mane.

We must have fallen like drunkards into a dream
Of listening, lulled by the thunder of the horses.
We awoke stiff; broad day had come.

Out through the gate the unprinted desert stretched
To stone and scorpion; our stable-horses
Lay in their straw, in a hag-sweat, listless and wretched.

Now let us, tied, be quartered by these poor horses,
If but doomsday's flames be great horses,
The forever itself a circling of the hooves of horses.

The poem, by the standard of Hughes's best writing, is not all that good; it is less controlled than Larkin's and has some of the quasi-medieval trappings of the romantic realm of Gormenghast. But it is unquestionably *about* something; it is a serious attempt to re-create and so clarify, unfalsified and in the strongest imaginative terms possible, a powerful complex of emotions and sensations. Unlike Larkin's, Hughes's horses have a violent, impending presence. But through the sharp details which bring them so threateningly to life, they reach back, as in a dream, into a nexus of fear and sensation. Their brute world is part physical, part state of mind.

They have, of course, their literary antecedents: the strange, savage horses which terrorize Ursula Brangwen at the end of *The Rainbow*. But this is part of their wider significance. Dr Leavis has come, apparently, to believe that D. H. Lawrence and T. S. Eliot represent the two warring and unreconcilable poles of modern literature. The best contemporary English verse, however, shows that their influences can be creatively reconciled. In the seriousness of what I have called the new depth poetry, the openness to experience, the psychological insight and integrity of D. H. Lawrence would, ideally, combine with the technical skill and formal intelligence of T. S. Eliot. If this were to happen we would have contemporary work which, like Coleridge's 'Imagination', would re-concile 'a more than usual state of emotion with more than usual order'.

My own feeling is that a good deal of poetic talent exists in England at the moment. But whether or not it will come to anything largely depends not on the machinations of any literary racket but on the degree to which the poets can remain immune to the disease so often found in English culture: gentility.

Introduction to *The New Poetry* (Penguin, 1962)

John Berryman

Delusions, Etc. was already in proof when John Berryman jumped off a bridge in Minneapolis onto the frozen Mississippi last January. So there is no question of its being a ragbag of uncollected work hastily gathered up as a memorial. The book is as he wanted it, the order of its poems and the emotional emphasis all his. Which seems to point to the fact that, up to the end, he was fighting against the way of dying he finally chose. For the emphasis is on the faith he had regained after 43 years away from the Roman Catholic Church. So *Delusions* begins and ends on a religious note, as though to defend himself against his own depression.

In all truth, it is not the religious note of a genuinely religious man. Berryman's poems to God are his least convincing performances: nervous, insubstantial, mannered to a degree and intensely argumentative. It is as though he had continually to reassure himself of his belief, or to reassure the Deity if He happened to be listening. There is, of course, a distinguished tradition for this kind of verse: John Donne and Hopkins, Berryman's great hero, were continually arguing with God in the tone of voice of men who knew that there was a lot to be said on both sides. But Berryman had a quirkier sensibility, less rigorous and logical than associative, diffuse, at times a bit scatterbrained.

He was, heaven knows, an enormously learned man who, unlike most poets on campus, took his professorial duties seriously and could swap footnotes with the best of pedants. But that just made it easier for him to plug the gaps in his arguments with abstruse references. Although Berryman knew a great deal about theology and even more about church history, his poetry was weakest when he set himself up as a religious thinker.

His real gift was different, less armored, less comforting and it emerged only slowly in his maturity. Essentially, it was a gift for grief. He had always been a poet of profound unease, touchy and irritable, as if his nerve ends were too close to the surface. In his early poems this edgy, bristling energy was brought to its own special perfection in the marvelous *Homage to Mistress Bradstreet*, which Edmund Wilson rightly called 'the most distinguished long poem by an American since *The Waste Land*.'

That continual sense of exacerbation, which was the young Berryman's most characteristic note, was expressed in *Homage* largely in the surface of the poem, in a texture compressed, twisted and tensed almost to breaking point. He turned private anguish into an intricate public style. Perhaps he could hardly have done otherwise since, during the fifties, the New Critical dogma of the impersonality of art ruled supreme. By the time he came to write his great cycle of Dream Songs the atmosphere had changed; the poets had become less wary of their emotions and vulnerability, and the public less reluctant to hear about them.

Berryman worked on the Dream Songs for well over a decade, gradually fighting his way clear of the contortions and obscurity of the early songs into something altogether purer and more central. The work began as a fragmentary diary of a middle-aged alcoholic with badly frayed nerves and an unremitting case of morning-after guilt. The man's name was Henry and Berryman strenuously insisted that he was not the poet, despite all the obvious similarities.

As the work progressed, Henry's gripes and hangovers faded away and the work became an extended act of mourning for a whole generation of friends and fellow-writers who had died tragically and before their time. R. P. Blackmur, the oldest, was only 61; none of the others made it beyond their fifties. Theodore Roethke died of a heart attack; Randall Jarrell was a possible suicide; Delmore Schwartz was found dead in a seedy hotel. Berryman wrote elegies on them all, urgent and agonized, as if his poetry were the only way of redeeming the futility of their deaths.

There was a power and richness of response in the second volume of Dream Songs, *His Toy, His Dream, His Rest*, which made it seem he had never before found a subject adequate to what he had to give. It read as though all the previous tension and eccentricity were ways of evading that overpowering 'irreversible loss' he mentioned in the book's preface. And that loss, the poems finally admitted, was the suicide of his father when Henry, like Berryman himself, was still a child. The death of his friends set him free to mourn that first, decisive death, and from there he could move on to his own dying, not simply to accept the inevitability of it but also, in a beautiful series of songs he called 'Opus Posthumous,' to mourn and celebrate it beforehand, in preparation. In the process of writing an elegy on his own brilliant generation, he was also writing an elegy on himself, as if there were no one else he could trust with the task.

The late Dream Songs are Berryman's masterpiece. *Love & Fame*, which came out in 1970, was a letdown in comparison – noisy, ostentatious, uneasy in the awkward sense of being desperately insecure. It seemed to have been written by that tetchy public figure he so often presented to the world: jagged, ambitious, as touchy about other men's success as his own, and passionately absorbed in all that shabby gang warfare which makes the literary life peculiarly unspeakable. The Dream Songs had rightly won him all the prizes, and now he seemed overwhelmed by the adulation which had been denied him too long.

Mercifully, all the noise and posturing has disappeared from *Delusions*. The handful of poems on fellow artists – Emily Dickinson, Georg Trakl, Dylan Thomas and Beethoven – are calmer, subtler. Only in the religious poems is there a reminder of his frantic style. Elsewhere the note is resigned and the theme, once again, is loss. But this time it is his own life, not that of his friends, which seems to be slipping away from him:

> *Age, and the deaths, and the ghosts.*
> *Her having gone away*
> *in spirit from me. Hosts*
> *of regrets come & find me empty.*
> *I don't feel this will change.*
> *I don't want any thing*
> *or person, familiar or strange.*
> *I don't think I will sing*
> *any more just now;*
> *or ever. I must start*
> *to sit with a blind brow*
> *above an empty heart.*

This is the most perfect poem in the book: the language, like the feeling, bleakly pared to the bone. It is a poem from rock bottom, too late for mannerism or for hope, almost too late even for grief: 'I don't think I will sing/any more just now;/or ever.' It doesn't take much hindsight to see that he had reached that state of terminal desolation where suicide began to seem to him not merely possible but inevitable. Perhaps that is why he was so careful to buttress each end of the book with poems to that God in whose eyes suicide is the most mortal of sins. D. H. Lawrence once wrote, 'Never trust the artist, trust the tale.' By these lights Berryman's religious verse seems like a willed, nervous defense against the appalling sadness which permeates the real poems at the heart of the book.

Yet at times the sadness is curiously optimistic. In one of the two belated Dream Songs in *Delusions*, Henry is reading late in Richard Blackmur's house in Maine:

> *Off the coasts was an island, P'tit Manaan,*
> *the bluff from Richard's lawn was almost sheer.*
> *A chill at four o'clock.*
> *It only takes a few minutes to make a man.*
> *A concentration upon now & here.*
> *Suddenly, unlike Bach,*
> *& horribly, unlike Bach, it occurred to me*
> *that one night, instead of warm pajamas,*
> *I'd take off all my clothes*
> *& cross the damp cold lawn & down the bluff*
> *into the terrible water & walk forever*
> *under it out toward the island.*

This, as it turned out, was the style of death he finally chose for himself, or would have chosen had the Mississippi not been frozen over. Yet it isn't quite the dead end, final and irreducible, that he wrote of in the first poem I quoted. In drowning himself, Henry is walking out towards the island. Maybe he will eventually arrive at that lost place in childhood towards which so many of his finest, saddest poems yearn.

Perhaps that is why it seems fitting that the last line of the whole book should be: 'all the black same I dance my blue head off!' Although mourning and melancholia became the great themes of Berryman's poetic maturity, a weird gaiety comes through his work, sometimes manic, always fragile, yet nevertheless irrepressible. It is part of the extraordinary energy which kept him going through all the difficulties he created for himself, particularly his wildly self-destructive bouts with the bottle. It was a kind of intensity of the spirit, buoyant, witty, inventive and, despite his late reconversion, *Delusions* is not particularly religious. It seems a pity that the vitality didn't win out in the end.

But perhaps the whole direction of his work made that impossible. For years I have been extolling the virtues of what I have called extremist poetry, in which the artists deliberately push their perceptions to the very edge of the tolerable. Both Berryman and Sylvia Plath were masters of the style. But knowing now how they both died I no longer believe that any art – even that as fine as they produced at their best – is worth the terrible cost. I doubt if Berryman thought so either. An eyewitness reported that just before he jumped he turned and waved goodbye. He was waving to no one in particular, since he had come to the bridge on his own. Maybe it was his way of saying sorry.

New York Times, 1972

Robert Lowell

ROBERT LOWELL WAS THE last of the brilliant generation of American poets who emerged after the last war – John Berryman, Theodore Roethke, Delmore Schwartz, Randall Jarrell – all of whom died before their time. Although Lowell lived longest, he was only 60 when he collapsed last Monday with a fatal heart attack in a New York taxi-cab.

He was a tall, stooping man with a benign, vaguely puzzled air but shrewd eyes which missed nothing. His thin, floating hair had recently turned white – perhaps because he had spent his last few unhappy years in England. He was born, in 1917, one of the Boston Lowells – who 'talk to the Cabots' – and, like Eliot, he was a Harvard man, though he did not stick it out, finishing at Kenyon College under the poet John Crowe Ransom.

Ransom, Tate and the other Southern poets of the Fugitive School influenced his speaking voice, which was full of strange Southern lifts and drawls, more than his style or his preoccupations. Technically, he was the heir of the great modernists, particularly Eliot, and he began by exploring the rhetorical possibilities of their legacy while adapting it to a sensibility palpably rawer and less protected. From the start, he had an unwavering command of language, an extraordinary range of imagery and a knack of stamping each line with his own utterly individual rhythm.

He published his first two books, *Land of Unlikeness* and *Lord Weary's Castle* in 1944 and 1946, when he was in his middle twenties. They won him all the prizes, including a Pulitzer, and established him immediately as an original, lavishly gifted new talent. This reputation was reinforced by his long poem, *The Mills of the Kavanaughs*, in 1951. All through the fifties Lowell's reputation grew. He became the darling of the New Criticism for which his rich, knotted poems were a godsend with their learning, their literary references and Catholic symbolism (he had been converted in 1940, but left the Church a few years later).

Then, in 1959, came *Life Studies*, a complete and unexpected change of direction and a book as revolutionary and influential in its way as *The Waste Land*. He turned his back on the symbolism and thickly textured Eliot-Jacobean language of his earlier work and began to write clearly, colloquially, about all the subjects which were taboo to the New Critics: his personal strains, domestic conflicts and the periodic breakdowns from which he had suffered for years.

> *Tamed by Miltown, we lie on Mother's bed;*
> *the rising sun in war paint dyes us red;*
> *in broad daylight her gilded bed-posts shine,*
> *abandoned, almost Dionysian.*
> *At last the trees are green on Marlborough Street,*
> *blossoms on our magnolia ignite*
> *the morning with their murderous five days' white.*
> *All night I've held your hand, as if you had*
> *a fourth time faced the kingdom of the mad —*
> *its hackneyed speech, its homicidal eye —*
> *and dragged me home alive . . . oh my Petite,*
> *clearest of all God's creatures, still all air and nerve . . .*

He wrote without nagging or hysteria, and also without abandoning the skill, intelligence and tautness of line of his earlier work. The poems were not less concentrated, they were simply concentrated in a different way and for different ends: to capture lucidly and without rhetoric the experience as it really was, not as it might have been in an ideal poetic world. The result was a kind of transparency: you looked through the poems to see the man as he was, troubled, witty, vulnerable, balancing precariously between tenderness and violence.

In *Life Studies* and the books that followed, Lowell transformed poetry in much the same way as the action painters, who were working in New York at the same time, transformed the visual arts; not by turning it towards abstraction — he once told me that what he was aiming for was 'a sort of Tolstoyan fulness' — but by his determination to cope artistically, with great concentration and directness, with the inner world, or with what another American poet, Hayden Carruth, called 'the existential core.'

In doing so, he altered the whole climate of poetry. His example set free other talented poets, most notably Sylvia Plath, who used the gains he had made to push on in their own different ways into different areas. After *Life Studies*, as after *The Waste Land*, nothing has quite been the same.

In Britain his originality was acknowledged, but grudgingly, as though it were not quite the done thing for a serious poet to lay himself on the line so nakedly. Perhaps this was true of his many minor imitators but with Lowell himself it was to ignore the great discipline and artistry which went into his apparent simplicity, and also to ignore his profound involvement in the technical skills he effortlessly deployed. He was continually rewriting his poems, as though to acknowledge both his own technical dissatisfaction and also the provisional nature of each work when measured against his artistic ambitions.

It was this aesthetic distance and discipline which set him apart from the minor exponents of the so-called 'Confessional' school. It also gave his poems a curiously general, almost impersonal resonance. When he wrote nominally about his own crack-ups he seemed in the process to be describing the symptoms of crack-up in the society around him. In a liberal and individual way he had always been intensely concerned with American politics and history. In 1943, for example, he served five months in a federal prison when he refused to be conscripted because he considered the Allied bombing of European cities morally indefensible. Much later, he turned down an invitation to the White House as a protest against President Johnson's Vietnam policy. He also campaigned strenuously when his friend Senator Eugene McCarthy ran for President. In his trilogy of plays, *The Old Glory*, and later in the poems collected in *History*, he was continually harping on the conflict between American political idealism and American violence.

Life Studies was followed in 1962 by *Imitations*, a brilliant collection of very free translations, then in 1965 by the equally stunning *For the Union Dead*, then by the lyrical but more regular *Near the Ocean* in 1967. After that he began a long series of shorter, tighter poems first collected as *Notebook*, then expanded and republished in three separate volumes, *History*, *For Lizzie and Harriet* and *The Dolphin*. None of these quite achieved the marvellous power and ease of *Life Studies*. He seemed stifled, almost stultified by the condensed forms he had imposed on himself. He abandoned them, however, a couple of years ago and was writing again in the freer, more open style of his best work. A new collection, ·Day by Day, has just appeared in the USA.

He was, I think, the finest poet of his greatly gifted generation – wide-ranging, subtle, powerful – and his influence on contemporary verse has been as profound as anyone's since Eliot. In private, he was a brilliant, allusive talker, and a courteous, most generous friend. He had been married three times, always to talented writers: Jean Stafford, Elizabeth Hardwick and Caroline Blackwood.

Observer, 1977

Sylvia Plath

SYLVIA PLATH BELONGS TO that curious band of poets – it includes Chatterton, Keats, Rimbaud – whose fame is inextricably bound up with their lives. Rimbaud apart, they died prematurely, in the full flower of their talent, 'just as he really promised something great, if not intelligible,' as Byron said of Keats. But Plath's case is more extreme than that of the others. Chatterton committed suicide when he was starving to death and became, as a result, the Romantic symbol of the rejected artist. But at least he didn't write about the act. Neither did Hart Crane or Hemingway or even, in so many words, Virginia Woolf. For Plath, death, and the rage and despair that attend it, were her subject, and she followed the logic of her art to its desolate end. Her last poem, 'Edge,' is literally her own epitaph. Her life and work are not just inextricable, they seem at times virtually indistinguishable.

Although Plath began in the 1950s and never relinquished the discipline and detachment she acquired in her apprenticeship, her work has been overtaken by more contemporary, less choosy attitudes: by the Warhol concept of art as news, as a form of celebrity, of art for gossip's sake. It is as good a way as any of avoiding the full effect of what she wrote. Most people know about her broken marriage, her outrage, her suicide, but I wonder how many of the thousands who fervently identify with the intensely autobiographical heroine of *The Bell Jar* have ever bothered with the difficult, unforgiving, oddly detached late poems.

Plath's case is complicated by the fact that, in her mature work, she deliberately used the details of her everyday life as raw material for her art. A casual visitor or unexpected telephone call, a cut, a bruise, a kitchen bowl, a candlestick – everything became usable, charged with meaning, transformed. Her poems are full of references and images that seem impenetrable at this distance but which could mostly be explained in footnotes by a scholar with full access to the details of her life. Her extraordinary last poems are concentrated and fast-moving; the images develop one from the other, eliding and expanding with the authority and directness of a peculiarly dazzling dream. I think she was able to take these aesthetic risks because the stuff she was transmuting was made up of the commonplaces of her everyday life, glassily clear and obvious to her. Her poetry was a kind of alchemy, turning dross into gold.

Unfortunately, the mundane details of Plath's life are hard to come by. She died in February, 1963, having published one volume of poetry, *The Colossus*, and her novel, which was written under a pseudonym and not much noticed at the time. *Ariel*, a modified version of a selection she had made of her late poems, appeared in 1965 to great acclaim. In 1971, *The Bell Jar* was published in the USA and became a best-seller. In the same year, two further selections of her later poetry appeared, but it was another ten years before the *Collected Poems* was published and won her, posthumously, the 1982 Pulitzer Prize for poetry. In 1975 came *Letters Home*, a heavily edited and abridged selection of her letters to her mother. In 1982, the journals which she had kept from her youth until the last days of her life were published – but only in the USA, only in excerpts, and with the crucial last couple of years missing. The novel she was working on when she died disappeared.

The tantalizing way in which the work dribbled out over the years, combined with the vivid use Plath made of her experience and the sanitized hints that could be pieced together from *Letters Home* and the journals, created a great need for a full biography. Plath's writing had provided her own version of her life and there was no way of checking artistic license against the hard facts. But a full-scale biography meant unlimited access to written materials and because Plath died intestate the rights to these were controlled by the Hughes estate. That meant, in effect, by her sister-in-law Olwyn Hughes, since her husband Ted Hughes has steadfastly refused to be involved in the biographical wrangling. Olwyn Hughes, however, seems to have been unwilling to cooperate with any biographer who did not share her point of view.

The experience of Linda Wagner-Martin seems to have been typical:

Olwyn was initially cooperative, and helped me in my research by answering questions herself and referring me to others who could be of assistance. As Olwyn read the later chapters of the book, however, and particularly after she read a draft of the manuscript in 1986, her cooperation diminished substantially. Olwyn wrote me at great length, usually in argument with my views about the life and development of Plath. Ted Hughes responded to a reading of the manuscript in draft form in 1986 with suggestions for changes that filled fifteen pages and would have meant a deletion of more than 15,000 words.

Of necessity I continued to correspond with Olwyn Hughes in order to obtain permission to quote at length from Plath's work. But on every occasion Olwyn objected to the manuscript, frequently citing Ted Hughes's comments (although . . . Ted Hughes refused to be interviewed directly for the book). I did make many changes in response to these comments. However, the requests for changes continued, and I concluded that permissions would be granted only if I agreed to change the manuscript to reflect the Hughes's points of view. When I realized that this tactic would continue indefinitely, I had to end my attempt to gain permission to quote at length if I was ever to publish this book.

Professor Wagner-Martin went ahead and published anyway, with a minimum of quotation, a mildly feminist but otherwise careful and even-handed account of the life. But she relied heavily on *Letters Home* and *Letters Home* is as much a work of fiction as *The Bell Jar*. Plath had a highly ambiguous and defensive relationship with her mother. She was not willing to allow her to see anything but the bouncy, straight-As, Phi Beta Kappa success and the possibility of appearing a failure was not something she could tolerate. One of the direst aspects of the break-up of her marriage was that her mother was on hand to witness her humiliation: 'The horror of what you saw and what I saw you see last summer is between us,' she wrote, 'and I cannot face you again until I have a new life.'

The good girl image of *Letters Home* may have been appropriate to Plath when she was serving her apprenticeship as a poet and the aesthetic ideal was the Parnassian high style of Wallace Stevens, polished, marmoreal, referring only to itself. Plath wrote some beautiful poems in this manner and the skills she acquired in doing so were vital to her mature work. But there is only a tenuous connection between the good girl and the impassioned, highly original artist she became.

More important, the competent, positive image that Plath took such pains to construct for her mother's benefit collapsed when her husband left her. Professor Wagner-Martin used this twist in the plot to point a feminist moral about male authority, marriage and victimization. Apart from that, her portrait of Plath was admiring and forgiving in precisely the way official biographies are supposed to be. The Plath estate thought otherwise and commissioned Anne Stevenson, an English-based American poet, to write an authorized version. Ms Stevenson, however, seems not altogether willing to take full responsibility for the outcome. She writes in an Author's Note, 'This biography of Sylvia Plath is the result of a three-year dialogue between the author and Olwyn Hughes, agent to the Plath Estate. Ms Hughes has contributed so liberally to the text that this is in effect a work of joint authorship.'

It might be reasonable to suppose that the agent to the estate of a best-selling author would want a biography that portrayed its subject in a good light. Far from it. The purpose of *Bitter Fame* is to correct the nice girl image projected in *Letters Home* and to present Plath as the engineer of her own destruction. In broad outline, the argument is simple: Plath was profoundly disturbed from the start and her sickness increased exponentially over the years. The first chapter is called 'The Girl Who Wanted to be God' and its first section ends:

> By the time Sylvia was a senior in high school she was already dependent on writing and success in publishing for social survival. She was afflicted, not with too much sense of her own value, but with too little. Wherever she was, that little pronoun 'I' which traveled around with her had to be bolstered, propped up by social approval, or she became, in her extreme words, a 'zero,' a 'hollow nothing.' Haunted by a fear of her own disintegration, she kept herself together by defining herself, writing constantly about herself, so that everyone could see her there, fighting and conquering an outside world that forever threatened her frail being.

Thereafter the picture builds steadily of a sick and fragile personality, probably borderline psychotic, subject to unreasonable and unreasoning rages and fits of jealousy, exaggerated enthusiasms and inky depressions, who spent her life secretly raging against a father who had abandoned her by dying when she was eight years old. In this scenario, her suicide becomes a final act of revenge, a vindictive evening of scores with the once beloved dead, and an act from which all the good will in the world could never have saved her. In case we miss the point, the book's final chapter is called 'Getting There' and it culminates in a statement by the doctor who was looking after her during her last months in London:

> I believe, indeed it was repeatedly obvious to me, that she was deeply depressed, 'ill,' 'out of her mind,' and that any explanations of a psychological sort are inadequate . . . I believe . . . she was liable to large swings of mood, but so excessive that a doctor inevitably thinks in terms of brain chemistry. This does not reduce the concurrent importance of marriage break-up or of exhaustion after a period of unusual artistic activity or from recent infectious illness or from the difficulties of being a responsible, practical mother. The full explanation has to take all these factors into account and more. But the irrational compulsion to end it makes me think that the body was governing the mind.

The doctor, it should be noted, has things several ways but ends up by making the body decisive. If her final suicide was brought on by 'brain chemistry,' then nothing and no one could have saved her and nobody was to blame.

The doctor himself had done everything he could: he saw her regularly up to the very end, tried unsuccessfully to get her into hospital, and arranged for help, both domestic and psychiatric. Despite all his precautions, 'she slipped through the net' and, like everyone else involved in the tragedy, he was devastated. It is also clear from the evidence that by the end of her last weekend (she gassed herself around 6 am on a Monday morning) she was, in truth, beyond help. The last person to see her alive was Professor Trevor Thomas, who lived in the flat below hers, and the person he saw sounds like someone undergoing a psychotic episode. She rang his bell around midnight, asking to buy stamps and insisting on paying 'or I won't be right with my conscience before God.' Ten minutes later he opened his door and found her still in the freezing hallway, standing as if in a trance. When he offered to call a doctor she refused, saying, he wrote, 'she was having a wonderful dream, a marvellous vision.'

Yet however far gone she was at the end, she also possessed enormous powers of recovery and was in touch with an incomparably rich inner world. Whence the power and beauty of her last poems, and also their extraordinary detachment. In her very last poem, 'Edge,' she imagined her children dying with her (in life she took elaborate precautions to make sure they did not):

> She has folded
> Them back into her body as petals
> Of a rose close when the garden
> Stiffens and odours bleed
> From the sweet, deep throats of the night flowers.

What matters here is not the Medea-like tragedy but the uncanny artistic detachment that allows the imagery to develop its own lucid, calm life. I can think of no better example of Coleridge's description of genius at work: 'unparticipating in the passions, and activated only by that pleasurable excitement, which had resulted from the energetic fervour of his own spirit in so vividly exhibiting what it had so accurately and profoundly contemplated.' 'Edge' was written on February 5, 1963, six days before Plath died. Whatever else, it is not the work of someone who is 'out of her mind' or governed by a rogue 'brain chemistry.'

Bitter Fame's other method of correcting the nice girl image of *Letters Home* is to demonstrate in detail how Plath's psychological instability turned her into a monster. To this end, Mss Stevenson and Hughes are unwavering in their single-mindedness. We are told of her 'enormous hostility,' 'egoistic fantasizing' and 'romantic self-aggrandizing,' that 'she was indeed cruel.' We hear of her 'exercising her talent for rewriting life to suit her audience,' 'her latent paranoia,' 'her psychological blindness,' and that she 'was drawn to Peter [Davison] chiefly for reasons advantageous to herself.' (This is, incidentally, 'A Peter Davison Book'.) When she took dancing lessons before going to Cambridge the authors comment, 'Alas, for all its medieval splendors, Cambridge was to have little to offer in the way of tango-dancing intellectuals,' and when Plath failed to find her boyfriend Richard Sassoon in Paris she is said to have been 'missing Richard's purse as much as his presence.' As to her famous, headlong marriage to Ted Hughes: 'Clearly, Sylvia wanted to secure Ted before he went alone to teach in Spain.' Of her often brilliant journals, they comment, 'One side of her reached back for a harmonious home life and commercial success; another abandoned itself to moony fantasies, black, silent furies or imaginary scenes of violence.'

Plath's own ambition was immense but she also believed passionately in her husband's genius and worked hard to get his poems published, typing them up and sending them out continually. When his first book, *The Hawk in the Rain*, won the New York Poetry Center competition – for which she, not he, had entered it – she wrote delightedly to her mother to tell her the news, adding that his success would make life easier for her when her own work was accepted; this is described as 'gloating.'

A little later we read, 'As always when under attack (or imagined attack), Sylvia fought back viciously,' that 'though not a ballerina, [she] nevertheless took pride in acting the prima donna throughout her life,' that she 'could never resist the gratuitous dig' (a nice one, that, in the circumstances), that 'her ambition to produce a publishable story or poem seemed to cancel out any normal regard for people's sensibilities, however dear to her the people were.' A friend of Olwyn Hughes is wheeled on to describe 'the sheer quantity of distress Sylvia was capable of causing her nearest and dearest. Her aggression was relentless.' A friend of Ted's grudgingly admits 'she very evidently loves him in the self-interested and possessive way of which she is capable,' and Davison describes her 'borderguard standards' and 'pointed malice.' We also get 'her gift for malice,' her 'character-istically extreme language,' and her 'irrational and uncontrollable rage.' There are also three references to Plath as a witch.

As for the poems: 'Rival' is called 'malevolent exorcism,' 'Mystic' 'the poem . . . of an uncompromising child,' and 'The Jailor' is 'frenetic overkill.' In 'Event' and 'Rabbit Catcher' 'she was making her self-justifying and unforgiving case in much the same terms as henceforth she would use to sow the seeds of the myth of her martyrdom.' 'Fever 103,' 'Purdah,' and 'Lady Lazarus,' 'penetrating the furthest reaches of disdain and rage, are bereft of all normal "human" feeling.'

But the cruellest dig of all is the comment on her pathetic, passing fantasy of having her mother move to Devon to be near her after her marriage failed: 'Clearly Sylvia, with her long-term future as a writer in mind, was angling for a baby-sitter as well as a supportive mother (and typist) who would live close at hand.'

In more than 350 pages of catty disparagement, nothing is said of Plath's charm, which was considerable, nor of her quizzical intelli-gence and profound love of poetry, nor of her courage and resilience in her last ghastly months.

But Mss Stevenson and Hughes's contribution to the demythologizing of Sylvia Plath is mild compared to the 25-page memoir by Dido Merwin, which is quoted extensively in the text and printed complete as an appendix to *Bitter Fame*. Mrs Merwin, we are told without any irony at all, 'had been brought up in what could be termed the English intellectual Squirearchy. However scanty her formal education, her conditioning had bestowed on her the advantages of an insider in the Georgian circles in which her family moved . . . Given her innate sense of belonging (something Sylvia never had), Dido easily attracted the attention of poets by admiring them and amusing them.' It is obvious there would have been no love lost between a condescending English dilettante with an eye for poets and a hard-driven, insecure and in some ways naive American professional writer like Plath. Whatever real or imagined outrages transpired, Mrs Merwin has apparently been waiting 25 years to get her own back. Her memoir is a work of sustained and quite astonishing venom and what is most tasteless about it is not that it should have been written about someone who can no longer defend herself but that it should be published in a biography commissioned and approved by the Plath estate.

Since her death, Plath has become a feminist cause, canonized as a great woman artist who was abused, put upon and betrayed by men. On every level, this is the crudest sentimentality and I suspect Plath, who liked men and trusted them, would not have appreciated it. Although she had close women friends in her last months – Elizabeth Compton, Winifred Davies, Susan O'Neill-Roe, Ruth Fainlight, Clarissa Roche, Jillian Becker (none of whom, apart from Mrs Becker, are given much space here) – *Bitter Fame* demonstrates in great detail that, both living and dead, Plath had a great deal more to fear from her own sex than from any man.

Ted Hughes himself has wisely kept his distance from this deconstruction of his wife's reputation. 'I have read through the text simply to check, and if necessary correct, the limited number of facts of which I can be reasonably certain,' he writes. 'That leaves the main bulk of the book to other people's reports, opinions, and interpretations, for which I take no responsibility.' In the troubled circumstances, this is the sanest response. Hughes has been much abused by the lunatic fringe of feminism. They have picketed him with placards blaming him for his wife's death and have so frequently defaced Plath's gravestone, trying to eliminate her married name, that she now lies in an unmarked grave. His crime is to have left her for another woman, although, if the evidence *Bitter Fame* amasses of her possessiveness, jealousy and insecurity is only fractionally true, he seems to have been motivated less by treachery than sheer despair. I myself have always believed, as Robert Graves wrote of another tragic couple, 'the hazards of their love-bed/Were none of our damn business.' Couples break up all the time and precipitate young marriages often lead to precipitate mutual unhappiness. Plath herself was sufficiently aware of this truism to seek help once a week from a therapist when she and her husband were in America.

Perhaps therapy helped her get in touch with some of her hidden drives and fears but the more important influence, I think, was her husband's own poetry. When they first joined forces Hughes was a far more mature poet than Plath. He was not only gifted with marvelous powers of observation, he also seemed in his finest poems – 'The Otter,' 'Pike,' 'Hawk Roosting' – to be in direct communication with his deepest instincts, with the dark underside of his imagination. I suspect that Plath was inspired by his example to try to do the same and what she found was very hard to handle.

When her father died Mrs Plath, we are told, 'fastidiously spared' her children his funeral. So Plath never had the chance to mourn him properly and all her natural grief and outrage at the terrible loss festered unaired below the bright, hardworking, brittle surface she presented to the world. Her earlier poems kept resolutely to that surface. They were always elegant and stylish, sometimes brilliant, but only rarely and briefly did they manage to engage the forces that really shook her being. In their different ways, both Hughes and Robert Lowell broke through the aesthetic carapace of '50s high style and tried to explore the volatile depths below. When Plath followed their example she tapped a great reservoir of pain that came roaring to the surface when her marriage broke up. As her biographers put it, in their characteristically snide way, Hughes 'became a facet, in her psychodrama, of the huge figure of Otto Plath, who also "deserted" her. This, in essence, was the myth she propagated in the marvelously achieved voice of Ariel.'

In the end, the myth matters a great deal less than the achieved voice. All the hard-won discipline of her long apprenticeship was taken for granted and what emerged was a free and utterly original voice of extraordinary range and power, a voice that shifted from ominousness, through anger, tenderness and fear, to the stillness and desolation of her final days. In poems like 'The Arrival of the Bee Box' and 'The Applicant' she even managed to master the accents of those sophisticated London *poules de luxe* who had given her, socially, such a hard time – contemptuous, sardonic, arrogant, the voice of a woman who has ordered her own death from Harrods and is appalled to see the delivery van arrive.

The artistic achievement of these last poems makes nonsense of the idea of Plath as a passive victim, abused by men and circumstances. Only in the last few days of her life did her courage and resourcefulness give way to paralyzing depression. Up until then, despite her upset and her anger, she seemed intent on making a new start out of the end of her marriage and she talked about it as a kind of freedom: 'Psychologically . . .' she wrote to Ruth Fainlight, 'I am fascinated by the polarities of muse-poet and mother-housewife. When I was "happy" domestically I felt a gag in my throat. Now that my domestic life . . . is chaos, I am living like a Spartan, writing through huge fevers and producing free stuff I had locked in me for years. I feel astounded and very lucky.' Perhaps she was whistling in the dark but she had the poems to prove she had turned personal disaster into a triumph. 'I am a genius of a writer,' she wrote to her mother; 'I have it in me. I am writing the best poems of my life; they will make my name.' She was right, of course, and apart from the fact that she did not live to enjoy the success she wanted so badly, the only tragedy is that the cult of Sylvia Plath is based on the suicide rather than on the pure, disciplined, hard-edged poems that were more intolerant of weakness in herself than in other people. *Bitter Fame* apparently sets out to destroy the myth, to expose her feet of clay and cut her down to size – but it does so vengefully, as though the myth were a fabric of Plath's own creation. It isn't. It depends wholly on the power of her work and if she has been badly served by the myth, that is because the myth is a great deal less interesting than the astounding poetry she wrote.

New York Review of Books, 1989

Ted Hughes

WHEN SYLVIA PLATH COMMITTED suicide, early in the morning on 11 February, 1963, she ceased to be merely a poet and became, like Thomas Chatterton, a symbol, a warning, a myth. Their importance had very little to do with their work; it didn't matter that Chatterton was a precocious faker who wrote nothing now worth reading and Plath was a genius at the height of her powers. For the Romantics, Chatterton was 'the marvellous boy' who was destroyed by an indifferent public (he was starving to death when he swallowed arsenic, in 1770). For the feminists, Plath was a terrible example of the raw deal women must expect in a world dominated by men. Ted Hughes, they said, married her, then dumped her for another woman when she became troublesome, leaving her to cope on her own with their children and her demons.

I doubt if Plath would have seen herself that way. She was too talented and ambitious to want preferential treatment and, by the end, when the poems were pouring out unstoppably, sometimes three a day, she was too convinced of her achievement to need anyone's say-so. It was Hughes who was left with the consequences: public accusations of murder and treachery, his name hacked off her tombstone again and again.

Despite the provocation, he has kept silent. Since Plath's death, Hughes has become Britain's Poet Laureate – the first major poet to hold the post since Tennyson – and has published a dozen collections of poetry and five books of prose, as well as anthologies and a number of books for children. But he has written very little about his wife, nothing at all about their life together, and refuses to speak to biographers or scholars or journalists.

For his detractors, Hughes's silence is another sign of his callousness; his supporters say it is the only dignified way of coping with intrusiveness and malice. The publication of *Birthday Letters* shows that his reticence was for public consumption only and for the last twenty years he has been gradually telling himself the story of his life with Plath in poems, the art-form he understands best and, unlike prose, one that will not run away with him.

Birthday Letters is an extraordinary book, a sequence of fairly short poems that reads like a novel. What Plath called 'the peanut-crunching crowd,' who want the gossip and don't much care for poetry, won't see it that way. To understand the narrative the reader needs to have read a biography of Plath and to know her work. Hughes's poems are full of references to hers – quotes, echoes, quick allusions. One or two – 'The Rabbit Catcher,' for example – are even straight rewritings, the same incident viewed from the other side of the mirror. In other words, they are scenes from a marriage, Hughes's take on the life they shared. Plath's version is in her last poems; part of her genius lay in her ability to take any trivial domestic incident and infuse it with significance. Hughes is doing something similar but his subject is Plath herself – how she looked and moved and talked, her pleasures, rages, uncanny dreams and many terrors, what was good between them and where it went wrong. He takes the bare bones on which the biographies have been hung – Cambridge, Spain, America, Devon – and does what no biographer, however diligent and impartial, could ever do: he describes what it felt like to be there with her.

Plath was a Fulbright scholar at Cambridge when they met. This was in 1956, when life in England was still pinched and deprived, though she hated the unheated houses and lousy plumbing less than the snobbery and crushing put-downs. Hughes was not that kind of superior Englishman. Although he had been at Cambridge, he was a northerner, a country boy who knew about foxes and otters and hawks, and she had already fallen for his poetry before she met him. The attraction between them was mutual, their courtship brief and dramatic. For Hughes, Plath was 'beautiful, beautiful America,' a land of impossible plenty. His first intimation of her coincided with 'the first fresh peach I had ever tasted. / I could hardly believe how delicious. / At twenty-five I was dumbfounded afresh / By my ignorance of the simplest things.' He seems never quite to have lost his sense of her foreignness and freedom, as though she had been cast in some more generous mold that made him feel shabby. When they married he was 'a post-war, utility son-in-law' and she was 'transfigured. / So slender and new and naked, / A nodding spray of wet lilac.'

In fact, she was a girl with a load of troubles on her back: a suicide attempt that had almost succeeded, a nightmare series of electro-convulsive shock treatments and, behind all that, an adored Prussian father who scared her stiff and died when she was eight. Hughes calls her father 'The Minotaur' and a large number of the 'Birthday Letters' chart Plath's gradual, fatal descent into his lair. As he describes it, it was Hughes who showed her how to get there and he did it in the name of poetry.

Plath was already an accomplished poet when she met Hughes. She had won prizes and published at least as much as he had. Her poems were skilful, polished but frozen, 'thin and brittle, the lines cold,' he says. In comparison, Hughes had already arrived; he had a hot line open to whatever it was that made him tick. It didn't matter that sometimes he used mumbo-jumbo to get where he wanted to be – astrology, hypnosis, ouija boards or the dottier forms of Jungian magical thinking. All that mattered was that the poems he fished out of the depths were shimmering with life, while the life in Plath's work was still locked away out of sight. Finally, provoked by his wife's violence into blind rage, he unwittingly handed her the key she had been looking for: ' "Marvellous!" I shouted, "Go on, / Smash it into kindling. / That's the stuff you're keeping out of your poems!" ' Always the good student, she did what she was told: she went down into the cellarage, key in hand. But the ghouls she released were malign. They helped her write great poems, but they destroyed her marriage, then they destroyed her.

Naturally, both of them behaved badly as the marriage disintegrated and Hughes makes no attempt to justify or excuse himself. He also doesn't soften her violent rages and jealousy or blur her crippling fears or make their life together seem other than a crazy highwire act – one slip and they were in the abyss. Quite simply, he is too good a poet and the form won't let him; poems are all about tone, and sentimentality would kill them dead. This is particularly true of *Birthday Letters* which sound curiously like Plath's late poems – tightly controlled despite their apparently free form, packed with images, fast-talking and full of foreboding. Hughes had helped Plath find her true voice, she had learned well and by the end she had overtaken him; her last poems were fiercer than his, cleaner and more original. Now, after a glum spell when his duties as Poet Laureate seemed to have got the better of him, she has helped him rediscover his full, delicate range. As I said, the book is about a shared life.

Some of the poems in *Birthday Letters* are as good as any Hughes, Britain's finest living poet, has ever written. They are also the saddest: all that love and talent gone to waste, her death, his grief. I wonder what would have happened if her second suicide attempt had failed like the first and she had somehow got out from under the shadow of her terrifying, dead father and had lived to be sixty-something and famous. It would be good to think that, like Hughes, she would have been able to write about her old love so generously and with such tenderness.

The New Yorker, 1998

Philip Larkin: Anthologist

THE OXFORD BOOKS OF sixteenth, seventeenth, eighteenth and nineteenth century verse are placid respectable tomes, scholarly, useful and incapable of giving offence to anyone. But the Clarendon Press has not had much luck with the present century. Their first attempt, edited by W. B. Yeats in 1936, was a monster of misrepresentation. Every anthology is a form of covert literary criticism; the editor is not merely choosing poems he likes, he is also passing judgment on the relative importance of his elect by the amount of space he allots to each. In Yeats's vision of judgment Edith Sitwell became the major poet of the age. He gave her 18 pages, three times as many as D. H. Lawrence or Ezra Pound, both of whom rated no more than Yeats's mystical friend A.E. Second to Sitwell came another friend, Dorothy Wellesley (who?), with 15 pages. Eliot and Yeats himself scored 12, Thomas Hardy a mere three and a half. The great poets of the war, Wilfred Owen and Isaac Rosenberg, did not appear because, Yeats announced in his plummy prose, 'passive suffering is not a theme for poetry.'

Philip Larkin's *Oxford Book of Twentieth Century English Verse* rights at least some of these wrongs. Hardy now gets 24 pages, the same as Auden and second only to Eliot's 29. Yeats has 21, Kipling 19. Poor Lawrence, however, still comes off relatively badly with 10 pages, the same as the unspeakable Sir John Squire. Larkin, by any reckoning one of the best poets around, allows himself only six pages, just one more than Donald Davie and one and a half less than John Wain, which is modesty indeed. Otherwise, he springs only one major Dorothy Wellesley-style surprise: he allots 18 pages to Sir John Betjeman, placing the Master of Metroland sixth in the contemporary immortality stakes.

Hardy, Kipling, Betjeman: clearly, Larkin is putting his emphasis on the Englishness of twentieth century English verse, on the native tradition that has continued despite the other, cosmopolitan, modernist tradition which descended from Eliot and Pound largely through the Americans whom Larkin, like Yeats, does not include. I suppose this is a valid perspective, particularly at this lateish point in the century when the ways of English and American poetry seem finally to have parted. But it produces a curious narrowness of range and tone, a feeling that, although over 200 poets get in, something important has nevertheless been left out.

As you would guess from his own poetry, Larkin has a preference not just for the restrained but also for the local, for those with an eye for the tiny particulars of a scene and an ear for the nuances of talk at a specific moment of time – in other words, for those who use English almost as though it were a regional dialect. Presumably this is why he includes so many examples of verse by novelists and essayists who were never poets: Eden Phillpotts, Arnold Bennett, Max Beerbohm, J. C. Powys, Gilbert Frankau, Francis Brett Young, V. Sackville-West, L. A. G. Strong, C. S. Lewis, Christopher Isherwood, George Orwell, Christopher Caudwell, Malcolm Lowry, Alan Sillitoe. Although his sense of place does not extend to Ireland – Patrick Kavanagh gets three pages, Thomas Kinsella a derisory 12 lines – the book seems, in the end, not so much an anthology of the century's best English poetry as a kind of social history in verse.

Unfortunately, Larkin's interesting taste for whatever is regional and period goes with an altogether less lovable distaste for work with its roots in the more ambitious modernist tradition. He likes his Auden casual not concentrated and, apart from Eliot, whom history has already chosen for him as the age's greatest poet in this language, he has little time for anything that is obscure, oblique or experimental. The most disgraceful example of this bias is Larkin's treatment of Geoffrey Hill, one of the few genuinely gifted and original poets now writing: he is allowed only one 16-line poem, published over 20 years ago when Hill was still an undergraduate. It would have been less insulting to have left him out altogether, and also, perhaps, more consistent with the editor's principles.

Randall Jarrell once wrote of the art of anthologising, 'You may leave out James Whitcomb Riley because you are afraid of being laughed at, but if you leave out Spenser you mean business.' Larkin has it both ways. He is clearly not afraid of being laughed at since he finds room for doggerel by G. D. H. Cole and 'Sagittarius' (Olga Miller); he even includes two pages of J. B. S. Haldane's jolly ruminations on cancer:

> *My final word, before I'm done,*
> *Is 'Cancer can be rather fun.'*
> *Thanks to the nurses and Nye Bevan*
> *The NHS is quite like heaven. . . .*

To my knowledge, this is the worst poetry in any anthology outside *The Stuffed Owl.*

Yet Larkin also, unmistakably, means business. He has collected together the work of more than 200 writers – it would be confusing to call them all poets – but still chooses to leave out old masters like David Jones and Samuel Beckett, as well as a number of the most interesting younger poets: Christopher Middleton, Edwin Morgan, Roy Fisher, Ian Hamilton and Seamus Heaney.

In his brief and pleasantly unpretentious introduction Larkin disclaims a detailed knowledge of the present-day scene. But that, finally, is no excuse; in these distinguished circumstances, someone should have told him, for there is no way in which this book can be read merely as a collection of Larkin's private and personal favourites. It is, quite simply, far too big. By including 584 poems by 207 poets he is implying, at least, some final and comprehensive view of the subject. After all, at no point in history have there ever been 207 *real* poets at work in one country; indeed, it would be hard enough to find a period which produced 207 *real* poems. Given the prestige of these Oxford anthologies, Larkin is pronouncing, whether he intended to or not, a definitive last word on the situation of modern English verse. He is responsible to all the schoolchildren who will have to slog through the book, and to all the vaguely interested, vaguely literary readers who don't know what they like and want to be told, and will ask for it for Christmas and birthdays. And this means that Larkin is responsible not just for his stunning omissions but also for his misrepresentations: Isaac Rosenberg, Hugh MacDiarmid, Keith Douglas, Alun Lewis, Henry Reed, William Empson and F. T. Prince, as well as poets I have already mentioned like Lawrence, Hill and Larkin himself, are vastly better than their slim representation here implies.

But perhaps Larkin is not to blame; perhaps this particular job is impossible. Given the necessary scholarship, it is easy to compile an anthology of poets long dead whom history has already ground down to size. The living and recently deceased are a good deal more recalcitrant. Instead of lying politely down, they crowd round the anthologist, often literally. At worst, he was at university with them, or has drunk with them in pubs, or feels sorry for them because he knows about their sordid private lives. At best, he owes them a debt of gratitude or nostalgia because he read them at an impressionable or poignant time. In any event, he shares their world.

As a result, any modern anthology has to be partisan, reflecting not just the editor's taste, or lack of it, but also his prejudices and, if he is a gifted poet like Larkin, the whole framework of values and habits out of which he has created his own art. The editor himself is in the book deeper than he admits, deeper than he knows. All of which makes for an illuminating, if infuriating choice.

But this, alas, is not the brief for an Oxford Book of anything. What is required is something synoptic and dignified, a comprehensive roll-call of the honoured almost dead to go with the memorial blue covers and gold lettering. Larkin has not provided that and never could have, although he has at least been fairer in his attempt than Yeats. His massive, mildly eccentric book has merely the trappings of authority, not the discrimination. He would have done better to settle for a larger selection from, at most, the three or four dozen poets he really likes: the Larkin Book of Modern Verse. Meanwhile, the poor reader who wants to know if poetry is alive and well, and where it is living, will have to go on shopping around as usual.

Observer, 1973

Thom Gunn

THOM GUNN PUBLISHED HIS first collection of poems, *Fighting Terms*, in 1954. He had graduated from Cambridge the previous year, but nearly all the poems in the book had been written while he was still an undergraduate. I was at Oxford at the time and, even now, I can remember the mixture of astonishment, pleasure and plain envy with which I first read a poem by Gunn in one of the little magazines we all wrote for. It was called 'Helen's Rape' and it began with a 'Now-hear-this' authority that reminded me of John Donne:

> *Hers was the last authentic rape:*
> *From forced content of common breeder*
> *Bringing the violent dreamed escape*
> *Which came to her in different shape*
> *Than to Europa, Danae, Leda:*
>
> *Paris. He was a man . . .*

This, I thought (and still think), was what the new poetry should sound like – powerful, confident, allusive, with the swagger of a young poet who has something original to say and an authentic voice to say it in, loud and clear.

The poems in *Fighting Terms* seemed especially miraculous in England in the miserable 1950s. Times were hard all over, of course: in the States, Senator McCarthy and the House Un-American Activities Committee were on the rampage, and Stalinists ruled the roost in the Latin Quarter, as well as in the Soviet Union and Eastern Europe. Yet, in retrospect, the '50s in the USA have begun to look like the decade when the American dream came true – a time of prosperity, full employment, moral certainty and calm, poor on civil rights but strong on civil rectitude – a kind of well-mannered and well-managed paradise, soon to be lost. It was also prime time for the arts in America: the Abstract Expressionist painters were at their peak and a dazzling generation of young writers were hitting their stride – Lowell, Berryman, Roethke, Cheever, Bellow, Mailer, Malamud, Roth and Updike.

It wasn't like that in England. The country was exhausted by the battering it had taken in the Second World War, demoralized by the loss of its empire and its status as a world power, and life in general was pinched and deprived. The conveniences Americans took for granted – plentiful food and central heating – were still luxuries most British citizens scarcely dreamed of and secretly despised. In those pre-Thatcher days, the British were not yet interested in pig-heaven. On the contrary, deprivation suited them fine. It was what they had been trained for, particularly the males of the species who had done time at expensive boarding schools. The battle of Waterloo was won on the playing fields of Eton, but only because Waterloo was a picnic after the rigors of Eton. A century and a half later, military life still felt like a spell at the Ritz to boys who had just left Public Schools. Reticence and rationing came to them naturally; enthusiasm made them wince. For Brits visiting the States, American abundance was as suspect and hard to comprehend as the American intellectual appetite and generosity of spirit. We Brits had behaved wonderfully during the war – with unflinching patience and good-humour – but once the fighting was over the wartime mentality lingered on: always apologize, never complain, but don't let the bastards grind you down. (The spirit of that impoverished time is caught best in Ealing comedies like *The Lavender Hill Mob* and *Kind Hearts and Coronets*, with their mixture of geniality and slyness, inertia and disrespect.)

This taste for deprivation had a deadening effect on literature in general and poetry in particular. What passed for the latest movement in English verse in the mid-fifties – the nine poets included in Robert Conquest's 1956 anthology *New Lines* were, in fact, labeled 'The Movement' – was glumly unadventurous. In Movement terms, the ideal poem was like a well-made essay; it had a beginning, a middle and an end, and it made a point. It was carefully rhymed, rhythmically inert and profoundly complacent. The one poet in the anthology who was able to make something original out of the restrictions of the style was Philip Larkin – a master of the wry, self-deprecating put-down and slangy half-rhymes ('sod all' with 'untransferable'). But, as everyone now knows, Larkin himself was mired in drabness. He seemed truly to have believed that life was as parsimonious with opportunities as he was with his own resources. He was a brilliant craftsman and he had a beady understanding of his own limitations, but generosity was not his style, neither in spirit nor in practice. If he had a philosophy of life – although the very idea of anything so high-flown would have made him shrink – it was summed up in one of his gloomy aphorisms: 'Sex is much too wonderful an experience to share with anybody else.'

Thom Gunn was born in 1929, seven years after Larkin, which meant that he was less easily resigned to the constraints which those who had come of age during the war took for granted. Although some of his poems appeared in *New Lines*, only one of them was from *Fighting Terms*, an untypically mild little number called 'Lerici' about the difference between Shelley, who was 'submissive' in his drowning, and Byron's mastery of the destructive element. It lacked the jolting rhythmical aggression of poems like Gunn's 'Lofty in the Palais de Danse' – 'You are not random picked. I tell you you / Are much like one I knew before, that died' – or the mysterious power of 'The Wound':

> The huge wound in my head began to heal
> About the beginning of the seventh week.
> Its valleys darkened, its villages became still:
> For joy I did not move and dared not speak . . .

In their different ways, the best poems in *Fighting Terms* – 'The Wound,' 'The Secret Sharer' and 'Carnal Knowledge' – are all about that huge wound in his head; that is, they are about psychic pain, the difficulties of growing up and coming to terms with your own identity.

Gunn had more than his fair share of difficulties to come to terms with. His mother had died when he was fifteen and his relationship with his father – a notoriously hard-nosed journalist who edited a London tabloid – was uneasy. Then, while Gunn was at Cambridge, he came to the conclusion that he was homosexual. In the buttoned-up 1950s, when the homosexual act, even between consenting adults, was a criminal offense (so was attempted suicide), this was a tough decision. It was tougher still at Cambridge, where the most powerful figure in the English department was F.R. Leavis. Like Matthew Arnold, Dr. Leavis believed literature was a moral discipline, a substitute for religion. His hero was D.H. Lawrence and behind the catch-phrases solemnly parroted by the doctor's disciples – 'maturity,' 'reverence,' 'poise,' 'the quality of felt life,' 'the free play of the vital intelligence' – was the belief that the moral and spiritual welfare of society was in the hands of us literary folk. We lusted after responsibility, and in the '50s responsibility meant marriage – the wife, the kids, the little home and the dog. Marriage (even a quarrelsome, unhappy marriage like that of Lawrence and Frieda) was the ultimate vindication of literary seriousness. According to Joan Didion, who was at Berkeley around that time, 'we were the last generation to identify with adults.'

Gunn was no exception, but his sexual preferences seem to have confused the issue for him: when homosexual activity is considered a criminal offense, how can the potential offender maintain a comfortable attitude toward moral seriousness and responsibility? Out of that confusion, I think, the best poems emerged. He himself prefers not to see it that way. 'I rejoice in Eliot's lovely remark that art is an escape from personality,' he wrote in 1979, in an essay about his life and poetry. He added, in a postscript:

> In my early twenties I wrote a poem called 'Carnal Knowledge', addressed to a girl, with a refrain making variations on the phrase 'I know you know'. Now anyone aware that I am homosexual is likely to misread the whole poem, inferring that the thing 'known' is that the speaker would prefer to be in bed with a man. But that would be a serious misreading, or at least a serious misplacement of emphasis. The poem, actually addressed to a fusion of two completely different girls, is not saying anything as clear-cut as that. A reader knowing nothing about the author has a much better chance of understanding it.

I wonder. 'Carnal Knowledge' is a fierce and upsetting poem, and whether or not it is autobiographical is beside the point. The poem works because it expresses a conflict everybody understands:

> *Even in bed I pose: desire may grow*
> *More circumstantial and less circumspect*
> *Each night, but an acute girl would suspect*
> *That my self is not like my body, bare.*
> *I wonder if you know, or, knowing, care?*
> *You know I know you know I know you know . . .*

I hardly hoped for happy thoughts, although
In a most happy sleeping time I dreamt
We did not hold each other in contempt.
Then lifting from my lids night's penny weights
I saw that lack of love contaminates.
You know I know you know I know you know.

Abandon me to stammering, and go;
If you have tears, prepare to cry elsewhere —
I know of no emotion we can share.
Your intellectual protests are a bore
And even now I pose, so now go, for
I know you know.

Anyone educated in England's sexually segregated schools did not have to read Freud to know that we are all to a certain extent bisexual. Yet that is not an idea people accept easily – maybe not even Gunn himself at the time. So when he came to write his autobiographical essay, a quarter of a century later, perhaps he was less bothered by the possibility that 'Carnal Knowledge' might, with hindsight, be knowingly misread than by the suspicion that he had lacked good faith when he was young, and had either deliberately misled his readers or had deceived himself about his true feelings. Yet in terms of the poem those hesitations are beside the point. What matters is that his ambiguous feelings allow him to express thrillingly the dividedness and dissatisfaction we all sometimes feel when we are in bed with the wrong person.

By 1957, when Gunn published his second collection, *A Sense of Movement*, he had made his choice and, as though to ensure there would be no further misreadings, he prefaced the book with a quotation from Corneille: '*Je le suis, je veux l'être.*' Coming out of the closet, even in a foreign language, was a bold gesture in the '50s, yet once the decision was made a curious, marmoreal calm settled on his verse. Gunn had always been an intensely literary poet. In those days, of course, when English was still an embattled subject in the universities – it had none of the status of 'serious' disciplines like classics and the sciences – everyone who studied it was literary to a degree that seems unimaginable now that English departments are vast and theory-ridden and so uninterested in value judgments that they teach Zane Grey and *Superman* more fervently than Shakespeare and

Milton. But even back in the days when great literature seemed to matter, Gunn was more literary than most. He had acquired his reading habits literally in the womb: his mother, he says, read the whole of Gibbon's *History* while she was pregnant with him; the house he was brought up in was full of books, and as a child he had devoured Victorian poetry and prose romances. Then came Cambridge, and his total immersion in Leavis's 'Great Tradition', and the discovery (also thanks to Leavis) that 'Donne and Shakespeare spoke living language to me.' A couple of years later, he won a fellowship in creative writing at Stanford, where he came under the influence of another literary moralist – Yvor Winters, who believed that 'the artistic process is one of moral evaluation of human experience.'

Winters had his own ideas about the Great Tradition. He was a powerful critic, but a minor poet, with an eccentric taste in minor poetry. He loathed Eliot and the Modernist movement, and opted instead for a different twentieth-century pantheon – Robert Bridges, Adelaide Crapsey, and Elizabeth Daryush, whom he called 'the finest poet since T. Sturge Moore.' (Sir Edmund Gosse dismissed Moore as 'that sheep in sheep's clothing.') Above all, Winters was a formalist. He believed in reason, order, and a kind of Elizabethan appropriateness of emotion and subject-matter, in what Gunn, in a Winters-like poem on Winters, called 'Ferocity existing in the fence / Built by an exercised intelligence.'

Gunn was one of the most talented writers to come under Winters's influence, and I do not think he was helped by it. The unease and energy that had made the early poems tick so ominously gave way to decorum, strict reasonableness and formal grace – to smoothly flowing rhythms and bland rhymes. Gunn turned his back on England, settled in San Francisco, and began to write explicitly about homosexuality. Yet, paradoxically, the more he wrote about the gay world – then still a marginal or forbidden subject, with its bars and predators and rentboys – the more decorous his verse became. 'I was much taken by the American myth of the motorcyclist, then in its infancy, of the wild man part free spirit and part hoodlum,' he wrote, 'but even that I started to anglicize: when I thought of doing a series of motorcyclist poems I had Marvell's mower poems in my mind as a model.' In case you have forgotten, Marvell's mower poems are some of the most sweet-tempered and formally perfect in the language.

Gunn himself seemed to embody this paradox in his person. On the rare occasions I met him, in San Francisco or London, he was dressed like Marlon Brando in *The Wild One* – T-shirt, jeans, cowboy boots and creaking leather jacket – yet his manner remained English in the best sense: polite, unassuming, diffident, fastidious. In those days, before poetry readings became a subdivision of show biz, with rewards to match, he was doing what most poets did to make ends meet: he was teaching literature to college kids. It was a job he says he enjoyed and certainly took seriously. He produced weighty essays – on Ben Jonson, Hardy, and Fulke Greville, Sir Philip Sidney's friend – that impressed the faculty at Berkeley sufficiently for them to offer him tenure. He tried it for a year, then left, preferring to teach only enough to pay the bills while he got on with his real work, writing poetry.

Essentially, there was no great clash between his job and his vocation. Gunn's *Collected Poems* run to almost five hundred pages, and all of them have virtues a serious teacher, like Winters, or Gunn himself, could recognize and teach: technical skill, lucidity, discipline. A large proportion of them are also rather dull. That, too, is par for the course. Coleridge was a great poet, but his reputation rests on five poems: 'The Rime of the Ancient Mariner,' 'Kubla Khan,' 'Dejection: an Ode,' 'Christabel' and 'Frost at Midnight' – a group that amounts to a mere fifty-five pages, or less than ten percent of the Oxford edition of his poetical works. Some poets – Eliot was one – write very little and publish only what they think is perfect, but for most the apprenticeship never ends. They keep on writing reams of dutiful verse in order to keep the bed aired, just in case the Muse chooses to pay a visit.

Gunn spent years perfecting his craft and applying it to the gay new world he now inhabited. And he meant what he had said about Marvell's mower poems. He has a poem on surfers that might have been written by Lovelace, a poem on a young drug pusher that sounds like a seventeenth-century ballad, a poem on a gay hustler in the manner of Thomas Gray's elegy on his cat. The more outrageous the experience – LSD trips, sexual orgies, group gropes – the more fastidious the verse becomes:

> I like loud music, bars, and boisterous men.
> *You may from this conclude I like the things*
> *That help me if not lose then leave behind,*
> *What else, the self.*

What else, indeed, can you conclude from such plonking, stately rhythms? Well, you might also conclude that, in poetry, leaving

behind the self is not always a virtue. Even when Gunn came under
the influence of Robert Duncan, in the late '60s, and began to write
free verse, his iron control never faltered. There were occasional
exceptions – for example, a miraculous poem on a cherry tree,
scrupulously observed, yet full of tenderness – but mostly Gunn
was off at a distance in the poems he wrote in the '60s and '70s, an
uninvolved technician, a watcher; he watched the scene, he watched
himself watching, and he watched himself being watched. It was 'I
know you know I know you know I know' all over again, though
without the confusion, the involvement, the cost.

Maybe all that this means is that Gunn was happy in San Francisco –
and happiness, for the past two centuries, has not been a great inspirer
of poetry. (Even Edward Lear's comic masterpieces are fuelled by loss,
regret and an abiding distaste for his ungainly self.) Yet apart from a
handful of early poems, Gunn has never shown much interest in the
style of exacerbated intensity that attracted his Cambridge contemporary, Ted Hughes. The virtues preached by Yvor Winters suited
him fine, and he summed them up in an epitaph on another Winters
disciple, J.V. Cunningham:

> *He concentrated, as he ought,*
> *On fitting language to his thought*
> *And getting all the rhymes correct,*
> *Thus exercising intellect*
> *In such a space, in such a fashion,*
> *He concentrated into passion.*

In Gunn's case, however, passion went missing for a long time, and
it returned in a different shape from its first visitation, when he was an
undergraduate. In the mid-'80s, the AIDS epidemic hit San Francisco,
and the gay community began to die. Twenty years earlier, Gunn had
used strict, traditional forms to describe his acid trips, because, he
wrote, 'the only way I could give myself any control over the
presentation of these experiences, and so could be true to them,
was by trying to render the infinite through the finite, the unstructured through the structured.' At the time, his plan didn't work out;
the LSD poems are so rigorously structured that the experience itself
becomes just another mildly intriguing event to be observed from a
distance. AIDS was different. It threatened him, it threatened his way
of life, and, most important, it was killing off his friends.

It was a terrible time, but to have presented it as merely terrible –
that is, as 'unstructured' – would have been to falsify it. And suddenly,
the technical skills he had labored over for so long came into their
own. *The Man With Night Sweats*, which was published in 1992 and
ends his *Collected Poems*, culminates in a series of elegies on his dead
and dying friends which are as fine and clear as anything Gunn has
written. Qualities in his verse which once seemed to exist in an
aesthetic vacuum now serve an urgent purpose: the scrupulous
attention to detail brings his friends back to life; the formal elegance
dignifies their dying; the restraint has something difficult to restrain –
pity for them, fear for himself:

> *When near your death a friend*
> *Asked you what he could do,*
> *'Remember me', you said.*
> *We will remember you.*

It sounds easy, but in fact it took him decades of hard labour in the salt
mines of technique and self-abnegation to write as simply as that.
Gunn, who had started out so brilliantly and full of purpose and then
seemed to lose his way, has ended up writing a handful of poems that
poets like Marvell, whom he fell for in his literary youth, would have
recognized and admired. In his own fastidious manner, he has joined
them.

The New Yorker, 1994

Seamus Heaney

FIELD WORK IS SEAMUS Heaney's fifth collection of verse. He published his first in 1966 and since then his output has been steady and discreet. Like his poetry: steady, discreet, reliable, and highly successful. He has won all the prizes and the reviews of his books have been so unanimous in their praise that now the question of his excellence is no longer discussed; the reviewers content themselves with explicating the subtleties of his textures or his references, as if he were some younger Eliot or Yeats.

It is all very peculiar, particularly in England where new voices have a notoriously hard time in being heard. Even more peculiar is the fact that recognition and success happened to Heaney instantaneously. The British jacket of his second book quotes five rave reviews of his first, three of them by university professors. This in itself would be extraordinary for any young poet anywhere. In England, where the divorce is absolute between the academies and what is called in the US 'creative writing,' it was more or less unprecedented. Maybe Rupert Brooke did as well, but it didn't happen to Ted Hughes at first, or even to Philip Larkin, however unassailable his status seems now; it still hasn't happened in Britain to Sylvia Plath.

Why, then, was Heaney an exception? Perhaps it has something to do with his being an Irishman. Since Congreve and Sterne there has always been at least one major Irish star on the British literary scene. Yeats and Joyce are long dead; Patrick Kavanagh outlived them but was too patchy and Dublin parochial; the gifted, underrated Thomas Kinsella departed for America, disappeared into the interior, and has scarcely been heard from since. The only obvious and natural contender is Beckett, but he has exiled himself to Paris, writes in French as much as English, and is experimental in a radical, forbidding way which many British academics, as well as the Great British Public, find hard to love. Heaney, if nothing else, is far less unsettling. Moreover, he comes from Northern Ireland and has written eloquently about that troubled and troublesome sore on the British conscience. But so, too, has Michael Longley, who comes from the same province and is also an excellent poet. Yet his books sell the usual derisory few hundred, while Heaney, like Larkin, numbers his admirers by the thousand. It would be good to believe that craft and restraint can still be so spectacularly rewarded, but I suspect, alas, that his popularity says less about these modest virtues than about contemporary English taste.

Heaney has in abundance a gift which the English distrust in one another but expect of the Irish: a fine way with the language. What in Brendan Behan, for instance, was a brilliant, boozy gift of the gab is transformed by Heaney into rich and sonorous rhetoric. He is a man besotted with words and, like all lovers, he wants to display the beauties and range and subtleties of his beloved. Unlike most, however, he disciplines his passion, reining it in for better effect. It is an admirable procedure, although there are times when the urge to make a nice noise gets the better of him:

> I dreamt we slept in a moss in Donegal
> On turf banks under blankets, with our faces
> Exposed all night in a wetting drizzle,
> Pallid as the dripping sapling birches.
> Lorenzo and Jessica in a cold climate.
> Diarmuid and Grainne waiting to be found.
> Darkly asperged and censed, we were laid out
> Like breathing effigies on a raised ground.

The last two lines are purely ornamental; they add nothing except a solemn, reverberating, Tennysonian grandeur.

It is something of a miracle for a poet writing at the latter end of the twentieth century to sound so Victorian without, at the same time, sounding merely pompous and secondhand. Heaney's skill in bringing off this difficult balancing act is, I suspect, the clue to his extraordinary popularity. The British have never taken easily or willingly to Modernism. Apart from Joyce and Beckett, the great experimental movement in literature was largely an American concern: Eliot, Pound, Crane, Moore, Stevens, Williams, all of them attempting in their different ways to break the links with English poetry and make it new in distinctly American or cosmopolitan ways. Modernism, in other words, was a literary Declaration of Independence. In contrast, the British adjusted to the times by a process of seepage, gradually adapting the old forms to the rhythms of twentieth-century speech: Yeats, Auden, Graves, and so on, down to Larkin. So they are comfortable with Heaney because he himself is comfortably in a recognizable tradition.

He is also a rural poet, born and brought up in the country and now wisely retired to it from the hurly-burly of literary life. Like Wordsworth, he suggests in one poem; whereupon his wife 'interrupts: "You're not going to compare us two . . .?" ' She's right, of course. Nevertheless, he is squarely in a hallowed tradition running from Crabbe and Clare, through Hardy and Edward Thomas, to excellent contemporary minor poets like Norman Nicholson and the dour R.S. Thomas.

Heaney's position in it, however, is far from countrified. He is an intensely literary writer: his poems on the Irish troubles sound like Yeats, his elegy on Lowell sounds like Lowell; he brings in heroes and heroines with beautiful names from Irish myth, and quotes Wyatt and Dante, whom he also 'imitates,' Lowell-fashion. There are, in fact, moments when his literariness turns into downright pedantry. For example, his third collection, *Wintering Out*, contained a four-line poem called 'Nerthus':

> *For beauty, say an ash-fork staked in peat,*
> *Its long grains gathering to the gouged split;*
>
> *A seasoned, unsleeved taker of the weather,*
> *Where kesh and loaning finger out to heather.*

It is a kind of latter-day Imagism, a rhymed and rhythmical celebration of one of the common, unassuming objects of this world in the spirit of William Carlos Williams's love poem to a dishmop or his red wheelbarrow on which so much depended. The difference is in the title and the last line, which send the conscientious reader scurrying to his reference books. Without, as it happens, much joy. Neither 'kesh' nor 'loaning' figure as such in the biggest Oxford dictionary, although they seem to be dialect variants of words which do: 'kex: an umbelliferous plant with a hollow stalk'; 'loan: an open uncultivated piece of ground near a farmhouse or village.' 'Nerthus' defeats all the encyclopedias on my shelves. No doubt I will be scornfully put in my place either for ignorance or for missing the point. But in a poem as brief, unsubstantial, and apparently simple as this, these verbal affectations get in the way; they themselves are ways of missing the point.

Unless, of course, the point is other than what it seems: Heaney is not rural and sturdy and domestic, with his feet planted firmly in the Irish mud, but is instead an ornamentalist, a word collector, a connoisseur of fine language for its own sake.

The exception is *North*, his fourth and best book, which opened with an imposing sequence of poems linking the grim Irish present with its even grimmer past of Norse invasions and ancient feuding. The tone was appropriately stern, but also distanced, the language spare, as though stripped back to its Anglo-Saxon skeleton. For the space of these dozen and a half poems Heaney seemed to have found a theme so absorbing that charm and rhetoric were irrelevant. The poems were as simple, demanding, and irreducible as the archaic trophies from the bog which they celebrated. And like an archaeologist, he pared away the extraneous matter and kept himself decently in the background.

That reticence and self-containment have largely gone from *Field Work*. He is back with the seductions of fine language, the verbal showman's charming sleights of hand. Consider, for example, the first stanza of 'Oysters,' the opening poem of the book:

> Our shells clacked on the plates.
> My tongue was a filling estuary,
> My palate hung with starlight:
> As I tasted the salty Pleiades
> Orion dipped his foot into the water.

First there is a verbal discovery, 'clacked,' the right and precise word to set the scene; then a precise evocation of the seawater taste of the creatures, 'My tongue was a filling estuary'; after that, Heaney takes off into graceful, expanding variations on the same theme. In other words, the poem does not advance into unknown territory, it circles elegantly around and around on itself until it ends where it began, with language: 'I ate the day / Deliberately, that its tang / Might quicken me all into verb, pure verb.' This is a twentieth-century expression of a nineteenth-century preoccupation, old aestheticism and new linguistics, Gautier filtered through Barthes.

Heaney's real strength and originality are not, I think, in his flashy rhetorical pieces, or in the poems in which he takes on the big themes that are unavoidable for a serious poet living in Northern Ireland. They are, instead, in modest, perfect little poems like 'Homecomings,' or the short sequence which gives this book its title, or the closing stanzas of 'The Skunk':

After eleven years I was composing
Love-letters again, broaching the word 'wife'
Like a stored cask, as if its slender vowel
Had mutated into the night earth and air

Of California. The beautiful, useless
Tang of eucalyptus spelt your absence.
The aftermath of a mouthful of wine
Was like inhaling you off a cold pillow.

And there she was, the intent and glamorous,
Ordinary, mysterious skunk,
Mythologized, demythologized,
Snuffing the boards five feet beyond me.

It all came back to me last night, stirred
By the sootfall of your things at bedtime,
Your head-down, tail-up hunt in a bottom drawer
For the black plunge-line nightdress.

Heaney's originality lies in his aroused, free-floating sensuality which pushes at the language, mingling the other senses – smell, sound, touch, taste – in visual images: 'The sootfall of your things at bedtime.' It is like one of those witty, elegiac conceits Herrick or Henry King would have been proud of: softness, silence and a vaguely erotic darkness, all lovingly fused in a single image. When Heaney is at his best he maintains a tender, fruitful muddle between the body of the natural world and the body of his wife. It is beautifully done in a way perfected most recently by poets like Snodgrass and Wilbur: pure and expert and deliberately low-key. It is also a different universe, less disturbed and disturbing, from the vivid, ominous, undeniable visitant in Lowell's 'Skunk Hour' who 'jabs her wedge-head in a cup / of sour cream, drops her ostrich tail / and will not scare.'

But that can only increase Heaney's standing with the custodians of contemporary British culture. Lowell once criticized American artists for what he called 'the monotony of the sublime.' He meant their fierce ambition, their continual all-out striving toward the ultimate Great American Novel/Poem/Painting, as though it were ignoble to settle for anything less than greatness. They order these things differently in England. There the prevailing vice is a monotony of the mundane and artistic ambition is thought to be slightly off, as though it were not quite gentlemanly to settle for anything more than the minor.

Heaney's work fits smoothly into this tradition. It challenges no presuppositions, does not upset or scare, is mellifluous, craftsmanly, and often perfect within its chosen limits. In other words, it is beautiful minor poetry, like Philip Larkin's, though replacing his tetchy, bachelor gloom with something sweeter, more sensual, more open to the world – more, in a word, married.

It is, however, precisely these reassuring qualities which have been seized on by his champions as proof of the fact that in Heaney Britain has, at last, another major poet. This seems to me grossly disproportionate both to the fragility of the verse and also to Heaney's own modest intentions. After all, he does not often come on like Yeats reincarnated and much of his excellence depends on his knowing his own range and keeping rigorously to it, no more, no less.

In the circumstances, his current reputation amounts, I think, to a double betrayal: it lumbers him with expectations which he may not fulfill and which might even sink him, if he were less resilient; at the same time, it reinforces the British audience in their comfortable prejudice that poetry, give or take a few quirks of style, has not changed essentially in the last hundred years. If Heaney really is the best we can do, then the whole troubled, exploratory thrust of modern poetry has been a diversion from the right true way. Eliot and his contemporaries, Lowell and his, Plath and hers had it all wrong: to try to make clearings of sense and discipline and style in the untamed, unfenced darkness was to mistake morbidity for inspiration. It was, in the end, mere melodrama, understandable perhaps in the Americans who lack a tradition in these matters, but inexcusable in the British.

These, as I understand them, are the implications of Heaney's abrupt elevation into the pantheon of British poetry. Few well-established critics care to cope with work outside a correspondingly established tradition and even fewer, in the words of the margarine advertisement, can tell Stork from butter. But their current dedication to safety, sweetness, and light seems, at this late stage of the game, a curiously depressing refusal of everything that is mysterious and shaking and renewing in poetry. They remind me of Ophelia in her madness:

> *Thought and affliction, passion, hell itself,*
> *She turns to favour and to prettiness.*

Anthony Hecht

ANTHONY HECHT WAS BORN in 1923, which means he belongs to the generation of writers who served in World War II and hit their stride in the 1950s. From the perspective of the cultural anarchy that was about to break loose, the Fifties are usually dismissed as a timorous and conformist decade: the cold war was at its height, nuclear catastrophe seemed imminent, Senator McCarthy was on the rampage, and liberals everywhere kept their heads well below the parapet.

That, certainly, was how it felt in exhausted postwar England, but – for this Englishman at least – the atmosphere was altogether livelier in the US, McCarthy notwithstanding. Instead of being cowed or stifled by the ubiquitous sense of menace, the Abstract Expressionist painters and their poetic equivalents – Lowell, Berryman, Plath – responded to it by turning inward; they used their private troubles as a mirror for the troubles all around, and the work they produced was anything but conformist. As for intellectual life, the arguing didn't stop or become less fierce, it merely changed focus; from Marx to Freud, from dialectical materialism to the New Criticism. For a brief period, literature seemed to replace politics and religion as a source of true values, just as Matthew Arnold had predicted, and even literary criticism seemed like a noble vocation.

In other words, the Fifties were a serious decade and the Fifties poets took their art seriously. It was a craft, a skill to be learned, a hard discipline, like drawing from life, that stayed with you no matter what you did with it later. That was one of its many attractions for Anthony Hecht when he was fresh out of the army and trying to put his life back together again, courtesy of the GI Bill of Rights. It was a long and difficult task and he had a lot to work at, starting with his childhood in New York. His family was upper-middle-class, but flaky and thwarted and downwardly mobile, always on the edge of financial ruin; his younger brother was crippled and epileptic; his parents loathed each other and didn't much care for their two children, whom they manipulated relentlessly in their shameful squabbles. Then the war came. Hecht was conscripted into the army, fought as a GI in Europe, and was present at the liberation of the Flossenbürg concentration camp, an annex of Buchenwald – experiences that darkened his already bleak view of the world, eventually helped to precipitate a breakdown, and seem to have stayed with him ever since.*

The GI Bill took him to Kenyon College, where he studied under John Crowe Ransom, began to teach, and published his first poems. Ransom himself was a gifted poet, witty, tender, gentlemanly, and technically conservative. From him, Hecht has written, 'one learned to pay keen attention to poetic detail.' He was also a master craftsman, which must have encouraged the younger poet's fascination with poetic forms and their uses. But unlike Lowell, who had preceded him at Kenyon, Hecht was a slow starter. He later suppressed half the poems in his first collection, *A Summoning of Stones*, because the general tone, he told Philip Hoy, was 'jaunty and distanced, cool and artificed . . . too full of devices.' In those days, essay-poems – poems with a beginning, a middle, and a moral at the end – were all the fashion on both sides of the Atlantic, though Hecht, even at the start, was too subtle a technician to settle for the thumping pentameters favored by his British contemporaries. Anyway, what he had to express was too complex for that complacent formula. At the root of all his best mature poems was darkness, or rather darkness and distaste, residues of his bleak childhood and whatever nightmares had their origins in his experience at Flossenbürg. He made poetry out of this, however, only by keeping it at a distance and applying great technical pressure.

Hecht, I mean, is a poet who has dealt with twentieth-century horrors most often in elaborate traditional forms. Like everyone of his period, he was profoundly influenced by T.S. Eliot, but what he took from him had little to do with experimental Modernism. Hecht's Eliot is

---

* Hecht discusses all this, and a great deal more, in a long and illuminating conversation with Philip Hoy, published in 1999 by Between the Lines. *Anthony Hecht in Conversation with Philip Hoy* is one of an excellent series which also includes book-length interviews with W.D. Snodgrass, Richard Wilbur, Thom Gunn, and Seamus Heaney, among others. Although they are called 'conversations,' Hecht's was conducted at a distance, and without benefit of a tape recorder: Hoy first sent him a list of one hundred questions, to which Hecht responded with intricate written replies; this was followed by a further fifty letters and faxes, and much rewriting.

the poet who replaced the languid Romanticism of the late nineteenth century with a new style of classicism – impersonal, controlled,
lucid, and highly intelligent. His Eliot was also the critic who backed it
up with essays on what William James might have called the 'tough-
minded' poets – Donne and the Metaphysicals, Ben Jonson, Dryden,
the Jacobean dramatists – who had somehow been pushed out of the
way during the rise of the 'tender-minded' Romantics. This was the
Eliot who wrote, in 'Tradition and the Individual Talent,'

> Tradition . . . cannot be inherited, and if you want it you must
> obtain it by great labour. It involves, in the first place, the historical
> sense, which we may call nearly indispensable to anyone who
> would continue to be a poet beyond his twenty-fifth year; and the
> historical sense involves a perception, not only of the pastness of
> the past, but of its presence.

This was precisely what a young man with a natural bent for
learning wanted to hear. So, too, was Eliot's famous comment, in the
same essay, on the extinction of personality:

> Poetry is not a turning loose of emotion, but an escape from
> emotion; it is not the expression of personality, but an escape from
> personality. But, of course, only those who have personality and
> emotions know what it means to want to escape from these things.

Hecht was a nonreligious Jew who wrote poetry because, among
other reasons, he wanted to deal with what he had seen firsthand: the
crimes committed against less fortunate Jews in Nazi Germany. He
was too intelligent, however, and far too fastidious ever to try to hitch
a lift from such outrage; 'I have,' he told Hoy, 'little sympathy or
patience with the poetry of moral indignation.' For Hecht, Eliot the
invisible poet was a perfect role model.

Hecht's way of keeping his volatile subject matter at an aesthetic
distance was to create characters and speak through them like a
novelist, just as Browning had done. This is nowhere more apparent
than in an extraordinary poem published in his second collection, *The
Hard Hours*, in 1967. It is called 'Behold the Lilies of the Field,' and in
it, without ever raising his voice, he contrives to describe something
altogether monstrous – the ritual humiliation, daily flogging, and
eventual flaying alive of the Emperor Valerian by the Persians in 260

AD. Unusually for Hecht, the poem is in free verse, but a free verse written with such attention to detail and so subtly monitored for pitch and tone that it seems as disciplined as the trickiest traditional prosody. It also has a tricky time-scheme, shifting from the American present to ancient Rome with no apparent change of gear. The poem begins, almost like one of Lowell's 'Life Studies,' with a man angrily recounting some wounding childhood memory of his hypocritical mother to a shadowy figure who might be a therapist:

> I don't think
> She knows what honesty is. 'Your mother's a whore,'
> Someone said, not meaning she slept around,
> Though perhaps this was part of it, but
> Meaning she had lost all sense of honour,
> And I think this is true.
>
> But that's not what I wanted to say.
> What was it I wanted to say? . . .
> Lie back. Relax.
> Oh yes. I remember now what it was.
> It was what I saw them do to the emperor.

Then comes the sudden change of scene and century and the terrible catalog of cruelties, glassily enumerated, which circle repeatedly back to the narrator's own torment, variations on the single theme of unwillingly bearing witness: 'And I was tied to a post and made to watch.'

On one level, it is a sidelong and beautifully reticent way of airing Hecht's Flossenbürg nightmare. Bearing witness, however, is only part of the torment. Valerian's story ends, as the mother's does, with the loss of honor. At which point, the mother unexpectedly reappears:

> His death had taken hours.
> They were very patient.
> And with him passed away the honor of Rome.
>
> In the end, I was ransomed. Mother paid for me.
> You must rest now. You must. Lean back.
> Look at the flowers.
> Yes. I am looking. I wish I could be like them.

He is talking about murderous rage as well as outrage, and the cold voice coldly describing the unspeakable things he 'saw them do to the emperor' is not quite as dispassionate as it seems. It makes you wonder what the soothing therapist was thinking, not just about the man's despair, but about the crippling sadism that lurks below it. And this is Hecht's particular strength: he knows how to tackle the ambiguity of feelings while keeping it at arm's length, ironically, and without benefit of Modernist experiment.

For Hecht, cruelty is a terrible side effect of what he called, in his poem 'The Venetian Vespers,' 'Something profoundly soiled, pointlessly hurt/ And beyond cure in us.' It is like a trapdoor that opens at his feet when he least expects it, usually when he is most in love with the world and how it looks. And this, paradoxically, is more often than you'd think because Hecht, for all his pessimism, is fascinated by the sheer sumptuous richness of things. He is a consummate painter of still life:

> They were green grapes, or, rather,
> They were a sort of pure, unblemished jade,
> Like turbulent ocean water, with misted skins,
> Their own pale, smoky sweat, or tiny frost.

He is equally hedonistic about his craft: he loves language as much as he loves the visible world, and handles rhyme and meter with the same scrupulous, almost sensuous attention to detail as he paints still life. As a result, he is, among his many other talents, one of the best translators around. In his versions of two long poems by Joseph Brodsky, 'Cape Cod Lullaby' and 'Lagoon,' he triumphantly performed the impossible, recreating the intricately melodious metrical forms that come naturally in Russian but seem to defy plain English. Similarly, in *The Darkness and the Light*, Hecht's most recent collection, he captures the lilt, wry wit, and lightness of touch of Charles d'Orléans in a way that makes the fourteenth-century French poet read like a contemporary:

> Back off, clear out, the lot of you,
> Vile Melancholy, Spleen, and Woe;
> Think you to dog me to and fro
> As in the past you used to do?

> Not anymore. 'Begone. You're through,'
> Says Reason, your determined foe.
> Back off, clear out, the lot of you,
> Vile Melancholy, Spleen, and Woe.

> *If you resurface, may God throw*
> *You and your whole damnable crew*
> *Back where you came from down below,*
> *And thereby give the fiend his due.*
> *Back off, clear out, the lot of you.*

At heart Hecht is a classicist and he is at his best with the Latin poets. Like Horace, he has the true satirist's gift for combining anger with elegance, without ever losing his balance. And although he is now nearing his eightieth birthday, his contempt for hypocrisy and vanity is still going strong, especially when they intrude on subjects he most cares for, like literature:

> *It's the same in the shady groves of academe:*
> *Cold eye and primitive beak and callused foot*
> *Conjunctive to destroy*
> > *all things of high repute,*
> > *Whole epics, Campion's songs, Tolstoy,*
> > *Euclid and logic's enthymeme,*
> *As each man bares his scalpel, whets his saber,*
> *As though enjoined to deconstruct his neighbor.*

>   *And that's not the worst of it; there are the Bacchae,*
>   *The ladies' auxiliary of the raptor clan*
> *With their bright cutlery,*
> > > *sororal to a man.*
>   *And feeling peckish, they foresee*
>   *An avian banquet in the sky,*
> *Feasting off dead white European males,*
> *Or local living ones, if all else fails.*

When Hecht is writing in public mode, like this, he has the gift for jaunty, far-fetched rhymes and the sharp eye for pretension of a latterday Byron. But he lacks Byron's swagger and, even when making fun of fools, his take on the human condition is as mirthless as it ever was. Poets in old age tend to look back, as though to take account of their lives, to bring vanished people and places back to life, and say goodbye. Hecht, however, is going down to the wire forgiving no one, with every detail clear-cut and no soft focus. This, for example, is how he remembers the overstuffed parlor of his parents' apartment:

> Green velvet drapes kept the room dark and airless
> Until on sunny days toward midsummer
> The brass andirons caught a shaft of light
> For twenty minutes in late afternoon
> In a radiance dimly akin to happiness –
> The dusty gleam of temporary wealth.

No phony nostalgia for Hecht; 'dimly akin to happiness' is as close as he gets to being reconciled to his bleak childhood.

There is just one poem that seems at first to be the exception because it expands with great delicacy on 'the pleasures of those childhood days':

> The sound of rain. The gentle graphite veil
> Of rain that makes of the world a steel engraving,
> Full of soft fadings and faint distances.

The poem ends, 'Who can resist the charms of retrospection?' Who, indeed? The answer is in the title, 'Lot's Wife.' Look back nostalgically, Hecht is saying, and you get turned into a pillar of salt.

He is still troubled by visions of cruelty. A number of these new poems are based on Old Testament stories, grimly reinterpreted as precursors for the Final Solution. And even the less cataclysmic tales are tainted by the desolation cruelty leaves in its wake: for instance, one of the elders who spies on Susanna as she bathes is a dirty old man with sadistic fantasies, stewing in 'the plush, delirious Minsky's of his mind.' The only biblical character who sounds not altogether desolate is Miriam, the prophetess and sister of Aaron, who is also the one who might be speaking for Hecht:

> I had a nice voice once, and a large following.
> I was, you might say, a star.

Her last words are,

> The past is past; it's no good to anyone.
> Many were lovely once, at least as children.

She sounds resigned, mature, almost forgiving – that is, until you recall Miriam's fate: because she bad-mouthed Moses, the good Lord, in his mercy, made her a leper. As in Beckett's *End Game*, Hecht's world is 'Light black. From pole to pole.'

Beckett also said, 'The prospect of death is always revivifying,' and sure enough, the atmosphere brightens wonderfully with the three poems that end this new collection. They are about making a decent exit, and the way they are written shows how it should be done – gracefully, tenderly, and *con brio*:

> Like trailing silks, the light
> Hangs in the olive trees
> As the pale wine of day
> Drains to its very lees:
> Huge presences of gray
> Rise up, and then it's night.

> Distantly lights go on.
> Scattered like fallen sparks
> Bedded in peat, they seem
> Set in the plushest darks
> Until a timid gleam
> Of matins turns them wan,

> Like the elderly and frail
> Who've lasted through the night,
> Cold brows and silent lips,
> For whom the rising light
> Entails their own eclipse,
> Brightening as they fail.

When Emerson, in 1837, wrote admonishingly, 'We have listened too long to the courtly muses of Europe,' he seemed, like a good democrat, to be objecting less to the influence of Europe than to its courtliness. One of Hecht's many achievements is to write with the courtly grace of Lovelace or Carew in a wry and wholly contemporary American voice.

New York Review of Books, 2002

Virginia Hamilton Adair

WHEN JEAN RHYS WAS told that her novel, *The Wide Sargasso Sea*, had won both of what were then Britain's most prestigious literary awards — the W.H. Smith Prize and that of the Royal Society of Literature — her bleak reaction to the good news was that it had come too late. That was in 1966, when Rhys was seventy-six years old, and *The Wide Sargasso Sea* was her first published work in more than a quarter of a century. But she had had five books in print before she disappeared from sight at the beginning of World War II, and that makes her positively precocious by Virginia Hamilton Adair's standards. Adair is now eighty-three and *Ants on the Melon* is her first collection of poems. Yet even if the book wins all the prizes it deserves she is unlikely to complain that recognition has come too late, because public recognition has never been what she was after. She has written poetry all her life — she began when she was six — but only for the purest of reasons: to please herself, to make sense of her life, and because she loves the possibilities and discipline of the art.

Ants is not a big book; it contains a mere eighty poems. But those eighty have been selected from literally the thousands Adair has written and this gives the collection an extraordinary authority. In part, it is the authority that comes with age: because Adair has waited so long to bring her poems together, there are no hesitations, no uncertainties; her voice is clear, assured, varied and utterly her own. Age also brings with it another kind of authority: it allows even a slight form to carry a great weight of experience.

> *Hearing the footsteps of thieves*
> *in the dark downstairs:*
> *what are you looking for?*
> *it has already been stolen*
> *over and over*

> *I listen to my breath stumbling*
> *in the dark rooms of my lungs:*
> *What does it hope to find?*
> *take it and welcome*
> *while I sleep*

That is called 'Break In' and it is hard to know which came first, the event or the metaphor. Was it real thieves who frightened Adair in the night or the sound of her uncertain breath? The power of the poem is in the way one becomes the other without any noticeable change of gear and a bewildering range of emotions – first a flicker of fear, then disdain, then weariness – is registered in ten quiet lines.

Poetry, especially the kind of lyric poetry Adair writes best, is usually a young person's gift. That is not because the young are necessarily more available to their feelings than the old, but because they are more convinced by them, less savvy, less bemused by all the qualifications that come with experience and seem natural to old age. Part of Adair's achievement is that she has not withdrawn into some turtle-shell of indifference. Her poems 'read' young – intellectually alert, open to feeling, full of life and curiosity – and when you add that freshness to the long perspective of age the results are extraordinarily moving. Writing about her widowed grandmothers, for instance, what she remembers most vividly is not their 'black shoes, black hose, black veils,/ black god-knows-what-else never seen' but their color and vitality:

> *I see the other at the backyard pump*
> *with a bowl of surplus pancakes*
> *for the birds: orioles, tanagers,*
> *jays and cardinals, wild with color*
> *and competition. I hear her cries*
> *of laughter as her blacksleeved arms*
> *hold the hotcakes aloft*
> *among the dip and swirl of brilliant wings.*

Like the birds, the poem itself is 'wild with color and competition' – the poet's competition with herself in the effort to bring the beloved old ladies back to life.

Adair's authority comes, too, from the fact that, published or not, she has always been a wholly professional poet. According to the poet

Robert Mezey, her neighbor in Claremont, California, who persuaded her to publish this book, she served a long apprenticeship in her craft. When she began writing as a child, poets were still expected to know about meter and rhyme. At secondary school, she wrote verse in Latin as well as English, and at Mount Holyoke, where she won all the poetry prizes, she did 'a rigorous year-long course in versification.' This stern training in the basic techniques of verse was, to her, like practicing scales is to the musician; it gave her the skills to do whatever she wanted. Whence her subtle, unobtrusive rhymes and the liquid inner rhythm of her verse, her instinct for the way each line of poetry moves and has its natural length and inflexion:

> Slow scythe curving over the flowers
> In yesterday's field where you mow,
> My cool feet flicked
> The dew from the daisies, hours,
> Hours ago! Ages and ages ago
> They flicked the dew
> From the yellow and snow-colored flowers you leisurely mow.

It takes years of hard work and practice to write with such ease and simplicity and deftness. It also takes the poetic equivalent of what musicians call perfect pitch.

Adair was brought up in a household in which poetry was part of the air she breathed. Her father, Robert Browning Hamilton, was an amateur poet – his poem 'Along the Road' was very famous in his time – and one of her earliest memories, Mezey says, is of looking through the bars of her crib while her father read to her from Pope's version of the *Iliad*. He went on reading poetry to her, or reciting it from memory, all through her childhood on the assumption that poetry was one of the necessary pleasures of life. Necessary but not sufficient. Like Wallace Stevens, Adair's father wrote poetry but had trained as a lawyer and earned his living as an insurance executive, specializing in surety bonds. As it happens, he and Stevens knew each other but, according to Mezey, when Virginia asked him if they had ever talked poetry, he answered, 'Certainly not.' His shocked reaction – like Marianne Moore's sniffy dismissal of poetic pretention, 'there are things that are important beyond all this fiddle' – was a fine antidote to literary self-importance and ambition, and his daughter never seems to have found any good reason to disagree with him.

Not that that stopped her publishing when she was young and starting out on an academic career. She went to Radcliffe for her MA, then to the University of Wisconsin at Madison to start a Ph.D., which she never completed, perhaps because she was too entranced by the sheer buzz of being young:

> I wear a ring with seven small diamonds
> and a couple more, a little larger.
> I am in love with at least two men, also
> the trumpet of Louis Armstrong, poetry,
> scholarship, ritual, ice-skating
> at 10 below zero, drinking Manhattans,
> dancing, Wisconsin lakes and woods,
> being in love with almost everything.
> A crisis looms ahead: a June marriage;
> but 10 months are too endless to be real.

She went back east to marry Douglass Adair, a handsome and talented young historian whom she had met at Harvard, and, once they were married, she did what well brought-up young women, however gifted, were supposed to do in those days: she adjusted her career to her husband's, followed him to wherever he was appointed, raised a family, did a little teaching, and went on writing poetry in her spare time. To judge from the poems, it was a good marriage, full of wit and passion, and she does not seem to have felt diminished by its demands.

She was also sporadically publishing poems in all the usual places – *The Atlantic Monthly, The New Republic, The Saturday Review* – and they were establishing a reputation for her among people whose judgment she valued. But literary fame was not what she wanted. 'To be acclaimed young is heady,' she wrote, 'later on a drag.' Adair seems to have had several good reasons for not wanting to be famous, some of them personal, some aesthetic. She came of age as a writer at a time when American poets, having finally severed their English connections and taken off on their own, were intensely preoccupied with style and stylishness. Yet she herself remained strangely uninfluenced by the prevailing modernist fashions. There is no trace in her work of Eliot or Pound or Stevens or Moore or Williams or even of Ransom, although her early fans included Gordon Chalmers, who brought Ransom to Kenyon. In *Ants on the Melon*, only some relatively dull poems she wrote during a spell in England, in the 1950s, show signs of outside influence; they are smooth and sonorous and heavily rhymed in a manner that was in favor with the British traditionalists at that time. In a way, Adair herself is a traditionalist – if that is what striving for excellence as something beyond fashion and personality means – but her casual, witty, powerful voice is wholly her own, and maybe she was afraid that it wouldn't be heard by an audience with fixed ideas of how a 'modern' poem should sound. She wanted to make it new in her own way without getting trapped into repeating herself in order to please her readers.

Her private reasons for not publishing a book were more complicated. She told Alice Quinn of *The New Yorker* that her three children resented her poetry:

> They didn't like me for writing. It took time from them. Sometimes, I'd think, if I don't get half an hour to myself, I'm going to go crazy. I could hear Douglass sort of shooing and shushing the children: 'Now, don't disturb Ginny. She's writing.' And I knew at that moment that they hated me for wanting to write, and I even hated Douglass for shooing them.

She also learned about the corrosive effects of ambition from her husband. Douglass Adair was a distinguished historian, a brilliant writer, a brilliant lecturer, who published articles and held down plush professorships – at Williamsburg, where he edited the prestigious *William and Mary Quarterly*, and at the Graduate School in Claremont. His academic reputation was unassailable, his colleagues admired him, and, because he was an unusually charismatic lecturer, he was, Adair has said, 'beset by female students.' But somehow it wasn't enough. 'I think my husband was really sort of tortured by a desire for fame,' Adair told *The New York Times*. That torture is the subject of a wry and bitter poem called 'The Professor Sings of Love':

> *Then when the great job came through*
> *it was for her, not me.*
>
> *'New England autumns together –'*
> *she murmured in my uneasy arms.*
> *Already I felt winter on the way.*
>
> *I wrote her, 'I am not Prince Consort,*
> *Nor was meant to be.'*

Ever the good sport, Kate responded
I was witty and wise . . .

Women, like teeth, should be strong
but not prominent.

The poem, of course, cuts both ways; Adair herself was assuredly no
Princess Consort. But her marriage was more valuable to her than her
literary career and, as with her children, her husband's peace of mind
mattered far more than a book.

As it happens, it ended tragically. After thirty-five years of apparent
happiness, without warning and for no obvious reason, Douglass
Adair went upstairs one afternoon and shot himself. His wife had
written tender, witty poems about their marriage – about making love
('Peeling an Orange'), about breeding like mice ('Where Did I Leave
Off?'), about family holidays ('Blueberry City'); even a poem about
her hysterectomy ('By the Waters') is full of life and appetite – and
although the poems she wrote after his suicide are often baffled, angry
and desolate, they remained tender and witty:

Lying entwined with you
on the long sofa

the hi-fi helping
Isolde to her climax

I was clipping
the coarse hairs

from your ears
and ruby nostrils

when you said, 'Music
for cutting nose wires'

and we shook so
the nailscissors nicked

your gentle neck
blood your blood

I cleansed the place
with my tongue

and we clung tight
pelted with Teutonic cries

till the player
lifted its little prick

from the groove
all arias over

leaving us
in post-Wagnerian sadness

later that year
you were dead

by your own hand
blood your blood

I have never understood
I will never understand.

The poem is called 'One Ordinary Evening,' and it is precisely the loving ordinariness of the scene, the contrast between Wagnerian erotic doom and the kind of carefree sex that begins and ends in laughter – 'the player/lifted its little prick/from the groove/all arias over' – that makes the closing lines so shocking.

To write about a subject so desolating with such control and simplicity, to write a love poem to someone dead and gone as though he were alive and present – alertly, with humor and affection – is a triumph, above all, of a tone of voice. But a tone of voice implies a listener and Adair says she was never much interested in the audience out there in the poetry-reading world. So whom was she writing for? Her answer would be that she wrote to please herself and that is the point of poetry. In other words, when any artist is at work, the last thing he has in mind is Freud's shabby trio of motives – fame, riches and the love of beautiful women – and even the impulse that sparks the work off becomes unimportant. All that matters is getting it right, making it cohere within itself, paring it down, taking up the slack, exploiting the medium for its own sake, because that is what the artist knows how to do. A poet like Adair does not necessarily have a richer inner life than other people; she simply understands better how to express it in language.

Yet for a poem to exist properly there has to be a reader, someone who listens and understands and registers the subtleties. Even the most reclusive poet has an audience in his head and Adair sounds anything but reclusive. She is also astonishingly lacking in self-absorption and conceit. The voice that comes off the page is convincing because it is so immediate; she seems to be talking right to you, without fuss, without affectation, expecting a response. So when she claimed that she wrote only to please herself, perhaps she was implying that her internal audience was classier and more discriminating than the fashion-conscious world of contemporary poetry. According to *The New York Times*, 'acceptance by the public had never much mattered to her. "While my father was living, and he lived to 94," she said, "if I showed him things and he liked them, then I was satisfied." ' Through her father, I think, the audience in her head extended to the poets both of them loved, especially Donne, Marvell and Herbert. With her pure diction and faultless ear for cadence, George Herbert is the one she is most like. But she also seems close to Zbigniew Herbert, the great Polish poet, who is likewise a master of clarity and irony. Indeed, despite the fact that Adair's voice is quintessentially American, she seems closest in spirit to contemporary poets from Central Europe, like Herbert and Miroslav Holub, who went on writing for their desk drawers, confident in their private values and sensibilities, knowing they had no audience while the Stalinists ruled the roost.

Writing beautifully is no guarantee of success. Andrew Marvell was famous in his time as a political satirist and for his Latin verse, but he had to wait three hundred years before he was recognized as one of the greatest lyric poets in the language. We are fortunate in comparison. Virginia Adair may be very old, but at least her wonderful first book has apeared while she is still with us.

New York Review of Books, 1996

Les Murray

THERE WAS A TIME when Australian artists with something new to say packed their bags, left the country and didn't return until they had made their reputations in more sympathetic surroundings. During the early '60s, for example, most of Australia's best painters were working in London: Sidney Nolan, Arthur Boyd, Charles Blackman, Colin Lanceley, Brett Whitely, Lawrence Daws, John Perceval. Also in town were the young Robert Hughes, the poet Peter Porter and Australia's own megastar in the making, Barry Humphries.

When Albert Tucker, the first of the painters to leave, got on the boat to Europe, he explained bleakly, 'I am a refugee from Australian culture.' London, of course, was famously swinging in the '60s, although a decade or so earlier its culture had been as timorous, narrow-minded and fiercely anti-Modernist as Australia's: Menuhin's first performance of Bartok's 2nd Violin Concerto and the Tate Gallery's exhibition of the great wartime canvasses of Picasso and Matisse provoked storms of outrage and derision. But these were mild compared to the whoops of Philistine delight inspired by the Ern Malley affair in Australia during the war.

Like Chatterton's Rowley poems and Macpherson's Otway, Ern Malley was an elaborate literary hoax. It was cooked up by two clever young conscript poets, Lieutenant James McAuley and Corporal Harold Stewart, as a joke, they claimed, to while away a boring Saturday afternoon in the Victoria Barracks in Melbourne. Unlike Chatterton and Macpherson, however, McAuley's and Stewart's intentions were wholly malicious. Rowley and Ossian were acts of homage to the Romantic-Gothick style; that is why Wordsworth and Keats worshipped Chatterton, and Ossian was revered throughout Europe − even by Napoleon. Ern Malley was designed simply to expose the sham of Modernist verse and the gullibility of those who promoted it. To this end, Ern's creators gave him all the appropriate credentials for a misunderstood genius: they made him a misfit and a loner who worked as a garage mechanic, sold insurance, then died at the age of twenty-five, leaving a sheaf of poems which his bereaved and appropriately uncomprehending sister Edna bundled up and sent to *Angry Penguins*, Australia's most belligerently avant garde magazine. Max Harris, the feisty editor, was convinced he had discovered another 'marvellous boy,' the Antipodes' answer to Chatterton and Rimbaud. With much trumpeting, he published Malley's complete works in a special edition of his magazine, with a brilliant imaginary portrait of Malley by Sidney Nolan on the cover. The hoaxers then tipped off the tabloids, and poetry – for the first and probably last time in Australian history – became front-page news. Harris was not merely made to look a fool, he was hauled up in court by the police and charged with publishing obscene material. McAuley and Stewart had their moment of triumph, but it was Ern Malley who had the last laugh: the poems they concocted for him turned out to be more interesting and enduring than anything they wrote under their own names. But the final triumph was for the Philistines: the Ern Malley affair set Australian culture back for years.

Although it was a literary scandal, it was the painters who bore the brunt of it. On one level this was inevitable: reading poetry is an acquired skill and the audience is always small; painting, in comparison, is a more visible art in every sense, and every ignoramus knows what he or she likes. More important, painters like Nolan and Boyd were major figures by any standards and, as poor Ern Malley was pretending to do, they were using Modernist techniques to create a specifically Australian art. For example, when Nolan hung a cow in a tree, it wasn't a homage to Chagall, it was something he had seen in the outback after a freak flood, and he had photographs to prove it. The painters were trying to do justice to the eerie Australian landscape, with its peeling gum trees and burnt hills and dazzling light – a light like that in Dante's Paradiso, so clear that there might never have been a cloud. Australia had one or two good minor poets at that time – especially the fastidious Judith Wright – but they were fettered to the Mother Country and, until Les Murray appeared on the scene a couple of decades later, none of them had the range or the talent or the sheer ambition of the painters.

Murray announced his arrival with extraordinary self-confidence:

It began at dawn with fighter planes:
they came in off the sea and didn't rise,
they leaped the sandbar one and one and one
coming so fast the crockery they shook down
off my kitchen shelves was spinning in the air
when they were gone.

They came in off the sea and drew a wave
of lagging cannon-shells across our roofs.
Windows spat glass, a truck took sudden fire,
out leaped the driver, but the truck ran on,
growing enormous, shambling by our street-doors,
coming and coming . . .

By every right in town, by every average
we knew of in the world, it had to stop,
fetch up against a building, fall to rubble
from pure force of burning, for its whole
body and substance were consumed with heat
but it would not stop.

And all of us who knew our place and prayers
clutched our verandah-rails and window-sills,
begging that truck between our teeth to halt,
keep going, vanish, strike . . . but set us free.
And then we saw the wild boys of the street
go running after it.

And as they followed, cheering, on it crept,
windshield melting now, canopy-frame a cage
torn by gorillas of flame, and it kept on
over the tramlines, past the church, on past
the last lit windows, and then out of the world
with its disciples.

'The Burning Truck' is the poem Murray puts first in *Learning Human*, his chronological selection of the poems he considers his best. Its subject is war and it was written around 1965, a time when Australian verse was still taking its cue from elsewhere and anti-war agit-prop was all the fashion. But the war Murray writes about is the World War II he experienced in his childhood, not Vietnam, and his attitude to it is anything but self-righteous. An incident that might have been full of dread – a low-level fighter raid – becomes instead a source of wild excitement, a child's delight in the anarchy and violence that erupts when rules are turned on their heads and the placid certainties of 'all of us who knew our place and prayers' are vacuumed up in a great liberating rush of adrenalin.

But that's not the whole story. Although 'The Burning Truck,' like all Murray's best poems, is suffused with energy and appetite, something deeper and stranger is going on below the surface. It is as though the poet himself were physically swept up in the backdraft of the excitement. He doesn't simply observe the incident and describe it; he somehow becomes it – becomes, that is, the burning truck 'growing enormous, shambling by our street-doors, / coming and coming . . . a cage torn by gorillas of flame.' He might as well be announcing his own arrival on the literary scene, and he expresses it as a curiously physical experience.

This fits with his conception of poetry as a process that brings mind and body and fantasy together all at once: 'You've got to be able to dream at the same time as you think to write poetry,' he has said. 'You think with a double mind. It's like thinking with both sides of your brain at once. And if you can't do that, you can't write poetry. You can write expository prose, but poetry is as much dreamed as it is thought and it is as much danced in the body as it is written. It's done in your lungs. It's done in every part of your muscles – you can feel it in your muscles.' That quotation comes from Peter F. Alexander's *Les Murray: A Life in Progress*, a shrewd, measured, meticulously researched interim biography, written with the poet's co-operation. Unfortunately, Alexander's book has been held up by litigation – maybe because much of it is about the shamefully bitter in-fighting that plagues the Australian poetry world.

Murray seems to have been a prodigy from the start – 'a word freak,' he called himself. He was speaking before he was two, toddling around the yard reciting nursery rhymes by heart; by four he was reading, devouring every book in the house; by the time he went to school, at nine, he had memorized great tracts of his mother's eight-volume encyclopaedia. Later he developed an extraordinary knack for picking up foreign languages effortlessly, as though by osmosis. (His first, and virtually only, steady job was in the Translation Unit at the Australian National University at Canberra. He gave it up to concentrate on his poetry.)

Being a prodigy, however, was not necessarily an advantage in the impoverished New South Wales backwater where the Murrays lived. Bunyah was populated by the kind of 'good country folk' Flannery O'Connor wrote about so sardonically – hard-scrabble farmers, suspicious of anything that smacked of pretension, especially books. 'We didn't dwell a lot on readers,' one of the locals told Alexander complacently. More importantly, Murray was a disturbed child, always on the go, intemperate, impossible to control. 'Semi-autistic' is how he described himself – the modern diagnosis would probably be Asperger's Syndrome – and his parents didn't know how to cope with him, even though his mother was a city girl and trained nurse, a cut above the neighbours. So his father did to his son what his own father had done to him: he thrashed him brutally for every mis-demeanor, and went on thrashing him until Murray was too big and fast on his feet to subdue.

The Murrays were stern Scottish crofters who had emigrated voluntarily to Australia in the middle of the 19th century and had been settled in Bunyah ever since. They owned land and had prospered, but Murray's grandfather was a vindictive, drunken brute who deliberately kept his son poor – not hard-up, but dirt poor, barely managing to scrape a living from a few head of dairy cattle. The house the poet's father built for his wife was a leaky wooden shack with a tin roof, unlined walls and stamped-earth floors covered with linoleum. It had two rooms – the parents' bedroom and a living room. A lean-to kitchen was tacked onto one end; at the other was a rickety porch which doubled as Murray's bedroom. There was no running water and no electricity. This dire poverty was a source of such shame for Murray's parents that they kept their son strictly apart from his many cousins in the farms around and refused to allow any of them into the house because, the poet told Alexander, 'Home was too demeaning to let the terrible frank eyes of kids see it.' Murray didn't begin to mix with other children until a little local school opened in the valley. By then he was nine years old and set in his ways as a loner and an autodidact.

Even at school, a cousin said, he was 'always in the back room, quarrying those books.' The books set him apart and so did his build. He was a big child, prodigiously strong and prodigiously fat. Australian culture is famous for its resentment of the unusual, its passion for cutting everyone down to size – they call it 'the tall poppy syndrome' – and later Murray suffered for his gifts at the hands of envious minor poets. His weight, however, was not a problem for him until went he went away to high school in a distant town. For two nightmare years he was taunted mercilessly for his obesity – especially by the girls. But by then his life was already in ruins. When Murray was twelve his mother died as a result of a miscarriage and his father, who had been too ashamed and embarrassed by his wife's pregnancy to call an ambulance, retreated into chronic depression. It was a dark time the poet never forgot or forgave:

> From just on puberty, I lived in funeral:
> mother dead of miscarriage, father trying to be dead,
> we'd boil sweat-brown cloth; cows repossessed the garden.
> Lovemaking brought death, was the unuttered principle.
>
> I met a tall adopted girl some kids thought aloof,
> but she was intelligent. Her poise of white-blond hair
> proved her no kin to the squat tanned couple who loved her.
> Only now do I realise she was my first love.
>
> But all my names were fat-names, at my new town school.
> Between classes, kids did erocide: destruction of sexual morale.
> Mass refusal of unasked love: that works. Boys cheered as seventeen-
> year-old girls came on to me, then ran back whinnying ridicule.

Like his father, Murray had always been prone to what Winston Churchill called 'the black dog' and he responded to depression by eating voraciously. (Years later, when he was fifty, he went into a depressive breakdown that lasted eight terrible years; by the end, his weight was up to an astonishing 350 lbs.) Yet although poets are generally a lean and hungry bunch, Murray has always seemed proud of his girth, as though it were an outward sign of his appetite for the visible world and the physicality of his language. One of his best poems is in praise of fat people and is dedicated to the famously fat actor, Robert Morley:

> Is it possible that hyper-
> ventilating up Parnassus
> I have neglected to pay tribute
> to the Stone Age aristocracy?
> I refer to the fat.

We were probably the earliest
civilized, and civilizing, humans,
the first to win the leisure,
sweet boredom, life-enhancing sprawl
   that require style . . .

It's likely we also invented some of love,
much of fertility (see the Willensdorf Venus)
parts of theology (divine feasting, Unmoved Movers)
likewise complexity, stateliness, the ox-cart
   and self-deprecation.

Not that the lists of pugnacity are bare
of stout fellows. Ask a Sumo.
Warriors taunt us still, and fear us:
in heroic war, we are apt to be the specialists
   and the generals.

But we do better in peacetime. For ourselves
we would spare the earth. We were the first moderns
after all, being like the Common Man
disqualified from tragedy . . .

Fatness and informality are principles of faith for Murray and he has written about them in many forms – 'The Quality of Sprawl,' 'The Dream of Wearing Shorts Forever' – always tenderly, wittily, yearningly. They go with his love of grunge, his terrible teeth and youthful reluctance to bathe, as though sheer size absolved him from having to bother about appearances.

They also go with his image of himself as a typical Australian, since Australians have a talent for informality and present themselves to the world – triumphantly in the recent Olympics – as easy-going, friendly, and hard to impress. (The levelling, envious, poppy-lopping is the down-side of this democratic spirit.) Even so, Murray was ahead of his time. As a student at Sydney University in the late '50s, he was slopping around in government-surplus tat while his contemporaries were still wearing ties, tweed jackets and brogues.

Zero Mostel once said, 'Success didn't go to my head. It went to my waistline.' Murray's girth seems directly proportional to his poetic reach and, among many appetites, his truest is for Australia itself. Unlike poor Ern Malley, Murray never wanted to imitate the

Modernist masters; he wanted to transform Australian vernacular and Australian back-country life into his own unique form of Modernism. 'My "reply" to the expat generations,' he said, 'is to succeed from home.' He has a Whitmanesque ambition to pin down the commonplace reality of his country in verse, to include everything, especially the everything that more finicky poets turn away from – the deprived and depriving world he was born to. Hence the fighting title of one of his recent collections: *Subhuman Redneck Poems*.

It doesn't always work. At times his ambition gets the better of him and his sheer technical proficiency becomes a burden. The rhyming seems too easy, the verbiage too lush, as though Murray the 'word-freak' had been seduced by his love of language and the thick taste of words in his mouth. He seems least effective in big, set-piece landscape poems like 'The Buladelah-Taree Holiday Song Cycle' and 'Flood Plains on the Coast Facing Asia,' which read like roll-calls of place-names and scenes, clogged with details, stuffed with adjectives, then suddenly clearing to a kind of King James Bible grandeur: 'the storm veers mightily on its stem, above the roof; the hills uphold it.'

But when he is truly attending to whatever is before his eyes the results are sometimes extraordinary:

> *Going out to pick beans with the sun high as fence-tops, you find*
> *plenty, and fetch them. An hour or a cloud later*
> *you find shirtfuls more. At every hour of daylight*
>
> *appear more that you missed: ripe, knobbly ones, fleshy-sided*
> *thin-straight, thin-crescent, frown-shaped, bird-shouldered, boat-keeled*
> *ones,*
> *beans knuckled and single-bulged, minute green dolphins at suck.*

It's all a question of tone: the casual leading into the rococo, setting it off, calming it down.

Casual is what Murray does best. To my mind, the most successful poems in the book are the simplest and most intimate. This, for example, to a fellow-poet:

> *Since you'd become happy,*
> *you told me, you'd stopped writing poems.*
> *I should wish you a long silence. I do,*
> *I do, if you mean it.*

And this, to his daughter on her wedding day:

> *this must be the secular human lot: health*
> *till high old age, children of character,*
> *dear friendships. And the testing one: wealth.*
> *Quietly we add ours: may you*
> *always have each other, and want to.*

Murray is a great virtuoso and he has used his manifold talents to put Australia literally on the poetic map. But virtuosity is an ambiguous gift; given its head, it takes over and descends into mere flamboyance – mannerism, word-play, language for language's sake. In 'Quintets for Robert Morley' he writes, 'Never wholly trust the fat man / who lurks in the lean achiever / and in the defeated, yearning to get out.' In his own case, the reverse is mostly true. Murray the fat virtuoso, flashing up and down the verbal keyboard, is less impressive than Murray the lean Australian – off-hand, unfooled and blithely at ease with himself.

New York Review of Books, 2001

Derek Walcott

WHEN DEREK WALCOTT'S FIRST book of poems was published in London in 1962, it came with the blessing of Robert Graves, one of the twentieth century's finest and most underrated poets, and a title from Andrew Marvell – 'In a Green Night.' The title was a muted gesture towards Modernism, since T.S. Eliot had been the major force behind the rediscovery of Marvell after two and a half centuries of neglect. But Eliot had cosmopolitan tastes and initially he had been drawn to the Metaphysical poets because they reminded him of Laforgue and Corbière. Graves, on the other hand, was linked to Marvell as though by natural right, as direct inheritor of a peculiarly English lyric tradition: classical, witty, idiosyncratic, pure. It was this tradition that Walcott had absorbed as a student in the British West Indies: 'Like any colonial child,' he wrote in his essay 'The Muse in History,' 'I was taught English literature as my natural inheritance. Forget the snow and daffodils. They were real, more real than the heat and oleander, perhaps, because they lived on the page, in imagination, and therefore in memory.'

The British empire may have had many failings, but in its glory days no one was sent out to administer the Pax Brittanica without a solid grounding in the classics, and the colonial schools and colleges benefited accordingly. Walcott himself has said that his education 'must have ranked with the finest in the world. The grounding was rigid – Latin, Greek and the essential masterpieces, but there was this elation of discovery.' It was also, by modern standards, sternly old-fashioned. At Oxford, fifty years ago, English literature stopped at the death of Keats and I assume it was no different at the University of the West Indies. If you were interested in what followed or – God forbid – in contemporary writing, you read it in your own time. Walcott was indeed interested and duly served his apprentice-ship with Eliot and Auden, but his heart wasn't in it. He is not an experimental poet and has never been easy with the fast-talking, hard-edged high anxiety that gives the Modernist writers their peculiar sense of strain. His natural style is melodious, meditative and even-paced, closer to Yeats than to Eliot or Pound, closer still to the Victorians – closer, in fact, to grand Victorians like Tennyson and Arnold than to their maverick proto-Modernist contemporaries like Clough and Hopkins.

Walcott has something else in common with these earlier masters: he writes long poems, poems with plots and characters and intricate philosophical themes, and the long poem is not an art-form that has fared well in the last hundred or so years. Pound tried it because he was determined to write the Great American Poem but – to me, at least – the *Cantos* are a gigantic magpie's nest stuffed with shiny objects, more like the journal of an eccentric scholar than an epic, and with no more inherent structure than, say, Berryman's daybook of griefs and gripes and hangovers, the *Dream Songs*. The most important long poem of the twentieth century is *The Waste Land*, though not by Victorian standards; it runs to a mere 433 lines and Eliot is said to have added the end-notes in order to pad the thing out to book-length. In other words, *The Waste Land* is a short poem that feels long because it traverses such a dense inner space.

Walcott's work has never been interested in that kind of jagged compression. His abiding preoccupations are complex and contem-porary – exile, alienation, and the troublesome area where black culture and identity meet white – but he deals with them from an aesthetic distance and his plangent, ruminative tone of voice needs length in which to flourish. He is also a craftsman, a sophisticated technician who likes to ring changes on that most traditional of meters, the iambic pentameter, and is fascinated by rhymes, half-rhymes and assonance. Although his work itself is in no way old-fashioned, it seems, like his classical education, to belong to a steadier, more spacious period before poetry became a specialized, minority interest and was, instead, as much a part of the general culture as the novel. You simply read it differently: silently but out loud, as it were, for the civilized and civilizing pleasure of listening to the music in your head.

Omeros, Walcott's Caribbean variations on Homeric themes, is a long book – 350 pages of *terza rima*. *Tiepolo's Hound*, which is also written in a technically demanding form – alternately rhymed couplets, a/b//a/b – is only half that length, but it is complex and multi-layered, and it evolves slowly, like a novel. It is a poem about exile and obsession and art, and it explores these themes through the stories of two lives, Walcott's and Camille Pissarro's, told in parallel, each illuminating the other.

They make a good pair: born in the West Indies exactly one hundred years apart and self-exiled to colder climates; two craftsmen doggedly devoted to their art and working against the current fashions. Both of them were outsiders from the start – children with talent and ambition in indolent backwaters, internal exiles whether they left home or stayed put. Their family backgrounds added to the confusion. Pissarro's was Sephardic Portuguese in what was then the little Danish colony of St. Thomas, in the Antilles, and he moved to France when anti-Semitism was about to erupt in the Dreyfuss affair. Walcott arrived in the States at the height of the Civil Rights movement and his beginnings were even more complicated than Pissarro's. His peculiarly English education, he once wrote, meant that 'My generation had looked at life with black skins and blue eyes,' but that was only half the story. His father was an Englishman, his mother West Indian; they were middle-class, English-speaking Methodists in a British colony, St. Lucia, where the fishermen and peasants were Catholic and spoke Creole French. Walcott eventually came to regard his complex heritage as a source of strength:

> I'm just a red nigger who love the sea,
> I had a sound colonial education,
> I have Dutch, nigger, and English in me,
> and either I'm nobody, or I'm a nation.

But that wry confidence didn't come easily and the contradictions he was born to haunt his work.

The exile always carries his homeland with him, though not necessarily as a paradise lost. Walcott is particularly eloquent about the way Pissarro's tropical childhood enhanced the chilly beauty of Paris and made it delectable, sharpening his appetite, modulating his palette, opening his eyes to a different order of light:

O, the exclamation of white roses, of a wet
grey day of glazed pavements, the towers

in a haze of Notre Dame's silhouette
in the Easter drizzle, lines banked with flowers

and umbrellas flowering, then bobbing like mushrooms
in the soup-steaming fog! Paris looked edible:

salads of parks, a bouillabaisse of fumes
from the steaming trees in the incredible

fragrance of April.

Walcott writes about painting subtly and with insight because it, too, is part of his inheritance. His father was a civil servant who painted in his spare time, but he died when the poet was a baby and Walcott got to know him by poring over the handful of paintings and art books which he left behind:

From my father's cabinet I trace his predecessors
in a small blue book: The English Topographical Draughtsmen,

his pencil studies delicately firm as theirs,
the lyrical, light precision of these craftsmen –

Girton, Sandby, and Cotman, Peter De Wint,
meadows with needle spires in monochrome,

locks and canals with enormous clouds that went
rolling over England, postcards from home,

his namesake's county, Warwickshire. His own
work was a double portrait, a cherished oval

of his wife in oil, his own face, with a soft frown
that seemed to clarify the gentle evil

of an early death. A fine sketch of a cow,
a copy of Millet's The Gleaners, *Turner's*

The Fighting Temeraire, *the gathering blow*
of a storm with tossing gulls, more than a learner's

skill in them, more than mimicry, a gift

'These objects had established my vocation,' Walcott wrote in a 1965 essay called 'Leaving School,' 'and made it as inevitable as that of any craftsman's son, for I felt that my father's work, however minor, was unfinished.' He duly took over where his father had left off. He started out as a painter as well as a poet and continued painting long after his literary reputation was established. *Tiepolo's Hound* is illustrated by a not particularly relevant selection of his watercolours, and on the back of the book is a photograph of the handsome young poet at his easel. Walcott's pictures are bright and delicate and pleasing, but they have none of the authority of his verse, as he himself readily admitted in an interview on British television:

> There's a very big difference between someone who can paint pretty well and somebody who's a painter . . . it's how the paint is moved along recklessly, you know, without any caution. And although I can paint pretty competent water-colours I just don't have that bursting confidence . . . It's all very Methodist.

Methodist and also methodical: he is, by temperament, a devoted craftsman who studied the masters and laboured at his technique, and not just when he was learning to paint. Even now, as a mature poet, he goes out of his way to make things difficult for himself, setting himself technical goals – book-length poems in tricky rhyme schemes – that few other contemporary poets would even attempt. But craft is only a necessary first step. Amateur painters labour to acquire it, but true artists, like Pissarro, take it for granted. For them, technical assurance and economy become something more mysterious: an instinct for the precise brushstroke in the precise place that brings an image suddenly to life.

This mystery is the dominant theme of *Tiepolo's Hound*. Walcott sensed it first at an art show in New York:

> *I remember stairs in couplets. The Metropolitan's*
> *marble authority, I remember being*
>
> *stunned as I studied the exact expanse*
> *of a Renaissance feast, the art of seeing.*
>
> *Then I caught a slash of pink on an inner thigh*
> *of a white hound entering the cave of a table,*

so exact in its lucency at The Feast of Levi,
I felt my heart halt. Nothing, not the babble

of the unheard roar that rose from the rich
pearl-lights embroidered on ballooning sleeves,

sharp beards, and gaping goblets, matched the bitch
nosing a forest of hose. So a miracle leaves

its frame, and one epiphanic detail
illuminates an entire epoch.

This moment of revelation became the poet's obsession, as though by studying the single slash of colour that made Tiepolo's 'spectral hound' leap out of the frame he could unravel the mystery of genius. The trouble was, he could never find the picture again, however diligently he visited exhibitions and trawled through art books:

I riffled through the derisive catalogue
determined that the fact was not a vision.

(The dog, the dog, where was the fucking dog?)
Their postures wrong. Nothing confirmed my vision.

He even made a pilgrimage to Venice, but grudgingly, with his patience wearing thin:

Devoted as a candle to its church,
the thigh flared steadily, more affliction

than quest now, I would end my search . . .

Cowardice, stubbornness, indifference
made too much of the whiteness of the hound.

When he drew a blank in Venice it occurred to him that maybe he had mistaken the artist; the creature was Veronese's, not Tiepolo's. So he started over, again to no avail. And the more he searched, the deeper the mystery became.

Walcott tells this story in tandem with Pissarro's, as two versions of the same quest, one misguided and frustrating, the other resolved, though not in the heart-stopping way Walcott would have predicted when he first saw Tiepolo's hound. For Walcott, Pissarro represents genius without flamboyance, the artist as craftsman, plugging away at his vision of light – light in Paris, light in Pontoise, endless subtle variations on a single luminous theme, 'so modest, so sublime!' His life was bleak and impoverished, his paintings didn't sell, and only a handful of fellow-artists recognised his gift. In old age, his hands were crippled by arthritis and he was almost blind, but he went on painting to the very end.

This is the secret Walcott was looking for: stubborn persistence allied to craftsmanship so habitual and refined that it becomes an instinct, a way of seeing; not the sudden flash of inspiration or High Renaissance drama, but a steady devotion to the world as it is:

> *Some critics think his work is ordinary,*
> *but the ordinary is the miracle.*
>
> *Ordinary love and ordinary death,*
> *ordinary suffering, ordinary birth,*
>
> *the ordinary couplets of our breath,*
> *ordinary heaven, ordinary earth.*

This is cool and measured and beautiful, and perhaps that's what Walcott means by 'Methodist.' In the poet's imagination Tiepolo's hound embodies the careless, flamboyant talent both he and his father lacked as painters. Pissarro's meticulous genius is less startling in comparison, but it is what Walcott is after in his new poem:

> *A silent city, blest with emptiness*
> *like an engraving. Ornate fretwork eaves,*
>
> *and the heat rising from the pitch in wires,*
> *from empty back yards with calm breadfruit leaves,*
>
> *their walls plastered with silence, the same streets*
> *with the same sharp shadows, laced verandahs closed*
>
> *in torpor . . .*

Walcott is doing in words for his beloved St. Lucia what Pissarro did in paint for the French landscape – fixing it in time with 'lyrical, light precision,' modestly and without fuss.

New York Review of Books, 2000

Vladimir Mayakovsky

HE WAS AN OUTSIZE figure in every way: a giant of a man, built like a heavyweight boxer, and with a boxer's bruised good looks and endless reserves of energy. In the unquiet but outwardly sedate days before the revolution he was a great shocker of the bourgeoisie, shouting down speakers at polite meetings, flaunting an obnoxious yellow tunic in the teeth of buttoned-up respectability, occasionally sporting a wooden spoon in his button-hole instead of a rose, preaching the death of the old forms, the elimination of punctuation, and a new poetry of machines. The violence and horror of the revolution and the early days of Communism, which drove even Gorki to a breakdown, acted on him as a stimulus: 'Mayakovsky entered the revolution,' wrote a contemporary, 'as he would his own home.'

For the good of the cause he put aside his lyrics and churned out slogans and posters as relentlessly as one of the production lines he so admired. By every account he was one of the all-time great readers of poetry, a spellbinder who could hold an audience for hours – in the flatfooted provinces as easily as in the capital. 'There would be no sense in calling him a writer,' wrote Kornel Chukovsky, one of his early critics and defenders, 'his calling is not writing but shouting his head off. He needs not paper but a larynx.'

True to form, he even seemed at one point on the edge of becoming a screen heart-throb; he wrote movies, starred in them and had his usual knock-down success. Women adored him and fell like corn. Those who loved him, he treated badly – he had at least one suicide to his credit. He reserved his epic passion for a couple of ice-cold bitches – one already married, the other with her sights on a French title – who treated him much as he treated the others: disdainfully.

He was the most famous and flamboyant Russian poet of his time. Lenin was intrigued but disliked him; he called his style 'hooligan communism.' But after his suicide Stalin proclaimed him the greatest. And immediately he became a paragon for party versifiers, taught in every school and reburied monumentally in a grandiose cemetery for party dignitaries. 'This was his second death,' wrote Pasternak. 'He had no hand in it.'

Giant? Monster? Showman? Charlatan? Genius? 'Everybody is right about Mayakovsky,' says Patricia Blake in her excellent introduction to *The Bedbug* and *Selected Poetry*. The problem is whether such gigantism is compatible with poetry; whether genius transformed into a public career doesn't ultimately negate an essentially solitary art; whether, in short, Mayakovsky sacrificed his gifts to his image as disastrously as he sacrificed them, in his later years, to his politics.

The questions are as alive now as they were 50 years ago, and as unsettled, despite Stalin's canonization of the man, or maybe because of it. Yet one quality no one denied him was his genius. The spiritual impact of the man was as overwhelming as his physical presence. But the nonsense, arrogance, ruthlessness were off-putting, the noise distracting. To see a legend spotlit in an auditorium and hear him declaim was one thing. To meet him afterwards in a living room and read his words silently to oneself was, apparently, something different and less earthquaking. We suffer the same ambiguity with some of our own flashier poets, though genius, alas, is not their problem.

Wiktor Woroszylski, a Polish poet and editor, has solved the contradictions surrounding Mayakovsky's life and work by producing 'a composite biography.' The phrase is Edward Nehls's, who used the technique in his great three-volume work on that other supremely controversial figure, D. H. Lawrence. The biographer does not allow himself the luxury of conjecturing, interpreting or judging; he doesn't even appear. He simply selects the sources and supplies certain factual links. For the rest, as Woroszylski says, 'only records of various kinds will be allowed to speak.'

These records include everything from fragments of Mayakovsky's own laconic autobiography, his strangely gushy love letters, through reviews, manifestoes, notes on public debates, editorials, government directives, to the reports of the Tsarist secret police who first arrested the adolescent Mayakovsky. 'It is closest, perhaps,' says the author, 'not so much to literature as to a film chronicle, made up of old shots and captions.' It is, in all events, a marvelously thorough and illuminating piece of work.

Mayakovsky was born in the deep backwoods of Georgia. When he was 12 his father, a decayed gentleman turned forester, died prematurely, and the penniless family – there were two older sisters – moved to Moscow. Almost immediately, Mayakovsky was involved in Bolshevik politics. He dropped out of school to become 'a professional revolutionary' and had been arrested three times before he was 16. By the time of his last arrest his talents as a showman were already obvious: he refused to stay in his cell and paraded the corridors, inciting his fellow prisoners and proclaiming himself their leader. He was 15.

Politics meant going underground, which in turn meant abandoning his education. Finally, he chose art school, where his ambition and aggression exceeded his shallow talent. But while there he met up with David Burliuk, a painter with a flair for promotion, who heard Mayakovsky's first, tentative poem and proclaimed him a genius. Mayakovsky never looked back. His motto had always been 'Hating prettiness': now he had a medium in which he could express all that rage and energy.

He had a genius for violent, far-fetched rhymes – which, as Patricia Blake explains, are more or less untranslatable – and for sudden, piercing imagery: 'I shall bring the dawn of my ultimate love, / bright as a consumptive's flush.' He also had a genius for exhibitionism and for that infighting endemic in Russian literary life, which has always been plagued with internecine rivalries between coteries, movements, poets' cafes and clubs, all squabbling, all hating each other, all utterly unforgiving.

In the days before the revolution, the gang warfare was harmless enough. In his unspeakable Futurist youth, Mayakovsky paraded in his yellow jacket, declaimed, abused, issued manifestoes with titles like *A Slap to the Public's Taste*, and nothing much was injured except public sensibility and private vanity. But after 1917 the same vicious squabbling had more sinister results; literary politics became as exacerbated and as deadly as the real thing. Like the party chiefs, the poets were fighting for keeps. While Lenin was still alive and the cultivated, impartial Lunacharsky was People's Commissar of Education, writers out of favor merely had difficulty in getting published and making a living. But when Stalin took over and his mouthpiece Zhdanov proclaimed the orthodoxy of Socialist Realism, those out of favor perished: Mandelstam, Babel and the great theatrical director Meyerhold died in the camps; Tsvetayeva, Yashvili, and even the foxy Fadeyev took their own lives.

But by that time Mayakovsky had already committed suicide. The record of his last years is infinitely depressing. He gave himself over to the Party. But the more vehement his Communism, the more fiercely the party hacks attacked him. His egotism and self-drama had always been supreme: when he was eighteen, he wrote a version of *Hamlet* called, quite simply, *Vladimir Mayakovsky*; after the revolution, he produced *Mystery-Bouffe* in which he transformed himself into the Messiah. Such arrogance was not likely to endear him to the official writers, whose mission was to reduce every talent to their own level of mediocrity. It was not, anyway, in Mayakovsky's nature to conceal his contempt.

Whatever good his 3000-line ode on Lenin might have done him he undercut by his plays, *The Bedbug* and *The Bathhouse,* which satirized the new breed of bureaucrats, avaricious, self-inflated, corrupt. In *The Bedbug* he did this, admittedly, in the name of an ideal Communist future, but even that seemed dehumanized and intolerable. Although well translated by Max Hayward, *The Bedbug* is a crude piece of work; the wild inventiveness of the poems seems clumsy and obvious when translated into stage business. Yet the satire cut all ways and, in the end, it was Mayakovsky himself who was most hurt.

In his last days, he abandoned his gifted friends in LEF – his left wing version of Futurism – and joined the nonentities of RAPP, the official association of writers. But he was too big for them and, in self-defense, they isolated him as though he were infectious, until such time as he should learn his lesson and diminish himself to their paltry stature.

This total isolation before his death was an intensification of the loneliness that had always obsessed him, however stunning his triumphs on the podium or in bed. Chukovsky called him 'a poet of catastrophes and convulsions.' yet his genius lay in being able to express a sense of universal foreboding and resentment through the medium of highly personal poems. 'Mayakovsky did not invent anything in his poetry,' wrote David Burliuk, 'His poems reflected the course of his life. They were like a ship's logbook.' But in trying to accommodate this intimate genius to party principles, he ended by knowingly strangling it. In his beautiful late poem, 'At the Top of My Voice,' he wrote. 'I / subdued / myself / setting my heel / on the throat / of my song.'

The best essay on Mayakovsky – oddly enough, not mentioned by Woroszylski – is by Trotsky: 'His voice out-thunders thunder. What is the wonder that . . . the proportions of earthly things vanish and that no difference is left between the small and the great? He speaks about love, the most intimate of feelings, as if it were the migration of peoples . . . No doubt, his hyperbolic style reflects in some measure the frenzy of our time. But this does not provide it with an over-all artistic justification . . . Mayakovsky shouts too often where one should speak softly, and so his cry, where cry is needed, sounds inadequate.'

English does not lend itself easily to this style of cosmic mega-lomania. The rather inept translations in Woroszylski's biography often reduce the poems to inflated gibberish. In comparison, the versions by Max Hayward and George Reavey really communicate a sense of the energy, subtlety and inventiveness which is always claimed for Mayakovsky. So does G. M. Hyde who, in his translation of the poem on Yesenin, also manages the weird off-rhymes. This latter is an appendix to Mayakovsky's brilliant essay *How Are Verses Made?*, one of the few documents about the practical business of writing poetry which genuinely carries conviction. That is, it is all about how it is done and not at all about esthetic theory. It is a wonderfully invigorating performance, simple, direct, utterly without side: the great master of rhythm admits he knows nothing about that old academic favorite, meter; he demonstrates the slow, painfully patient labor through draft after draft, to find precisely the right cadence and word. I know nothing quite like it.

In the end, all the skill and devotion in the world were not enough. His last play, *The Bathhouse*, had been savaged – and he hated criticism. He had cut himself off from his friends and his new allies would have nothing to do with him. Lila Brik, his great love, was finished with him and had gone abroad; his other passion had married her French count. And God knows what betrayals he felt, at last, he had committed on his own poetic gift. He had always been a gambler and a risk-taker. On April 14, 1930, he played Russian roulette for the third time, and lost. Contemptuous to the last, he wrote in parenthesis in his suicide note: 'I do not recommend it to others.'

Ten years earlier, the dying Alexander Blok had been asked why he no longer wrote poetry. 'All sounds have stopped,' he replied. 'Can't you hear that there are no longer any sounds? . . . I close my eyes so as not to see those apes.' The apes in question were the ignorant and unprepared masses, as well as the place-holders and apparatchiks for whose sake Mayakovsky stripped his poetry and turned it into propaganda. But that wasn't enough and, in the end, they got him, too. Only after he was safely dead could they transform him, at Stalin's command, into a cultural hero.

New York Times, 1971

Zbigniew Herbert

ZBIGNIEW HERBERT HAS HAD an exemplary Central European education. He was born in 1924 in Lwów in eastern Poland, the son of a lawyer and professor of economics whose great-grandfather spoke only English (hence his literary British surname). In September 1939, when Herbert was fifteen, Lwów was swallowed by the Russian whale. Twenty months later, the Germans marched in and Herbert finished high school underground, fighting in the Resistance. At the end of the war he went to university to study both his father's disciplines: he took a master's in economics at Kraków, then a master's in law at Toruń, where he stayed on to study philosophy. In 1950 he moved briefly to Gdańsk, then on to Warsaw where for six years he held down a series of menial, Kafkaesque jobs: in a bank, in a shop, as a clerk in the management office of the peat industry, in the department for retired pensioners of the Teachers' Cooperative, and in the legal department of the Composers' Association.

During the Nazi occupation his poems had been published irregularly in underground magazines and they continued to appear more or less in the same unofficial way during the grim Stalinist period after the war. Although he was a precocious poet, he had to wait until Khrushchev's thaw in 1956, when he was thirty-two, to publish his first book of poems. The second appeared the following year, two large collections representing a decade and a half of work, which established him as the leader of his exceptionally gifted generation. It is typical of his ironic indifference to success that he celebrated this recognition with an apologetic poem dedicated to the desk drawer which in sterner times had been his one true audience; his 'rebel's fist stiff in dissent,' he wrote, had given him a subject and an excuse, and his new liberty to publish what he wants is only responsibility in another guise:

such is freedom one has again
to invent and overthrow gods

He has been inventing and overthrowing gods ever since, a party of one, permanently and warily in opposition. Although he lived abroad from 1965 to 1971, when the conditions in Poland were relatively relaxed, and was abroad again in the late 1970s – in 1979 he was awarded the Petrarch Prize, Germany's greatest cultural accolade – he returned home immediately after the troubles started in Gdańsk, in 1980, and has stayed there since. His international reputation is now too secure for the authorities to harm him, yet he refuses to accept their embrace. His new collection, *Report from the Besieged City*, was first published by internees in the Rakowiecka Prison in Warsaw in 1983.

To understand modern Polish poetry it is necessary also to understand something of what the country went through during the Nazi occupation: 6 million killed out of a population of 30 million; dozens of villages destroyed and their inhabitants massacred, in the style of Lidice and Oradour; Warsaw razed and emptied of its million inhabitants, the Nazis boasting that they would turn it into 'a second Carthage'; Governor General Hans Frank's infamous Operation AB which aimed at the total elimination of the country's intelligentsia and succeeded in murdering 3,500. There was an old historical grudge between the Germans and the Poles, and it was settled by twentieth-century totalitarian methods.

All this instilled in the survivors a distaste for rhetoric and artistic pretension that amounted almost to a hatred of poetry itself. Tadeusz Różewicz, who is three years older than Herbert, looked on art as an offense against human suffering and reduced his poems to a minimalist notation stripped of meter, rhyme, even of metaphor. 'Modern poetry,' he wrote, 'is a struggle for breath.' Herbert, too, eschews all punctuation and every unearned gesture. 'He lowers his voice rather than raising it,' John and Bogdana Carpenter write in the introduction to *Report from the Besieged City*, 'the rhythm of his poems sometimes approaching the level of a whisper, or silent thinking.' Yet despite the lack of punctuation, the argument of his poems is unfailingly lucid and the voice, however low, is clear and precise. This clarity is the core of everything Herbert has written. Despite the historical catastrophes he has lived through, he is a classicist, like Eliot, whom he reveres, and Piero della Francesca, about whom he has written eloquently in his collection of essays, *Barbarian in the Garden*.

Or perhaps he is a classicist because the continuing Polish catastrophe has placed such curious burdens on its writers. It is a nation that has held itself together for the past two centuries only by a collective effort of will. For 150 years Poland was partitioned between Russia, Prussia, and Austria, reemerging between the world wars, then swallowed up again, first by the Germans, then by the Russians. All this puts a special strain on writers, for in an occupied or one-party nation literature takes on the patriotic, educative, and moral burdens normally assumed by the state. It becomes, for instance, a forum for national debate in which political issues are discussed in guise of imaginative writing. Whence the Polish penchant for allegory and what they call 'Aesopian language.' Whence, too, the strange phenomenon of the underground presses, during both the Nazi occupation and the present troubles, continuing to print poetry and fiction along with political leaflets. In the Polish context, a poem or story can seem as rousing and urgent as a fighting handbill, and is probably more effective.

One of Herbert's earliest poems, written when he was in his teens, first appeared in this clandestine way. It is called 'Two Drops' and is prefaced by a quotation from the nineteenth-century poet Slowacki – 'No time to grieve for roses when the forests are burning' – which the young Herbert, writing at a time when all of Poland was on fire, then proceeded to turn on its head:

> The forests were on fire –
> they however
> wreathed their necks with their hands
> like bouquets of roses
>
> People ran to the shelters –
> he said his wife had hair
> in whose depths one could hide
>
> Covered by one blanket
> they whispered shameless words
> the litany of those who love
>
> When it got very bad
> they leapt into each other's eyes
> and shut them firmly
>
> So firmly they did not feel the flames
> when they came up to the eyelashes
>
> To the end they were brave
> To the end they were faithful

To the end they were similar
like two drops
stuck at the edge of a face

It is a beautiful poem; given the circumstances in which it was written and the poet's age at the time, it is extraordinary. The theme is one that Herbert has repeated, in one form or another, throughout his work: that the feeling that can flower between people, however frail, is somehow a match for history, however violent. Most young poets would have been satisfied with that ultimate existential gesture – making love while the bombs fall, as if a kiss could annihilate annihilation. Herbert, however, uses it to affirm less obvious, more abiding virtues: bravery, faithfulness, restraint (grief becomes merely 'two drops / stuck at the edge of a face'). In the end, the poem is not about a gesture of defiance but about dignity; it is classical in the true Roman sense.

Herbert has never deviated from this passion for *virtù*. The hero of many of his later poems is Mr. Cogito, a battered descendant of Valéry's luminously intelligent M. Teste, and also a descendant of Descartes who exists because he thinks about his existence. In other words, Mr. Cogito is a witness whose duty it is to serve truth not art, to think dispassionately about what he has seen, and to speak up for morality, however inappropriate it may seem:

go upright among those who are on their knees
among those with their backs turned and those toppled in the dust

you were saved not in order to live
you have little time you must give testimony

be courageous when the mind deceives you be courageous
in the final account only this is important . . .

That is from 'The Envoy of Mr. Cogito,' Herbert's stern and moving last testament that ends his 1977 *Selected Poems*. But independence and courage, like clarity and restraint, have little chance against what he calls 'the babble of the speaker's platform the black foam of news-papers.' The best he can do is elevate plainness into an aesthetic and moral principle. In an early poem, 'A Knocker,' he wrote wryly of his style, as though it were a limitation beyond his control:

my imagination
is a piece of board
my sole instrument
is a wooden stick

> *I strike the board*
> *it answers me*
> *yes—yes*
> *no—no*

In the latest collection, 'Mr. Cogito and the Imagination' repeats the same theme less hopefully, but as an article of faith:

> *he wanted to make it*
> *an instrument of compassion*
>
> *he wanted to understand to the very*
> *end*
>
> *…*
>
> *and so to bring the dead back to life*
> *to preserve the covenant*
>
> *Mr. Cogito's imagination*
> *has the motion of a pendulum*
>
> *it crosses with precision*
> *from suffering to suffering*
>
> *there is no place in it*
> *for the artificial fires of poetry*
> *he would like to remain faithful*
> *to uncertain clarity*

Early and late, Herbert has avoided 'the artificial fires of poetry' by using irony, that most classical of instruments and the enemy of rhetoric, of inflation, of distortion. But irony is also the weapon of the powerless, as Herbert himself pointed out – ironically, of course – at the end of a prose poem called 'From Mythology':

> Then came the barbarians. They too
> valued highly the little god of irony.
> They would crush it under their heels
> and add it to their dishes.

For Herbert, irony has always been a two-edged instrument that turns on the poet as readily as on the outside world. But in the earlier poems he used it playfully to rewrite his beloved classical myths in modern, deflationary terms – Arion, for instance, becomes 'the Grecian Caruso' – and even, in some of his love poems, as an improbable way of expressing desire without indiscretion:

> *Inadvertently I passed the border of her teeth and swallowed her agile tongue. It lives inside me now, like a Japanese fish. It brushes against my heart and my diaphragm as if against the walls of an aquarium. It stirs silt from the bottom.*
>
> *She whom I deprived of a voice stares at me with big eyes and waits for a word.*
>
> *Yet I do not know which tongue to use when speaking to her – the stolen one or the one which melts in my mouth from an excess of heavy goodness.*

This youthful playfulness has seeped away over the years as his confidence in the power of truth and intelligence, as well as of irony, has weakened. The tone of his recent poems is grim, like the situation of his country and of the civilized standards on which his work is based. 'I avoid any commentary I keep a tight hold on my emotions I write about the facts,' he says in the title poem of *Report from the Besieged City*.

'Then came the barbarians': when he called his prose collection *Barbarian in the Garden* he was implying that he himself was the barbarian outsider reacting to the civilized gardens of France, Italy, and ancient Greece. Yet these elegant, meticulous, oddly passionate essays return continually to the theme of vanished cultures and their violent destruction – the Templars, the Albigensians at Montségur, the Greek colonists at Paestum – as though his underlying concern was always the modern barbarians from East and West who have erupted into the precarious culture of his own country.

In the poems, too, the focus constantly shifts backward and forward between past and present. 'Report from the Besieged City' is both about Poland after December 1981, when General Jaruzelski declared 'a state of war,' and about Poland as it has been through the centuries, a crossroad for invading barbarians:

> *in the evening I like to wander near the outposts of the City*
> *along the frontier of our uncertain freedom*
> *I look at the swarms of soldiers below their lights*
> *I listen to the noise of drums barbarian shrieks*
> *truly it is inconceivable the City is still defending itself*

> *the siege has lasted a long time the enemies must take turns*
> *nothing unites them except the desire for our extermination*
> *Goths the Tartars Swedes troops of the Emperor regiments of the*
>   *Transfiguration*
> *who can count them*
> *the colors of their banners change like the forest on the horizon*
> *from delicate bird's yellow in spring through green through red to winter's*
>   *black*

Invading armies have become so much a condition of Polish life that Herbert describes them as if they were manifestations of nature itself – that is, dispassionately and with an eye for their 'delicate bird's yellow' beauty.

It is this objectivity – the rigorousness with which he avoids the easy outs of self-pity, melodrama, even nostalgia – that preserves the classical spirit in Herbert's work. Mr. Cogito's imagination may cross 'with precision from suffering to suffering,' but as it does so the precision matters as much as the suffering. Whatever his subject, the steady light of his intelligence imposes on it a kind of serenity of which the classics themselves are part, since they enable him to view the unruly present in the long, cooling perspective of history. What he wrote of his idol, Piero della Francesca, is also true of his own work: 'Over the battle of shadows, convulsions and tumult, Piero has erected *lucidus ordo* – an eternal order of light and balance.'

Czeslaw Milosz once wrote that Herbert survived the war and Stalinism because of 'his personal qualities – good health, toughness, an orderly mind.' Those qualities have also kept him from being abstract in his classicism, or pedantic, or superior. His poetry is founded on a belief in ordinary human values – love, dignity, intelligence, common decency – as the only true defense against the barbarians. 'History teaches us that nations and their achievements can be destroyed in an almost total manner,' he said in an interview quoted by the Carpenters in their introduction to the 1977 *Selected Poems*. 'During the war I saw the fire of a library. The same fire was devouring wise and stupid books, good and bad. Then I understood that it is nihilism which menaces culture the most. Nihilism of fire, stupidity, and hatred.'

Herbert has steadily opposed nihilism with neither rhetoric nor anger, but with sanity – wakeful, ironic, evenhanded, intransigent:

The pebble
is a perfect creature

equal to itself
mindful of its limits

filled exactly
with a pebbly meaning

with a scent which does not remind one of anything
does not frighten anything away does not arouse desire

its ardour and coldness
are just and full of dignity

I feel a heavy remorse
when I hold it in my hand
and its noble body
is permeated by false warmth

> *— Pebbles cannot be tamed*
> *to the end they will look at us*
> *with a calm and very clear eye*

Herbert is the only contemporary poet I know who can talk about nobility and, more important, sound noble without also sounding false. It is a note that is rare in the arts of any period. The Romans had it, so did Shakespeare, Donne, and Milton. But it hasn't been much in evidence in recent years and perhaps it took someone who has witnessed close-up – 'with a calm and very clear eye' – some of the worst horrors of this century to speak out for *virtù* and endurance without sounding sentimental.

The strengths Herbert praises in his poems – steadfastness and independence, imperviousness to cant, contempt for the bullies – have their corollary in the purity of his style. He has been marvelously served by his translators but perhaps his persistent lucidity has made their task a little easier. All of them remark on how much is lost in translation. Despite that, his poems, even in English, seem to me finer than anything currently being written by any English or American poet.

New York Review of Books, 1985

Czeslaw Milosz

FOUR YEARS AGO MILAN KUNDERA published in these columns an essay called 'The Tragedy of Central Europe.' The tragedy in question was not so much war and occupation, the massacres, destruction, and humiliation at the hands of ignorant invaders; it was, instead, the loss of what Central Europe once embodied: European culture. Central Europe, for Kundera, was not just a collection of small and vulnerable nations with difficult languages and tragic histories; it was the intellectual and artistic center for the whole of Western civilization and the last stronghold of the intelligentsia, a place where essays counted for more than journalism, and books had more influence than television.

Long before Kundera wrote his article Czeslaw Milosz had described a typical day in the life of Central European man. On August 1, 1944, the day the Warsaw uprising unexpectedly began, Milosz and his wife were caught in heavy gunfire while on their way to a friend's apartment to discuss – what else? – poetry in translation. Face down for hours in a potato field, with machine-gun bullets zipping over his head, Milosz refused to let go of the book he was carrying. After all, it was not his to throw away – it belonged to the library of Warsaw University – and anyway, he needed it – assuming the bullets didn't get him. The book was *The Collected Poems of T.S. Eliot* in the Faber & Faber edition. All in all, it was a very Polish situation: bullets and modernism, the polyglot in the potato field, ashes and diamonds.

Milosz has all the other characteristics of Central European man. He was born in Lithuania, a country that has vanished utterly into the Soviet maw, the bulk of its people transported by Stalin to somewhere beyond the Urals. Like his great Lithuanian predecessor Adam Mickiewicz, Milosz writes in Polish and is fluent in several languages. He has also suffered a typically Central European fate – exile. Half his long life has been spent teaching in Berkeley. In other words, he is a man whose only true home is in books, in language; he carries his country around in his head.

The one language Milosz might be expected to speak is German. He claims, however, to understand only two phrases, *Hande hoch!* and *Alle männer vrraus!*, mementos of the five years he spent in Warsaw during the Nazi occupation. His fellow Polish poets, Zbigniew Herbert and Tadeusz Rózewicz, also got their education during the war; whence the starkness of their poetry – Rózewicz's minim-alism, Herbert's austere, ironic morality. But they were both teenagers when the Germans marched in and the terrible years of Hans Frank's Government-General were their high school. Milosz, however, was born in 1911 and had published two books of poetry before 1939, so his style was formed in less savage times and what was lost – 'a world gone up in smoke' he called it in a poem written in 1941 – concerned him as much as what was being done.

What the war taught him as a poet had to do, above all, with priorities:

> I could reduce all that happened to me then to a few things. Lying in the field near a highway bombarded by airplanes, I riveted my eyes on a stone and two blades of grass in front of me. Listening to the whistle of a bomb, I suddenly understood the value of matter; that stone and those two blades of grass formed a whole kingdom, an infinity of forms, shades, textures, lights. They were the universe. I had always refused to accept the division into macro- and micro-cosmos; I preferred to contem-plate a piece of bark or a bird's wing rather than sunsets or sunrises. But now I saw into the depths of matter with excep-tional intensity.

That is from Milosz's brilliant and understated autobiography, *Native Realm*. The experience of total war taught him the supreme value not of art but of life itself, of brute survival in a wholly destructive element.

In *The Captive Mind*, his somber denunciation of the sovietization of Eastern Europe, he described a similar experience, transposed into the third person, and drew the necessary aesthetic conclusions:

> The work of human thought *should* withstand the test of brutal, naked reality. If it cannot, it is worthless. . . . A man is lying

under machine-gun fire on a street in an embattled city. He
looks at the pavement and sees a very amusing sight: the
cobblestones are standing upright like the quills of a porcupine.
The bullets hitting against their edges displace and tilt them.
Such moments in the consciousness of a man *judge* all poets and
philosophers. Let us suppose, too, that a certain poet was the
hero of literary cafés, and wherever he went was regarded with
curiosity and awe. Yet his poems, recalled in such a moment,
suddenly seem diseased and highbrow. The vision of the
cobblestones is unquestionably real; and poetry based on an
equally *naked* experience could survive triumphantly that judgment day of man's illusions. In the intellectuals who lived
through the atrocities of war in Eastern Europe there took
place what one might call the *elimination of emotional luxuries*.
Psychoanalytic novels incite them to laughter. They consider
the literature of erotic complications, still popular in the West,
as trash. Imitation abstract painting bores them. They are hungry
– but they want bread, not hors d'oeuvres.

Before the war Milosz's sense of impending doom had earned him the
title of 'catastrophist.' In the face of a catastrophe greater than he could
ever have imagined his own early prose appeared to him paltry and
self-indulgent. So did his youthful literary ambitions. He peddled a
pamphlet of his verse – printed by an underground press and sewn
together by his wife-to-be – in the same spirit and for the same motive
as he peddled black-market cigarettes and blood sausage: because he
was penniless. Poetry had become, in every sense, a means of survival,
a matter of life and death.

The poems he wrote during the war and published in 1945 as
Rescue are a kind of atonement for his earlier frivolity and a reparation
made to those who did not survive. The two prose passages I have
quoted are glosses, in their different ways, on 'Dedication,' the famous
poem that ended the 1945 volume:

You whom I could not save
Listen to me.
Try to understand this simple speech as I would be ashamed of another.
I swear, there is in me no wizardry of words.
I speak to you with silence like a cloud or a tree.

What strengthened me, for you was lethal.
You mixed up farewell to an epoch with the beginning of a new one,
Inspiration of hatred with lyrical beauty,
Blind force with accomplished shape.

Here is the valley of shallow Polish rivers. And an immense bridge
Going into white fog. Here is a broken city,
And the wind throws the scream of gulls on your grave
When I am talking with you.

What is poetry which does not save
Nations or people?
A connivance with official lies,
A song of drunkards whose throats will be cut in a moment,
Readings for sophomore girls.
That I wanted good poetry without knowing it,
That I discovered, late, its salutary aim,
In this and only this I find salvation.

They used to pour millet on graves or poppy seeds
To feed the dead who would come disguised as birds.
I put this book here for you, who once lived
So that you should visit us no more.

The war released Milosz into an adult world where rhetoric, dogma and ambition seemed so much childishness. This adult world, however, did not exclude childhood. At the heart of *Rescue*, among poems about ruined Warsaw and the destruction of the ghetto, about grief, deprivation, and random death, is a beautiful sequence called, ironically perhaps, 'The World.' The poems are short, calm, so simple as to seem almost translucent, and their subject is the lost world of Milosz's childhood in the deep Lithuanian countryside (the same world that he later wrote about – less convincingly, I think – in his autobiographical novel, *The Issa Valley*). In their restrained and tender way, they bring 'news / From a world that is bright, beautiful, warm, and free,' and they make Milosz's subsequent exile seem inevitable. They confirmed him as a poet whose continuing theme, however stern and 'naked' the reality he dealt with, was always that of loss.

In Central Europe the war did not end when what Richard Eberhart called 'the fury of aerial-bombardment' was over. The Stalinist repression that followed merely translated the problem of

survival into different terms: moral instead of physical, personal truth
in the face of state-imposed hypocrisy. The kind of poetry imagined
by Milosz and those like him – poetry that occupies the moral high
ground yet is proof against ridicule and impervious to pretension –
became more urgently necessary and correspondingly less easy to
publish. 'A new, humorless generation is now arising, / It takes in
deadly earnest all we received with laughter,' Milosz wrote in 1946,
when he was a Polish diplomat in New York. Five years later, having
decided that historical inevitability and the good of the cause were no
longer excuses he was willing to tolerate, he went into exile, first in
France, where *The Captive Mind* was vilified by Sartre's captive left,
then in California. It was not an easy decision. 'I was afraid to become
an exile,' he wrote, 'afraid to condemn myself to the sterility and the
vacuum that are proper to every emigration.' For the poet, whose
work partly depends on nuances and allusions that only his country-
men can pick up, the vacuum of exile is inevitably more absolute than
for the prose writer:

> *Novels and essays serve but will not last.*
> *One clear stanza can take more weight*
> *Than a whole wagon of elaborate prose.*

But not in translation. Although Milosz supervises the English versions
of his work and has been well served by his collaborators, his poems
have a richness and sinuous flow that make you believe that a good
deal has been lost in translation.

The vacuum of exile exists in many forms, the two foremost being
the loss of audience and the loss of subject matter. Eventually, Milosz's
poems did filter back into Poland, though not officially until long after
he had defected, so for years his effective audience was reduced to
bickering and malicious café clubs of fellow exiles. But for a poet
whose subject matter was loss, who already considered himself to be in
exile, like Adam, from some lost Eden of Lithuanian childhood,
physical exile merely strengthened him in his themes and preoccupations. As a result, 'the sterility of exile' has never been Milosz's
problem. *The Collected Poems* runs to more than five hundred pages
and his serious, wondering, adult tone of voice never lapses into
affection or self-consciousness.

Perhaps this is because Milosz has always been a poet of place, a
marvelous describer of everything from details – 'the tiny propellers of

a hummingbird' – to atmosphere. It is ironic that he should have written so vividly *in Polish* about California:

> *With their chins high, girls come back from the tennis courts.*
> *The spray rainbows over the sloping lawns.*
> *With short jerks a robin runs up, stands motionless.*
> *The eucalyptus tree trunks glow in the light.*
> *The oaks perfect the shadow of May leaves.*
> *Only this is worthy of praise. Only this: the day.*

His long years in the perennial Californian spring, however, have not softened his vision of the world or of his business in it. 'Ill at ease in the tyranny, ill at ease in the republic,' he says of himself, and from that unease is born his steady concentration on the essentials of the poet's task when everything superfluous has been removed: 'gradually, what could not be taken away / is taken. People, countrysides. / And the heart does not die when one thinks it should.' All that is left is language. 'You were my native land; I lacked any other,' he writes in a poem on 'My Faithful Mother Tongue.' And the poem ends, 'what is needed in misfortune is a little order and beauty.' This need for the beauty and order of poetry as an alternative to the disorder of homelessness has been Milosz's constant theme. At the end of *Unattainable Earth*, published in 1986 and his last book before the *Collected Poems*, there is a poignant poem on the 'Poet at Seventy.' It is followed by a kind of prose footnote that encapsulates his whole life's effort:

> To find my home in one sentence, concise, as if hammered in metal. Not to enchant anybody. Not to earn a lasting name in posterity. An unnamed need for order, for rhythm, for form, which three words are opposed to chaos and nothingness.

Milosz's pursuit of order and beauty has been curiously disinterested. Someone once said that 90 percent of the *Oxford Book of English Verse* is about God or death or women. Not so in Milosz's poetry. He is a Catholic and the Church figures in his verse, though less for God's sake than because its rituals recall his early upbringing. As for women: in his whole *Collected Poems* I found only a single love poem – an exceptionally beautiful one called 'After Paradise.' That leaves death, and the truth is that the people who appear in his poems are mostly ghosts from the past. Milosz is a poet of memory, a witness; his real heroes are the dead to whom his poems make reparation. Perhaps exile makes it hard to forget the past and part of its burden for the poet is the need to bring the imagination to bear on people and places that no longer exist. But, as he explains in a marvelous late poem called 'Preparation,' living emotions keep getting in the way:

> Still one more year of preparation.
> Tomorrow at the latest I'll start working on a great book
> In which my century will appear as it really was.
> The sun will rise over the righteous and the wicked.
> Springs and autumns will unerringly return,
> In a wet thicket a thrush will build his nest lined with clay
> And foxes will learn their foxy natures.
>
> And that will be the subject, with addenda. Thus: armies
> Running across frozen plains, shouting a curse
> In a many-voiced chorus; the cannon of a tank
> Growing immense at the corner of a street; the ride at dusk
> Into a camp with watchtowers and barbed wire.
>
> No, it won't happen tomorrow. In five or ten years.
> I still think too much about the mothers
> And ask what is man born of woman.
> He curls himself up and protects his head
> While he is kicked by heavy boots; on fire and running,
> He burns with bright flame; a bulldozer sweeps him into a clay pit.
> Her child. Embracing a teddy bear. Conceived in ecstasy.
>
> I haven't learned yet to speak as I should, calmly.

Like other major witnesses of this century – Primo Levi, Zbigniew Herbert – Milosz is a moralist: his work does not pronounce or make judgments; it simply takes as its criterion human decency – disinterested, modest, and not willingly misled:

> poems should be written rarely and reluctantly,
> under unbearable duress and only with the hope
> that good spirits, not evil ones, choose us for their instrument.

New York Review of Books, 1988

T.E. Hulme and Wilfred Owen

1

ONE OF THE MYSTERIES of the Modernist movement in literature, especially during its experimental heyday in the first decades of the last century, is how few British writers were involved. Nearly all the dominant figures writing in English were either American or Irish – Eliot, Pound, Yeats, Joyce, Stevens, Marianne Moore – and even a generation later, a master technician like Auden at his innovative, nervy peak was never Modernist and experimental in a way that came naturally to Beckett. The line of English verse in the 20th century runs directly from the Victorians, via Hardy and Housman, to Larkin and Hughes, almost as if Modernism had never happened.

With hindsight, it seems obvious that American poets needed to experiment in order to break free. When Ezra Pound talked about making it new he meant, among other things, creating a poetic language that could adapt itself to American vernacular rhythms, a language not bound by Shakespeare's iambic pentameter and un-constrained by a tradition that stretched back to Chaucer. The tradition Pound laid claim to began with Dante and the troubadours, bypassed Chaucer, and included Fenellosa's ideograms, as though writing with an American accent meant being free to pick and choose from world literature.

Pound, of course, loved to parade his learning, especially in Edwardian London where he was greeted, at first, as a hick from Idaho. (Graves accused him of getting his ideograms from the sides of tea-chests.) But showmanship aside, Pound's brand of eclectic cosmopolitanism was a great source of creative energy. His early poems were conventionally lush; two of them were later included in the *Oxford Book of Victorian Verse*, where they seem not at all out of place; he became a Modernist by modelling himself on Gautier and Laforgue, and translating the Latin of Propertius. Similarly, Eliot made his home in England but found his style, he said, across the Channel: 'The kind of poetry that I needed, to teach me the use of my own voice, did not exist in English at all; it was only to be found in French.' Having discovered his own voice, Eliot then went on to apply what he had learned to English literature, which he reinterpreted from a continental perspective, notably in his brilliant and influential essay 'The Metaphysical Poets,' in which he praised Donne and his followers for qualities he admired in Laforgue and Corbière.

What the French had to offer, in practical terms, was *vers libre*. Technically, *vers libre* was an escape from the tyranny of traditional forms – from the classical French Alexandrine and the English iambic pentameter. But free verse in the technical sense mattered less than freedom itself. Like all new movements in the arts, Modernism was driven by the Oedipal urge to pull down the old order and start afresh, and in the first decade of the 20th century the old order meant late, decadent Romanticism. There was no better antidote to the hypnotic chanting of poets like Swinburne than the casual and ironic *vers libre* of the new French poets.

When Pound arrived in London, in 1909, aged 24 and eager to spread the word, one Englishman with cosmopolitan tastes was already preaching death to Romanticism and defending abstract art, though he was a poet only briefly and in passing. *The Complete Poetical Works of T.E. Hulme*, published by Pound as an appendix to his own collection, *Ripostes*, in 1912, consisted of five short poems, and by the time it appeared Hulme had more or less abandoned the art of poetry. Apart from that brief guest appearance, all Hulme published during what Robert Ferguson, his biographer, rightly calls his 'short sharp life' was a handful of essays, mostly written for A.R.Orage's magazine, *The New* Age, and two translations, one of a book by Bergson, the other by Sorel, both with critical introductions. In 1924, seven years after Hulme was killed in action, the poet Herbert Read edited a collection of his work, *Speculations*. It amounted to 271 short pages, including the index.[1]

---

[1] There were later collections of his scattered work, but they did not appear until long after his reputation was established: *Further Speculations*, ed. Sam Hynes, University of Minnesota, 1955; *The Collected Writings of T.E. Hulme*, ed. Karen Csengeri, Oxford, 1994.

Hulme's influence, however, was out of all proportion to his output. According to Ferguson he was 'one of the half-dozen mid-wives of the Modernist aesthetic in poetry', and Eliot called him 'the forerunner of a new attitude of mind, which should be called the twentieth-century mind.' Hulme was a mathematician turned phi-losopher, always belligerently his own man, an abstract thinker who loved concrete details and precision, who evolved a subtle intellectual basis for non-representational art and thought his way through to the spare, unadorned verse style that later became Imagism, and whose famous essay on 'Romanticism and Classicism' became one of the key texts of Modernism. Half a century after Hulme's death, Saul Bellow's Herzog was still arguing in favor of his definition of Romanticism as 'spilt religion': 'There is something to be said for his view. He wanted things to be clear, dry, spare, pure, cool, and hard. With this I think we can all sympathize. I too am repelled by the "dampness," as he called it, and the swarming of Romantic feelings.'

No one gets to influence the intellectual life of a whole century simply by being clever or iconoclastic or original or even right. Hulme, who eschewed personality as a Romantic symptom, was himself a man of extraordinary presence and nobody who tangled with him remained neutral. He was the son of a prosperous Stafford-shire businessman who disapproved of him, a powerful young man, self-confident and lazy, with a passion for women and what Ferguson calls 'gladiatorial' arguments. According to Wyndham Lewis, who once finished hanging upside-down from the railings of Soho Square after a run-in with him, Hulme was 'a very large and imposing man, well over six foot, broad-shouldered and with legs like a racing cyclist. He had an extremely fine head, which it was his habit to hold on one side, as if listening (a bird-like attitude) really rather reminiscent of an antique bust.' Lewis also said, 'He was a very rude and truculent man. He needed to be' – presumably because Hulme, like Lewis, was an avant garde artist condemned to work in a cultural world which dismissed Eliot's 'Prufrock' as 'absolutely insane.' Both men were trouble-makers, but for Hulme provocation was a way of life.

At school he had founded a debating society, and he went on founding clubs where he could argue for most of his life. At Cam-bridge, where he read mathematics, he started the Discord Club, a collection of rowdies who lived up to the club's name by behaving dreadfully. Hulme, as founder-president, set the standards and was duly sent down after five terms for riotous behavior. Eight years later, his college allowed him back – this time to read philosophy – but he lasted only a few months before he was chased out for seducing the teenage daughter of one of his professors. Hulme was a teetotaller, so drink was never his excuse. He behaved badly on principle because he was permanently in revolt against convention. It was a revolt that manifested itself in many ways, from his compulsive philandering to the radical and original thinking that went into his aesthetics. This is what Ferguson has to say about it:

> [One] day . . . Hulme was apprehended by a policeman while urinating in broad daylight in Soho Square. 'You can't do that here,' he was told. Still buttoning his trousers, Hulme turned to him and replied, 'Do you realise that you're addressing a member of the middle class?' The policeman then apologised and walked on. Connoisseurs of the episode assume that Hulme was caught short after a night's drinking, but [Ashley] Dukes states expressly that the incident took place 'in broad daylight'. Hulme, moreover, remained unshakeably teetotal. If a rational explanation is possible a clue might be that note in 'Cinders' [a journal of thoughts and aphorisms published in *Speculations*] in which he referred to the 'resolution to shake off social convention and do it', a compulsion he apparently experienced so strongly at times that he called it 'the knife order'. It may be that Hulme was performing his devotions to the god of the knife order that day in Soho Square, and that he urinated where and when he did precisely *because* there was a policeman standing nearby.

There is another pertinent 'knife order' in 'Cinders': 'Passion is action, and without action but a child's anger.' Hulme, who was passionate and not at all childish, devoted a great deal of energy to provoking intellectual action and making people think. 'He led people up the garden path, made them agree to things, and then left them in the cart,' said J.C. Squire, one of the ringmasters of literary London. 'He used to twinkle at me across their heads. I couldn't help smiling but I did think "what a bad man you are."' Jacob Epstein, the American sculptor whose work Hulme promoted and on which he based his theories of abstract art, put it more kindly: Hulme 'had a quality . . . of great urbanity, and his broad-mindedness, I maintain, only ceased when he met humbug and pretentiousness.'

Hulme devoted himself to battling against what he called 'the state of slush in which we have the misfortune to live' and he did so with supreme confidence, indifferent to what people thought of him, flaunting his burly, unpoetic presence and provincial accent, as if they too were part of the argument. Here he is addressing the Poetry Society in London:

> A reviewer writing in the *Saturday Review* last week spoke of poetry as the means by which the soul soared into higher regions, and as a means of expression by which it became merged into a higher kind of reality. Well, that is the kind of statement that I utterly detest. I want to speak of verse in a plain way as I would of pigs: that is the only honest way. The President told us last week that poetry was akin to religion. It is nothing of the sort. It is a means of expression just as prose is and if you can't justify it from that point of view it's not worth preserving.

Hulme was a subtle and sophisticated thinker and his style of argument was not usually as belligerently forthright as this. But it was always intensely personal and that, I think, is the secret of his influence. In a BBC interview in 1959, Pound remarked:

> I came on six lines of Hulme's the other day – no importance unless you think that it is important that a guy who left only a few pages of poetry should have a style so unmistakable that you come on it and you know that it's Hulme's.

Hulme's prose is even more unmistakable than his verse. According to Kate Lechmere, one of his two great loves, he had a 'certain stand-easy laziness–insolence about him,' and you can hear it in his style, especially in the great essay on 'Romanticism and Classicism':

> The great aim is accurate, precise and definite description. The first thing is to recognise how extraordinarily difficult this is. It is no mere matter of carefulness; you have to use language, and language is by its very nature a communal thing; that is, it expresses never the exact thing but a compromise – that which is common to you, me and everybody. But each man sees a little differently, and to get out clearly and exactly what he does see, he must have a terrific struggle with language, whether it be with words or the technique of other arts. Language has its own special nature, its

own conventions and communal ideas. It is only by a concentrated effort of the mind that you can hold it fixed to your own purpose. I always think that the fundamental process at the back of all the arts might be represented by the following metaphor. You know what I call architect's curves – flat pieces of wood with all different kinds of curvature. By a suitable selection from these you can draw approximately any curve you like. The artist I take to be the man who simply can't bear the idea of that 'approximately'. He will get the exact curve of what he sees whether it be an object or an idea in the mind. I shall here have to change my metaphor a little to get the process in his mind. Suppose that instead of your curved pieces of wood you have a springy piece of steel of the same types of curvature as the wood. Now the state of tension or concentration of mind, if he is doing anything really good in this struggle against the ingrained habit of the technique, may be represented by a man employing all his fingers to bend the steel out of its own curve and into the exact curve which you want. Something different to what it would assume naturally.

There are then two things to distinguish, first the particular faculty of mind to see things as they really are, and apart from the conventional ways in which you have been trained to see them. This is itself rare enough in all consciousness. Second, the concentrated state of mind, the grip over oneself which is necessary in the actual expression of what one sees. To prevent one falling into the conventional curves of ingrained technique, to hold on through infinite detail and trouble to the exact curve you want. Wherever you get this sincerity, you get the fundamental quality of good art without dragging in infinite or serious.

Apart from Coleridge's description of Shakespeare at work in *Biographia Literaria*, Hulme's, I think, is the subtlest and most inward account of the creative process ever written. And the secret is in the tone of voice. Hulme writes like a man wholly at ease with himself, casually, conversationally, thinking on his feet and trying to impress no one, intent only in saying what he has to say as precisely and clearly as he can – just like the artist he describes. His cool, demystifying approach embodies the spirit of Modernism to which Eliot and Pound aspired, and his informality, so uncharacteristic of that stuffy period, makes him seem as contemporary now as he must have seemed when Eliot read him in the '20s and Bellow in the '50s.

Hulme treated the warfare in Flanders with as little fuss as he wrote his prose. In his letters home he admits merely to being 'exasperated' or 'annoyed' by the inconvenience of being shot at. He wrote just one war poem, but, because it fulfills his 'great aim' of 'accurate, precise and definite description,' it captures, like few others, the grim resignation of daily life on the Western Front:

Over the flat slopes of St. Eloi
A wide wall of sandbags.
Night,
In the silence desultory men
Pottering over small fires, cleaning their mess-tins:
To and fro, from the lines,
Men walk as on Piccadilly,
Making paths in the dark,
Through scattered dead horses,
Over a dead Belgian's belly.

The Germans have rockets. The English have no rockets.
Behind the line, cannon, lying back miles.
Before the line, chaos:

My mind is a corridor. The minds about me are corridors.
Nothing suggests itself. There is nothing to do but keep on.

The poem survives because he recited it to Pound while convalescing from a bullet wound in 1915, and Pound transcribed it. Hulme himself couldn't be bothered to write it down. On September 28, 1917, four days after his thirty-fourth birthday, he was blown apart by an enemy shell, apparently too absorbed in thought to hear it coming.

2

Hulme died a few months after Wilfred Owen began to write the poems for which he is now remembered. It is as well they never met because Owen was in every way Hulme's opposite – a mother's boy, short, slight, frail, shy, and sharply aware of his lower-middle class background. His father was a railway official, his devouring mother, as in D.H. Lawrence's ballad, 'was a superior soul, / a superior soul was she, / cut out to play a superior role / in the god–damn bourgeoisie.'

Without the means to do so, she consoled herself with evangelical piety, hypochondria, and a suffocating, self-serving devotion to her three children.

Wilfred was her oldest and her darling, the one she pinned her thwarted ambitions on, and he only got out from under her spell in the last year of his life, which was also the time he was writing his finest poems. Even then, the letters he had written her continuously did not cease. According to Dominic Hibberd's magisterial biography, 'Over five hundred and fifty of Wilfred's known letters are addressed to Susan [his mother], some of them marked private; one is addressed to her and Tom [his father] together, and only four to Tom alone.' Her younger son, Harold, resented her, her grandchildren and nieces thought she was hypocritical and affected, but for Wilfred, Hibberd says, she was 'an ideal listener . . . his audience throughout his life . . . [and] in some of his adult letters he writes to her almost as a lover.' Throughout his teens he labored to please her, working as a pupil-teacher to acquire his secondary education, then as an assistant to an evangelical country vicar, spreading the word, doing good works, and cramming his spare time with extra-mural courses to qualify him for a university scholarship. But he lost his faith and failed the scholarship. To escape his mother's disappointment as well as his own, he left England and went to teach English at a Berlitz School in Bordeaux.

He had been writing poetry since his adolescence – lush, melodious verse in the manner of Keats – but France changed him. He discovered harmless pleasures like smart clothes, good food and wine – his pious mother deplored the demon drink – and came to terms with his homosexuality. He also met a real poet for the first time, Laurent Tailharde, a sixty-year-old disciple of Mallarmé and friend of Verlaine, who introduced the young Englishman to their work and seems to have fallen briefly in love with him. Hibberd thinks that reading French poetry and trying to translate it led Owen to his great and liberating innovation, the use of half-rhymes and assonance – keeping the consonants and changing the vowels: 'laugh / leaf / life', 'blood / bled', 'smell / smile – which Edmund Blunden later named the 'pararhyme.' Owen called it, more modestly, 'my Vowelrime stunt,' but when Robert Graves read the poems he understood the technical implications straight away and sent him a letter saying, 'Don't make any mistake, Owen; you are a damned fine poet already & and are going to be more so . . . you have found a new method . . .

those assonances instead of rhymes are fine – . . . Puff out your chest a little, Owen, & be big – for you've more right than most of us . . . You must help . . . [us] revolutionize English Poetry.'

When Graves wrote that, in 1917, he had been in the army for three years and knew that the sweet-toned, pastoral innocence of the Georgian poets – the verse equivalent of the music of composers like George Butterworth and Peter Warlock – could not properly express the reality of trench warfare. Just as Freud had responded to the Great War by positing a death instinct beyond the pleasure principle, Graves knew that something darker and more dissonant was needed. He himself never managed it, although he went on to write some of the most beautiful love poems of the 20th century, nor did Sassoon, despite his anger and stylish satires. Perhaps both of them were too much the officer-and-gentleman, too full of sporting spirit and ideals of honor and bravery.

Owen had these, too, but with a difference. Although he was the least warlike of men, nothing was lost on him and he had a gift for learning from experience, using it, and changing himself in the process: from studious mother's boy, to pious lay-assistant, to French-ified dandy and finally, astonishingly, to first-rate officer – efficient, hard-working, knowledgeable, brave, and an excellent marksman. But because his mother's presence was always with him he saw the senseless slaughter through her eyes. Whence, I think, his famous preface to the poems he did not live to see published: 'I am not concerned with Poetry. My subject is War and the pity of War. The Poetry is in the pity.' This was not a perspective that came easily to poets like Graves and Sassoon, who had been raised in the harsh, motherless atmosphere of an English Public School.

In his brilliant book on the war poets, Paul Fussell writes, 'The innocent army fully attained the knowledge of good and evil at the Somme on July 1, 1916, . . . one of the most interesting [moments] in the whole long history of human disillusion.'[2] Owen arrived at the Somme six months later and within weeks was enduring what he called 'seventh hell' – almost dying of cold when pinned down in No Man's land, watching one of his men choke to death in a gas attack, nursing a blinded sentry while he died, then another terrible vigil, pinned down again, with the shattered remnants of a friend's body all around him. Within six months, he was sent back to base with shell-

[2] Paul Fussell, *The Great War and Modern Memory*, O.U.P., 1977, p.29

shock and ended up in Craiglockhart Hospital, near Edinburgh. Craiglockhart was doubly lucky for Owen: his psychiatrist encouraged him to face his nightmares by writing poems about them, and Siegfried Sassoon, a fellow-patient, was there to read them and urge him on. The result was the beginning of an extraordinary creative spell, like Keats's 'marvellous year,' in which Owen wrote all his greatest poetry.

Like Keats, Owen's subject was death, but his journey into 'the inwardness of war' was also the end of Romanticism for him. In a poem called 'A Terre,' which Owen called 'a photograph' and Hibberd thinks was based on something the poet had seen in a field hospital, a shattered, dying soldier yearns for life in any form and on any terms – as a rat, a maggot, a microbe:

> Certainly flowers have the easiest time on earth.
> 'I shall be one with nature, herb, and stone',
> Shelley would tell me. Shelley would be stunned.
>
> The dullest Tommy hugs that fancy now.
> Pushing up daisies is their creed, you know.

Shelley had been another of the young poet's idols and by the time Owen bids him farewell the pararhymes are doing their dissonant work and the pentameters are stirring in their groove.

Owen was killed on November 5, 1918, one week before the Armistice, so it is impossible to know if his poetry would ever have developed along the lines Hulme had proposed. All that is certain is that he knew what his subject must be and it was far from Romantic. The previous New Year's Eve, he had written to his mother:

I go out of this year a Poet, my dear Mother, as which I did not enter it. I am held peer by the Georgians; I am a poet's poet.

I am started. The tugs have left me; I feel the great swelling of the open sea taking my galleon.

Last year, at this time, (it is just midnight, and now is the intolerable instant of the Change) last year I lay awake in a windy tent in the middle of a vast, dreadful encampment. It seemed neither France nor England, but a kind of paddock where the beasts are kept a few days before the shambles. I heard the revelling of the Scotch troops, who are now dead, and who knew they would be dead. I thought of this present night, and whether I should indeed – whether we should indeed – whether you would indeed – but I thought neither long nor deeply, for I am a master of elision.

But chiefly I thought of the very strange look on all the faces in that camp; an incomprehensible look, which a man will never see in England, though wars should be in England; nor can it be seen in any battle. But only in Étaples.

It was not despair, or terror, it was more terrible than terror, for it was a blindfold look, and without expression, like a dead rabbit's.

It will never be painted, and no actor will ever seize it. And to describe it, I think I must go back and be with them.[3]

As the disasters of the 20th century unfolded, that 'blindfold look' became, I think, the underlying theme that Modernist masters like Eliot, Yeats in his maturity, Kafka and Beckett strained to express. Maybe Modernism would have been less an American-Irish affair if potentially major poets like Owen and Isaac Rosenberg, as well as a whole generation of English poets who had yet to develop, had not been slaughtered in the Great War.

New York Review of Books, 2003

3 Wilfred Owen, *Collected Letters*, ed. Harold Owen and John Bell, O.U.P., 1967, p.521

Edward Lear

'ONE DAY THERE APPEARED at luncheon sitting opposite us a rosy, grey-bearded, bald-headed, gold-spectacled little old gentleman who captivated my attention . . . Something seemed to bubble and sparkle in his talk and his eyes twinkled benignly behind the shining glasses. I had heard of uncles; mine were in America and I had never seen them. I whispered to my mother that I should like to have that gentleman opposite for an uncle. She smiled and did not keep my secret. The delighted old gentleman, who was no other than Edward Lear, glowed, bubbled and twinkled more than ever; he seemed bathed in a kindly effulgence. The adoption took place there and then; he became my sworn relative and devoted friend.'

Lear at that time was nearly 60 and the little girl who adopted him was one of a long line of entranced children whom he drew to him like the Pied Piper. Thomas Hardy might have classified their devotion as one of life's little ironies since Lear himself had had a childhood so desolate that he spent the rest of his life trying to get over it.

He was born in 1812, the penultimate of 21 children of a wealthy stockbroker. Six of them died in infancy and seven more died before their mother succumbed in 1844 to what the doctors genteelly but accurately described as 'general decay'. Lear was 32 by then but, for him, his mother had effectively disappeared from his life 28 years before when 'the morning came of that hateful day' on which his father unexpectedly defaulted at the Stock Exchange. This disaster was later inflated by Lear into a full-scale Victorian melodrama: the grand family mansion in rural Holloway sold, the bankrupt father languishing for four years in King's Bench Prison, four sisters dying of mortification when they were sent out to work. Not true, says Lear's biographer, Vivien Noakes. All that is certain is that the house in

Holloway was rented out for a year and that when the Lears eventually moved back they had been stripped of their middle-class pomp – 12 carriages before the crash – and thereafter endured a continual, nagging lack of money.

Lear was to be short of cash for the rest of his life. But more important for the ugly, shortsighted, affectionate little four-year-old was that when disaster struck his mother abandoned him. Although she continued to live in the same house, she handed the child over to his sister Ann and had nothing further to do with him.

Ann was 22 years older than Lear and so devoted to him that she remained a spinster for his sake. Nonetheless, Lear never recovered from the shock of his mother's abrupt withdrawal of her love. Even in middle age the trauma was still so vivid that he could use it, in a letter to a friend, as an unanswerable argument against marriage: 'There is nothing of which I have so distinct a recollection as the fearful gnawing sensation which chills & destroys one, on leaving scenes & persons, for which & whom there are no substitutes . . . I say, there is nothing I so distinctly remember, because those feelings are with me already taking the form of past matters, never again to recur . . . Not that one has actually *outlived* the possibility of their repetition, but rather, I *prevent* them by keeping them at arm's length: I *won't* like anyone else, if I can help it . . . all the rest of my short foolish life.'

A year or two after that first disaster, when Lear was five or six, he began to be visited by his 'Terrible Demon', epilepsy. Violent, regular fits plagued him for the rest of his life, sometimes as many as 20 a month, each marked in his diary by a little cross. He could tell when they were coming, so not even his closest friends knew he was epileptic. But the disease forced him into isolation since it was a secret he was unwilling to share with anyone. When he was seven the 'Demon' was joined by 'The Morbids' – cycles of paralysing depression that got worse and more frequent as he grew older. They, too, were linked with feelings of loss and abandonment; the first occurred after one of the very rare occasions when he spent a happy evening with his usually forbidding and unapproachable father.

At 15 he went out to earn his living as a commercial artist. At 20 he sowed a few timorous wild oats and reaped venereal disease. As a young man, he was gauche and uncoordinated. In middle and old age, he was overweight and drank too much. His inclinations were homosexual and for years he was hopelessly in love with a pillar of rectitude with an eminently Victorian name, Franklin Lushington.

Neurotically restless, he was almost 60 before he committed himself to owning a house, which then brought him nothing but chagrin. He fretted constantly about his lack of recognition and lack of money. He was chronically asthmatic and bronchial. His eyesight was dreadful, his nose was too big.

A gloomy life then, depressed, lonely, frustrated, full of doubt and illness. But set against all that was a natural sweetness and sense of fun that drew to him a large circle of loving friends, ranging from the Viceroy of India, the Lord Chancellor, the 12th, 13th, 14th and 15th Earls of Derby and a wide assortment of distinguished contemporaries, through Tennyson and Holman Hunt, to his faithful Greek servant Giorgio. All were faithful, devoted and as protective of him and his interests as he would allow them to be. 'He is one of those men of real feeling it is so delightful to meet in this cold-hearted world,' said a friend. Children recognised that instinctively and adored him without reserve.

He was also, despite his illnesses, a man of tremendous energy. He worked all day and every day. When he wasn't working he travelled incessantly, mostly on foot. He plodded around Italy, including parts rarely visited by Europeans in those days: Calabria, the Abruzzi, Sicily. He walked through Greece and wildest Albania, visited Mount Athos and Corsica, and twice sailed up the Nile. He went to Palestine and was nearly killed by bandits at Petra, 'the rose-red city'. When he was over 60 he drove himself to fever and exhaustion on a monstrous trek around India and Ceylon.

Perhaps the discomforts of travel were easier to bear than sitting still and facing his depression:

> There was an old man whose despair
> Induced him to purchase a hare:
> Whereon one fine day, he rode wholly away,
> Which partly assuaged his despair.

But he was also driven by professional curiosity, financing his endless journeys by producing literally thousands of watercolours and paintings which he sold irregularly and gratefully for paltry sums, and beautifully illustrated journals that he published at his own expense.

Although he was a brilliant watercolourist and draftsman, and gave drawing lessons to Queen Victoria, his real pride was his grandiose, boring landscapes in oils. He seems to have thought watercolour to be somehow trivial and that only in oils could he achieve the substance and reputation – the stately Victorian solemnity – he yearned for. So at the age of 38, four years after he had taught the Queen, he enrolled as a student at the Royal Academy and learnt to draw from the antique alongside students half his age. He also aspired to be adopted into the Pre-Raphaelite Brotherhood and went to school, painfully, with Holman Hunt, who condescended to him. But oils were not his natural medium. They killed off his liveliness and delicacy, deadened his intuitions and turned a spontaneous gift into hard labour. He called his oil paintings 'Tyrants', but because they cost him so much in time and painful effort he priced them out of the market.

He also had a genius for drawing animals. When Lear was 20, the Earl of Derby saw his 'Illustrations of the Family of Psittacidae, or Parrots' and invited him to Knowsley Hall to paint the creatures in his famous private zoo. As usual, Lear spent his spare time in the nursery, and to amuse the children began to write his 'Book of Nonsense'. When he eventually published it, it brought him the success and recognition he always lusted after as a painter, but he took a sideways, unwilling pleasure in this and let his publishers fleece him. He sold the entire rights of the book in a fit of pique for £125, then watched it go into 19 editions in his own lifetime.

In 1886, two years before Lear died, the arbiter of Victorian art, John Ruskin, bestowed on him – though not on his paintings – the accolade he had always sought: 'I don't know of any author to whom I am half so grateful for my idle self as Edward Lear. I shall put him first of my hundred authors.' In a way, Ruskin was speaking for everyone, for in practice, if not in theory, Lear is now one of the most famous poets in the language. 'The Owl and the Pussycat' is probably known by heart by more people than any poem of Shakespeare. More important, almost 100 years after his death, some of the so-called 'Nonsense' has come to look, by any standards, like very good poetry indeed.

Around 1867, Lear finally made up his mind that he could never marry and would therefore be lonely for the rest of his life. A handful of the poems that followed this bleak decision – 'Pelican Chorus', 'The Jumblies', 'The Dong with the Luminous Nose', 'The Courtship of the Yonghy-Bonghy-Bó' – are sustained, beneath their playfulness, by the same uneasy sense of loss, a mixture of grief, guilt and nostalgia for something loved that is irrevocably gone, that is the authentic note of Victorian poetry:

Often since, in the nights of June,
We sit on the sand and watch the moon;
She has gone to the great Gromboolian plain,
And we probably never shall meet again!
Oft, in the long still nights of June,
We sit on the rocks and watch the moon;
She dwells by the streams of the Chankly Bore,
And we probably never shall see her more . . .

That may not quite have the assured, swelling diapason of 'Break, break, break/On thy cold grey stones, O Sea!' Lear lacked the assurance, the self-conscious eminence of his friend Tennyson, and so would never indulge his depression without also making it slightly ludicrous. (Mariana's famous complaint – 'She said, "I am aweary, aweary/I would that I were dead!" ' is transformed in Lear's diary into: 'He only said, "I'm very weary/The rheumatiz he said/He said, it's awful dull & dreary/I think I'll go to bed." ') But this sense of his own absurdity, combined with his uncannily subtle ear, make Lear's best poems seem far more lively and less cloying to our taste than many of the more respectable monuments of Victorian verse.

Children adored him because all through his long life he remained in touch with the child he himself had once been. This emerges in his letters – in direct proportion to his depression – as a manic, punning jollity. But in Lear's poems the line was also open to the grief of his terrible childhood; it is present in the haunting, plangent rhythms and unexpected, almost unwarranted depths, as it is perhaps present in the delicate brushwork and shimmering surfaces of his landscapes.

Lear was that rare phenomenon, an utterly harmless man; the eccentric old bachelor and everybody's uncle who was also a genius – funny, irritable, quirky, hypochondriac, yet full of sweetness. But that was a quality that somehow made him nervous; he dared not commit himself fully to anyone and would only express his loneliness and frustrated love in the safely insulated medium of nonsense. For that reason, his contemporaries condescended to him but, as Auden wrote, 'Children swarmed to him like settlers. He became a land.'

Observer magazine, 1985

Andrew Marvell

MARVELL HAD A REPUTATION during his lifetime, but not as a lyric poet. He was renowned as a political insider and combatative parliamentary backbencher, as a satirist and pamphleteer. Early in Marvell's career, Milton, who was his friend, recommended him for a government post as a man 'of singular desert for the State to make use of'; a Frenchman who met him later in Saumur described him, less sympathetically, as 'a notable English Italo-Machiavellian'. Margaret Thatcher would have called him 'one of us'.

Marvell's credentials for a place in the political establishment were impeccable. His father was a Church of England minister, M.A. Cantab., Master of Hull Grammar School, lecturer at Holy Trinity Church, and famous enough to be included in the contemporary guide book to the great and good, Fuller's *Worthies of England*, where he is described as 'Most *facetious* in his *discourse*, yet *grave* in his *carriage*, a most excellent preacher.'

Andrew Marvell, the poet, was born in 1621, went up to Trinity College, Cambridge, in 1633 and published his first verses, in Latin and Greek, in 1637, when he was sixteen. A year later, his mother died and his father remarried. Marvell's response was to leave Cambridge and convert briefly to Catholicism. But his clerical father found him in London and bustled him back to university and that, effectively, was the end of his unconventionality. He stayed at Cambridge until his father died in 1641, then went down without taking his M.A. and spent five years – 1642–1647 – travelling on the continent, possibly as tutor to a rich young Englishman, Edward Skinner.

By 1653, when Milton wrote his recommendation, Marvell was attached to the household of one of the most powerful men in England: he was tutor to the daughter of General Fairfax, who had recently retired as commander-in-chief of the Parliamentary forces.

Lord Fairfax was an enlightened and liberal man and he had resigned his command because he refused to invade Scotland. His post was then taken by his less forgiving lieutenant-general, Oliver Cromwell, and in due course Marvell went on to tutor Cromwell's ward and prospective son-in-law, William Dutton. This apprenticeship to the great and good of his own generation was eventually rewarded and Marvell landed the government job he wanted; he joined Milton as Latin Secretary to the Council of State in 1657. Two years later, he was elected M.P. for Hull and he held the seat until he died in 1678. By then, his fame as a political pamphleteer and satirist was established; a generation after his death, Swift wrote admiringly of *The Rehearsal Transprosed* and called Marvell a 'great genius'.

For Swift, Marvell's genius was in his satires, but he also had a considerable reputation as a Latin poet. According to Aubrey, 'He was a great master of the Latin tongue; an excellent poet in Latin and English; for Latin verses there was no man could come into competition with him.' Some of those Latin poems were published in Marvell's lifetime, as were his political satires in English (most of them anonymously), but the poems that eventually made him famous were not printed until 1681, three years after his death, and it took another two and a half centuries for his real achievement as a poet to be recognised. Dr. Johnson ignored him, except for a passing reference in his life of Milton; the two Romantics who noticed him – Hazlitt and Lamb – thought him quaint and whimsical; the late-Victorian scholars edited him in the same archeological spirit as they edited Suckling or Aurelian Townshend. It was not until 1921 that Marvell properly entered the pantheon. Grierson began the process in the introduction to his famous anthology of *Metaphysical Lyrics and Poems*, where he wrote, 'Apart from Milton, he is the most interesting personality between Donne and Dryden, and at his best a finer poet than either,' and T.S. Eliot completed the job with his marvellous essay celebrating the 300th anniversary of Marvell's birth.

In that tercentenary essay Eliot wrote, 'To bring the poet back to life [is] the great, the perennial, task of criticism,' and he performed the miracle for Marvell brilliantly in the space of a couple of thousand words. Even so, three hundred years seems a long wait in oblivion for the author of some of the most formally perfect poems in the language. Indeed, oblivion seems to have set in almost before the ink was dry: very few of the poems on which his reputation now rests were published in Marvell's lifetime and they seem not even to have circulated widely among his friends, since not many manuscripts survived.

There is nothing unusual about this. In the 16th and 17th century, gentlemen – members of the professional classes as well as courtiers – did not write verse for the general public – not even for that small section of the general public that could read. For Marvell and the Caroline courtly poets, as for Donne and his followers, poetry was not a profession, it was a social grace, like singing or swordsmanship, an accomplishment friends might appreciate and admire but not something to be flaunted before strangers. They passed their poems in manuscript to their friends, who, in turn, made copies for their friends, and occasionally they allowed their verse to appear in courtly anthologies, depending on the occasion and the other contributors. But printed collections were mostly published posthumously. Posterity, or even a poetic reputation outside their immediate circle, was not their concern. What Thomas Sprat, the historian of the Royal Society, wrote in praise of Abraham Cowley, was also true of Marvell: 'he never willingly recited any of his Writings. None but his intimate friends ever discovered he was a great Poet by his discourse.' Marvell published his satires because they were an adjunct to his public career as a politician. The rest of his poetry was a private pleasure written for his own enjoyment and for that of a few friends.

Whence Marvell's confidence in his sophistication. He was writing for people who shared his interests and education, who would pick up his references, appreciate his wit and elegance, and were equally attuned to the Latin and Greek classical tradition that deeply permeated everything he wrote.

This shared sophistication gave Marvell a certain freedom as well as a certain strength. He needed an intimate audience because, despite his public career, he was an intensely private person and his poems mostly reflect that privacy:

> Two Paradises 'twere in one
> To live in Paradise alone.

Phiip Larkin, Hull's other poet and also unmarried, once remarked, 'Sex is much too wonderful an experience to share with anyone else;' Marvell's couplet expresses more elegantly the same bachelor yearning for the uncluttered life. He was always a fastidious poet, detached and reserved, but sometimes the line is blurred between critical distance and plain distaste for the heat and muddle of the ordinary human condition.

The greatest of his poems depend on this fastidiousness. Although he eventually became a staunch republican, until 1650 his sympathies had been with the Royalists, and the 'Horatian Ode', which was probably written in June 1650, is far from a celebration of Cromwell's martial triumphs. It is, instead, a reluctant tribute to the necessity of force from a man who had no taste for it:

> So restless *Cromwel could not cease*
> In the inglorious Arts of Peace,
>   But through adventrous War
>   Urged his active Star. . . .
> 'Tis Madness to resist or blame
> The force of angry Heavens flame:
>   And, if we would speak true,
>   Much to the Man is due:
> Who, from his private Gardens, where
> He liv'd reserved and austere,
>   As if his highest plot
>   To plant the Bergamot,
> Could by industrious Valour climbe
> To ruine the great Work of Time,
>   And cast the Kingdome old
>   Into another Mold.

Marvell's own preference was for the private garden and his disaste for restlessness was as great as his disdain for go-getting industrious valour. He was a political liberal in an illiberal time, but he understood the realities of political power. That did not prevent him from being shocked by the sacrilege of regicide or from admiring the nobility with which the king went to his death. Although Marvell was a Puritan and a devoted Parliamentarian, he was never a religious fanatic and his particular style of highly civilised sophistication did not take willingly to violence. Hence his famous comment on the Civil War:

> Whether it be a war of religion or liberty it is not worth the labour
> to enquire. Whatsoever was at the top, the other was at the
> bottom; but upon considering all, I think the cause was too good

to have been fought for. Men ought to have trusted God – they ought to have trusted the King with the whole matter.

He was evidently a man not taken in by propaganda and the triumph of the 'Horation Ode' is in its even-handedness in the teeth of his own natural aversion to the butchery perpetrated in the name of religious and political principles. He balances Cromwell's zeal and ruthlessness against the king's grace and dignity, admires the loser and judges the winner without ever compromising his own standards.

Fastidiousness, alas, is as rare in political poetry as it is in politics itself – which is why the 'Horatian Ode' is such an extraordinary achievement. But there is another side to Marvell's particular style of fastidiousness which prevents some of his great poems from being quite as great as they first appear. 'To His Coy Mistress' seems like a perfect love poem until you compare it with 'Good Morrow' or 'The Anniversary' or 'A Valediction: of weeping' or any of a dozen of Donne's other finest poems, and then Marvell seems oddly impersonal, almost disembodied. The difference is that Donne writes as though he were talking, urgently and directly, to someone standing right in front of him; the poems are as swift and immediate as an overheard conversation. Marvell, in comparison, is celebrating not love or a living woman but what Eliot called 'one of the great traditional commonplaces of literature. It is the theme of O mistress mine, of Gather ye rosebuds, of Go, lovely rose; it is in the savage austerity of Lucretius and the intense levity of Catullus.' That commonplace is the theme of carpe diem, and Marvell plays skilled and beautiful variations on it, but I am not convinced he had anyone particular in mind when he was writing.

Anyone, that is, apart from himself. The first half of the poem is less concerned with passion than with absurdity: the absurdity of the rituals of courtship, of false modesty, of his own inadequacy as a lover:

> Thou by the Indian Ganges side ·
> Should'st Rubies find: I by the Tide
> Of Humber would complain . . .

The coy mistress gathers exotic treasures in exotic places while he is left to grumble in the dour northern town he was brought up in. The joke is clearly at his own expense. So is the 'vegetable love', given the passion he expresses elsewhere for fruits and flowers and gardens. The sudden quickening of pace and feeling, the 'surprise' both Eliot and Grierson rightly admired – 'But at my back I alwaies hear / Times winged Chariot hurrying near . . .' – has nothing to do with his mistress's charms; it is provoked by the prospect of his own mortality and it leads him into accepting images of violence – the cannonball tearing 'with rough strife, / Thorough the Iron gates of Life' – that go flatly against his own peaceful predilections. As I have written elsewhere, 'the real and moving poem is about time, death, waste and the *need* to love, rather than about love itself.'[1] The poem starts as variations on a literary theme, as a brilliant and inventive exercise, then gets swept up into a passionate, private but quite different concern.

Marvell did write love poems – poems, that is, full of delight, excitement and surprise – but all of them, in their different ways, were inspired by innocence rather than passion. His real love poems are about gardens and unspoiled nature, about young girls in bud, about mowers, shepherds and shepherdesses. In a word, they are about Eden and, like Milton's, Marvell's Eden was a garden enclosed by untamed nature. For Marvell, however, Eden had an English name and an English location. I think it was Lord Fairfax's estate at Nun Appleton House, where Marvell lived during the turmoil of the Civil War, with his charming young pupil and her sympathetic father, who had just retired from public life on a matter of principle. Fairfax's principles seem to have been much the same as Marvell's and that congeniality, combined with Nun Appleton's gardens, woods and spreading fields, seem to have inspired most of his best poems.

The Elizabethans resurrected the pastoral tradition as part of their rediscovery of Greek and Latin poetry and Shakespeare – above all, in *The Winter's Tale* – then adapted it to the English landscape. Marvell brought these two elements together in a unique and special way. Since his own poetry was rooted in the classics, he naturally followed the classical conventions – shepherds and shepherdesses courting, spurning, languishing – but he used them as an excuse for a Shakespearian relish in detail:

> *Oh what unusual Heats are here,*
> *Which thus our Sun-burn'd Meadows sear!*
> *The Grass-hopper its pipe gives ore;*
> *And hamstring'd Frogs can dance no more.*

1 A. Alvarez, *The School of Donne*, 1961

> *But in the brook the green Frog wades;*
> *And Grass-hoppers seek out the shades.*
> *Only the Snake, that kept within,*
> *Now glitters in its second skin.*

His poems are full of this kind of loving and precise observation: 'the hatching *Thrastles* shining eye', 'the Fountains sliding foot', 'Grass, with moister colour dasht,/Seems as green Silks but newly washt;' or this extraordinary description of the woodpecker:

> *He walks still upright from the Root,*
> *Measuring the Timber with his Foot;*
> *And all the way, to keep it clean,*
> *Doth from the Bark the Wood-moths glean.*

This is nature poetry *avant la lettre*, but nature poetry written by someone who loved the subject for its own sake and without the pressure of Wordsworth's unrelenting egocentricity.

Marvell and Milton were two of the foremost classicists of their day and I think the sweet and pure simplicity of Marvell's pastorals – many of the dialogues sound as though they were written to be set to music – were deliberate attempts to re-create in English the lucid calm of Virgil's *Eclogues*, just as Milton's clangorous blank verse was a re-creation of Vergil's epic beat.

The pastoral, in its various forms, was also high fashion in the 17th century, in much the same way as working-class culture was fashionable in the 1950s. This was a period when courtiers dressed up as shepherds and shepherdesses, artful formal gardens were a source of great pride to their owners and people paid fortunes for tulip bulbs. Marvell duly paid homage to 'skilful gardeners' and floral clocks, but his real passion was for the 'wild and fragrant innocence' of the natural world before its fall into art and worldliness.

It is a critical commonplace that his favourite adjective was 'green'. In his not very large body of work, excluding the satires, he used the word two dozen times – so often that it almost seems a stylistic tic. According to William Empson, 'it is connected . . . with grass, buds, children, an as yet virginal prospect of sexuality, and the peasant stock from which the great families emerge.'[2] It is also connected with

2 William Empson, 'Marvell's Garden,' *Some Versions of Pastoral*, London, 1950, p.127

strong feeling. Whenever Marvell needed to imply special approval, a special intensity of feeling, a special kind of beauty, he uses 'green'. At times, the word seems so right and so simple that only genius could have chosen it:

> *He hangs in shades the Orange bright,*
> *Like golden Lamps in a green Night.*

But the habit was so deep-rooted in him that he also used 'green' at moments when, to anyone else, it might have seemed obvious and flat:

> *So Architects do square and hew,*
> *Green Trees that in the Forest grew.*

That is the final couplet of one of his most complex and subtle poems, 'A Dialogue between the Soul and Body', and the line-break ensures that 'green' gets plenty of emphasis. For Marvell, it implies the unviolated innocence of nature; for the uninitiated, it seems self-evident and a little feeble.

'Green', I think, was Marvell's shorthand for paradise and happiness, a word so soaked in private allusions that it generated its own mystery. Just what that mystery was is the subject of 'The Garden', the strange poem in which he described, ironically and with all sorts of jokes at the expense of classical myth and conventional love poetry, a condition the Book of Common Prayer calls 'the peace that passes all understanding'.

'The Garden' was probably written when Marvell was with the Fairfaxes in Yorkshire – there are jaunty variations on the same theme in stanzas 71–77 of 'Upon Appleton House' – and it reads like an answer to his 'Horatian Ode'. It starts with a farewell to arms, Oliver Cromwell-style – 'How vainly men themselves amaze / To win the Palm, the Oke, or Bayes' – but its real subject is paradise and true happiness. Paradise is lonely and asexual – it begins with 'delicious solitude', 'when we have run our Passions heat' – and true happiness is a transcendental state achieved by what was, for Marvell, a kind of magical thinking through which his favourite word formed what mathematicians call a 'strange loop' with itself:

> *Annihilating all that's made*
> *To a green Thought in a green shade.*

In 'The Exstasie', John Donne and his mistress achieved a similar mystical revelation, eye to eye and sweaty palm to sweaty palm; but to make it perfect, 'Else a great Prince in prison lies', they had to come back down into their bodies and make love. In contrast, Marvell's mystical ecstasy is a solitary experience and at its climax his soul takes flight into the landscape:

> Casting the Bodies Vest aside,
> My Soul into the boughs does glide:
> There like a Bird it sits, and sings,
> Then whets, and combs its silver Wings.

For Marvell, perfect bliss, the *raptus* of passion, was an out-of-body experience.

The nearest his poems ever came to sensuality was in the strange panegyric to murdered innocence, 'The Nymph complaining for the death of her Faun'. Like the 'Coy Mistress', this, too, starts out as variations on a conventional theme; there is an ancient and honoured literary tradition of poems lamenting the death of a favourite pet: Catullus on Lesbia's sparrow, Ovid on Corinna's parrot, Skelton on Philip Sparrow. But none of them carries the curious sensual charge of Marvell's poem:

> Upon the Roses it would feed,
> Until its Lips ev'n seemed to bleed:
> And then to me 'twould boldly trip,
> And print those Roses on my Lip.
> But all its chief delight was still
> On Roses thus its self to fill:
> And its pure virgin Limbs to fold
> In whitest sheets of Lilies cold.
> Had it liv'd long, it would have been
> Lilies without, Roses within.

To me, that sounds closer in spirit to Freud on polymorphous perversion than to Catullus or Ovid. In her trance of blood and virginity, Marvell's Nymph has less in common with Lesbia or Corinna than with Count Dracula.

The poem may have begun as a sidelong reaction to the violence of the Civil War – scholars have suggested that 'the wanton troupers' are

the Scottish Covenanting Army which invaded England in 1640 – and
it segues into a conventional story of pastoral seduction and betrayal,
complete with all the usual puns on 'dears' and 'hearts'. But once the
nymph is left alone with her faun it becomes a panegyric on the
eroticism of innocence. For all its grace and tenderness, it seems a great
deal more aroused than any of Marvell's other love poems.

It is also more moving. The poem is, of course, a lament and Marvell
seems always to have been irresistibly stirred by feminine grief. Even
'Mourning', one of his most glib and cynical poems, deepens when
confronting the strangeness and grandeur of a weeping woman:

> *How wide they dream! The* Indian *slaves,*
> *That sink for Pearl through Seas profound,*
> *Would find her Tears yet deeper Waves*
> *And not of one the bottom sound.*

In 'The Nymph complaining . . .' grief and innocence come together
to create something even richer and stranger:

> *See how it weeps. The Tears do come*
> *Sad, slowly dropping like a Gumme.*
> *So weeps the wounded Balsome: so*
> *The holy Frankincense doth flow.*
> *The brotherless* Heliades
> *Melt in such Amber Tears as these.*

The lines are some of the most beautiful Marvell ever wrote and they
compress into a kind of solemn, slow-motion hallucination of grief all
the elements that spoke to him most eloquently: man-ravaged nature
– 'the wounded Balsome' – as well as Christian and classical myth –
'the holy Frankincense' and 'the brotherless *Heliades*'.

As I said earlier, gentleman poets wrote, at most, for an intimate
audience of friends. When Marvell was a young man and writing his
finest poems, he was living a secluded pastoral life deep in the
Yorkshire countryside and his only audience was General Fairfax
and his little daughter Mary. One way of amusing them was the game
of wit, as played both by Donne and by late, decadent but at that time
highly fashionable Metaphysical poets like Cleveland and Cowley. It
was a game Marvell was supremely adept at and he brought to it his
own peculiar brand of perfection.

'The Definition of Love', for example, is an extended scientific-mathematical conceit in the manner of Donne and Lord Herbert of Cherbury, but Marvell handles it with a difference. Instead of using his cleverness as a means of seduction and blinding the lady with science, he takes the title literally and produces an extended essay in abstraction in which the imagery and the argument work cunningly together to prove the impossibility of love. He starts with solid allegorical figures, with tinsel wings, iron wedges and decrees of steel, then gradually flattens them out and refines them away; the round globe of 'Loves whole World' loses a dimension and is 'cramp'd into a *Planisphere*' which is then reduced to the lines of a geometrical figure. The result is rueful and charming but it is not a love poem; it is what the poet says it is, a definition of a love too refined to exist.

In its own terms, it is an elegantly logical performance, but Marvell's logic was altogether different from Donne's. Donne was always arguing fiercely, trying to prove a point or make an outrageous case or get a girl into bed. His poems are full of logical copulas – 'therefore', 'thus', 'and so'. His followers admired and imitated this mannerism; it was part of what Donne himself called his 'masculine perswasive force'. But those outside the select circle were less impressed. When Donne and his followers were labelled 'Metaphysical' – the word was applied to them long before Dr. Johnson wrote his famous essay on Cowley – it was a derogatory term, an accusation. It implied that he sounded like the Schoolmen, the mediaeval neo-Aristotelian philosophers who wasted their time in pointless casuistry, debating endlessly about how many angels could dance on the head of a pin. It implied that he was old-fashioned, out of key with the new scientific spirit of the Royal Society or the burgeoning rationality of the Enlightenment.

In comparison, Marvell's logic seems measured, Roman and far less aggressive. He uses the classical syllogism – thesis, antithesis, synthesis – less because he has anything urgent to prove than because it imposes on the poems a perfect formal shape. The result is a Platonic ideal of the Metaphysical poem – polished, smoothed over, made abstract and fixed for all time, as though in amber.

Marvell's other way of amusing his captive audience at Appleton House was to take the Metaphysical conceit and push it into absurdity. This had already been done unwittingly by John Cleveland, a Cambridge don whose dreadful verse was briefly but hugely popular. (His 1647 *Poems* went through twenty editions, thirteen of them in two

years, compared with two editions of Milton's 1645 *Poems*.) For
Dryden, 'Clevelandism' meant punning, 'wresting and torturing a
word into another meaning'. It also meant outlandish conceits by
which, as Dr. Johnson said, 'the most heterogeneous ideas are yoked
by violence together'. The motive behind both processes was a
donnish desire to show off the author's learning and ingenuity at
whatever cost:

> *I like not tears in tune, nor do I prize*
> *His artificial grief who scans his eyes.*
> *Mine weep down pious beads, but why should I*
> *Confine them to the Muse's rosary?*
> *I am no poet here; my pen's the spout*
> *Where the rain-water of mine eyes runs out*
> *In pity of that name, whose fate we see*
> *Thus copied out in grief's hydrography.*

This has all Cleveland's dotty faults and pretentions: the bad pun ('scan'),
the ridiculous comparison (weeping eyes and rain-spouts), the knowing
polysyllabic reference to an arcane science (hydrography). Above all, it
has the prime distinguishing mark of Clevelandism: an utter inappropriateness to the occasion, which in this instance was the death by
drowning of Edward King, Milton's friend and the subject of 'Lycidas'.

Marvell took this crass formula and transformed it into high art. He
had always been a master of the subtle pun ('Deaf with the drumming
of an Ear') and the elegant conceit ('A Soul hung up, as 'twere, in
Chains / Of Nerves, and Arteries, and Veins'). But he was also a master
of the absurd. Whence the notorious figure of 'the Antipodes in Shoes',
which Eliot accused of being one of those 'images which are over-
developed or distracting; which support nothing but their own mis-
shapen bodies'. In context, however, it seems altogether less offensive:

> *But now the* Salmon-Fisher's *moist*
> *Their* Leathern Boats *begin to hoist;*
> *And, like* Antipodes *in Shoes,*
> *Have shod their* Heads *in their* Canoos.
> *How* Tortoise *like, but not so slow,*
> *These rational* Amphibii *go?*
> *Let's in: for the dark* Hemisphere
> *Does now like one of them appear.*

This is the last stanza, the 97th, of a very long poem and I do not believe that Marvell, a supremely self-confident craftsman, has let the Metaphysical style run away with him at this crucial moment. He is not going over the top with a far-fetched image, he is merely being playful.

He had, in fact, stolen the conceit from 'Square Cap', one of Cleveland's most popular poems: 'The antipodes wear their shoes on their heads.' Marvell then shows what can be done with it: he prepares the way with a pun – *'Leathern Boats'* suggests 'boots' – expands it into the solemn pedantry of the following couplet – 'How *Tortoise* like, but not so slow . . .' – and ends with absurdity – the comparison of the dark coming down over the hemisphere with the coracles over the heads of the fishermen. It is ridiculous, of course, but that is precisely the point of the exercise. Cleveland, as a university wit, used the Metaphysical conceit to show off his cleverness and his learning. Marvell, a classicist and perfectionist, saw the conceit for what it mostly was, a literary joke in not very good taste, and used it accordingly: with mock seriousness at conventional occasions for conventionally exaggerated praise of his patron, and playfully when his patron's daughter makes her entry. The last stanza of the poem is the climax of this playfulness, the moment when it moves over into what was, at that point, an entirely new form: comic verse. Marvell may have been the finest inheritor of the line of wit that descended from Donne and Jonson, but he was also the initiator of another tradition entirely, a tradition that reached its peak two centuries later with Thomas Hood, Lewis Carroll and Edward Lear. There is a direct line from 'Upon Appleton House' to 'The Hunting of the Snark' and 'The Dong with the Luminous Nose'.

There is a portrait of Marvell in the National Portrait Gallery: a cupid's bow mouth with a full lower lip, a pencil moustache so carefully trimmed that it might almost be a shadow, the eyebrows long and fine and arched, the expression disdainful and withheld. 'He was of middling stature,' wrote Aubrey, 'pretty strong sett, roundish face, cherry cheek't, hazel eie, browne haire. He was in conversation very modest, and of very few words: and though he loved wine he would never drinke hard in company, and was wont to say that *he would not play the good-fellow in any man's company in whose hands he would not trust his life*. He kept bottles of wine at his lodgeing, and many times he would drinke liberally to refresh his spirits, and exalt his muse.'

It sounds like a peculiarly English combination: a public servant fastidious in his art and his politics, a bachelor with a gift for amusing children, a lover of nature and gardens, Latin and Greek poetry, innocence and privacy, a man who was obscurely vulnerable to women's grief but never vulnerable enough to marry, who wrote like an angel when he was young, then settled into a middle age of politics and controversy and solitary drinking. A couple of centuries later, all this would have been a recipe for eccentricity and unhappiness. But Marvell was writing at a time when people seemed to have been less at the mercy of their private inadequacies and he used his to produce some of the most classically perfect poems in the language. They are classical in the true, Latinate sense: chaste and musical, lucid and restrained, long on invention and elegance, short on appetite, monuments to a style of civilisation that is now as remote and foreign as that of classical Rome and Greece themselves.

Introduction to *Andrew Marvell, The Complete Poems*, Everyman edition, 1993

Prose

Jean Rhys

The Work

WHEN JEAN RHYS PUBLISHED her first book, a collection of short stories called *The Left Bank*, in 1927, it came with an enthusiastic preface by Ford Madox Ford. He was presumably rather less enthusiastic about her first novel, *Quartet*, which appeared the next year. It is the story of a young woman, left penniless when her husband is sent to prison, who drifts into an affair with an older man, egged on by his crushingly understanding and emancipated wife. Writing of *The Left Bank*, Ford had praised his protégée's 'passion for stating the case of the underdog.' It turned out that the underdog heroine had an uncanny eye for the hypocrisies and secret brutality of those on top and an equal gift for expressing, without dramatics, the pain and confusion of her own condition. Ford himself was the model for the novel's unspeakable Mr. Heidler.

Three more novels followed in the 1930s: *After Leaving Mr. Mackenzie* in 1930, *Voyage in the Dark* in 1934, and *Good Morning, Midnight* in 1939. Then silence. Like one of her heroines, Miss Rhys went to earth, or just went under, and the books went out of print. It was nearly twenty years before she was traced, after the BBC broadcast a dramatized version of *Good Morning, Midnight*. She was living in Cornwall and had accumulated, in her two decades underground, the extraordinary stories which made up the collection *Tigers Are Better Looking*. She was also writing, and compulsively rewriting, another novel, *Wide Sargasso Sea*, which was finally published in 1966. It is a masterpiece but so in its different way is *Good Morning, Midnight* which had sunk with remarkably little trace. This time, however, Miss Rhys got the recognition she had deserved for so long – though none too soon. She is now 83. Harper & Row has published hardcover editions of most of her books in America; Popular Library has a softcover edition of *Wide Sargasso Sea*; Vintage softcover editions of *After Leaving Mr. Mackenzie* and *Good Morning, Midnight*.

To my mind, she is, quite simply, the best living English novelist. Although her range is narrow, sometimes to the point of obsession, there is no one else now writing who combines such emotional penetration and formal artistry or approaches her own unemphatic, unblinking truthfulness. Even the narrowness works to her advantage. She knows every detail of the shabby world she creates, knows precisely how much to leave out – surprisingly much – and precisely how to modulate the voice which controls it all, at once casual and poignant, the voice of the loser who refuses, though neither she nor God knows why, to give up. Because of this voice, the first four novels read as a single, continuing work. They have the same heroine – although she goes by different names – the same background of seedy hotels and bedsitters for transients in Montparnasse and Bloomsbury, and they recount the single, persistent, disconnected disaster of a life in which only three things can be relied on: fear, loneliness and the lack of money.

Money, above all, is the permanent anxiety, the spring that moves the plots and people. When the heroines have it, they blow it recklessly on clothes and drink, knowing it won't last, anyway. Without it, they twist like cornered animals and humiliate themselves by begging from contemptuous family or ex-lovers, or by sleeping with men they don't want. When Mr. Mackenzie stops Julia Martin's allowance, blood money to end an affair, she has to face London again and her impoverished, acidly genteel uncle and sister. ('Norah herself was labelled for all to see. She was labelled "Middle class, no money." ') She drifts into an affair with the not quite spontaneous, vaguely stunted Mr. Horsfield, then out of it again – Mr. Horsfield buys the ticket – back to the familiar demimonde of Paris, with no money, no future and no longer even sure of her looks.

In *Good Morning, Midnight*, Sasha Jansen is older, already in her forties, and the plot is reversed. She has been holed up in London trying to drink herself to death when she is rescued by a friend and packed off to Paris to recuperate and buy herself clothes. But her Paris is haunted: her baby died there; her marriage broke up; affairs have torn her to shreds. There are bars she can't enter, hotels she daren't pass, and at every moment of inattention the past comes back at her in piercing detail. Her world is unstable and superstitious, as threatening and volatile as nitroglycerin. So she drifts, holding herself in, absurdly prone to tears, until she is picked up by a gigolo who is deceived by her fur coat into thinking she has money. Together they perform a kind of mating dance, at once cynical and anguished, in which each seeks to use the other as an instrument for a revenge on life. They end, of course, more injured than before. But then what else is possible, since they are both walking wounded?

' "Look," he says, still speaking in a whisper. He throws his head up. There is a long scar, going across his throat. Now I understand what it means – from ear to ear. A long, thick, white scar. It's strange that I haven't noticed it before.

'He says: "That is one. There are others. I have been wounded."

It isn't boastful, the way he says this, nor complaining. It's puzzled, puzzled in an impersonal way, as if he is asking me – me, of all people – why, why, why?'

This one question – why? – reverberates through all of Miss Rhys's work. She is far too shrewd to try to provide an answer other than the inevitable one: 'This happened and then that happened.' In other words, that's how things are. She is also far too pure an artist to allow herself the luxury of self-pity. Like the gigolo, she is 'puzzled in an impersonal way.' So the moments of drama and confrontation – when the subterranean terror and despair seem about to burst through – remain strictly moments, done briefly, without comment or fuss, from the outside. Her mind flicks away from them, quick as a fly, and settles on a small detail off to one side: her make-up is wrong, the light falls oddly, a bell rings, a car hoots or a cliché comes to life. ('Now I understand what it means – from ear to ear.') And this, as she does it, is far more unnerving than any full-throated howl of anguish could ever be. She is like the girl in the Max Beerbohm story who looks life straight in the face out of the very corners of her eyes.

She is like a Beerbohm heroine in other ways, too. Miss Rhys's apparently autobiographical heroines have been, in their time, chorus girl, mannequin, artist's model, even a part-time prostitute. In other words, they are in the Muse business, the stunning vulnerable girls who, when Miss Rhys began writing, more usually inspired books than wrote them. At the beginning of *Voyage in the Dark* the 19-year-old virgin chorus girl is reading *Nana*; at the end she, like Nana, is on the game, but chillingly and without any of Zola's unearned polemic. This makes the world Miss Rhys creates seem strangely unprecedented, glassy clear yet somehow distorted, as though she were looking up at things from the bottom of a deep pool. She makes you realize that most other novels, however apparently anarchic, are rooted finally in the respectable world, that their authors came to their subjects from a position of strength and with certain intellectual presuppositions, however cunningly suppressed. She, in contrast, has a marvelous artistic intelligence – no detail is superfluous and her poise never falters as she walks her wicked emotional tightrope – yet is absolutely non-intellectual; no axe to grind, no ideas to tout.

She also writes from a position of weakness: as though orphaned, her women have no one to fall back on, no money, no will to get on, and one skin too few to protect them against an endlessly hostile world. Julia Martin, like all the others, is 'too vulnerable ever to make a success of a career of chance.'

Yet that is the only career she has ever had, drifting from man to man, loan to loan, injury to injury, waiting appalled until her looks finally fail and there is nothing left. In the money or out of it, the heroines have a certain chic, a certain emotional style, but they are never respectable and the middle-class world knows this and treats them accordingly. 'If all the good, respectable people had one face,' says Julia, 'I'd spit in it.' But inevitably it is they who end up spitting in hers.

Miss Rhys is particularly expert in the chill hypocrisy of the English. 'I got the feeling,' says a foreigner in one of her stories, 'that I was surrounded by a pack of timid tigers waiting to spring the moment anybody is in trouble or hasn't any money. *But tigers are better-looking, aren't they?*' This sense of being an outsider unwillingly involved in the intricate social games the British play is constant in Miss Rhys's work. Perhaps this is because she spent the first 16 years of her life in the West Indian island of Dominica, where her Welsh father was a doctor. The dream of a tropical paradise as irretrievably lost as her innocence haunts *Voyage in the Dark*. But it was another quarter of a century before she was able to face it head-on.

Wide Sargasso Sea is her only novel to be set in the past and with a heroine not immediately identifiable with the author, except in her being, like all the others, one of those who are defeated as though by a natural right. Antoinette Cosway is a nineteenth-century Creole heiress, inbred, hovering on the borderline between innocence and decadence, at once besotted by her exquisite West Indian island and menaced by it, as her mother has been menaced by their freed slaves and eventually driven out of her mind by them. An Englishman, stone cold and destructive as all Miss Rhys's Englishmen are, marries Antoinette for her dowry, betrays her and glassily drives her mad in her turn. His name is not given, but the book ends at Thornfield Hall, the setting of *Jane Eyre*. Antoinette, that is, has become the first Mrs. Rochester, crazy and shut away in an attic, her own tenuous life merely an obstruction to other, sturdier lives, waiting her release by fire.

It is a hallucinatory novel, as detailed, abrupt and undeniable as a dream, and with a dream's weird and irresistible logic. It is also the final triumph of Miss Rhys's stylistic control. Despite the exotic setting and the famous, abused heroine, there is no melodrama. The prose is reticent, unemphatic, precise, and yet supple, alive with feeling, as though the whole world she so coolly describes were shimmering with foreboding, with a lifetime's knowledge of unease and pain.

The purity of Miss Rhys's style and her ability to be at once so deadly serious and offhand makes her books peculiarly timeless. Novels she wrote more than 40 years ago still seem contemporary, unlike those of many more popular authors. More important, her voice itself remains young. She was about 30 before she began to write – apparently having other things on her mind before that – yet the voice she created then, and still uses, is oddly youthful: light, clear, alert, casual and disabused, and uniquely concerned in simply telling the truth.

New York Times, 1974

The Life

JEAN RHYS WAS 76 years old before she had a literary success. Her first five books – a collection of short stories and four novels, published between 1927 and 1939 – had been praised sporadically for their style, disliked generally for their sordid subject matter and sold hardly at all. Fame of a kind came finally in 1966 with the publication of *Wide Sargasso Sea*, which won her what were then two of Britain's most prestigious literary awards, one from the Royal Society of Literature, the other the W.H. Smith Prize. Rhys refused to go to either presentation ceremony. She pleaded ill health, but the truth was she was too old, too shy and too distrustful of her fellow writers to cope with the razzmatazz. She was also beyond caring. According to Diana Athill, her friend and publisher, her reaction to the good news was that it had come too late.

She was right, of course. In literary terms, nothing was going to make up for forty years' neglect. But Rhys didn't think in literary terms. To an extraordinary degree, the world of letters figured hardly at all in her life and interests and ambitions. Until her last years, when she became successful and therefore sought after, she met few other writers and with those she did meet she was so formal and shy that they lost interest and rarely tried to see her again. If she had to communicate with a fellow author, she preferred to do so by letter. The 1984 selection of the letters she wrote after 1931 contains none at all to anyone of a comparable literary stature.

The reason is that, although there were times when she wrote obsessively, her real life was elsewhere and writing was secondary to it. 'I never wanted to write,' she wrote to her friend Peggy Kirkaldy. 'I wished to be happy and peaceful and obscure. I was *dragged* into writing by a series of coincidences . . . [and] need for money.' Obscure she certainly was until the last few years of her very long life – she was 88 when she died – but happy and peaceful never, and her belated success was no compensation for the unspeakable mess she made of the business of living. Maybe she thought that if recognition had come earlier a little money might have eased the strain and made the need to behave badly less overpowering.

Carole Angier puts it more starkly: success had come too late, she says, because 'by the time it came she had too much to hide.' In her will Rhys specifically asked that no biography of her should be written unless it was authorized in her lifetime. She never gave that author-ization. Instead, she began to write her memoirs, published post-humously as *Smile Please*. Her objections to a biography were partly a matter of principle: 'I have not met other writers often. A few in Paris . . . Even fewer in England. That does not matter at all, for all of a writer that matters is in the book or books. It is idiotic to be curious about the person.' She wrote that in a fragment of a diary published at the end of *Smile Please*. But as Ms Angier shows, Rhys's objections were not just a matter of principle: the style of the writing – offhand yet purified and austere – was utterly at odds with the style of the life.

Yet her books were autobiographical to an exceptional degree.

Rhys had great imagination and no invention at all: she had no gift for plots, she couldn't dream up situations she herself had not already been in, the people she wrote about are the people she knew. This is an honorable tradition, of course. Even Shakespeare rarely bothered to think up his own plots; he either reworked them from other people's plays or lifted them from Plutarch or Holinshed. Rhys's invention was even more straitened: she stuck to the facts of her life, the people and places and disasters she had lived with, and then refined them, reduced them to their essence, made them perfect.

As Ms Angier explains in the introduction to her notes, for years Rhys kept a series of notebooks that she used partly as a diary, partly for rough drafts that were later worked up – or down – into fiction. She sometimes claimed that the notebooks were all fiction, fiction in diary form, but Ms Angier argues convincingly that this was not true. This allows her to plot Rhys's life by moving continuously to and fro between the notebooks and the finished work. She has also done a great deal of legwork: she has examined the archives, interviewed everyone who knew Rhys when she was old and combed the work of those, all of them now dead, who knew her in her dazzling but confused youth. The result is sympathetic, even-handed and psychologically shrewd, and I am quite certain Rhys would have hated it because of what it reveals of the life she wanted to keep hidden.

It is a fascinating story, of course, which is why Rhys did not want it written. Writing is usually a staid and lonely profession and writers generally do not lead interesting lives. Some, like Conrad, lead interesting lives in their youth, then settle down and write about them later, but most, like oysters, need only a small irritation to get them going. Rhys herself was doomed to an interesting life. Or rather, she led four lives, two of them 'interesting' in the direst way and all of them, until the last years, spiralling remorselessly downward.

The first lasted until her middle thirties when she met Ford Madox Ford who got her writing and helped publish her first book, a collection of stories called *The Left Bank*, in 1927. Then came her second life with her second husband, Leslie Tilden Smith, a failed literary agent turned publishers' reader, who encouraged her to write, typed her manuscripts and sent them off to be published. According to Ms Angier, the bulk of her work was written between 1928 and 1938 when she was with him. When *Good Morning, Midnight*, one of her masterpieces, sank without trace in 1939 she sank with it, dragging Tilden Smith down with her. After he died in 1945, she married his cousin, Max Hamer, a crooked, unsuccessful solicitor and one of God's losers, like Rhys herself. The writing stopped and her trajectory on the downward spiral went more or less out of control until she was rediscovered a decade later and began, sporadically, to write again. She died in 1979, acclaimed by the Establishment she despised – she was awarded the CBE – and even modestly solvent, a condition she found hard to believe in after a lifetime's penury.

The first 'interesting' decades of her long life gave her most of her material. She was born Ella Gwendoline Rees Williams in 1890 on the island of Dominica, known to its inhabitants as 'the Cinderella of the West Indies' and 'the third world's third world.' Her father was Welsh, a romantic figure who had run away to sea before becoming a doctor and emigrating to the Caribbean in search of a career and a wife. Her mother came from an old Dominican family, originally Scots, sugar merchants who had come down in the world after the abolition of slavery. Rhys seems to have felt herself an outcast in her own family and maybe she was: a baby sister had died exactly nine months before she was born, so perhaps her mother was still in mourning for the dead child; she certainly seems to have preferred Rhys's younger sister. Ms Angier reels off a catalogue of injuries Rhys felt was done to her in her childhood, mostly by her mother, a decent but uncomprehending woman who believed, like all the other Victorians, in strict propriety and corporal punishment. But I have the impression that Rhys played this card too hard, as though to excuse her own subsequent bad behavior – her indifference, her rages, her fecklessness. It is more likely that unhappiness was the country of her heart and there were times when this puzzled her, so she sought excuses and someone to blame.

She left Dominica for England when she was 17, spent a term at a school in Cambridge, then two terms at Beerbohm Tree's Academy of Dramatic Art. She said later that she left the Academy because her father died and there was no money to pay the fees. Not true, says Ms Angier; her father did not die until a year later. She left because she had not much talent and a grating West Indian accent that no amount of elocution lessons could modulate into the obligatory Edwardian upper-class drawl. Later she developed a soft, almost whispering voice. But in the land of Professor Higgins and Eliza Doolittle she would have had a hard time making it as a lady.

She couldn't act and she didn't want to go home to Dominica and her disapproving mother. All she had were marvelous looks and a vague instinct for trouble. So she joined the chorus of a touring company, which in those days was not considered a proper option for a well-brought-up doctor's daughter. In a way, turning chorus girl was one of the few deliberate choices Rhys ever made. She seems to have fallen into her other careers – mannequin, mistress, good-time girl, wife, mother, even novelist – as a result of what Updike has called 'drift and whim,' allied to a profound passivity which manifested itself in everything from her inability to get out of a relationship to her pathological unwillingness to finish her books and let them go. It is characteristic of Rhys, who always thought of herself as not belonging anywhere, that her one crucial choice should have been to move socially downward into the demimonde. In those days, the chorus line was not a stepping stone to a career on the stage. The best a chorus girl could hope for was to catch the eye of a rich young 'masher' in the stalls and get him to marry her. But that happened very rarely and most of the girls thought in terms of free dinners and presents and casual affairs. The next step down was prostitution and Rhys, in due course, took it, although not for long.

First, she found herself an ideal lover. His name was Lancelot Grey Hugh Smith and he was a stockbroker from a grand banking family, vastly rich. He was also twice her age, patient, subtle, intelligent and, for a time, as besotted with her as she was with him. But after 18 months he pensioned her off, albeit gently and regretfully, and she never really recovered. What she did do, however, was write it all down in a notebook which, she claimed, she put in the bottom of her trunk and forgot all about until she dug it out and turned it into *Voyage in the Dark*, the most poignant of all her books, published in 1934, 25 years after the event. Ms Angier doesn't altogether believe that this burst of writing happened spontaneously, out of the blue: 'she'd been writing out her sadness in poems since she was a child; she'd probably been writing it out in a sporadic diary for years. She went on doing this for ten more years; indeed, for all her life.' Whatever the truth, her writing began in heartbreak and stayed that way.

Meanwhile, she went on the skids, drank heavily, slept around for money, became pregnant and had a back-street abortion. In 1919, after seven years of dingy Bloomsbury bedsitters and Soho nightclubs and casual affairs, she married Jean Lenglet, a French-Dutchman, and moved with him to Paris. Lenglet, like Rhys, was a demimondain – a journalist, *chansonnier* and con man who lived by his wits and not always above the breadline. They scraped by hand-to-mouth in the

Latin Quarter and had a baby son who died when he was three weeks old. When Rhys described his death in *Good Morning, Midnight* she used a kind of shorthand for heartbreak – spare, ironic and without a trace of self-pity. It is one of the bleakest, most moving things she ever wrote, but the reality, as described by Ms Angier, was equally bleak and altogether shabbier. The baby died because of Rhys's profound incompetence and even profounder indifference. He had been left by an open window in January and developed pneumonia; the parents took their time before they called a *sage femme* who called a doctor; while the baby was dying in the *Hospice des Enfants Assistés*, Rhys and Lenglet were getting giggling drunk on champagne, trying to pretend the disaster wasn't happening.

But 'this catastrophe changed their luck,' says Ms Angier. Friends took pity on them and wangled Lenglet a job with the Interallied Disarmament Commission. For a time, they lived it up in Vienna and Budapest, but naturally the good times didn't last. Lenglet got involved in a currency swindle and they had to flee precipitately, with the police on their tails. By then, Rhys was pregnant again. Their daughter Maryvonne was born in Brussels, but motherhood was never one of Rhys's talents. After two weeks, she dumped the new baby in a clinic and went off to London to hustle money. That was in May, 1922; it was November before they came to collect the child, then promptly dumped her again in a French clinic where she remained until she was three. By that time Rhys and Lenglet were separated and Maryvonne was mostly left to fend for herself in one institution or another. During the '30s she spent summer holidays with her mother but most of the little parenting Maryvonne received was done by Lenglet and when World War II broke out she returned to Holland to be with him. Eventually, Rhys made what were, for her, determined efforts to repair the damage and Maryvonne did what she could to be a dutiful daughter, but they were never easy together.

Back in Paris, Rhys and Lenglet were penniless again. She had already tried and failed at a number of jobs – mannequin, shop assistant, governess, guide. Finally, she translated some of her husband's articles and tried to peddle them to the English newspapers. Nobody wanted them but their prose seems to have impressed Mrs H. Pearl Adam, a formidable lady journalist. She asked to see the diary-notebook Rhys had kept in Paris and Vienna, tinkered with it, then passed it on to Ford Madox Ford, that great discoverer of unknown young writers. Ford, who recognized a natural when he saw one and was also a great womanizer, was entranced both by the prose and the author. She had, he wrote in his preface to *The Left Bank*, a 'singular instinct for form,' 'a terrifying insight and a terrific – an almost lurid! – passion for stating the case of the underdog.' He set about teaching her how to perfect her talent: how to cut out the extraneous details, condense the narrative, avoid cliché and melodrama, and pare away until the prose rhythms followed, with uncanny precision, the sidelong, casual, flickering movement of her sensibility.

Rhys was a perfect pupil for Ford: a prodigiously gifted tabula rasa. Thirty years later, Alwynne Woodward, vicar of Cheriton Fitzpaine, the Devon village where Rhys was then living, and one in her long line of rescuers, said that she was 'almost without education – but with a wonderful mind.' She read a great deal, of course, but undiscriminatingly, anything that came to hand, without direction, without ulterior motives, trash as avidly as 'good' books. Instead of getting her to read the great English novelists, Ford pointed her at French writers he thought she would find sympathetic. 'He told her,' says Ms Angier, 'if she wasn't sure of a passage to translate it into French: "If it looked utterly silly one got rid of it." ' Twenty years later, Samuel Beckett, another of this century's great stylists, also found his voice through French, although his approach was more radical: he gave up English altogether, wrote only in French, then translated himself back triumphantly into his native tongue. For both, despite their differences, the result was a prose style utterly their own which owed no debts to the great – or even to the not-so-great – tradition. This, combined with Rhys's contempt for the respectable world and the ease with which she took for granted life at the bottom of the heap, makes her work seem curiously contemporary.

The big literary figures of the '20s and '30s – not just pop stars like Aldous Huxley and Maugham, but Lawrence, Woolf, even Joyce – often seem dated now, trapped by the intellectual and cultural rhetoric they were reacting against, while Rhys, who had no cultural baggage, no intellectual preoccupations, no axe to grind, wrote then as though she were writing now. In her short story 'Till September Petronella,' the shock is not at the end, when the narrator lets herself be picked up like a common prostitute, but halfway through, when she looks at a calendar and sees the date – July 28th, 1914. Her prose is contemporary in the way a poem by Donne is contemporary: you hear the voice speaking directly to you; her reality is your reality. It is a prose close to poetry not in the lush sense usually implied by the term 'poetic prose' but because it is condensed, elliptical, emotionally precise.

Rhys had a taste for older men and Ford, like Lancelot Smith, became, in Ms Angier's words, 'lover, father and friend; and teacher and patron too.' He launched her as a writer, but in doing so he was sharpening a knife for his own throat. When Lenglet's sins caught up with him and he was sent to prison, charged with illegal entry into France and offenses against the currency regulations, Rhys moved in with Ford and his stolid, complaisant mistress, Stella Bowen. Rhys was in her middle thirties by then, although she looked at least ten years younger, and she had refined her natural passivity into a fine art. Ford was captivated by what he called her 'Creole indolence' and Lenglet suffered for it. She didn't show up for his trial, answered his passionate letters coolly, visited him irregularly, and left him to fester in the knowledge that he was 'betrayed, cuckolded and let down.'

All four protagonists eventually wrote about this miserable affair – Bowen in her memoirs, the others in novels – though Rhys had the last word artistically in *Quartet*. What is common to them all, even to Rhys – especially to Rhys – is how badly she behaved: venomously, abjectly, sullenly, as though driven by an overpowering need to lose. What is also common to them all is how much she drank. Rhys herself makes no attempt to disguise this. The heroines of the four novels she published in the '30s – *Quartet*, *After Leaving Mr. Mackenzie*, *Voyage in the Dark*, *Good Morning, Midnight* – are all trying, in varying degrees, to drink themselves to death. It is their way of forgetting their mislaid happiness, of blotting out the confusion and perpetual money worries. What she fails to mention, however, is that when she drank another person entirely emerged. The odalisque languor, passivity and charm dropped away, along with the whispering voice. She became a nightmare figure, full of rage – violent, obscene, hoarse, murderous. Stella Bowen called her 'a doomed soul, violent and demoralized' and Ford, quite simply, was terrified. (He wasn't alone in this. In 1977, a good-natured and brisk young nurse, who was looking after Rhys in Devon, momentarily thwarted her and was frightened out of her wits when her sweet, 87-year-old charge leapt out of her wheelchair and became a taunting, threatening witch, straight out of the girl's worst nightmares.)

Ford pensioned her off and left for a lecture tour in the States, Lenglet fled to Holland and went into a poorhouse, Rhys stayed in Paris and wrote *Quartet*. Briefly, in 1927, she took her daughter out of the institution she had been dumped in and joined her husband in Amsterdam. By that time he had contrived one of his characteristic transformations: he had gone from inmate to manager of the poor-house and had then been fired for embezzlement. They spent a few weeks as a family – the only time the three of them lived together – but the marriage was over. By 1928, Rhys had drifted back to London and moved in with Leslie Tilden Smith, whom she eventually married.

Ford had turned her into a writer but it was Tilden Smith who nurtured her talent and kept her going: he cooked, cleaned, typed, edited and sold her books to the publishers. More important, he even managed to make her let go of the manuscripts – always the hardest part for her – when he thought they were finished. But at a cost. Her drinking got worse and so did her drunken rages. She taunted him unceasingly, threw his typewriter out the window, blacked his eyes, tore his face. He was a self-effacing, generous man, with a real passion for literature, and he put up with it because he loved her for a time and, when that ended, because he loved her talent. And under his diffident, stoic care, at least she was writing. According to Ms Angier,

Jean conceived and probably wrote the majority of her lifetime's work, published and unpublished, between 1927 and 1939: four novels, eight stories (of which two reached novel length), a mass of autobiographical writing, and a further lost novel. Only her early diaries and her first volume of stories . . . came before; and about fifteen stories, her final version of *Wide Sargasso Sea*, her unfinished autobiography and a few commissioned pieces after.

But the books didn't sell and the drinking got worse. In 1935, one year after the appearance of *Voyage in the Dark*, she was hauled up before the magistrates at Bow Street court, along with the hapless Tilden Smith, on the charge of drunk and disorderly. *Good Morning, Midnight*, her masterpiece, was published in April 1939, four months before the Germans marched into Poland, and according to Rhys 'the war killed it,' although in fact the reviewers had already made sure there wasn't much left to kill. They had always criticized her for her amorality and for what they thought of as her sordid subject-matter – sex and money and drink, topics the Brits warm to reluctantly and only when they come gift-wrapped in 'life-affirming' Falstaffian disguise. On those terms, *Good Morning, Midnight* does not admit a chink of light into its darkness. Like her other novels, it has an unhappy ending, but this time the unhappiness is so abrupt, unexpected and yet inevitable that the effect is not tragic, with all that implies of nobility and waste, it is simply unnerving, a horror made more horrific by being muted and factual and assented to (The last words are 'Yes – yes – yes . . .'). It is also the product of extraordinary artistic control and perhaps it was this combination of high art and low life that made Rhys's work so hard to stomach at the time she was writing. She didn't write about low life as a literary subject – *à la* Zola, *à la* socialist realism – she wrote about it as the reality she lived with. Her view is the view from the bottom, the underdog's Ford called it, and her themes are underdog's themes: fear, loneliness, lack of money. Her method, however, is that of high art, pure and fastidious, and she uses it to create a wholly orginal tone of voice, casual and clear and disabused, the voice of the vulnerable young woman Rhys herself might have been if booze and failure in her real life hadn't turned her into a vengeful hag.

By 1939 she was a chronic alcoholic, sinking fast. In 1940, Tilden Smith joined the RAF, perhaps thinking he would have more chance fighting the Nazis than fighting his sodden wife. Without him to take care of her, she fell apart. In July 1940, she was arrested again for being drunk and disorderly and the local paper wrote up the trial:

> Police Constable Haverson stated defendant was unsteady on her feet, her appearance was dishevelled, and her breath smelt strongly of spirits. She broke out into a stream of abuse of the English race, declaring, according to one witness, 'I am a West Indian, and I hate the English. They are a b— mean and dirty lot.' The disorderly conduct . . . arose only after one of the witnesses had thrown water over her. Mrs Tilden Smith was very distressed because no news had been received of her daughter in Holland since the invasion of that country.

'It's terrible to think of this –' writes Ms Angier. 'Jean on a country road, raging at England; someone throwing a bucket of water over her. And this was the woman who had already written some of the finest prose of our century.' If you set this against America's long line of alcoholic writers who managed to keep a canny grip on their careers, despite their bad habits, you begin to understand both the degree of Rhys's self-destructive rage and helplessness, her total lack of any sense of herself as an artist, and also of England's blank, self-satisfied indifference to talent. Ms Angier's biography often reads like a morality tale about art and life and the deadly cost of one to the other. But there are long stretches when it turns, quite simply, into a horror story.

Because of his wife's drunkenness Tilden Smith had to resign his commission in the RAF and go back to his miserable dogsbodying for publishers in London. But because he was around, at least Rhys kept writing – short stories and long bouts with her notebooks which she later turned into fiction. But the strain of the marriage got to him at last and he died just after the end of the war at the age of sixty. He smoked heavily and he had a dicky heart, but he came from a long-lived family and his daughter thinks he should 'have lived for years and years.' But that was reckoning without Jean Rhys and the monster she became when she drank.

All through her life Rhys was terrified of loneliness. She was also profoundly incompetent in practical matters: she couldn't type, she couldn't drive, she couldn't manage any mechanical device more intricate than a corkscrew. Since she never much cared for other women, she needed a man about the place, however dreadfully she then treated him. Soon after her husband died, she moved in with his cousin, Max Hamer, and within two years they were married. Hamer was eight years older than Rhys and, like her father, he had been a sailor. He was invalided out of the Navy after twenty years' service, then trained as a solicitor, but on his good days he retained the military bearing of a naval officer and the tweedy, blue-eyed English gentle-man's demeanour that Rhys always fancied. Unfortunately, he was as unworldly as she was and as penniless, and he neither knew about nor cared for literature. They were together for twenty years and, all in all, it was a dreadful marriage. Yet although she made him suffer as she had made her other husbands suffer – she was still beating him up when he was old and dying – she always talked fondly of him after his death, perhaps because, as a loser himself, he was never judgemental towards her.

They settled in Beckenham, a dreary south London suburb and a very long way from the Latin Quarter. Without someone to en-courage her and prod her on Rhys stopped writing altogether and devoted her attention exclusively to booze. There were vendettas with the neighbors, screaming matches, physical fights. She was arrested for throwing a brick through a window, for assault, for wandering around in the street, drunk and disorderly, in her night-gown and slippers. In the space of two years, she was brought up before the magistrates nine times. She became a local freak show, a joke people pointed at, a bag lady. She took to stuffing her handbag with papers 'to prove everything I say now,' including a story that nobody believed, that she was a writer called Jean Rhys. She also spent a week in the grim women's prison, Holloway, and was ordered by the court to undergo a psychiatric examination. The fact that she was sixty years old and a great writer made no difference at all.

For a brief moment, her writing identity was resurrected. An actress called Selma vaz Diaz had come across *Good Morning, Midnight* and adapted it as a dramatic monologue for BBC radio. The BBC didn't pay much but they were sticklers for professional etiquette and they required the author's permission. Rhys's publishers didn't know where she was, nor did the British Consul in Paris. There were rumors that she was dead but no death certificate could be found. So vaz Diaz put an advertisement in the *New Statesman* and Rhys, by some miracle, saw it. The next time she was arrested she was waving a piece of paper and saying 'something about the BBC.' Her enemy next door said she was 'impersonating a dead writer called Jean Rhys.'

This remission from her sodden, violent, mindless way of life was as short as all her other highs. Before vaz Diaz paid her first visit, Rhys was back in front of the magistrates again. Then a worse disaster struck: her husband was brought to trial at the Old Bailey, charged with larceny and obtaining money by false pretenses, sentenced to three years in prison and struck off the Solicitors' Roll. Rhys disappeared. Ms Angier can find no trace of her until she surfaced a year later in Maidstone, where Hamer was doing time.

Bruno Bettleheim once suggested that paranoids seemed to function quite well in the concentration camps because the terrible reality of the world they had been thrust into effortlessly outstripped their wildest fantasies. On a smaller scale, disaster seemed to strengthen Rhys and make her sane. She stopped drinking – or so she told her daughter – and began, briefly, to write again. In the diary she kept while staying at a pub called the Ropemakers' Arms in Maidstone she turned her, by now, extensive courtroom experience into a kind of spiritual trial, with counsels for the prosecution and defense and herself as prisoner at the bar. When the prosecutor asks her why she says she must write she replies, 'If I stop writing my life will have been an abject failure. It is that already to other people. But it could be an abject failure to myself. I will not have earned death.' She was 62 when she wrote this and the dream of being 'happy and peaceful and obscure' had long been washed away by booze and penury and rage. When she was younger she could get by on her looks and charm but now her looks were gone. (Or so she thought. When I met her she was in her middle eighties but she dressed and made herself up with enormous care to emphasize her marvelous velvet-blue eyes and she still had the slim legs and shy, flirtatious manner of a young girl.) She tended her writing as scrupulously and obsessively as she once tended her physical appearance, and made her prose into what she herself had once been – beautiful. It was the only way left to justify the waste she had made of her life.

Of course, her good resolutions didn't last. Hamer, who was 70 by then, was released after serving two years. They drifted west to wherever the rent was cheapest – a yacht moored up for the winter in a Welsh estuary, unheated summer chalets in dreary seaside towns – and the boozing and violence started again, compounded by regular bouts of 'flu, 'twice a year and regular as clockwork.' Gradually, however, her luck changed. In 1957 the BBC finally broadcast Selma vaz Diaz's version of *Good Morning, Midnight*, along with a *Radio Times* article that said she was working on a new novel. The writer Francis Wyndham, a fan who, the year before, had described her as 'the late Jean Rhys,' read the piece and arranged a contract with a London publisher.

The book was *Wide Sargasso Sea*, the advance was £25, and it was another nine years before it was published. The fact that it was published at all was mostly due to the devotion and pertinacity of Wyndham and Rhys's editor, Diana Athill. But they were in London and she was mostly holed up in a draughty jerry-built bungalow in deepest Devon. She always found writing hard and she was terminally disorganized; she wrote on scraps of paper and left them scattered all over the cottage, in 'plastic bags and hatboxes, . . . under the bed and the sofa, . . . on top of wardrobes and inside kitchen cupboards.' Without someone like Ford or Tilden Smith at her elbow to put the manuscript in order, and wrestle it away from her and her obsessional revising, the progress was glacial. She told me that most of the notorious rewriting of *Sargasso* was not rewriting at all; she was simply copying it out again and again, maybe changing a word or two in the process. Hamer died the year the book was published and she dedicated it to him, although he probably hadn't read a word of it and, knowing what it had cost them both, must assuredly have hated the thing.

It was time for a happy ending, but in fact success changed nothing at all. The boozing and rages continued as before and Rhys behaved shamelessly to anyone who came too close. Near the end, she almost destroyed Diana Melly who, because she loved the books and was enchanted by the old lady when she was sober, invited her to spend a winter in her London house. Diana's husband, the jazz singer and writer George Melly, nicknamed this Woman Who Came to Dinner Johnny Rotten.

Rhys was right when she said that only through writing could she earn death. In all other ways, she was a monster and the effect of Ms Angier's well-meaning biography is to make the reader doubt if any book, however original, however perfect, could be worth the price Rhys and those close to her paid. No wonder she did not want her biography written. Her prose was pure and self-denying and it kept very close to the facts of her life. In doing so, it distilled them, shaped them, made them seem inevitable. But the facts behind the art are shabby and demeaning: booze, rage, sexual manipulation, cultivated passivity, dire ingratitude and a blank indifference to husbands, lovers, children, friends and relatives. Ms Angier's biography is a powerful argument against biography itself: Jean Rhys was one of the finest writers of the century but the best way to read her work is to know nothing about the woman who wrote it.

New York Review of Books, 1991

Malcolm Lowry

DOUGLAS DAY'S SCRUPULOUS AND level-headed biography of Malcolm Lowry fails, understandably, to raise one important question: Why should anyone ever want to be a writer? In Lowry's case everything was against it. He himself wrote of one of his transparently auto-biographical heroes: 'He is disinterested in literature, uncultured, incredibly unobservant, in many respects ignorant, without faith in himself, and lacking nearly all the qualities you normally associate with a novelist or a writer.' In Professor Day's milder words, Lowry was no 'natural.' The early drafts of his works are clumsy and curiously naive, and he had to batter them into shape by, literally, endless rewriting. His one masterpiece, *Under the Volcano*, took him 10 years to complete and went through four separate drafts, the last of which itself went through at least four stages. Even after it had been published and made his name, he still talked vaguely of revising it yet again.

He was also a novelist without a subject. Or rather, his only subject was himself. He was, apparently, utterly unaware of other people and of his surroundings. The only substantial characters in his books are recognizable versions of Lowry, and even the extraordinary descriptions of Mexico in *Under the Volcano* read, for all their detail, like inner landscapes, exacerbating shades of his private inferno. Perhaps that is why he thought of himself as a poet *manqué*, although his verse is mostly trite and talentless. Like many others, he believed mistakenly that to be a poet it is necessary above all to be miserable. Although his friends insist that a weird, wry, self-deprecating jollity kept breaking through, misery was his usual condition. But then he could scarcely have been otherwise, since a good part of his anguish was inspired by the intolerable and unnatural strain of his vocation as a writer. Which brings us back where we started in the vicious circle.

There was, of course, another source of both his misery and his art:

he was massively, compulsively, suicidally alcoholic. He would drink anything he could lay his hands on: gin by preference but, if there was nothing else around, even after-shave lotion. In retrospect, his boozing seems, like Hart Crane's or Dylan Thomas's, an heroic activity, gargantuan, something almost to admire, that makes the rest of us seem fiddling and petty-minded. In fact, it was the purest agony for everyone who knew Lowry, particularly for his devoted second wife Margerie, and also for Lowry himself. 'Lowry was frightened of writing,' says Day, 'or frightened of failing at writing; and drunkenness offered a good excuse for not writing, and so not failing . . . Lowry drank in order to avoid writing, sobered up in order to write, then drank in order to avoid writing – and so on.'

He was, however, an alcoholic before he was a writer. He seems to have picked up the habit before he went up to Cambridge University when, inspired by all the wrong reasons and wrong novels, he disastrously worked his passage on a freighter from England to the Far East. When the other crew members, already contemptuous of him because he was a toff, roared off to the brothels at every port, Lowry, still virgin and terrified of syphilis, asserted his manhood by getting ostentatiously drunk. By 1933, the year his first and undistinguished novel, *Ultramarine*, was published and he himself was only 24, he was already in a clinic being dried out.

Day allows himself some rather superficial Freudian chat about oral compulsion and its roots in infancy – the weakest pages in his book and mercifully uncharacteristic of his otherwise untheoretical sympathy for the man – but the truth seems to be that Lowry had one of those conventional British childhoods which would drive anyone to drink. His father was a wealthy Methodist, athletic, abstemious and moralizing, an international cotton-broker, always off round the globe on business trips. Lowry's iceberg of a mother often went with him, leaving Malcolm, the youngest of her four sons, in the care of the usual incompetent and sadistic nannies. At 7 he was bundled off to boarding school and when, two years later, he contracted an eye infection which lasted for four years, his mother refused to have him home during the holidays, finding his bandaged eyes too unattractive to be endured. He went on to an unspeakable minor public school where, miraculously, this fat, sickly, unlovable duckling changed into a champion golfer, enthusiastic rugger-player and swimmer, and resident wit in the school magazine.

This mixture of hearty and esthete stayed with him for the rest of his life. In the relatively idyllic days of his second marriage, when he lived in a shack in the woods outside Vancouver, B. C., and worked on *Under the Volcano*, he drank little, chopped wood, did calisthenics and swam heroic distances. Until his tragic end, he retained the powerful arms, barrel-chest and pot belly of the ruined athlete. Perhaps even his wild bouts with the bottle had in them an element of physical bravado, since he had extraordinary powers of recuperation and survived, before he finally committed suicide, every brutality British medical psychiatry could throw at him: pentathol, shock treatment, apomorphine, aversion therapy and the threat of lobotomy.

By the time he went up to Cambridge, he was already a romantic figure: he had been to sea, worked with the avant-garde Conrad Aiken in America and broken the record at Hoylake golf course. He studied English – which meant, in effect, that he devoted himself to booze and his first novel – and was lucky to scrape a Third (a barely passing grade) in the days when it would have taken real genius to fail. Yet everyone who knew him was convinced that genius was what he had. Day finds this early recognition puzzling, since Lowry's brilliance was at best sporadic and his insecurities were enormous. I think that what is involved has nothing to do with achievement; it is, instead, a question of energy and generosity. As a young man Lowry was, in both senses of the word, careless of his gifts. He may not have cultivated them assiduously, but he also never hoarded them. He had about him the authentic buzz of life, witty, passionate, knowing and, above all, vulnerable. Emotionally, he was one of the big spenders.

Yet the bars of every literary capital are crawling with figures whom their friends call geniuses but who seem to the outsider merely drunkards, spongers and masters, or mistresses, of self-pity. All of them are constantly threatening to write a great book and none of them do so, because their lives are subtly arranged to provide them with excuses not to work. Given a modicum of talent and showman-ship it is, after all, relatively easy to appear a genius in the smoke and confusion of a poets' pub. But to produce the written proof requires not only talent but also concentration, routine, self-knowledge and an infinite tolerance for the boredom of hard work.

In Lowry's case it also required a large capacity for pain. What set him apart from the literary riff-raff was his ability, slowly, almost reluctantly, to transform all the misery, guilt, rage and self-destruc-tiveness which once kept him from writing into his inspiration. He prepared himself for his masterpiece by a progressive descent into his own exclusive inferno. First, he made a disastrous marriage to a tinny, impatient, promiscuous American girl whom he hardly knew. Within a few months he was impotent and she was unfaithful. When she walked out on him in Paris he followed her to New York, where her infidelities and his alcoholism increased. He finished up, raging, in Bellevue Hospital. It was a crucial experience, says Day:

'Lowry had, in effect, played about with the concepts of drunkenness, madness, oblivion; but now, suddenly, the doors of Bellevue closed behind him . . . and he found himself in a world that was infinitely worse than anything he had imagined before. . . . There is no better place . . . to learn how hideous life can be than in the psychiatric section of a large public hospital; and Lowry, who was no fool, must have seen this and realized what a poseur he was, and how protected he had been.' Out of this he wrote his appalled, unfinished novella, *Lunar Caustic*, which was, deliberately, his own version of Rimbaud's *A Season in Hell*. More important, Bellevue made him understand that hell was, in truth, the country of his heart. So he set about exploring it.

With his unerring instinct for trouble, he chose Mexico as the setting and his wife again as the instrument. Their respective drinking and infidelity increased until he became paranoid and began to hallucinate. When his wife left him for the last time in December, 1937, he stayed on for half a year, penniless, persecuted, half-mad, jailed in Oaxaca, drunk everywhere. Years later, when his great book was written and he was married again, this time successfully, he went back to Mexico to exorcize the ghosts. Instead, they exorcized him. The authorities had kept a fat dossier on his first stay; a policeman showed it to him with the comment: '*Borracho, Borracho, Borracho.* Here is your life.' Lowry and Margerie were deported.

By then it didn't matter. He had produced his improbable masterpiece and, although he went on fitfully and compulsively writing, even the sympathetic Day can find little to recommend in his last work. Not that his life had become suddenly easier, despite Margerie's extraordinary forbearance and devotion. For a man besotted with hell, the fates are always obliging. A crooked landlord in Vancouver kept him poor, his beloved shack in Dollarton burnt down, taking with it the manuscript of another novel, while the huge success of *Under the Volcano* drove him, literally, berserk; he twice tried to kill Margerie, and only a constitution of triple brass kept the drink from killing him.

Finally, back in England in 1957, a tormented decade after the triumph of *Under the Volcano*, he rounded off 30 years of boozing with an overdose of sleeping pills.

Earlier accounts of Lowry's death have tended to camouflage his suicidal intentions. Day leaves no doubt at all, although he admits that Lowry was so sodden and upset that he may possibly – just possibly – have been making merely one more grandiose gesture toward self-destruction, which failed because barbiturates proved less controllable than booze. But it is characteristic of Day's book that he neither whitewashes Lowry nor accuses him. Day, a professor of English at the University of Virginia, is fair-minded and sensible to a degree quite remarkable in an academic biographer of a contemporary figure.

Maybe he is lucky in that everything is still not known; the laundry and liquor bills have yet to be put through a computer; more important, there are still mountains of notes and drafts to be sifted. Yet I doubt if Day has the temperament to build the usual scholarly mausoleum. He is too skeptical, too humane, as suspicious of the elaborate allegorical interpretations that have been foisted on the books as he is of hagiography. He even makes occasional mistakes: Someone at the Oxford University Press should have told him that O.T.C. stands for Officers' Training Corps, not Course, and even on the longest day the sun has never yet risen at midnight in the Lake District.

Yet, Lowry as Day presents him – flawed, hopeful, impossible – is always believable, a genuine portrait of the artist as both a young dog and an old monster. Day remarks of Lowry the undergraduate 'he must have been an utterly miserable young man' and then goes on to show how utterly miserable, despite his gifts, and insufferable, despite his seductiveness, Lowry remained throughout his life. The climax of his awfulness came in New York after the triumphant publication of *Under the Volcano*. At parties in his honor he refused to open his mouth, he missed appointments, staged melodramatic death scenes and was perpetually drunk. As Day describes it, his behavior had little to do with despair, it was simply the stupid cunning and perversity of a spoiled child with a grown man's ability to insult, brutalize and destroy.

Yet perhaps for someone as dedicatedly and omniverously suicidal as Lowry, success was literally intolerable. Once he had made his name and a good marriage – Margerie not only typed and edited everything he wrote, she also actively collaborated with him: 'Nothing Lowry

wrote after 1939,' says Day, 'was, strictly speaking, entirely his own' –
he had nothing left to write about. So he systematically set about
destroying both: Random House dropped him; Margerie threatened
to do so. Yet maybe even that didn't really matter. When he wrote
Under the Volcano, he not only created a great work of art, he also
created himself. He was no longer one of the addled, faceless gang of
literary dabblers. He had transformed his weaknesses, failures and
sporadic illuminations into something marvelous. And that is a terrible
responsibility.

He once wrote to his British publishers, 'There are a thousand
writers who can draw adequate characters . . . for one who can tell
you anything new about hell fire. And I am telling you something
new about hell fire.' But that, as it turned out, was all he was telling;
unlike Dante, he had no talent for paradise or purgatory. So perhaps
he finally killed himself because he knew that he could no more cope
with happiness in his art that he could in his life. After all, the first
nightmare of every writer is to have produced no serious book at all.
But the second nightmare is to be a one-book man.

New York Times, 1973

Norman Mailer, Joseph Heller, Philip Roth

HENRY JAMES SAID THAT no one could survive being an American success, and that was back in the age of innocence before they invented the book tour. James hadn't been shuttled around the country from one broadcasting station to the next or lain on a bed in Washington, DC, and been interviewed, live, by a disc jockey in Washington State. The tribulations involved in achieving modern American literary success have grown in direct proportion to the publishers' anxiety about protecting their investments. The better known the author, the larger the advance he commands, and the more frantic the promotion he is subjected to. Yet at the end, if a book sells 50,000 copies and edges onto the best-seller list, its author can console himself only with the thought that, although he may have been seen and heard by millions, he has been read, at best, by an average of one thousand people in each state of the Union.

To the writer this may be of no great importance since he submits to this trial by interview not, as Freud said, because 'he longs to attain to honor, power, riches, fame, and the love of women,' but because he needs to sell enough copies of his last book in order to have the financial security to get on with the next. But the effect on his readership is something else: a commercially marketed author ceases to be an anonymous story-teller known only through what he writes; he becomes a face on TV or a voice from the speakers, a personality. And gradually, the audience comes to prefer the personality to the work because personalities are less demanding than art, and the sometimes scandalous lives of writers can be more diverting than the books they produce.

To complicate the issue, the direction of art in the second half of this century – from the existentialists and action painters through Lowell's *Life Studies* and Plath's last poems to the zanier reaches of confessional verse – has been to break down the barrier between the artist and the work. The two complement each other, and art becomes a fragment with a frame around it, a temporary clearing of calm and order that emerges from the chaos of life and then is swallowed up in it again. Caught between an aesthetic theory that insists on the indivisibility of art and life and marketing techniques that peddle the author as a property in his own right, fewer and fewer readers, one suspects, bother to distinguish fantasy from truth. In the confusion, Roth comes to equal Portnoy, Heller, Yossarian, and Mailer is a literary creation in his own right.

This is an ironic fate for Philip Roth, since he is among the most 'literary' of modern American novelists. He is a graduate of the Arnoldian Fifties when literature was considered the supreme discipline for aspiring young moralists – more serious than politics, more subtle than religion. His idols are the monks of fiction – Flaubert, Kafka, Babel, James – recluses dedicated to perfection, for whom failure was more real than success because they at least knew how far short they had fallen from what they might have done. E.I. Lonoff, the Babel redivivus of *The Ghost Writer*, has pinned above his desk, as a permanent warning against pride, Henry James's sad credo: 'We work in the dark – we do what we can – we give what we have. Our doubt is our passion and our passion is our task. The rest is the madness of art.' Roth himself seems to have more in common with Lonoff than with Nathan Zuckerman, the hero of his last three novels – *The Ghost Writer, Zuckerman Unbound* and *The Anatomy Lesson*. Unlike Lonoff, Roth gives interviews, but mostly in order to emphasize the monastic tedium of his life in rural seclusion, working every day, avoiding the world of literary gossip and promotion, using his reputation to help publish novelists from iron curtain countries who, without him, might not have easily found an audience in the West. (He is general editor of the excellent Penguin series 'Writers from the Other Europe.')

In short, an exemplary life in literature: dedicated, boring, solitary. Yet he is established in the popular fantasy as a man obsessed – with sex, with Jews, with himself. It is true he is obsessed, but mostly, it seems, as a book-keeper or a philologist is obsessed – that is, with the detail of his work, and what it costs him in freedom. As Nathan Zuckerman puts it in *The Anatomy Lesson*:

He thought he had chosen life but what he had chosen was the next page. Stealing time to write stories, he never thought to wonder what time might be stealing from him. Only gradually did the perfecting of a writer's iron will begin to feel like the evasion of experience, and the means to imaginative release, to the exposure, revelation, and invention of life, like the sternest form of incarceration. He thought he'd chosen the intensification of everything and he'd chosen monasticism and retreat instead. . . . When, some years later, he went to see a production of *Waiting for Godot*, he said afterwards to the woman who was then his lonely wife, 'What's so harrowing? It's any writer's ordinary day. Except you don't get Pozzo and Lucky.'

Unfortunately for him, in modern America the life of a literary loner with a bestseller to his credit is as suspect and vulnerable as any other life that goes public. Roth deals with the discrepancy between the ideal of literary life and its glum reality by milking the situation for black comedy. In a recent *Paris Review* interview (Fall 1984) he had this to say of the Zuckerman trilogy:

> I decided . . . to focus on the unreckoned consequences of a life in art in the world that I knew best. I realized that there were already many wonderful and famous stories and novels by Henry James and Thomas Mann and James Joyce about the life of the artist, but none I knew of about the comedy that an artistic vocation can turn out to be in the USA.

Foremost among those unreckoned consequences is the great, hallu-cinating, unhinging phenomenon of success American-style: neither honor nor power but riches, fame, and the love of women leading to more riches, more fame, more women – an inflationary spiral ending in a condition much like Rimbaud's systematic derangement of the senses.

The Zuckerman trilogy spans twenty years, from the complacency of Eisenhower to Nixon's Watergate. In the opening book Zucker-man is an awe-struck young apprentice, fresh out of college, getting his first astonished glimpse of a life in art. By the second book he is already in shock from the effects of a scandalous best seller; his father dies cursing him, and all the nuts in New York believe he owes them.

The Anatomy Lesson is set in 1973, about ten years later. Zuckerman is still rich, still famous, still beset by women, but now the effect is, literally, to prostrate him. He spends much of the book flat on his back on a play mat, his head supported by a thesaurus, martyred by an undiagnosable pain in his neck and shoulders, and ministered to by an eager team of young women. The thesaurus is a glum reminder of his youthful promise: 'Its inside cover was inscribed "From Dad – You have my every confidence," and dated "June 24, 1946." A book to enrich his vocabulary upon graduation from grade school.' Vain hope. Physical pain and the depredations of a life in art have stopped him writing. The young man who had felt daring when he and Lonoff passed a whole evening sipping – but not finishing – one small brandy apiece, now survives on vodka, Percodan, and marijuana.

The Zuckerman trilogy is about obsession, a subject that has always provoked Roth's best writing. Young Zuckerman is obsessed with the nobility of the literary vocation. Ten years older and a good deal wiser, unbound Zuckerman is obsessed with the squalid backlash of fame. In *The Anatomy Lesson* vocation and success have rotted down to a debilitating physical pain which, in turn, becomes the object of his obsession. Zuckerman consults doctors, osteopaths, psychoanalysts, dolorists; he spends an excrutiating week in traction; he gobbles Butazolidin, Robaxin, Percodan, Valium, Prednisone, as well as booze and dope; he reads medical books as compulsively as he once read the Great Masters and is authoritative no longer on life and art and morals but only on his own private anatomy of melancholy:

> His rib cage was askew. His clavicle was crooked. His left scapula winged out at its lower angle like a chicken's. Even his humerus was too tightly packed into the shoulder capsule and inserted in the joint on the bias.

It is the comedy of a man who can't stop himself. No matter how dire the circumstances, Nathan Zuckerman remains a straight-A student of pain who always does his homework.

Literature has become, literally, a pain in the neck, and so, too, has the literary demimonde, particularly as personified by Milton Appel, Harvard professor, literary critic, and inquisitorial defender of the faith, who has savaged our hero for betraying all those moral standards the young Zuckerman had been brought up to revere. Appel thereby becomes another obsession and much of the first part of the book is taken up with Zuckerman's increasingly deranged attempts to answer his tormentor in kind. Appel's chief crime is another of the 'unreckoned consequences of a life in art' in modern America: a dogged literalness that refuses to distinguish between the author and the characters he has invented. 'Life and art are distinct, thought Zuckerman; what could be clearer? Yet the distinction is wholly elusive. That writing is an act of imagination seems to perplex and infuriate everyone.'

It is on this issue that Zuckerman and Roth seem most at one, since Roth himself is now ritually chastised by critics for his self-absorption and narrowness of range. When the *Paris Review* asked the inevitable question, he answered:

Nathan Zuckerman is an act. It's all the art of impersonation, isn't it? That's the fundamental novelistic gift. . . . Making fake biography, false history, concocting a half-imaginary existence out of the actual drama of my life *is* my life. There has to be some pleasure in this job, and that's it. To go around in disguise. To act a character. To pass oneself off as what one is not. To *pretend*. . . . You don't necessarily, as a writer, have to abandon your biography completely to engage in an act of impersonation. It may be more intriguing when you don't. You distort it, caricature it, parody it, you torture and subvert it, you exploit it – all to give the biography that dimension that will excite your verbal life.

What excites Roth's verbal life – and provokes his readers – is, he seems to suggest, the opportunity fiction provides to be everything he himself is not: raging, whining, destructive, permanently inflamed, unstoppable. Irony, detachment, and wisdom are given unfailingly to other people. Even Diana, Zuckerman's punchy twenty-year-old mistress who will try anything for a dare, sounds sane and bored and grown-up when Zuckerman is in the grip of his obsession. The truly convincing yet outlandish caricature in Roth's repertoire is of himself.

When Roth talks about exciting his verbal life he apparently means exactly what he says. He writes as skillfully as any novelist around, yet the texture of his prose is curiously plain and undemonstrative. His strength is a virtually infallible ear for the rhythm not just of sentences but of whole paragraphs. Lonoff put it best: 'I don't mean style . . . I mean voice: something that begins at around the back of the knees and reaches well above the head.' But this reliance on voice and impetus and buzz has its price, notably Roth's cavalier attitude toward his plots. Like *Zuckerman Unbound, The Anatomy Lesson* finishes with most of its loose ends untied. Halfway through the book Zuckerman abruptly decides to abandon literature, return to school – that contained, magical world of his childhood when everyone who mattered thought he was wonderful – and become a doctor. He takes off for Chicago, where he went to the university, leaving behind his four mistresses. But three of them – Diana, the streetwise WASP, devoted Jenny, the artist, and Jaga, the Polish exile – are too sharply drawn, too full of quirky life, to be left blankly in the lurch. Jaga in particular is a marvelous character, vulnerable and cynical, with a black, Eastern European slant on the world. Yet she, like the others, is simply abandoned when Zuckerman takes off on the next lap of his crazed odyssey. The plot and the people matter less than the opportunity for another voice, another caricature.

En route for Chicago, Zuckerman stops being the nice Jewish boy who wants to be a doctor, assumes the name of the detested Milton Appel, and pretends he is the worst of all possible Jewish boys, a porno king, master of the orgy and professor of dirty rhetoric. This pseudo-Appel's tirade becomes more anarchic, more furious, more unbuttoned as the beloved Chicago of Zuckerman's student days recedes from him. It ends the only way it can when Zuckerman, in a Jewish cemetery, surrounded by the gravestones of all those obdurate forefathers whose grip on his life he feels he will never pry loose, falls and breaks his jaw. And this, as Roth puts it in the *Paris Review*, is the final solution to his Jewish problem:

> It isn't what it's talking *about* that makes a book Jewish – it's that the book won't shut up. The book won't leave you alone. Won't let up. Gets too close. 'Listen, listen – that's only the half of it!' I knew what I was doing when I broke Zuckerman's jaw. For a Jew a broken jaw is a terrible tragedy.

The book closes with Zuckerman, all passion spent, moving wanly around the hospital as a patient, discovering for himself what everyday suffering looks and smells and sounds like. Nothing is resolved except his rage – neither the pain in his neck, nor his unsatisfactory career, nor the girls he left behind. But at least the voice sounds quieter, as though Zuckerman, released from his monk's cell into the mundane, unliterary horror of lives at the ends of their tethers, is at last, mercifully, at a loss for words. But this is not quite the end of Zuckerman. Later this year the trilogy will appear in one volume together with a novella-length epilogue, 'The Prague Orgy.' It sounds like another version of the black comedy of the unreckoned consequences of a life in art – but this time in Czechoslovak style, with Zuckerman as an appalled onlooker.

Like Roth, Joseph Heller has never been much concerned with plots. Even in *Catch-22* the most important incidents – Milo's bombing of the squadron, the death of Snowden – were buried deep in the novel like truffles, sniffed at, lost, circled, lost, and found. The plot of *God Knows* is common property: the life and hard times of David, king of Israel, chiefly as recounted in the First and Second Books of Samuel and retold in the voice of an aging pilot from *Catch-22*. There are no surprises there, although Heller moves in circles as usual, starting with David on his deathbed (Kings I) and moving backward and forward in time as the mood takes him. No surprises, either, in the choice of subject matter: in 1970 Dan Jacobson took an incident from David's troubled reign and based on it an acid and elegant novel, *The Rape of Tamar*. But Jacobson's short book was traditional fiction – full of vivid physical presences and convoluted motives. *God Knows*, though more than twice as long, is curiously bodiless by comparison. Only Abishag the Shunammite, the exquisite virgin who warms the ancient king's bed, is described in (loving) detail. The rest are voices. Or rather, one voice: the whole book is a monologue, sometimes rambling, often repetitive – after all, the narrator is very old – but sustained by a nagging, wisecracking, self-justifying energy given only to those who are absolutely convinced of the purity of their motives. Even on his deathbed, the king is still 'David, the boy wonder,' cocky and indulged, wounded, self-righteous, gifted.

Like most spoiled children, David is carrying on a nonstop, sulky argument with Dad. Not with Jesse, his real father, who scarcely merits a mention from his upwardly mobile son, but with God Himself by Whom David feels himself to have been irretrievably wronged and to Whom he will no longer speak:

I've got this ongoing, open-ended Mexican stand-off with God. . . . He owes me an apology, but God won't budge so I won't budge. I have my faults, God knows, and I may even be among the first to admit them, but to this very day I know in my bones that I'm a much better person than He is.

David is also involved in a Mexican standoff with Bathsheba, the great love of his life as well as the great lay: he wants to make love to her once more for old times' sake; she wants him to name her son Solomon as his successor. These two wrangles provide the novel with suspense: Will He, won't He? Will she, won't she? The rest is grumbling reminiscence about the rough ride David has had since God, in His questionable wisdom, chose David himself to succeed Saul to the throne of Israel: the years in the wilderness with either Saul or the Philistines at his throat; the troubles with his sons, brothers, nephews, in-laws, wives. (Michal, Saul's daughter, is the first Jewish American Princess; when she helps David escape the assassins sent by her father, her last words are, 'Do you have your mouthwash?') All in all, life has not been quite what he had expected when he slew Goliath and charmed everyone with his poems and his singing.

The story is not important. The wars, treachery, love affairs, and family feuds are an excuse for a monologue that has less in common with *The Rape of Tamar* than with Mel Brooks's 2000-Year-Old Man:

> Some Promised Land. The honey was there, but the milk we brought in with our goats. To people in California, God gives a magnificent coastline, a movie industry, and Beverly Hills. To us He gives sand. To Cannes He gives a plush film festival. We get the PLO. Our winters are rainy, our summers hot. To people who didn't know how to wind a wristwatch He gives underground oceans of oil. To us He gives hernia, piles, and anti-Semitism.

The gags never stop, and they come in all shapes and sizes. They are clever one-liners ('Like cunnilingus, tending sheep is dark and lonely work; but someone has to do it') and stand-up comic tirades ('and that's another thing that pisses me off about that Michelangelo statue of me in Florence. He's got me standing there uncircumcised! Who the fuck did he think I was?'). To have a biblical king who talks like some disreputable Uncle Max from Brooklyn is one source of Heller's jokes. The other is his use of famous quotes. David, as he himself sees it, is not just a poet, he is *the* poet who was subsequently plagiarized by everybody from Shakespeare to Auden. Above all, he was plagiarized by his son Solomon, the family dimwit ('that *putz*'), who solemnly scratches down on a clay tablet his father's throwaway lines. One purpose of David's monologue is to set right the literary accounts by recording who said what to whom:

'Comfort him with apples' was the suggestion of Abner, captain of all Saul's host. 'Stay him with flagons.'

When apples and flagons failed to work, someone in attendance suggested music as a remedy known to have charms to soothe a savage breast.

'No shit?' said Abner.

The jokes are so plentiful and at times so good that it seems churlish to complain that they don't add up to much, particularly when Heller himself appears, in a recent interview (*Conversations With American Writers*, by Charles Ruas), to be that rarest of famous novelists, a genuinely modest man:

> Given enough time with any dialogue I write, I can have some-body make a remark which will produce a response. And it will be funny. . . . Comedy for me is something to use, and because I do it easily, I don't do it sparingly. . . . If you ask me to justify [this] in literary terms, I can't. I just have a feeling it's right. . . . I'm a pretty cheerful guy. All I'm trying to do is write good novels. . . . I'm doing what I can, and luckily what I can do is interesting to people.

What he can also do is write movingly about the downbeat emotions of middle age: affection, exasperation, forgiveness. But the one thing his freewheeling imagination seems in this book unable to encompass is a world very different from a Catskill resort. *Catch-22* was crammed with characters with lives of their own. *God Knows* has no one except a King David re-created in the image of an aging Jewish funnyman. It is the Gospel According to Henny Youngman, entertaining but cen-terless and not quite coherent, unless you postulate an audience that merely wants a novel to be a vehicle for a performance.

Norman Mailer has been grappling with the problem of American success for the whole of his career. He is a master of the public occasion – daring, clever, imaginative, charming, fast on his feet – and no one has tried harder to close the gap between the author and the work, producing theories and writing books that illustrate them with extraordinary persistence. Each novel seems another stage on the journey he charted more than a quarter of a century ago in 'The White Negro,' his essay on the psychopath as 'existential hero,' the

'frontiersman in the Wild West of American night life,' who 'murders
– if he has the courage – out of the necessity to purge his violence, for
if he cannot empty his hatred then he cannot love.'

The cast of *Tough Guys Don't Dance* are psychopaths without
exception. They drink too much, they take dope of all kinds and
have sex in every possible combination, indiscriminately. They also do
monstrous things to one another without a moment's afterthought:
chop off heads, blow out brains, flail about with blunt and sharp
instruments. 'There's a peculiar pleasure in shooting people,' one of
them says. 'It's much more intoxicating than you'd think.' But not for
the reader. Psychopathology of the kind Mailer dramatizes here seems
to me to be a recipe for weariness, not excitement. The people are
dreadful without being interesting and their violence doesn't mean a
thing – 'existentially' or otherwise – except as a means of alleviating
their drugged boredom or goosing the plot.

The book is a thriller with psychic overtones and a sturdily
Maileresque hero. Tim Madden is a one-time boxer, barman, million-
aire's gofer and convict who has settled in Provincetown and become
a writer. One morning he wakes up with a hangover to find blood on
the seat of his Porsche and a severed blond head in the secret hole
where he hides his marijuana. He remembers nothing of the previous
evening. Has he finally crossed the forbidden line and become a killer,
or is he simply a provoker of murder in others?

As a thriller, the book is closer in spirit to Mickey Spillane than to
Dashiell Hammett. Hammett, with his elegant plots and glacial clarity,
would have disdained Mailer's remorseless use of coincidence and his
sloppy prose ('A faint sound, husky and sensual as the earth itself,
stirred in her throat. It was marvelous'). Above all, he would have
disdained the way Madden glories in violence. Hammett's laconic
private eyes may accept mayhem as part of the day's work, but in the
end it sickens them and their toughness becomes a burden. For
Madden violence is a manly, purifying force he aspires to: 'With
anger such as ours, murder – most terrifying to say – could prove the
cure for all the rest.'

Those are much the same words as Mailer used in 'The White
Negro' to justify private violence as the mirror image of the large-scale
forces at work just below the bland surface of modern society. But
now he no longer seems concerned with civilization and its discontents. The psychic forces invoked in *Tough Guys* are vaguer and more
gothic, and Madden's attitude to them is curiously passive for an

existential hero: 'I'm prey to the spirits,' he says of one of the murders. 'If I did do it, I was in some kind of coma. I would have been carried to it by the spirits.'

The spirits take many forms in the novel. Punchdrunk Harpo, the best-drawn character in the book, hears spooky, prophetic voices on the wind, while the ghosts of the whores and smugglers of Hell Town – Provincetown's nineteenth-century red-light district – whisper to Madden continually. But the spirits are also there as an excuse, as a way of invoking a mood with the least possible effort: 'Was there a real fever in the air? . . . I suppose the spirits were tugging at the beer-drenched sponge of whatever collective mind was here.'

Mailer here seems a long way from the precision and persistence with which he once explored the destructive element. In *Advertisements for Myself* he announced, 'I am imprisoned with a perception which will settle for nothing less than making a revolution in the consciousness of our time.' Central to that perception was the belief that literature must cope with the violent underside of the psyche. Twenty-five years and nineteen books later that perception has been frittered away in random nastiness. Despite seven corpses, the dark forces exist in *Tough Guys* not as manifestations of another world or another style of awareness but as nothing more interesting than the fumes from the dope and booze ingested by one and all during the long Provincetown winters.

New York Review of Books, 1986

Robert Stone

IN JUST FOUR NOVELS in almost twenty years Robert Stone has established a world and style and tone of voice of great originality and authority. It is a world without grace or comfort, bleak, dangerous, and continually threatening:

> Keochakian took hold of Walker's lapel.
> 'People are watching you,' he said. 'Always. Evil people who wish you bad things are watching. You're not among friends.' He turned away, walked a few steps and spun round. 'Trust no one. Except me. I'm different. You can trust me. You believe that?'
> 'More or less,' Walker said.

Keochakian is one of those who flourish in Stone's predatory world; he knows the percentages – he is Walker's agent – and is not encumbered by scruples. The less fortunate and less buoyant go under – the boozers, addicts, crazies, and, occasionally, the saints – victims one and all.

Stone has a Hobbesian view of life – nasty, brutish, and short – but is also fiercely contemporary, and not just because he has a marvelous ear for the ellipses and broken rhythms and casual obscenity of the way people talk now. Stone is contemporary because he takes for granted the nihilism that seems to be a legacy of the Vietnam War, that fracturing of the sensibility which began in the Sixties with the disaffected young and continues, in these more conservative times, out there in the streets with the hustlers and junkies, the random violence and equally random paranoia. He is one of the few writers who are at once culturally sophisticated – full of sly quotes and literary references, strong on moral ambiguities – and streetwise.

Perhaps this is because Stone came to literature from a wholly unliterary direction. His father, a railroad detective, vanished before he was born, and his mother was a schizophrenic, an educated woman who ended up as a bag lady, sleeping in doorways, on fire escapes, around Manhattan with her small child. At the age of five, Stone was committed to St. Ann's orphanage in New York, where the priests taught him about literature and language (he still reads Latin poetry for pleasure), and the New York streets filled in the rest (he was a prominent member of a West Side gang called the Saxons). He was expelled from school for atheism and finished his education in his spare time while serving in the Navy and merchant marine. This, I assume, is why he is authoritative beyond the range of most other American writers about the psychopaths and sadists who cruise the lower depths. Rinaldo Cantabile, the gangland punk in Bellow's *Humboldt's Gift*, is a commedia dell'arte figure, stylized and eccentric; but Danskin in *Dog Soldiers* and Pablo in *A Flag for Sunrise* are created from the inside, convincing, menacing, and as undeniable as the brutes Stone must have had to cope with from the moment he entered St. Ann's orphanage.

Stone seems to have left the Navy in time to catch the Sixties at their craziest. He was, for a spell, one of the merriest of Ken Kesey's Merry Pranksters, but unlike the others, he used what was on offer and turned it into literature. Dope is a powerful force in all his novels, but as an addiction that influences behavior and defines personality, not as a source of illumination. In Stone's books people trail their habits after them like mangy dogs and the doors of perception remain resolutely shut. Perhaps because of the stern Catholicism of the orphanage or because his deprived childhood gave him nothing to drop out from, Stone seems never to have been tempted by the ersatz religion of the psychedelic movement, or by its cosy community spirit, least of all by its cult of speechlessness. (In *Dog Soldiers*, the following conversation takes place between Marge, the junkie heroine, and Dieter, a Kesey-like guru who has given up drugs and been abandoned by his followers: ' "Years ago," he said gravely, "something very special was happening up here." "Was it something profound?" "As a matter of fact, it was something profound. But rather difficult to verbalize." "I knew it would be." ')

Stone seems to have regarded drugs and booze as membership dues, a generational hazard, but literature and his hard-earned education were ways of bringing coherence and stability to an otherwise notably incoherent life. He was that most unexpected phenomenon, a serious artist among the freaks, a man in love with language among the deliberately inarticulate. His subject is the wayward violence of people at the ends of their tethers and on the edges of society, but his method is measured, orderly, and instilled with a black, bone-yard wit, as though Joseph Conrad, that other mariner turned novelist, had taken on the world of Elmore Leonard.

The characteristic Stone note is a combination of high culture and street smarts, an elegant formality slightly disproportionate to the seedy situation at hand: 'Axelrod was in the process of discovering an unwholesome stain on his sleeve.' Axelrod, in fact, has just been struggling with an unruly, vomiting drunk, but the slow-motion circumlocution – 'was in the process of discovering' – and school-masterly disapproval – 'unwholesome' – set the moment off as though in quotation marks, as though a man of sensibility were describing a scene that defies all sensibility.

Stone uses this mock formal style to keep his distance from heroes who have in common an unswerving instinct for trouble: stoned Rheinhardt, in *A Hall of Mirrors*, who baits a stadium full of primitive Christian rednecks; Converse, in *Dog Soldiers*, conned by misplaced bravado into smuggling three kilos of heroin from Vietnam to California; Holliwell, in *A Flag for Sunrise*, who shambles drunkenly across Central America, trailing guilt, self-pity, and destruction. All of them, in their different ways, are skilled provokers of violence in others, yet all somehow manage not to be dragged under with their betters. They have this tenacity in common, along with an understanding of the precariousness and unjustifiability of their miserable existences:

In the course of being fragmentation-bombed by the South Vietnamese Air Force, Converse experienced several insights; he did not welcome them although they came as no surprise.

One insight was that the ordinary physical world through which one shuffled heedless and half-assed toward nonentity was capable of composing itself, at any time and without notice, into a massive instrument of agonizing death. Existence was a trap; the testy patience of things as they are might be exhausted at any moment.

Another was that in the single moment when the breathing world had hurled itself screeching and murderous at his throat, he had recognized the absolute correctness of its move. In those seconds, it seemed absurd that he had ever been allowed to go his foolish way, pursuing notions and small joys. He was ashamed of the casual arrogance with which he had presumed to scurry about creation. From the bottom of his heart, he concurred in the moral necessity of his annihilation.

He had lain there – a funny little fucker – a little stingless quiver on the earth. That was all there was of him, all there ever had been. . . .

He was the celebrated living dog, preferred over dead lions.

(*Dog Soldiers*)

Each of Stone's heroes has been more half-assed than his predecessor, each concurs in 'the moral necessity of his annihilation,' and each survives.

Gordon Walker, in *Children of Light*, is the most shuffling of them all. He is an aging actor and screen writer, with a boozer's face, a bad coke habit, and an incurable itch for trouble. When the book opens he is greeting the shining California morning with vomit and dysentery followed by valium, vodka, and cocaine. All this before breakfast. Walker is more than usually bewildered because his wife of twenty years, in an unprecedented burst of sanity, has left him and his two sons are off somewhere in the East, beyond his reach in every way. He is adrift, a one-man disaster zone looking for a place to settle; dimly, he even knows it:

What we need here is less craziness, he told himself, not more.

Then he thought; A dream is what I need. Fire, motion, risk. It was a delusion of the drug.

For Walker, the dream is Lu Anne Bourgeois, a much-married Louisiana girl and Hollywood actress with whom he had, ten years before, the great love affair of his life. Lu Anne is 'his dark angel,' another unbridled spirit, another abuser of alcohol and controlled substances, with a precarious grip on reality and an instinct for self-destruction greater even than his own. But Lu Anne differs from Walker in one vital respect: she is a certified schizophrenic who has done time in straitjackets and padded cells and now lives in a twilight world populated by hallucinations she calls 'the Long Friends.' The Long Friends are creatures from the graveyards of her Louisiana childhood. They talk French and bicker among themselves, like maiden aunts, over questions of precedence and family history; they leave on the air an old-fashioned smell 'like sweet wine and lavender sachet.' In appearance, however, they resemble the nightmare figures of Bosch and Max Ernst:

> The creature was inside her dresser mirror. Its face was concealed beneath black cloth. Only the venous, blue-baby-colored fore-head showed and part of the skull, shaven like a long-ago nun's. Its frail dragonfly wings rested against its sides. They always had bags with them that they kept out of sight, tucked under their wings or beneath the nunnish homespun. The bags were like translucent sacs, filled with old things. . . . Their faces were childlike and absurd. Sometimes they liked to be caressed and they would chew the tips of her fingers with their soft infant's teeth.

Stone has always had a talent for creating menace out of the most casual encounters. (His friend Kesey once said of him, 'Bob Stone is a professional paranoid. He sees sinister forces behind every Oreo cookie.') But what is extraordinary about the Long Friends is that he makes them as real to the reader as they are to Lu Anne, and rather less frightening than the brutes who surround her in her working life.

Lu Anne is at Bahia Honda, in Mexico, shooting a movie that Walker had written for her years before. She is managing to keep a fragile hold on herself thanks to pills and her psychiatrist husband, Lionel — a surprisingly sentimentalized figure, by Stone's standards, with a 'strong, lean hand,' and a 'dry, bitter laugh.' But even before Walker arrives, she has secretly stopped the pills because they take the edge off her acting, and her husband has walked out, taking their children with him and abandoning Lu Anne to the Hollywood pack.

Their leaders are the Drogues, the young director, his wife, and his famous, ancient father:

> A director himself for almost fifty years, Drogue senior had been publicly caned, fired upon by sexual rivals, blacklisted, subpoenaed and biographied in French.

The Drogues are like the Callahans in *A Flag for Sunrise* and Antheil and Charmian in *Dog Soldiers* — rich, sleek, impregnable, and full of contempt:

Young Drogue displayed open palms. 'Hey, Lionel, I never suggest. If I want to say something I just up and say it.'

. . . He sighed. 'I just thought everybody should understand everybody else's feelings. See, we're Californians. Compulsive communicators. We're overconfiding and we're nosy. Don't mind us.'

For the Drogues, Walker and Lu Anne are mere irritants, barely worthy of their attention because they have 'no survival skills.' Lu Anne's madness is a risk they are willing, temporarily, to take because ' "She has a way of being crazy," old Drogue said, "that photographs pretty well." '

Stone's time at sea has left its mark on the way his novels develop. Each of them is a journey, with one character slowly making his way toward his appointment with fate, crosscut with scenes of what is waiting for him at his destination. The best and strongest parts of *Children of Light* describe Walker's gradual progress south to Bahia Honda. In a seedy hotel full of seedy, menacing people, he has a sad fling with Shelley, his agent's assistant, who loves him:

> She was a clamorous presence, never at rest. Even quiet, her reverie cast a shadow and her silences had three kinds of irony. She was a workout.

He visits Quinn, an aging stuntman and procurer of drugs, and together they contemplate the cheerless distance between their battered present and their risk-taking youth:

> [Quinn] was leaning back in the rocker looking at the sky. Walker turned to follow his gaze and saw two people hang-gliding high above the next ridge. They were beautiful to watch and, Walker thought, incredibly high. They seemed to command the wind that bore them.
> 'Shit,' Quinn said, 'look at that.'
> 'Does it make you paranoid?' Walker asked.
> 'Nah,' Quinn said. 'Makes me fucking cry, is what. Think that isn't kicks, man? That's the way to do your life, Gordo. Look the gray rat in the eye.'
> 'I think we all do that anyway.'
> 'We're little worms,' Quinn said. 'We piss and moan.'

Stone has claimed that he always smuggles a line from Gerard Manley Hopkins into each book; this – with its poignant yearning for the beauty of a physical world irretrievably lost – is his late-twentieth-century answer to 'The Windhover.'

Walker's last stop before the movie location is to collect downers from 'Er Siriwai, M.D., Ph.D., who, born on the roof of the world and reading, Mulliganlike, at the Royal College of Surgeons, Dublin, arrived in America to . . . become Physician to the Stars'; also their drug pusher and 'something very like a medical hit man.' The doctor has evaded prison by skipping across the border to Mexico where he established a laetrile clinic for the unfortunates he quaintly calls his 'customers.' He and Walker are two of a kind; both have sold out to the glamour and easy money of Hollywood. The doctor, who discourses in Indian-Irish of great elegance, passes due judgment on his old pal:

> 'I had a list once. Gordon – not a written list, of course, but a private mental list – of people I thought were supremely talented. Or good at certain things. Or clever but spurious. Or talented but lost or wasted it. I wasn't just a sawbones, y'see, indifferent to the artistic aspects of the motion picture. I cared' – he touched his heart – 'and I loved, I appreciated the work of the people I met in practice. But in your case, Gordon, though I love you dearly, old son, I can't for the life of me remember the things you did. Or where on me little list you figured.'

Neither, perhaps, can Walker. And that is the whole point of his journey.

Stone has a marvelous gift for fixing a character in the fewest possible lines. Even the walk-on parts buzz with life and individuality:

> The woman before him looked like a great many other women one saw in Los Angeles; she was attractive, youthful a bit beyond her years. She seemed like someone imperfectly recovered from a bad illness.

Yet *Children of Light* lacks the narrative denseness and control of the earlier books, in which every figure had his own part in the plan and met his own special fate. Each stage of Walker's journey south is rich in wit and detail, but each is complete in itself, a picaresque incident on the road that gives another angle on Walker's depression and destructiveness, but otherwise contributes nothing to the scheme of things.

The plot begins to move – and then too quickly – only when Walker arrives at the movie location. Stone has sold his previous books to Hollywood and clearly knows, and loathes, that world. Bahia Honda seethes with malice and vanity, with predators and their prey. The most corrupt and troublesome is Dongan Lowndes, a one-time novelist turned highbrow reporter. To Walker, as a literary man, Loundes is the most vicious of all creatures, 'an unhappy writer,' but Lu Anne recognizes him as a foul presence with whom the Long Friends are unusually comfortable. Lowndes's rancid ill-will, Lu Anne's madness, and Walker's cocaine-induced fecklessness combine to create a disaster. There is blackmail and a drunken brawl; the lovers take off; Lu Anne has her big mad scene, then swims out to sea and drowns.

Although the tragedy is inevitable – given Walker's bad habits and Lu Anne's vulnerability – the payoff seems oddly hurried and un-convincing. Apart, Walker and Lu Anne are subtle and disturbing figures; together, they lapse into actorly whimsy:

'Life too much for you, brother? Huh? What says the gentleman?'
  'The gentleman allows that things are tough all over.'
  'Gordon,' she demanded, 'are you listening to me?' She took her glasses off and gave him a look of pedagogic disapproval. 'Show the courtesy to listen to the person in the same bed as yourself.'

The plot, in its turn, also lapses into theatrical conceit. Before the book opens Walker has been playing King Lear and he is 'still up on Lear-ness, chockablock with cheerless dark and deadly mutters, little incantations from the text.' Throughout what follows the mutters and incantations continue and the novel's climax is an updated, topsy-turvy version of Lear's mad scene: a storm, a ruined shelter, Lu Anne naked, bleeding, raving and wallowing, literally, in pig shit, with Walker as the Fool, trying to soothe her, trying to survive.

Perhaps this shrillness and melodrama make sense in view of the drugs consumed. Walker snorts coke as often and as heedlessly and with as little apparent effect as the heroes of Hemingway's later books knocked back whiskey. But in the carefully established, beady-eyed world the lovers have left behind, it seems more like *grand guignol* than *King Lear*.

It also seems far more slanted than anything Stone has written before. He has always kept apart from the current fashion that confuses fiction with the art of the self and is suspicious of anyone with a gift for narrative. Stone, who has a strong imaginative grip on the contemporary American scene and writes like an angel – a fallen, hard-driving angel – is also a marvelous storyteller. He does not take sides and is as much at one with Pablo, the murderous speed freak, as he is with Holliwell, the liberal intellectual.

In comparison, *Children of Light* seems self-indulgent. Walker and Lu Anne are the only characters with whom Stone seems to have any sympathy, and gradually Walker, the zonked-out disorderly writer, takes over the whole stage. Early in the book he is continually overwhelmed by irrational attacks of panic; later everything drops away so that this unfocused sense of disaster can be fulfilled. Even Lu Anne, whose madness has been defined with such precision, delicacy, and restraint, becomes a mere crazy – a flailing, horrifying puppet. Her final mad scene is the exact point where the narrative unravels into histrionics, as if Stone had lost patience with the harsh and unsavory world he has so elegantly created and settled for something more stagy but less demanding. It is a solution on which Lu Anne herself has passed judgment, in a sane moment, while pondering one of the more overblown stage directions in Walker's script:

> So much popcorn, she thought. To get the character you had to go down and inside to where your grief was. The place your truest self inhabited was the place you could not bear.

This is the kind of truth Stone is reaching for in *Children of Light*. But to get at it he has sacrificed the intricate, gallows-humor detachment that has made him, in his previous books, one of the most impressive novelists of his generation.

New York Review of Books, 1986

William Styron

IN JUNE 1985 WILLIAM Styron went involuntarily on the wagon. Booze has been an occupational hazard for modern American writers – Faulkner, Hemingway, Fitzgerald, Cheever, O'Neill, Hart Crane, Berryman, Roethke are just the tip of the iceberg – and Styron was a serious drinker in the great tradition. He drank not just to wind down after the frustrations of a day in front of a blank page, he also used drink, he says, 'as the magical conduit to fantasy and euphoria, and to the enhancement of the imagination . . . as a means to let my mind conceive visions that the unaltered, sober brain has no access to. Alcohol was an invaluable senior partner of my intellect, besides being a friend whose ministrations I sought daily.' Note the passing contempt for the 'sober brain'. The style may be overblown but it is not at all apologetic. Styron was not just addicted to booze, he really loved the stuff.

Then, suddenly and without warning, his body rose up against his habits; he became allergic: 'I discovered that alcohol in minuscule amounts, even a mouthful of wine, caused me nausea, a desperate and unpleasant wooziness, a sinking sensation and ultimately a distinct revulsion.' Styron was left to cope, unprepared and unaided, with the pains of withdrawal and with the more shadowy emotional distress that drink, for decades, had so agreeably obscured.

W.C. Fields said he felt sorry for non-drinkers because they knew when they got out of bed in the morning that that was the best they were going to feel all day. Without booze, Styron felt lousy in bed and out: prone to sudden anxieties and panics; unable to sleep for more than a couple of hours on end; unable to write and oppressed by the conviction that everything he had previously written was valueless. Nothing gave him pleasure – neither family nor friends, food or sex, not even his beloved Connecticut farm. In no time at all, what began as withdrawal symptoms had turned into a full-blown chronic depression.

It was not helped by having just passed that gloomy landmark, his sixtieth birthday. More important, in order to sleep he was dosing himself with a tranquillizer called Halcion, which at that time was the latest wonder pill in America, prescribed as readily as aspirin and a great deal more enthusiastically. Halcion has since been found to be addictive and to have severe depressive side-effects – it has been banned in Holland – and Styron's recovery did not begin until the doctors took him off the drug when he was eventually hospitalised.

Alcohol withdrawal, age, a dangerous drug: whatever the reason, his depression deepened steadily as the months passed. The 'dreadful, pouncing seizures of anxiety' became more acute until, one day when he was walking in the woods, a honking flight of Canada geese went over:

> the flight of birds caused me to stop, riveted with fear, and I stood stranded there, helpless, shivering, aware for the first time that I had been stricken by no mere pangs of withdrawal but by a serious illness whose name and actuality I was able finally to acknowledge. Going home, I couldn't rid my mind of the line of Baudelaire's . . . 'I have felt the wind of the wing of madness.'

From then on, his panic intensified and the physical symptoms became more exaggerated. In a dreadful parody of old age, he acquired the shuffling gait and muttering voice of the senile, along with their habits: hypochondria, forgetfulness, confusion. The climax came in Paris, where he had gone to receive a glamorous literary prize. A series of gross social blunders made him blurt out the excuse he had hidden even from himself: " 'I'm sick," I said, "*un problème psychiatrique*." '

The next day, he rushed back to New York to consult a psychiatrist. But the psychiatrist turned out to be smug, insensitive and no help at all. These things happen, of course; the world, particularly the world of American psychiatry, is full of pompous incompetents. Even so, it seems strange that Styron, a sophisticated man with knowledgeable friends, did not find himself a more sensitive and intelligent therapist, once he realised what crassness he was being exposed to.

The reason, I suspect, is that an astute psychotherapist might have given him some insight into the inner forces that had brought him so low. And insight, despite the apparent frankness with which Styron discusses his troubles, is not quite what he seems to have been after. For example, no sooner has he mentioned the taboo word 'madness' than he issues what amounts to an elaborate personal disclaimer:

> madness results from an aberrant biochemical process. It has been established with reasonable certainty . . . that such madness is chemically induced amid the neurotransmitters of the brain . . . which for unknown reasons causes a depletion of the chemicals norepinephrine and serotonin, and the increase of a hormone, cortisol . . .

This is by no means, in Jane Austen's words, 'a truth universally acknowledged', nor is his later assertion, when he describes his father's depression: 'the genetic roots of depression seem now to be beyond controversy.' There may indeed be biochemical and genetic reasons why one person is predisposed to madness and depression and another is not, but they are never the whole story. The glib conviction with which Styron puts the blame on circumstances beyond his control reads to me like a sly way of distancing himself, of refusing responsibility for the unbearable panic and despair that overcame him.

This evasiveness is everywhere in the texture of the prose. Styron is often a powerful writer, but he has never been strong on concision. He has a rolling, ambling style that gets its effects cumulatively over a long distance. The prose of *Darkness Visible*, however, accumulates very little except commonplaces. It is slipshod, stuffed with clichés – the Picasso Museum in Paris is 'this sumptuous showcase of bright genius' – puffed up with empty grandiloquence – 'the intolerable equipoise of history'. At his worst moment, when he has decided to take his own life, Styron says he had trouble writing a suitable suicide note 'which I wished to infuse with at least some dignity and eloquence'. In the end, he says, 'I couldn't manage the sheer dirgelike solemnity of it.' Well, he's managed it here. Instead of the humour and pace that inform his novels, even at their blackest, *Darkness Visible* seems to have been written on a single sustained note: outraged bewilderment that these terrible things – and they were truly terrible – should have happened to him.

But if you listen carefully, another theme emerges. When Styron was gripped by what Churchill, another famous depressive, called 'the black dog', he yearned above all for collapse and asylum. He wanted to let go, to be taken care of. 'Why wasn't I in hospital?' he asks in a brief moment of clarity. And as soon as he is hospitalised, he begins to recover. This sounds to me like a perfectly natural reaction both to his crisis and to forty years' hard labour as a novelist. Yet curiously, Styron makes very little of it. Perhaps he considers it a sign of weakness and, although he is enormously frank about his suffering, the idea of weakness seems much harder for him to stomach. Maybe it doesn't fit with that tradition of hard-drinking, hard-living, hard-writing American novelists to which he, with distinction, belongs. But the truth is, if the sixty-something-year-old body can rebel against the habits of a lifetime, so can the spirit. I wish Styron had let down his guard a little and written about that.

Sunday Times, 1990

Alice Munro

'MAN IS BORN UNTO trouble, as the sparks fly upward,' Eliphaz the Temonite told Job. In Alice Munro's stories, it is the women who are born that way and the men, mostly, who cause it. 'You flare up,' says Carla, in the title story of Monro's new collection. 'That's what men do,' her husband Clark replies. Carla, being young and confused, doesn't answer back. After all, she is old enough to know that she's complaining about nothing worse than impatience and irritability: he picks fights at the local store, squabbles with clients of their nickel-and-dime riding school, and is chronically sullen with her. Trivial stuff, nothing to worry about. But Carla travels a long way in the course of a short story, and by the end 'what men do' has come to seem altogether more sinister than mere moodiness.

There are two runaways in the story – first Flora, their pet goat, then Carla herself – and, as Munro describes them, they sound very alike:

> At first [Flora] had been Clark's pet entirely, following him everywhere, dancing for his attention. She was quick and graceful and provocative as a kitten, and her resemblance to a guileless girl in love had made them both laugh. But as she grew older she seemed to attach herself to Carla, and in this attachment she was suddenly much wiser, less skittish – she seemed capable, instead, of a subdued and ironic sort of humor.

Carla herself is too young for irony, too brimming with emotion, and when the little goat disappears her despair seems like the culmination of 'her seesaw misery with Clark.' She spills out her unhappiness to Sylvia Jamieson, the recently bereaved neighbor she cleans for, and Sylvia, being sympathetic, practical and sophisticated –

she is a college teacher, her late husband was a famous poet –
encourages her to make a break for freedom.

Nobody lives happily ever after in Alice Munro's stories, so the plan
doesn't work out: Carla chickens out of a new life in Toronto a mere
two bus-stops from home and she never sees the lost goat again. Only
later, when all is seemingly forgiven and her marriage appears to be
flourishing, does she hear, at second hand, that little Flora had
reappeared miraculously out of the night at Sylvia Jamieson's house,
just in time to defuse what might have been a violent confrontation
between Carla's outraged husband and her would-be saviour. But
Clark doesn't mention it and somehow the little creature disappears
once more on the short trip home in the back of his truck. The only
traces of her Carla can find are some 'little dirty bones . . . [and] a skull
that she could hold like a teacup in one hand. Knowledge in one
hand.' She has learned, in other words, what her husband means when
he says, 'That's what men do,' though, like the bones, this knowledge
is a secret she keeps to herself:

> It was as if she had a murderous needle somewhere in her lungs,
> and by breathing carefully, she could avoid feeling it. But every
> once in a while she had to take a deep breath, and it was still there.

Not that Munro's women are any more trustworthy than her men.
At night, in bed, Carla had whispered stories in her husband's ear –
dirty stories in which their late neighbor, the distinguished poet, tries
to seduce her on his deathbed – all lies, of course, but they turn her
husband on. Similarly, the motives of worldly-wise Mrs Jamieson are
not as disinterested as they seem. She has a crush on Carla and loves
her not altogether purely or maternally for qualities she herself has
grown out of – for her impetuosity and innocence, for her churning
emotions and youthful bloom and the dazzling way she swings
between ungainliness and grace. All three characters are held tight
together by an erotic tension as unbreakable as a net of spun steel.

No one writes more subtly about sexual attraction than Alice
Monro – coolly, discreetly, but without ever lessening its fatal power.
By hints and inflections, she transforms the old cliché 'physical
chemistry' into an irresistible force, real and urgent. Her people
are drawn together subliminally by a smell, a touch, a tilt of the
head, a smile, by some sudden sense of physical ease and emotional
understanding that sets off an invisible process, unquestionable and

irreversible, and happens involuntarily, without anyone quite mentioning it:

> And Neil said to Grace, 'You didn't want to go home yet, did you?'
>
> 'No,' said Grace, as if she'd seen the word written in front of her, on the wall. As if she was having her eyes tested. . . .
>
> Describing this passage, this change in her life, later on, Grace might say — she did say — that it was as if a gate had clanged shut behind her. But at the time there was no clang — acquiescence simply rippled through her, the rights of those left behind were smoothly cancelled . . .
>
> She was not used to driving in a convertible with the top down, wind in her eyes, wind taking charge of her hair. That gave her the illusion of constant speed, perfect flight — not frantic but miraculous, serene. . . .
>
> Grace and Neil did not talk, of course. As she remembers it, you would have had to scream to be heard. And what she remembers is, to tell the truth, hardly distinguishable from her idea, her fantasies at that time, of what sex should be like. The fortuitous meeting, the muted but powerful signals, the nearly silent flight in which she herself would figure more or less as a captive. An airy surrender, flesh nothing now but a stream of desire.

That is from 'Passion,' the most extraordinary of the stories in Munro's brilliant new collection. Grace and Neil have just met and there is no future for them. She is twenty years old and uneasily engaged to Maury, Neil's young half-brother, whom she doesn't really fancy; Neil is in his mid-thirties, an alcoholic, with a sulky wife and two small children. But it is precisely the impossibility of their situation, their shared conviction that happy endings are not for them, that draws them together:

> She'd thought it was touch. Mouths, tongues, skin, bodies, banging bone on bone. Inflammation. Passion. But that wasn't what had been meant for them at all. That was child's play compared to how she knew him, how far she'd seen into him, now.
>
> What she had seen was final. As if she was at the edge of a flat dark body of water that stretched on and on. Cold, level water.

Looking out at such dark, cold, level water, and knowing it was all there was.

It wasn't the drinking that was responsible. The same thing was waiting, no matter what, and all the time. Drinking, needing to drink – that was just some sort of distraction, like everything else.

All Munro's stories rest on this bedrock of depression, 'this lack of hope – genuine, reasonable and everlasting.' 'Reasonable' seems a strange word to use about chronic melancholy, but that is precisely how she makes it seem – partly, no doubt, because her tone of voice is so reasonable, her writing so wary of overstatement, so allusive and accurate and restrained.

Most of the women who interest Munro are discouraged as though by natural right, since they come from nowhere and have been brought up without families. Or rather, they are discarded baggage from broken homes, raised by elderly relatives and with parents who have died or split up, moved off, lost touch and take no interest in them. So they assume from the start that love doesn't last, marriages go sour and people generally are unfaithful. Munro has always been ironic and clear-eyed about the heart's trickery, but her work has darkened as she has got older and, although she never allows it to muddy her style, her pessimism in these new stories is relentless. Sometimes it appears in nothing more than passing comments, flashes of disillusion masquerading as common sense – 'Outings . . . were what people did before they understood the realities of their lives'; 'The semblance of love would be enough to get by on until love itself might be rediscovered' – and sometimes, though rarely, she speaks out loud and clear:

It was all spoiled in one day, in a couple of minutes, not by fits and starts, struggles, hopes and losses, in the long-drawn-out way that such things are more often spoiled. And if it's true that things are usually spoiled, isn't the quick way the easier way to bear?

Her message does not change: good things occasionally happen, love of a kind exists, but not for keeps; you glimpse it, then it's taken away.

Munro's women are full of curiosity, both intellectual and physical – savvy, distrustful and not to be trusted, easy in their skins, uneasy in their souls. And that was not how women were supposed to be back in the 1950s, where many of these stories begin. When Maury takes

Grace to see Elizabeth Taylor in *Father of the Bride*, she is enraged because

> That was what men – people, everybody – thought [girls] should be like. Beautiful, treasured, spoiled, selfish, pea-brained. That was what a girl should be, to be fallen in love with.

Pea-brained, of course, is how Maury would prefer her to be – pea-brained, demure and domesticated – though his mother, who reads books and encourages Grace to do the same, knows better and Grace puts up with Maury for the pleasure of his mother's company. With Neil, her intelligence and the depression that, for both of them, seems to go with the responsibility for being intelligent is part of the sexual charge. But then, Neil comes into her life and is gone again within twelve hours.

All these young women are also doomed to disappointment because of the places they come from – doomed, that is, by their intelligence to live three-dimensional lives in two-dimensional worlds. Grace is learning how to cane chairs from the great-uncle who raised her, but she has matriculated in fifteen high school subjects, instead of the regulation five, because 'she just wanted to learn everything you could learn for free. Before she started her career of caning.' In the hick town in provincial Canada where she lives, canniness is admired but books, learning, and the life of the mind in general are a disadvantage, a social deformation that will work against her when she decides to settle down to the real business of a woman's life – marriage, child-rearing, house-keeping.

It is the same for Juliet, whose life is told in three interlinked stories:

> In the town where she grew up her sort of intelligence was often put in the same category as a limp or an extra thumb, and people had been quick to point out the expected accompanying draw-backs – her inability to run a sewing machine or tie up a neat parcel, or notice that her slip was showing. What would become of her, was the question.

Juliet has had a better start in life than Grace; her father is a schoolteacher with non-conformist ideas, her mother stylish and eccentric, and she herself is naturally bookish, a twenty-one-year-old prodigy, with a BA and MA in Classics, who is working on her

Ph.D. But she leaves town, travels west, falls for a married man, moves in with him and bears him a child. When the news of her bohemian lifestyle reaches the townsfolk back home, her father is forced to give up his job, her flaky mother gets religion, and Juliet becomes what the rubes she was brought up with always suspected − a scandalous freak.

Munro's stories about Juliet are a triptych with all the weight and complexity of a much longer novel: first the young woman's westward train journey across Canada, in which she meets her man, Eric; then her visit back home with her baby daughter to see her parents; finally, Juliet in later life and once more alone, Eric drowned at sea, her daughter swept off by some phoney cult. Juliet herself has been famous for a while as a TV personality, but fame, unlike loneliness, doesn't last, and anyway, it is not what she is after.

On that first train journey west, Juliet falls asleep while reading a passage on cosmic justice in a book about Greek thought:

> The book slipped out of her hands, her eyes closed, and she was now walking with some children (students?) on the surface of a lake. Everywhere each of them stepped there appeared a five-sided crack, all of these beautifully even, so that the ice became like a tiled floor. The children asked her the name of these ice tiles, and she answered with confidence, *iambic pentameter*. But they laughed and with this laughter the cracks widened. She realized her mistake then and knew that only the right word would save the situation, but she could not grasp it.

Juliet is an intellectual young woman, at ease in the world of dead, white, male culture, and readying herself for an academic life. But there is nothing academic about her dream. It is a writer's dream of aesthetic perfection − those beautifully even tiles of ice − in which everything depends on the right word in the right place. In one of Munro's earlier stories, an unhappy, abused little girl overhears her father reciting to himself while he works:

> The cloud-capped towers, she heard him say once.
> 'The cloud-capped towers, the gorgeous palaces.'
> That was like a hand clapped against Rose's chest, not to hurt, but astonish her, to take her breath away. She had to run then, she had to get away. She knew that was enough to hear.

For people like Rose and Juliet, the key to happiness – the key to everything – is language and the astonishing things you can do with it.

Writerly epiphanies like these are unusual for Munro, who seems not to care much for literary folk and their excuses, preferring ordinary troubled women with ordinary troubled lives in which nobody gets away with anything. But I think it is that openness to the power and mystery of words that makes Munro's work special and explains – at least, in part – how she manages to compress so much into the span of a short story. Her prose, I mean, has the economy and perfect pitch of good poetry, where everything depends on judgment, balance, and an ear for how words move and interact. Writing of this kind has nothing to with the vanity that passes for 'poetical prose.' On the contrary, one of the great pleasures of reading Munro is in her lack of ostentation, her skill in pinning down a scene or a character or even some moment of revelation in a passing detail and without ever raising her voice:

> She was reminded of her mother, Sara. Sara's soft, fair, flyaway hair, going grey and then white.

That is Juliet widowed and growing old, haunted by the daughter who has walked out of her life and, implicitly, by the mother she, Juliet, has also betrayed in her own way. But that is as far as her sorrow gets and there is no self-pity in her. Later, she says of her vanished daughter:

> I could tell you plenty about what I've done wrong. But I think the reason may be something not so easily dug out. Something like purity in her nature. Yes. Some fineness and strictness and purity, some rock-hard honesty in her.

I can think of no better way of describing Alice Munro's work.

New York Review of Books, 2005

Martha Gellhorn

IN 1934, WHEN MARTHA Gellhorn was twenty-five years old, she joined a team of sixteen writers hired by Harold Hoskins of the Federal Emergency Relief Administration to tour the country and report to him and the President about the state of the nation during the Great Depression. The pay was $35 a week, plus train vouchers and $5 a day for expenses, but it seemed lavish compared to the misery she saw. She went first to North Carolina, then to New England, then west, increasingly outraged by both the poverty, degradation and patience of the unemployed, and the greed and stupidity of the people who were supposed to be helping them. In Coeur d'Alene, Idaho, writes Caroline Moorehead,

> she talked to a group of men, farmers and ranchers in their former lives, who were being exploited by a crooked contractor . . . [She] told them that the only way to make themselves heard would be by doing something dramatic, like breaking the windows of the FERA offices. The next morning, she moved on to Seattle. The men did exactly what she had suggested, and broke the windows of their local FERA office, and immediately the FBI, alerted to a possible communist uprising, terrified that the jobless would stop being docile and turn violent, descended on Coeur d'Alene, where they were told that it had all been done at the suggestion of the relief lady. Before long, the contractor was arrested for fraud, the men went back to work, and Martha was recalled to Washington and sacked. She had become, she wrote to her parents in triumph, a 'dangerous communist.' As she saw it, it was an 'honorable discharge.'

It was an honorable discharge with a difference, however, and it had a peculiarly American fairy-tale ending. Eleanor Roosevelt was an old friend of Martha's mother Edna, and she and the President, Martha wrote later, 'were worried about my finances because I would not find another job with the FBI scowling.' So they invited the troublesome girl to stay at the White House while she turned her reports to Hoskins into a book about the 'defeated army of the unemployed.' Martha accepted without much enthusiasm, offended equally by the First Lady's dreadful food and the splendid gold-and-white plates it was served on. She told her friends that she had become the President's 'mascot or pet or poodle,' stuck it out grudgingly for a few weeks, then moved to a friend's summer house in Connecticut, where there were fewer distractions.

This episode was typical of a life that was always strangely divided and full of dramatic reversals. The pattern had already been set four years earlier when Gellhorn dropped out of Bryn Mawr at the end of her junior year and went to Paris with $75 in her pocket and no job in prospect. Counting the centimes and knowing no one was not just a novel experience for a young lady from a well-to-do background, it also, she claimed, had a permanent effect on her. When she made a selection of her journalism sixty years later, she called the book *The View from the Ground* because, she wrote, being poor in Paris had given her 'a sense of what true poverty means, the kind you never chose and cannot escape, the prison of it. Maybe that was the most useful part of my education. It was a very high-class education, all in all, standing-room at ground level to watch history as it happened.'

Gellhorn was always a stickler for the truth, but in this instance she seems to have exaggerated her plight. It was true she had been very poor in Paris – but she was broke student-style, not down and out, like Orwell – and ground level was not her natural habitat. With her blonde hair, long legs and perfect figure – she did exercises all her life to keep her weight at 125 pounds – she was as glamorous as a film star, and glamour goes a long way, especially in Paris, when it is combined with wit and self-confidence. It wasn't long before she was seen in smart salons in the company of Bertrand de Jouvenal, a successful journalist who, having been seduced by Colette and immortalized as Chéri, was, says Moorehead, 'one of Paris's most desirable lovers.'

Gellhorn was a stylish figure in her writing as well as her life, but stylishness, for her, was a moral issue, involving courage, a concern for social justice, and a determination to set the record straight. She was driven, she said, by 'some terrible curiosity, a real desire to know what it is all like.' This need to see things for herself, combined with her fearlessness and her love of action, took her repeatedly to report on trouble spots: China during the Sino-Japanese War, Spain in the Civil War, Finland when the Russians invaded. As a war correspondent in Europe during World War II, she stowed herself away on a hospital ship and landed on Omaha Beach, went on a night patrol during the Battle of the Bulge, and wangled a trip on a bombing raid over Germany. She went to Africa, Vietnam and, at the age of 85, to Brazil to investigate the murder of street children. She traveled light and often dangerously, was willing to put up with squalor, and tried to align herself with the Have-nots. But whenever she returned, the Haves were waiting to welcome her back. Her circle of friends included Roosevelts, Whitneys, Adlai Stevenson, Senator Fulbright, George Kennan, Diana Cooper, Bernard Berenson, Leonard Bernstein, H.G. Wells, Sybille Bedford; her two husbands were Ernest Hemingway and Tom Matthews, the patrician editor of *Time*.

Gellhorn never seems to have thought about or even noticed the contradiction between her principles and her connections, perhaps because she had been trained not to. Her parents were rich, enlightened, happily married and liberal; 'the Gellhorn house,' Moorehead says, 'was one of the very few white homes in St. Louis where black people came regularly for meals.' Her German father was a prominent gynecologist and obstetrician, a tough-minded man who had settled in America because he believed in Jeffersonian democracy and the Constitution; her mother was an early suffragette and social reformer whose family, according to Martha, were 'great swells.' Martha and her three brothers were brought up to think for themselves and amuse the adults as well as each other. (Whoever made their father laugh was given a penny, and that was a lesson that stayed with her; laughter, Martha said when she turned seventy, was 'the central and loveliest fact of life.') Lying, bragging, self-pity and boring people were cardinal sins. So were gossip and hearsay; at the Gellhorn dinner table, the children were expected to stick to 'personal observation or experience.'

It was an ideal training for a reporter who was determined to get the facts and write clean prose, and who saw herself as a witness for the underdog. And because Martha's parents were apparently close and loving, her upbringing might even have seemed the basis for a happy life. Love, however, seems to have passed Martha by. She had countless affairs during her long life but most of them were loveless.

Men swarmed around her because she was glamorous, brave, charming and clever, and she went to bed with them when it suited her – to pass the time or get her own way, for vanity, convenience, curiosity, pity, relief from boredom, and sometimes for affection – but not for love and rarely for pleasure. Sex, she said, 'was always painful,' and, except for some brief relationships beginning in her forties, physical tenderness was beyond her.

Motherhood also defeated her. In the chaos at the end of World War II, she adopted a baby from an Italian orphanage. She did so for all the right reasons – pity, concern, outrage for what was happening to the street children – but also impulsively, rather as she might have rescued a pet from the dogs' home, because she needed an object to lavish affection on, without pausing to consider what bringing up a child might involve. Gellhorn's passion for truth and curiosity about the world never extended to her own inner life. 'Freud made her laugh,' Moorehead remarks tartly, 'but he does not seem to have made her think.'

For a while motherhood seemed blissful, but then her terrible aptitude for boredom intruded. She dumped the boy first with hired help, then in boarding schools, while she went off on her travels or got on with her social life or shut herself away to write. The child was called Sandy and when he was a baby she loved him for being plump and happy; later, when plumpness turned to fat and the miseries of adolescence set in, she bullied him mercilessly about his weight, his laziness, his moral and intellectual shortcomings. Sandy dropped out of school early, took odd jobs, became a drug addict, served time in jail, and it was years before he pulled his life together. He was, she said, her 'greatest failure of all.'

Gellhorn's relationship with her father was also troubled. She yearned for his approval, but he was a hard man with high standards and he had no patience with her youthful pretensions. Like her, he believed in telling the truth and his reaction to her first novel, written when she was twenty-six, was harsh:

It will be pretty dark for you if you remain in the groove you have been plowing these past six or seven years. Strangely, that has been the only thing you haven't tired of, this self-deception . . . it's you and only you that can pull you out of this slough of self-pity and self-abasement and make you a person of lasting worth . . . 'I want to write, I want to write' that is your eternal wail. Then why the devil don't you? If you really want to write, write by all means, but do it NOW . . . instead of capitalizing on your yellow hair and your lively, spicy conversation.

Martha's response was her book about the Great Depression, *The Trouble I've Seen*, which he read in manuscript 'without stopping,' he told her, 'and with breathless interest.' He died a couple of months later, leaving his daughter believing she had failed him.

Martha's one enduring – and mutual – love was for her sweet-natured mother, Edna:

> She approved of me always – she alone, in my whole life. Yet she did not approve all my acts; only she gave me the benefit of the doubt, saying she could not believe my motives would ever be ugly. She said I made endless mistakes and the main loser and sufferer was me; but she did not blame me for my nature, the basis of my mistakes.

For all her devotion, however, Edna had no illusions about her daughter's troubles and was appalled by the unrelenting rage that possessed her: 'With Martha there is such hate that it is terrible. She starts with God and hates him violently. She does not know where to place her hate so just hates everything and everybody.'

Martha seems to have agreed: 'I feel angry, every minute, about everything,' she once said. She also said, 'You can do anything you like if you are willing to pay the full price for it,' and for her the full price meant putting her chronic anger and dissatisfaction to use. She did so partly by turning them on herself when she wrote, constantly purifying her prose, simplifying, sharpening, cutting away the flourishes and clichés, sticking relentlessly to facts. When she was still young she had written to Jouvenal:

> The great temptation is to do what I call 'fine writing,' the beautiful mellow phrases and the carefully chosen strange words. That I must avoid like the plague; only the simple words; only the straight clear sentences. I am terribly frightened of 'style.'

Moorehead thinks Gellhorn's achievement as a writer is based on her deep distaste for rhetoric, combined with her flair for 'the subject picked out by the memorable and seemingly insignificant detail.'

Gellhorn despised herself for lacking imagination, but she never compromised her truthfulness and she turned into an art what Moorehead calls 'a talent for describing the ordinariness in tragedy, the horror of war framed by the smallest of scenes.'

In theory, Gellhorn and Hemingway should have been a good match. He was the master of clean prose; they both put a high value on courage and the willingness to face danger. When she went to join him in Spain before they married, she wrote to a friend, 'I'm going to Spain with the boys. I don't know who the boys are, but I'm going with them.' That elation sustained her for a while and the months in wartime Spain seem to have been the best she and Hemingway had together, though the signs were bad even then. Hemingway wrote a disagreeable play, *The Fifth Column*, about their time in besieged Madrid, featuring himself as Philip Rawlings, a gloomily dedicated secret agent posing as a feckless journalist, and Martha as Dorothy Bridges, a Junior League blonde with the 'longest, smoothest, straightest legs,' but nothing much else in her favor. In Rawlings's view, Moorehead writes,

> Dorothy is 'lazy and spoiled, and rather stupid and enormously on the make,' a 'bored Vassar bitch' who can't cook, but who can write quite well . . . when she is not too idle. Dorothy has had 'men, affairs, abortions, ambitions' and is now desperate to marry Rawlings. At the end of the play, having decided not to make an 'absolutely colossal mistake,' he abandons her; she is, after all, only a 'very handsome commodity . . . a commodity you shouldn't pay too high a price for.'

Moorehead says 'Hemingway had sent messages to his women this way before,' but Martha, astonishingly, chose to read the play as 'an affectionate parody of herself.'

Even a woman as hard to fool as Gellhorn was dazzled, it seems, by the prospect of marrying America's most famous and influential author – *Life* magazine sent Robert Capa, then her closest friend, to photograph them on their honeymoon. She also admired and envied Hemingway as an artist. Although she wrote novels all her life and set great store by them, they are no longer much read and even Moorehead can find little to say in their favor. Gellhorn's reputation is based on her journalism and journalism, for her, was a second-class art: 'Books matter,' she said, 'but magazines are for people on trains,' and the book Hemingway was writing about the Spanish Civil War, *For Whom the Bell Tolls*, was in her view a masterpiece:

> She worried constantly that her writing was flat, and her own vocabulary bored her . . . 'I have been thinking about writing until I am dizzy and a little ill. And I have decided that what I have is patience, care, honor, detail, endurance and subject matter. And what I do not have is magic. But magic is all that counts' . . . Hemingway, she said, had magic. When she read bits of his new novel, she could see it, 'clear as water and carrying like the music of a flute.'

Reading Hemingway was a pleasure but living with him was a nightmare – and not only because the sex, as always, was dreadful for her. She was as tidy as a sailor and he turned out to be an untidy slob. He was also a drunk, a bully, and a braggart who constantly distorted reality to fit his fantasies. She hated him for that, called him an 'apocrophiar' and refused to go along with his self-serving altera- tions of the truth. The marriage lasted five years. After they parted, Moorehead says, Martha was 'adamant, to the point of legal threats, that no mention ever be made of Hemingway's name in connection with her own.' 'A man must be a very great genius,' she wrote to her mother, 'to make up for being such a loathsome human being.'

She had found that intimacy made her claustrophobic. The open road, she said, was her 'first, oldest and strongest love,' and she preferred friends to lovers, especially men friends, like Robert Capa, for whom she felt no sexual attraction:

> Lovers somehow never seemed serious; there was something I couldn't quite believe – and even in the most anguishing intox- icating depths of a love affair, I would always rather be with my friends, who were my own people and where I belonged . . . I only loved the world of men – not the world of men-and- women.

Later, before her second unhappy marriage, she remarked wryly, 'I guess this life is not my job and I do not do it well and as a result I am never really happy.' But friends made her happy and she had plenty of friends. After living in Mexico, Spain and Africa, she ended up shuttling between a cottage in Wales and an apartment in London, and it was there, when her old friends were dying off, that she was rediscovered, to her delight, by the young:

> At around the age of seventy, in the late 1970s, after the bad spell in which writing had become so tough and the fiction seemed to have dried up, Martha began to meet what she affectionately called 'my chaps.' They were women as well as men, writers for the most part, or in some way connected with the world of writing, but television people too: not teenagers, who bored her, but people in their late twenties and thirties with work and adventures behind them, early loves dissolved, current relationships floundering, people who did things . . . Martha liked people who shaped their own lives, who, like her, traveled to look and ask and carry back what they had seen; and after ill health severely reduced her ability to see and get about, she relied on the chaps to bring her the news she had once gathered for herself, to report from the war fronts, both real and emotional.

The chaps gathered around her because they admired her work and her stylishness; she welcomed their company because they made her laugh and didn't bore her. They also made her feel young. She had always been vain about her looks and, like everyone else, she hated growing old. She kept going in her testy, witty way until getting about at all was impossible, her eyesight had almost gone, and she had cancer of the ovary and the liver. In her ninetieth year, she bundled up the last of her papers, tidied her apartment, got into bed and took an overdose. 'Dying,' she had told a friend, 'is a very hard business, however achieved.' She herself did it without fuss, like an old Roman stoic.

When Gellhorn was, as she put it, 'rediscovered by the kids' she felt 'like a geriatric debutante' and couldn't believe her luck. Now she has been lucky again, posthumously. Caroline Moorehead has written fine biographies of Bertrand Russell, Freya Stark, and Iris Origo, but they were historical figures, whereas Gellhorn was a close friend of Moorehead's parents, Lucy and Alan Moorehead, the writer, and Caroline was later one of Gellhorn's 'chaps.' This lifelong friendship gives the biography a special edge and immediacy, as if Gellhorn were hovering over it, checking out the facts and monitoring the prose, although Moorehead never allows this to cloud her judgment. She deals subtly and sympathetically with her subject's skewed inner life and the implacable demands she made on everyone, especially herself. She knows the woman too well to pretend that her behavior wasn't often inexcusable or that her anger, boredom and selfishness didn't make others suffer more than she did. Moorehead is as scrupulous and unfooled as Gellhorn could have wished but, unlike Martha, she is forgiving, and that somehow adds to the authority of her book. It is a model biography, at once fond and disabused. Even a writer as hard to please as Martha Gellhorn would have approved of it.

New York Review of Books, 2004

English Jews

WHEN THE LATE CECIL Roth retired, in 1968, after his ninth term as president of the Jewish Historical Society of England, he felt he should apologize for devoting his life to such a 'modest cabbage patch.' This was, of course, the polite and appropriate thing to do; being English means always having to say you're sorry and Roth, who was the first Reader in Jewish Studies at Oxford, was a very English figure. John Gross, who met him at the open house Roth kept on Saturday afternoons for Jewish students, describes him as 'a tall man, with thick glasses, lots of teeth, lank black hair parted in the middle (it was often mistaken for a wig) and a spluttery voice' – in short, a typical Oxford don, except that 'his conversation abounded with what you might call the higher Jewish gossip.'

In contrast, there is nothing in the least apologetic about Todd Endelman's lucid style or his comprehensive and authoritative history *The Jews of Britain, 1656 to 2000*. Yet even he seems constrained by the uneventful story, as though to talk about Judaism without dwelling on suffering were historically – or even politically – incorrect:

Anglo-Jewish history in recent centuries is undramatic, at least in comparison to the travails of Jews in other lands. Show trials, pogroms, accusations of ritual murder, economic boycotts, and other persecutions that punctuated the histories of other Central and East European communities were absent, as were political revolutions, like those in France and Russia, that rapidly transformed the circumstances of Jewish life . . . While the absence of violence and turmoil in their history did not disturb Britain's Jews, who saw it as a mark of their good fortune, the same cannot be said of their historians. For them, the absence of persecution is a problem: it eliminates a familiar framework – Jews as a persecuted minority — and a set of related concepts and terms with which to view the history of Britain's Jews. One eminent historian concluded that British Jewish history was so tranquil it did not merit professional attention.

If the British Jews are lucky to have been spared the violence that makes history interesting, so too is England. It is an island nation, with a once powerful navy to protect it, and it fought its wars abroad. Hitler's bombers apart, the last battles fought on English soil were during the Civil War of 1642–1649, when Oliver Cromwell's Parliamentarians defeated the Royalist army of Charles I. Partly in response to the havoc that followed the execution of the king and the establishment of parliamentary democracy, Cromwell allowed the Jews to return. (The original community, never larger than four or five thousand, had been expelled in 1290.) He did so not for the usual reasons — because he needed their financial skills and resources — but because, Endelman writes,

In the intoxicating atmosphere of those tumultuous times, many supporters of the parliamentary cause — politicians, preachers, scholars, and ordinary people alike — expected the conversion of the Jews and the coming of the millennium in the near future . . . Believing that redemption was at hand and that the repeal of the [expulsion edict of 1290] would appease God's anger over the innocent blood being shed in England, they urged that the Jews be allowed to trade and dwell in England 'under the Christian banner of charity and brotherly love'.[1]

And that is how it happened. When the Jews eventually resettled in England, in 1656, they did so informally and as equals, not shut away in ghettoes and subject to special laws, but as full citizens with the same rights as any other Englishmen. Some areas were barred to them: 'they could not hold civil office,' writes Endelman, 'become freemen of the City of London, attend ancient universities, or enter certain professions, since doing so required the taking of an oath "upon the true faith of a Christian." ' But those barriers crumbled one by one and by the middle of the 19th century all of them had disintegrated. In

---

[1] Endelman is quoting a petition sent to Sir Thomas Fairfax, whose daughter Mary was tutored by Andrew Marvell. It adds a topical edge to the lines, 'And you should, if you please, refuse/Till the conversion of the Jews.'

terms of British law and civil rights, a Jew, in Claude Montefiore's words, was simply 'an Englishman of the Hebrew persuasion.'

. The Jews returned to England at the moment when the country was acquiring virtues the rest of Europe lacked: tolerance, freedom of worship, parliamentary democracy. Over the next three centuries, Britain was to become, in Ian Buruma's words, 'the fabled land of common sense, fairness and good manners, the revered country governed by decent gentlemen with grand titles and liberal views, that half-mythical place where liberty, humour and respect for the law always prevailed over the radical search for human perfection.'[2] That comes from the last chapter of *Voltaire's Coconuts*, Buruma's brilliant study of Europe's love-hate relationship with England. The name of the chapter is 'The Last Englishman' and its subject is Isaiah Berlin, a Russian Jew, born in Riga. The title is not altogether ironic since Berlin, Buruma thinks, 'was his own greatest creation,' and what he created was a quintessence of the English moral decency that harried European Anglophiles yearned for, although his inspired talk and astounding intellectual range were an altogether less typical delight.

For Buruma, the symbol of 'the tolerant society that had attracted the French *philosophes*' is Bevis Marks, the Sephardic synagogue, consecrated in 1701, in the heart of the City of London. He admires it not just because it is beautiful and elegant and untouched – surrounded now by skyscrapers but still lit by candles – but because it was 'built by a Quaker . . . [and] held together by beams donated by Queen Anne.' Three centuries ago, no other European country would have welcomed the Jews so open-handedly, and for those lucky enough to be exposed to it after a long history of discrimination, tolerance of that order was a heady and seductive mix. But it rarely comes free and in England the price of tolerance was Englishness.

The famous English class system, which nails people by accent and behavior – by the nuances of their vowels and the cut of their tweeds and by how they handle the cutlery at dinner – is an invisible web that keeps everyone remorselessly in place. But it is founded on the belief that simply being English is already an inestimable head-start and the only way to be English is scrupulously to obey the customs of the country.

[2] Ian Buruma, *Voltaire's Coconuts*, London, 2000, p.299

The class system, however, did not hinder social mobility. There were, Endelman writes,

> fewer obstacles to Jewish integration in England than elsewhere in old regime Europe. Jews who wanted to mix in landed society – and had acquired the necessary qualifications – were generally able to do so. Crude stereotypes alone were not sufficient to keep them out. The gentry and aristocracy did not constitute a closed caste and were accustomed to absorbing a flow of new wealth from below. The barriers between upper and middle ranks were penetrable and elastic, unlike elsewhere. Property, even Jewish property, counted and could not be ignored.

The same rules applied further down the social scale:

> On the eve of the mass migration from Eastern Europe [around 1870], the majority of Jews in Britain were middle class. They were native English speakers, bourgeois in their domestic habits and public enthusiasms, full citizens of the British state, their public and personal identities increasingly shaped by the larger culture in which they lived.

That is certainly how it was for my own forebears, for example, who arrived in England, dirt poor, sometime in the eighteenth century, settled in London's East End, scraped a living as 'general dealers' – i.e. pedlars – and pen-cutters, worshipped at Bevis Marks, and married illiterate wives who signed their marriage certificates with a cross. Three generations later, their grandchildren – my great-grandparents – had moved across town and were living it up in Bloomsbury mansions and vast apartments overlooking Regent's Park.

In the United States, that would have been just another success story, though it would probably have happened faster: as they say, the difference between the International Ladies Garment Workers' Union and the American Psychoanalytic Association is one generation. That is all it takes in the melting-pot to produce an authentic American, and where you start – Jewish or Catholic or Confucian – matters not at all. On the contrary, many Americans claim to be proud of their roots and believe that ethnic differences make the stew rich. Not so in England, despite the tradition of tolerance that has made London as cosmopolitan and multi-racial as New York. The immigrants arrive, speaking their old languages and following their old customs, and the great, slow-moving river of London churns them together and turns them into something else. That something else includes British citizenship, the right to vote, and a British passport but, no matter how long they stay, it never quite washes away the sense of being foreign. Even Quakers and Catholics, Endelman writes, felt set apart, as though they, too, didn't quite belong (and today many Muslims probably feel they hardly belong at all).

The only solution was disguise and impersonation, like spies in deep cover. Hence the spectacle that so baffled me as a child on the rare occasions when my parents, who were not religious people and went only to please my grandparents, took me to synagogue: the crowds of English gents in Savile Row suits and bowler hats, looking as if they had just stepped out of a painting by Magritte, reciting prayers in a language I didn't understand printed in a script I couldn't read. Hence, too, the example of a poet Endelman omits from his catalogue of British Jewish writers: Siegfried Sassoon, a lapsed Sephardic Jew with a Wagnerian first name, who called his autobiography *Memoirs of a Fox-Hunting Man.* Anglo-Jewry represents the Diaspora in its most extreme form: not assimilation, but worshipping as a Jew and behaving like a goy.

In America, Jews are constantly asking, 'Is it good for the Jews?' In England, they put the question differently: 'Does it give the Jews a bad name?' They are concerned, that is, with appearance and behavior. During the last three decades of the 19th century, for example, a massive influx of poor Yiddish-speaking Jews from Eastern Europe, fleeing the pogroms and conscription in the Tsar's army, provoked a thunderous editorial in *The Jewish Chronicle*, the community's long-established newspaper: 'As long as there is a section of Jews in England who proclaim themselves aliens by their mode of life, by their very looks, by every word they utter, so long will the entire community be an object of distrust to Englishmen.'[3] In England, where appearances matter a great deal, social embarrassment and anti-Semitism are always entwined.

And not only for the Jews. The government, too, felt constrained by a gentleman's code. According to Endelman, the Aliens Act of 1905 was designed solely to limit the influx of *Ost-Juden*, but 'the

---

[3] This reaction was not confined to England. The dismay of middle-class Central European Jews confronted by Orthodox *Ost-Juden* is a recurrent theme in the work of the Austrian-born Israeli novelist Aharon Appelfeld. I assume Muslim fundamentalists have a similar effect now on their acculturated brethren.

restrictionists in Parliament felt compelled to deny their anti-Semitism. In other national legislatures, it was a badge of honor.' This does
not mean the English liked the Jews, they simply expressed their
dislike more obliquely than elsewhere. Even the lower classes were
too polite for pogroms, so they made do with the Shylock stereotype:
Jews were crafty, untrustworthy, and obsessed with money – swarthy
figures with hooked noses, waiting to do down innocent Gentiles.
Further up the social ladder, the class system kicked in and anti-
Semitism became a subtle form of snobbery: being Jewish was a social
gaffe, like dropping your aitches; it didn't matter how well-mannered
or cultured they might be, Jews, by definition, weren't gentlemen.

   Or rather, that is how they were made to feel. John Gross calls his
memoir of 'growing up English and Jewish in London' *A Double
Thread*. He might equally have called it 'A Double Bind,' though from
the outside it seems like a success story – from the Pale of Settlement
to the Beefsteak Club in three generations. Gross himself is a
distinguished man of letters, with all the credentials an English
gentleman needs: a good school, an Oxford degree, a spell as a fellow
of King's College, Cambridge, and as editor of the *Times Literary
Supplement*. More importantly, his father, the central figure of the
book and a powerful influence on his son, was also a gentleman in the
true sense: 'He was patient, forbearing and slow to condemn. He got
on with people; he took it for granted that we had to live in a world
where there were, in the great phrase, "all sorts and conditions of
men".' As Gross describes him, he sounds like Chaucer's 'parfit, gentil
knight,' despite the fact that he was a Yiddish-speaking Orthodox Jew
who had been studying at a yeshiva when his parents emigrated from
Eastern Europe in 1913. In London, they settled in the East End
where he continued his Talmudic studies, then switched to medicine,
was accepted at Bart's Hospital – not easy for a Polish Jew, in those
days – qualified as a doctor, and set up practice in Whitechapel. His
patients were Cockneys, Jews, Irish, and, later, West Indians, all of
them poor, and he stayed there the rest of his life.

   Because of the war, however, his wife and two sons got out for a
while. They were evacuated briefly to a farm in Shropshire – 'the first
non-Jewish home I had ever stayed in,' Gross says, and it remains, in
retrospect, a pastoral idyll. They moved on to a village in Sussex, and
finally settled in Egham, a placid little town in Surrey, not far from
London. There were very few Jews in Egham and also no anti-
Semitism that Gross can recall: 'I never suffered on account of being

Jewish, never felt that my future was hemmed in, never endured either literal or metaphorical blows. The general attitude I encountered was one of casual acceptance.' Egham also gave him a crash course in Englishness, and Englishness is what Gross does best. He has an encyclopaedic memory for the details of life in Britain during the 1940s and '50s: for vanished brands and the jingles that advertised them, for music hall songs, intimate review artists, old movies and their now forgotten stars, for comic magazines like *Beano* and *Dandy*, *Hotspur* and *Wizard*, and the radio shows that kept the young cheerful – 'ITMA,' 'Children's Hour,' 'Saturday Night Theatre.' Gross's recall of these 'thousand trivial facts' is so effortless and vivid that he seems almost ashamed of it. Then he adds, disarmingly, 'All very pedantic, no doubt; but pedantry – caring about small things – can sometimes be a sign of love.'

All the while, Gross was growing away from his Jewish roots. He was a shy, timid child, maybe a little depressed, who made few friends and kept to himself: 'I hated scenes. I longed to distance myself from what I privately thought of (I don't know where I had picked up the phrase) as "Jewish emotionalism".' I don't think he picked the phrase up; he breathed it in with the Egham air. He was also not religious by nature: 'with Cyril Connolly, . . . I believed in the Either, the Or and the Holy Both.' But he was loyal to his family, his community, and, above all, to his beloved observant father:

> To have made a clean break with Judaism would have felt like making a clean break with myself. Wavering became a way of life, and by the age of eighteen I had settled, or seemed to have settled, for a world of token observance and demisemi-belief.

This two-way pull between the religion he didn't believe in and the life he was making for himself is the central theme of Gross's book. Why faith, or his lack of it, should still vex him so much in this secular society is a tricky question, but, for Gross, the answer is clear:

> For many Jews, whatever the larger historical balance sheet, anti-Semitism is the heart of the matter, the only significant reason why they still feel Jewish. For all Jews, inevitably, having to take account of it represents 'the last attachment': discard religion, cut your communal ties, and prejudice is still liable to turn up at the feast. But to have had a religious upbringing at least ensures

that in your own mind you are a Jew first, and the object of other people's dislike second. And after that – well, it has been said that to be Jewish is to belong to a club from which no one is allowed to resign.

Gross tells his story reticently and modestly, a style Endelman might interpret as a typically Anglo-Jewish way of dealing with the society around him. As Endelman sees it, England's 'genteel intolerance' emasculated the Jews, gnawed away at their collective identity, and kept them on the margins of Jewish intellectual life. As a result, Judaism in Britain was steadily diluted in the ambient gentility, until the Holocaust and the foundation of the state of Israel gave British Jews a cause to rally around.[4]

As a historian, Endelman has a low opinion of English contributions to Jewish scholarship and sectarian debate, and that leads him to harsh conclusions about 'the intellectual poverty of Anglo-Jewry . . . and the cultural barrenness of the landscape.' On this side of the Atlantic, the two issues seem less clearly related. For the last three centuries, more or less since the Jews resettled in England, intellectuals of all denominations have usually steered clear of religion; and we have the declining Church of England to prove it. But secular intellectual life in Britain is by no means poverty-stricken, and English Jews like Gross, by coming at it from a skewed angle, with a different load of prejudices on their backs, have changed it just as profoundly as England changed them.

New York Review of Books, 2004

---

[4] How long that new sense of identity will last is not certain. Fifty years ago, fashionable Marxists yearned for, and laid claim to, working-class credentials they did not have. Since the fall of communism, ethnicity has replaced Marxism, and what Buruma calls 'sentimental solidarity' has shifted from the proletariat to the world of the grandfathers.

And finally . . .

The Grateful Dead

NOT LONG AGO, A man I'd met in Las Vegas called me here in London and I couldn't think why. He and I had met at the poker table and that is not a place where people exchange confidences. He vaguely knew that I was a writer back in the real world, and I vaguely knew he was a lawyer. What I did not know was that the Grateful Dead were his clients. Now they were in town, he said, at the end of a European tour that had taken in Sweden, Germany and France; would I like to meet them?

He might as well have asked me if I wanted to be young again. I had never heard the Grateful Dead live – in fact, I had never been to a rock and roll concert – but the name itself was enough to bring back my youth and the '60s and that wild, vanished time. I found it hard to imagine those mellow, spaced-out San Franciscans in gloomy London, but it was not an opportunity to pass up. So 'Yes,' I said, 'yes, please,' and the man from Vegas took me to meet them back stage at the vast auditorium at Wembley.

Back stage, when the Dead perform, looks like a cross between Houston Mission Control and a shantytown: towering banks of electronic consoles with digital read-outs and flickering lights, and behind the consoles a row of little shelters cobbled together from the metal-bound traveling cases in which the group's gear is transported from gig to gig. The shelters had folding chairs and trestle tables, and the members of the band used them, between numbers, for R & R. The space between the high tech and the shanties swarmed with technicians, stagehands, wives, girlfriends and an astonishing number of small blonde children, most of them wearing earmuffs to protect them from the overwhelming din of the amplified music.

When we arrived at 5.30, a couple of hours before the performance was due to start, Bob Weir and Phil Lesh, the rhythm guitarist and the bass guitarist, were out on the front of the stage, playing riffs and fiddling obsessionally with the controls of their instruments. Jerry Garcia, the lead guitarist, was lounging at the back beside one of the consoles. 'I always have bad nerves before a show,' he said. 'How would you like to get up there in front of ten thousand people and make a fool of yourself? What we do is kinda precarious and we don't always succeed. In fact, many times we fail. So we go out there knowing there's a good possibility we'll lose our footing and fall. Maybe that's what keeps the audience interested. They know we're taking a chance and no matter how many times they come to a show it's never going to be the same twice in a row. I mean, I've been to every show we've done – right? – and I can't say I'm bored. I can never predict what anyone else in the band is going to play. They always surprise me. We surprise each other. It's like throwing logs on the fire. I guess we're still developing, still working at it. In that sense, we're all students of the same phenomenon. It has the effect of permanently renewing youth.'

As it happened, Garcia didn't look nervous, but neither did he look youthful. He looked, instead, like a benign, slightly disreputable college professor: white beard and thick white hair, spectacles, expansive waistline. He is forty-eight years old, two years younger than Phil Lesh, five years older than Bob Weir who is the youngest of the five musicians who got together in 1965 and became the Grateful Dead. Four of them are left – the fifth, Ron 'Pigpen' McKernan died of drink in 1973 – and apart from Weir, who has a ponytail and a face with a lot of mileage on it, none of them looks much like a pop star. Lesh looks as if he would be more at home with a soldering iron in his hand than a bass guitar: he has a clever, bespectacled face, receding chin and the vaguely puzzled air of what we English call a boffin – a backroom scientist. Mickey Hart, one of the two percussionists, is small and intense, with a deep chest and heavy forearms, the kind of guy you see hanging out, between climbs, at Camp 4 in Yosemite. The other drummer, Bill Kreutzmann, with his silver hair, silver moustache and spreading belly, might have stepped out of a Western movie – the rancher who sends his boys into town to shoot up Henry Fonda in reel 5.

The only one in the band who looks the part is the pianist, Bruce Hornsby, but he's a recent recruit and still in his thirties. 'I'm trying to bring some of that teenage-idol thing to the Dead,' he said.

'I'd be glad to be teenage anything at this point,' Garcia replied.

'I've got to where things are beginning to fall apart, but what's comforting about age is everyone's falling apart with you. I don't see anyone getting any younger.'

'Yeah, but some are falling apart slower,' Hornsby said.

Garcia did not seem disconcerted: 'It's a matter of use, man, good use. I enjoyed it when I had it, whatever it was. It all went to a good cause.'

The Dead have been playing together for a quarter of a century – an eternity in the pop music business – and when they started they were plumb in the center of the hippie subculture. They became the house band for Ken Kesey's Merry Pranksters, then, when Kesey left for Mexico, they were taken up by Owsley Stanley, the eminence grise of LSD. They used to play for free in Golden Gate Park to the waifs of Haight-Ashbury and they took part in all the famous '60s manifestations: the 'Be-In,' the 'Summer of Love,' the Monterey Pop Festival. Most of the other groups of the period have disbanded, the poets and novelists and gurus have run to fat and fallen silent and joined the system, but the Dead have gone on doing their thing, improvising along the way. 'It takes a long time to improve at anything,' Mickey Hart said. 'When you're in training with your brothers it changes all the time because the rhythms of life are different. It feels better now than it used to. There was too much chaos back then, although that's where we found the music. Now we have families and they can enjoy the music with us. It seems like a good way to go through life.'

Back in the '60s, the Dead were kids playing to other kids. Now they are middle-aged and they are still playing to the kids. That is what is most remarkable about them – even more than the music. The Dead are a touring band – they play seventy or eighty concerts a year – and everywhere they go their fans, who call themselves Deadheads, go with them. A few of the Deadheads are relics of the '60s. (There are said to be about a thousand people who catch forty or fifty shows a year.) But most of them are in their teens or twenties. What unites the Deadheads is not nostalgia for a period when few of them were alive but fervor for the band, companionship, and a sense of shared adventure. Before each concert, they set up a bazaar outside the auditorium where they barter, or sometimes sell, memorabilia, tie-dyes, psychedelic tee shirts, tapes, drugs, and, above all, tickets. (The concerts sell out in advance and, although the Dead try to cut out the scalpers by running their own ticket-sales office, not all Deadheads are lucky with their applications.) But the real purpose of the bazaars is fellowship; they are places where the fans can meet, exchange Grateful Dead arcana and talk about what's happened along the way.

'The people who are our audience now are the same sort of people who were our audience originally,' Jerry Garcia said. 'They are looking for something different, something to enlarge their own personal myth. Touring with us becomes, like, their war stories: "Remember that time we were travelling with the Dead and had three flat tyres in Des Moines and had to wake up a farmer in the middle of the night?" That kinda thing. It's part of the adventure of finding yourself, of moving through life. It gives you an excuse to go out and do it for yourself. It used to be there were a lot of ways of finding out about yourself: join the circus, hop a freight train, hit the road with Jack Kerouac. Now it's got to be where there are only a few ways left and we're one of them.' Garcia, like the other members of the band, is modest, lively and good humoured, and he has no trace of showbiz glitz. He is also old enough to be father to most of the Deadheads. So maybe the kids love the Grateful Dead because they are proof that getting old may – just may – be OK after all. It doesn't necessarily mean giving up, battening down the hatches, and becoming rigid and boring.

Whatever the reason, when the concert starts the sense of community is overwhelming. 'The audience is a nation unto itself,' Bob Weir had said, and what a large segment of that nation does is dance. That night, the Dead played for four hours, with only one break, and the audience danced with them from start to finish. I noticed one figure in particular who swayed and gyrated, coiled and uncoiled himself ecstatically and without pause. He looked like a blonde John the Baptist, gaunt and thin, with his hair down to his shoulders and a straggly beard. But the oddest thing about him was he was wearing a printed cotton skirt. 'A lot of Deadheads do that,' I was told. 'It's not a sexual statement. They just prefer dancing in a skirt.'

An Oxford undergraduate I know told me he had gone along to the concert expecting to meet a lot of middle-aged hippies and to be bored. 'But it was nothing like I expected,' he said. 'Sure, there were plenty of beards and long hair and tie-dyes. Also huge numbers of Americans. You could pick out the English types: they were the spotty guys in glasses, wearing parkas. But no one was there to see pop stars. What counted was the strange atmosphere, the friendly attitudes, the good humour. The guy next to me, whom I'd never set eyes on before, swung round to me in the middle of it with a beatific smile and said, "I'm going bald, man. I feel genuine at last." It was a great occasion. I was mesmerized, despite myself. It's music that just takes you away. I was carried along by it and by the crowd and by my own disjointed thoughts. I found myself dancing, dancing for hours, and I left in a daze.' He also told me that the friends he had gone with, who are partial to Indian food, had baked a special dish for the concert: psychedelic samosas.

From where I sat in the shadows at the back of the stage, where the technicians monitored the winking control panels and the vibrations from the giant speakers came up from the floor, through my chair, into the base of my spine and up into my skull, I could see the band in the dazzling spotlights and, beyond them, the huge, packed auditorium. Heads bobbing, bodies swaying, up-stretched arms waving like seaweed to the music. An ocean of people, lights coming and going across them, balloons rising and falling in the darkness above, everyone moving raptly to the rhythm, voices joining in the lyrics, hands clapping in time to the beat. It was like dream space out there, a vast echo chamber for what was happening on stage. The Grateful Dead were singing 'Trucking,' one of the songs that have made them famous, and the audience was singing along with them. They were not quite in unison, yet the understanding and the flow of affection between the kids out front and the ageing, genial figures on stage was flawless. Despite the decibels, the band seemed curiously relaxed. They smiled at each other, or to themselves, when the music really got to them; they smiled at the smiling young faces beyond the lights. The Grateful Dead began in the hippie drug subculture, but that is no longer the point. Who needs LSD when you are getting that kind of response from ten thousand loving fans? 'What a long, strange trip it's been,' they sang.

The New Yorker, 1990